Championship Triathlon Training

George M. Dallam, PhD

Steven Jonas, MD

Human Kinetics

Library of Congress Cataloging-in-Publication Data

Dallam, George M., 1959-
 Championship triathlon training / George M. Dallam, Steven Jonas.
  p. cm.
 Includes bibliographical references and index.
 ISBN-13: 978-0-7360-6919-9 (soft)
 ISBN-10: 0-7360-6919-4 (soft)
 1. Triathlon--Training. I. Jonas, Steven. II. Title.
 GV1060.73.D35 2008
 796.42'57--dc22

                        2008004225

ISBN-10: 0-7360-6919-4
ISBN-13: 978-0-7360-6919-9

Copyright © 2008 by George M. Dallam and Steven Jonas

Acquisitions Editor: Laurel Plotzke; **Developmental Editor:** Leigh Keylock; **Assistant Editor:** Laura Podeschi; **Copyeditor:** Jan Feeney; **Proofreader:** Sarah Wiseman; **Indexer:** Betty Frizzéll; **Permission Managers:** Carly Breeding and Martha Gullo; **Graphic Designer:** Nancy Rasmus; **Graphic Artist:** Francine Hamerski; **Cover Designer:** Keith Blomberg; **Photographer (cover):** SportsChrome; **Photographer (interior):** Photos on pages 64 and 67 by Vaughan Photography, all other photos by Neil Bernstein unless otherwise noted; **Photo Asset Manager:** Laura Fitch; **Visual Production Assistant:** Joyce Brumfield; **Photo Office Assistant:** Jason Allen; **Art Manager:** Kelly Hendren; **Associate Art Manager:** Alan L. Wilborn; **Illustrator:** Gary Hunt; **Printer:** Sheridan Books

Human Kinetics books are available at special discounts for bulk purchase. Special editions or book excerpts can also be created to specification. For details, contact the Special Sales Manager at Human Kinetics.

Printed in the United States of America   10 9 8 7 6 5 4 3 2 1

Human Kinetics
Web site: www.HumanKinetics.com

United States: Human Kinetics
P.O. Box 5076
Champaign, IL 61825-5076
800-747-4457
e-mail: humank@hkusa.com

Canada: Human Kinetics
475 Devonshire Road Unit 100
Windsor, ON N8Y 2L5
800-465-7301 (in Canada only)
e-mail: info@hkcanada.com

Europe: Human Kinetics
107 Bradford Road
Stanningley
Leeds LS28 6AT, United Kingdom
+44 (0) 113 255 5665
e-mail: hk@hkeurope.com

Australia: Human Kinetics
57A Price Avenue
Lower Mitcham, South Australia 5062
08 8372 0999
e-mail: info@hkaustralia.com

New Zealand: Human Kinetics
Division of Sports Distributors NZ Ltd.
P.O. Box 300 226 Albany
North Shore City
Auckland
0064 9 448 1207
e-mail: info@humankinetics.co.nz

Contents

Foreword

I first met George Dallam in the summer of 1996 when he was coaching the USA Triathlon national resident team in Colorado Springs, Colorado. The first thing that I noticed about George was his passion for engaging with and supporting his athletes. He was coaching many of the triathletes who had already been selected as the best in the country. During my summer in Colorado Springs, I saw how closely George worked with his athletes, treating each as an individual. He tailored his recommended program for each one of them, taking into consideration both their strengths and their weaknesses. When I left Colorado Springs that summer for my junior year at Wake Forest University, I realized that I wanted to be coached by George Dallam. I was hoping that he would have some time in his busy schedule for me. And he did. After my graduation in 1998 I started working with George full-time. He has been the only triathlon coach I've had since then.

George and I have been through a lot together. He was my coach when I competed at the 2000 and 2004 Olympic Games as well as for the 2008 Olympics in Beijing, China. I admire George in so many ways. What I admire most is his ability, as a professor of exercise physiology at Colorado State University at Pueblo, to take his scientific understanding of how the human body works and translate it into his approach to coaching. Using his knowledge base in science, he knows how to help athletes perform at their best, time and again. He has been able to help me reach all of my goals in triathlon—many of which I did not believe I could attain.

Not only is George an exercise scientist, but he is also accredited at the highest level as a triathlon coach. He has helped to write and teach many of the triathlon coaching certification courses that USAT offers. He has traveled around the country and the world speaking about coaching athletes at the highest level in our sport. He is also an amazing athlete. He raced at or near the front of many regional triathlons in the sport's early days. To this day he competes in age-group races in Colorado and around the country. I wouldn't want to be at a race and see George Dallam toe the start line beside me!

George has a wonderful family, with whom I've become very close. Susan Dallam is an amazing woman, teacher, wife, and mother. As George is passionate in his coaching and teaching, so is Susan in her own work as a teacher of children. Together they have raised a wonderful boy in George Jr. I am grateful to Susan for allowing me to spend so much time with her husband over all these years.

George has made me the athlete I am today. He always offered words of encouragement, and he knew what to say to me after a bad race as well as after a good one. He is a man who never seeks the limelight, but he deserves so much credit from me and so many other athletes. I thank George from the bottom of my heart.

Hunter Kemper
2000 and 2004 Olympian
Six-time U.S. elite national champion ('98, '99, '01, '03, '05, '06)
2005 USOC Male Sportsman of the Year
2005 Jim Thorpe All-Around Award winner
2005 ITU World Ranked No. 1
2003 Pan American Games gold medalist

Acknowledgments

I would like to thank the following people who were significant to the completion of this book. My wife, Susan, and son, George E., are the center of my universe and supported me through the long hours. My parents, Ann and Bud, raised me to be an independent thinker, athlete, and coach. My coauthor, Steve Jonas, provided wisdom, editorial talent, good humor, and the viewpoint of the "ordinary mortal."

Mentors, colleagues, and friends have guided me in the coaching and scientific process: Nicholas Romanov, Randy Wilber, Jay Kearney, Graham Fletcher, Dave Morris, Robert Robergs, Vivian Heyward, and Tim Yount. A legion of other coaches, physicians, and sport scientists provided theories, insights, rebuttal, and support. Many elite athletes were willing to try new ideas and training methods and give me feedback on their results over the years, including Hunter Kemper, Amanda Stevens, Ryan Bickerstaff, Michael Smedley, Marcel Vivian, Lisa Rainesberger, and Callahan Hatfield. The original Olympic Training Center resident team and Collegiate Camp athletes were willing to begin the great experiment: Nick Radkewich, Jill Newman (Chalmers), Susan Bartholomew (Williams), Michelle Blessing, Andy Kelsey, Cameron King (Randolph), Doug Friman, Keith Casserly, Laura Reback (Bennett), Becky Gibbs (Lavelle), Rick Duda, and Josh Dapice. I'd also like to thank Colorado State University at Pueblo, the United States Olympic Committee, and USA Triathlon for their continued support over the years. Finally, special thanks are in order for Steve Vaughan for helping with the photography and Ryan Bickerstaff for providing the natural log equations.

George Dallam

Introduction

Championship Triathlon Training is about achieving your peak performance in triathlon and duathlon. The peak that *you* can achieve depends on who you are—your age, your natural athletic abilities, your genetically determined potential and limitations, your athletic experience, and your availability of time.

Do you want to become an Olympian, be a top elite triathlete, have a productive pro career, compete for a medal in a large age group, or compete for a medal in a small one? Do you want to achieve a top age-group USA Triathlon national ranking, take part in as many races as you can manage in a season at whatever speeds you can manage over a long period, or simply compete in a few races a year and finish happily and healthily in whatever races you do for however long you race? This book will help you achieve any of those goals and more. You might be fast, middling-fast, or slow. You might be young, middle-aged, or older. You might do 3 races a year or 13. Regardless, in this book you will find advice that will help you to reach your peak as you define it for yourself. That is, peak performance is something to be individualized, just as training for it is.

Multisport athletic events have become one of the fastest-growing categories of sport on the planet. Competitors are drawn to the opportunity to challenge themselves physically and mentally and to do something different with their lives. They revel in the physicality of training. They jump at the chance to do endurance races that provide for variety instead of sameness. And they get satisfaction and enhanced self-esteem from achieving their racing goals.

Several training elements are necessary for success in multisport racing at any level: training your mental skill set, training for technique (your physical skill set), and training for strength, speed, and endurance. Throughout *Championship Triathlon Training*, all of these elements are addressed. You'll discover a set of principles to guide your multisport training process; the primary set of psychological skills for success in training and racing; the elements of technique in swimming, cycling, and running that you can master to improve performance and reduce injury; the rationale and methods for developing sport-specific strength and peak power; a specific system to extend sport-specific power into a complex endurance training program; specific examples of multisport training programs using the concepts presented in this book; triathlon-specific training methods and skills for racing; the basic nutritional concepts that support successful training; and the specific means to address health issues relating to participation in triathlon. Many of the ideas presented are well established and widely held; others are on the cutting edge of training methodology and not yet widely known or used. Enjoy them all on your way to a lifetime of healthy and successful participation in endurance sports.

Throughout the book you'll notice a mixture of metric and English measurements (such as miles, kilometers, yards, meters, pounds, kilograms). The choice of metric or English in each example reflects the more common usage of the two measurement systems used in the United States for athletic facilities and events. Most of the shorter and intermediate running distances are expressed in metric (for example, 400 meters, 5K, 10K); half-marathon and marathon distances are expressed in miles. Most swimming distances in this book are expressed in yards, because the majority of public training facilities available to triathletes are short-course 25-yard pools. To use the English-distance formulas we present at a metric pool, recognize that the metric distance of the stated numeric amount exceeds its English counterpart by approximately 10 percent and adjust accordingly. For the purposes of identifying appropriate training intensities as discussed in chapter 5, the effect of this difference in distance will be marginal. Most cycling distances are expressed in English measurements, but a few examples appear in metric because they reflect common race distances. There are a few metric conversions included in the book, but for the sake of saving space and maintaining readability, most English measurements appear without metric conversions. If you need to convert English measurements to metric, several conversion sites are available on the Internet for that purpose.

Essential Training Elements and Guidelines

Training for triathlon, or any endurance sport, is simply a matter of adapting to gradually increasing training stressors. In many cases, however, the optimal rate of adaptation, and any racing performance improvements that may result from it, can be inhibited or lost if you use training methods that go against the basic concept. For instance, common training beliefs such as "the harder you train, the more you will improve" can derail successful adaptation. This chapter describes the basic model for successful adaptation (training) that we feel is most effective, as well as a set of principles to guide that process.

Chain-Link Training Model

In the physiological training model advocated in this book, strength, speed, and endurance at various distances are viewed as separate components that are combined to help you achieve your goals. The most effective approach to physiological training involves developing each element as a link in a physiological chain. Appropriate balance, recognizing that each element in turn both limits and facilitates the development of the next, is essential for achieving a positive outcome at whatever speed and distance you are competing. The model, assuming application to the specific movements used in triathlon, has the following components:

Strength → Peak power → Anaerobic power and speed → Aerobic capacity → Race-specific power and speed → Endurance power and speed

Each link in the training chain is essential for reaching performance potential at the next link. Each link in the chain is also integrated with all of the other links. This point is important because triathletes at all levels may fail to deal properly with the first link, strength, the most fundamental limiter on performance. That happens because triathletes experience their first and greatest improvements in performance by emphasizing the development of the sustained-energy (endurance) elements of training. Triathletes often regard both strength and speed training as supplemental, if they do it at all. In fact, peak power is often sacrificed during endurance training. The loss of peak power, primarily through the loss of muscle mass, can cause physiological capacities and race times to decline. Weight training, when done properly, is a central element for succeeding and diminishing risk of injury at virtually all levels of multisport competition. This book shows you how doing both weight training and speed training can make endurance training even more fun and improve your performance at the same time. The model for this training (and all training) is one based on tolerable rather than maximal efforts. The psychological basis is to *perform progressively harder work* rather than to work harder, a phrase that will make more sense as you experiment with the approach.

Training Process

The primary purpose of engaging in physical training is to improve performance. You can sustain higher workloads by gradually increasing the work levels in training as adaptations occur. The primary signal that adaptation has occurred is a reduction in effort at a given workload. Consequently, you can then increase that workload without unreasonably increasing your effort level to sustain it. Following is a description of the adaptive process and the principles that guide the process.

Adaptation

Successful competition in any sport is not a random act. It is produced by talent and the application of sport-specific principles of training and skill development. It is common to perceive the sports of swimming, cycling, and running as natural motions that all people can perfect through trial and error and harder training. On the surface, that appears true—the greatest initial improvements come by getting out there and doing it—but maximizing ability requires much more. Interestingly enough, the "more" required usually does not consist of more time, effort, or mental commitment. Rather, what takes you to your highest ability is the *most effective application* of time, effort, and commitment. To accomplish this task, recognize that the training process is one of progressive adaptation over time. Exercise training is a simple concept that can be understood from the perspective of the Hans Selye model of stress adaptation, illustrated in figure 1.1.

Accommodation

When a stressor (in this case, exercise training) is applied to the human organism that results in movement away from homeostasis (central, balanced resting state), the organism is temporarily weakened, as illustrated by sector 1 in figure 1.1, the

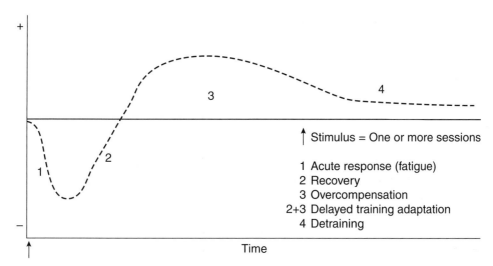

Figure 1.1   The stimulus causes fatigue, adaptation, and recovery.

Reprinted, by permission, from M.H. Stone, M. Stone, and W.A. Sands, 2007, *Principles and practice of resistance training* (Champaign, IL: Human Kinetics), 263.

acute response (fatigue). However, the healthy human body has an incredible physiological capacity to reorganize itself in response to stressors and become better able to tolerate them in the future, as shown through sectors 2 and 3 in the diagram, recovery and overcompensation. Triathletes, then, become able to swim, bike, and run longer and faster as a result of the application of training stress. This is referred to as accommodation of the training stressor, leading to successful adaptation.

Deterioration

By contrast, if the organism is not provided the necessary time to recover from the stressor, then further application of the stress will cause deterioration of the organism, which is known as failure to adapt. In humans, adaptation occurs largely through the synthesis of new proteins, which can take varying amounts of time. Consequently, determining the time course for adaptation is difficult to generalize. Failure to fully adapt is marked first and foremost by declining performance in spite of increasing effort. This phenomenon occurs if an inappropriate level of training stressor is reapplied somewhere between sectors 1 and 2 before adaptation. An example of this is running a track workout in the morning and then attempting to run it again in the afternoon. You would not be able to achieve the same performance times or would do so at a higher physiological effort. This is also referred to as overreaching or overtraining. In some cases, both coaches and athletes attempt to overreach in order to produce what they believe will be a greater adaptive effect later. They subscribe to the belief that if some work is useful, then more must be better. That might be true in certain limited instances, but most often, athletes who overtrain find their performance in both training and racing compromised. At the other extreme, performance also deteriorates when the stressor is reapplied too late or with inadequate intensity to maintain the current level of adaptation. This outcome is known as detraining.

Maintenance

Periodically applying a training stressor that allows the adaptation to be sustained over time without further improvement is known as maintenance of the adaptation. Surprisingly, specific adaptations can often be maintained with less frequent applications of the stressor than were applied to create accommodation in the first place. In other words, once you reach a certain speed for a certain distance, as long as the stimulus is still reapplied periodically, you are able to maintain that level of adaptation without training as frequently. This concept is the basis for the training system referred to as periodization, or the cyclical application of various training stressors. Once one element of training is developed, it can then be maintained in a cycle with a reduced frequency of application while another aspect of training is developed.

Adaptation Ceiling

The process of adaptation does not continue indefinitely. With applications of increasing stressors, the amount of improvement potential decreases, ultimately reaching some genetically determined ceiling. That is, no matter how much more you increase a stressor, there's a genetically determined limit to how much you can decrease a racing time or increase a weight or number of repetitions lifted. As you approach that ceiling, greater amounts of the stressor are then needed in order to create relatively smaller adaptations; this is known as the principle of diminishing returns. For example, your biceps muscles do not continue to get bigger after five weeks of 20 repetitions of biceps curls at 10 pounds. If you want your biceps muscles to get even bigger, you need to increase the weight. But, as the principle of adaptation ceiling states, there's a limit to how big your biceps muscles can get, no matter how heavy the weights are. The art of developing appropriate multisport training involves applying training loads (stressors) in appropriate amounts, with progressive increases designed to bring you as close as possible to your ceiling for adaptation for each sport, simultaneously and in combination, as you use the training loads in the races. This ceiling is reached only after many years of intelligent training.

Training Principles

For optimal performance in training and racing, you need to follow established scientific principles of training. These principles are learned through observation, analysis, experimentation, and experience.

Individuality Each person responds uniquely to training stressors and has a particular ability to tolerate a total training load. This is the principle of individuality. The pattern or rate of accommodation can be determined only through experience. Therefore, any uniform group training program will undertrain some participants and overtrain others. To avoid this problem, you must individualize training stressors as much as possible. But there are some benefits of training in groups, such as establishing camaraderie and friendly competition. Ideally, you can achieve individuality without completely sacrificing all the benefits of group training.

Progressive Overload Increasing the adaptation level requires gradual increases in the amount of stressor applied. You advance in small steps, applying greater stressors only as the physiological response indicates adaptation to the previous level. Doing so more rapidly invites the potential for failed adaptation, or overtraining, and one of its principal outcomes: injury.

Specificity The nature of the stressors applied must be similar or identical to the nature of the movement you are training to improve. This is called specificity. While not all training must exactly replicate triathlon racing conditions (see the principle of physiologically balanced training), to the extent possible the movement patterns used in training that is not sport specific should *resemble* those used in swimming, cycling, and running.

Progressive Application General adaptation to exercise stress should proceed from the most nonspecific training stimuli to the most race- and movement-specific training stimuli. This principle of progressive application allows for accommodation of specific stressors at each level of training, followed by maintenance while the next level is accommodated. This concept is the basis of training periodization, a systematic training approach that many elite endurance athletes follow.

Physiologically Balanced Training Humans reach their capacity for ongoing movement only when all the links in the chain are developed in appropriate balance. This principle is called physiologically balanced training. The links include movement-specific aerobic capacity, fractional use of oxygen, economy of movement, anaerobic energy production, muscular endurance, peak muscular strength and power, joint flexibility, and efficient neurological movement patterns. If physiological balance were not required, then specificity would dictate that all training simply duplicate racing conditions.

Another way to think of this principle is that all speeds in each sport must be developed in an appropriate balance. For example, to fully develop speed in a 10K race, you would need to train at your best 100-meter, 400-meter, 1,600-meter, 10K, and marathon running paces. Along with such workouts, you must develop strength, balance, and dynamic flexibility for specific movements. The amount, type, and timing of each form of training stressor will vary from person to person according to genetic capacity.

Trisport Training Reinforcement   Training stressors should be balanced across all disciplines in triathlon so that you develop efficiency in all sports simultaneously and according to the way in which triathlon races are conducted. This principle is an extension of specificity and is well illustrated by the experiences of many successful multisport athletes who come to triathlon from an elite single-sport background. Most find that to become great triathletes, they must first become weaker in their first chosen sport, meaning that they have to find an appropriate balance in their overall triathlon training in the context of their genetic makeup and abilities in the sports.

Recovery   Training stressors should be applied in tolerable blocks followed by time for recuperation and full accommodation. "Tolerable" needs to be defined for each person. This principle of planned restoration has evolved from the experience of those who use periodization training and primarily reflects experience rather than scientific principles to date. Even the best-trained athletes appear to be able to accommodate only three or four cycles of progressive increases in a specific exercise stress, particularly in training sessions that approach and exceed race intensity. This leads to the ongoing use of a three-to-one pattern of building training stressors (three parts building, one part restoration). You can use this concept on a weekly (microcycle), monthly (mesocycle), and even yearly (macrocycle) level in developing the long-term training plan.

Increased Adaptation Through Reduced Pain   Training stressors should be applied in a way that focuses on increasing work in relative comfort rather than on working as hard as possible in a training session. This is also an emerging idea based on experience rather than science. It is in direct opposition to the traditional "no pain, no gain" approach of many athletes and coaches. Since this principle focuses on making training as much fun as possible, its application will improve your ability to accommodate the stresses of training in a gradual way. This improves consistency in training and often leads to greater gains over time as you avoid overtraining and its principal outcomes, injury and decreased motivation.

You implement this concept by creating training sessions at all levels of intensity that you can complete progressively yet with acceptable physiological and psychological strain. An example involves breaking down a target training session into several parts, each of which you can complete without extreme physical or psychological discomfort.

Maintenance of Efficient Movement   The approach used for increasing training stress should center on the maintenance of efficient movement technique at progressively more demanding levels of training. In this way, additional training stress is added only as it reinforces effective movement mechanics. This is another principle derived from experience rather than from scientific study. It contrasts with the traditional method of training as hard as possible in any session, regardless of any diminution in the quality of technique. This is an

Training in such a way as to minimize pain during workouts can make triathlon a fun and rewarding experience.

extension of the principle of increased adaptation through reduced pain. An example involves limiting the number or speed of repetitions in a swimming set based on some measurable outcome of biomechanics, such as distance per stroke. For instance, you might currently be able to complete 10 × 100-yard repetitions of freestyle swimming at your target velocity and a constant stroke count of 16 strokes per length. However, to continue to hold the current velocity in additional repeats, you would have to modify your stroke and increase stroke count due to increasing fatigue. This principle indicates that you will benefit more by waiting to add more repetitions until a later training session, once your effort at the current velocity is reduced by adaptation and you can maintain the current stroke count.

Progression Based on Adaptive Response   Accommodation to training stressors can be evaluated most objectively through physiological monitoring involving technological and personal feedback. To do otherwise is to guess appropriate training loads. You or a coach should use some systematic set of objective measurements to track your response to each increase in training load. This is the principle of progression based on adaptive response. Consistent with the other principles, adjustments can then be made as necessary. These measurements can be as simple as the use of the subjective rating of perceived exertion (RPE; see chapter 5, page 120) or heart rate for a measurable work output during training and recovery periods. They can also be as complex and expensive as ergometer-based testing with measurements of $\dot{V}O_2$, lactate, or other metabolites.

Such physiological measurements can help you evaluate your current state of accommodation relative to any given training load. But you should not use them as the basis for determining training intensity, currently the most popular approach. The training load itself, reflective of your capacity to perform work over a given time or distance, becomes the basis for determining the correct training intensity. The physiological response to that load is then used in confirming tolerable amounts of the training to perform in any one effort and in evaluating adaptive progress from one training session to another. With the availability of inexpensive heart rate monitors, somewhat more expensive miniature global positioning systems (GPS) for measuring velocity and distance over the road, and onboard power meters for cycling, the practical application of this principle is well within your grasp for all three sports. You can improve this process further by systematically measuring general indicators of adaptation between training sessions. The list includes measures such as body weight, blood pressure, resting heart rate, and handgrip strength along with rating scales for quality of sleep, general sense of fatigue, desire to train, mood, and appetite.

Determining Limits in Training Volume Human feedback involves using objective and honest evaluation of the physiological response to training stressors to avoid overtraining, which is difficult to judge objectively for yourself. If you aspire to reach your potential, an objective observer (such as a coach or training partner) becomes vital, regardless of your own level of knowledge, in letting you know when further increases in overall training load are nonproductive. For example, although it may be tempting to perform extra training sessions when time allows, if the extra load overwhelms your ability to adapt to your most fundamental training sessions, then the extra work has become nonproductive. With the "more is better" philosophy so prevalent in endurance sports, it often takes a coach to help you see that you have reached your volume limits. You apply the principle by making small increases in training load until you reach the point where adaptation in your key training sessions is no longer occurring. This is determined through evaluation of a combination of measures of general training status, such as sleep quality, mood, and desire to train, combined with measurement of specific responses to key training sessions, such as heart rate and sense of effort at a given workload.

Motivational Training Environment Central to mobilizing and maintaining motivation is the ability to continually evaluate performance, make progressions based on that feedback, and then experience improvement as a result—all of which tie in with progression based on adaptive response and determining limits. This is the principle of the motivational training environment. It involves creating ways to receive feedback on the success of the task while you are performing it and using that feedback to create goals. This might include measuring outcomes such as physiological responses in relation to workload, biomechanical outcomes relating to the use of a movement pattern, or physiological or psychological outcomes relating to the use of a psychological skill. As a result, day-to-day training progress and motivation are driven by regular feedback illustrating skill development or physiological adaptation rather than based only on achieving improved maximal performance efforts. An example is in the construction of a swimming set in which your objective is to retain a given stroke count or reach a certain stroke rate. By counting strokes (either directly or via technology), you can receive ongoing feedback in relation to the desired result. A psychological example involves using a breathing and visualization technique to attempt to reduce heart rate while running at a given speed on the treadmill.

Summary

Optimal preparation for competition in triathlon requires the application of a full spectrum of physiological stressors (both exercise training and environment) in a progressive manner designed to improve adaptive response to the conditions you will face in races. Then you employ a complex training program based on a variety of work intensities to develop your capacity for producing neuromuscular and metabolic energy. Training sessions should emphasize general physiological development and the specific demands of triathlon events through the use of triathlon's movement patterns—swimming, cycling, and running. Monitoring of the physiological response to these workloads provides the most effective means of guiding progressive application over time. In this environment, where feedback and relative comfort are provided and failure to progress is minimized, you tend to have the greatest enjoyment in the training process and the best conditions for fostering motivation.

Chapters 4 through 8 provide specific details on putting together the pieces of a training plan. But first, chapter 2 addresses the mental aspects of creating the motivational environment.

2

Training the Mind

To most sedentary people, a sport like triathlon can appear to be a form of masochism, a grueling experience that is nearly impossible for all but the very special (or crazy) person to complete. A common myth is that exercise is painful, or at least it has to be if it is to be beneficial. And many doubt that enjoyment can be associated with the training process. But for experienced and successful triathletes, nothing could be further from the truth. If done properly, triathlon training can be extremely enjoyable. To make this happen, successful triathletes, regardless of ability, need to learn how to train in the optimal motivational environment. Systematically training psychological skills in both practice and competition is the focus of this chapter. Creating an enjoyable and motivational training environment not only enhances the training experience but leads directly to success in racing as well.

Motivational Environment

At its extremes, exercise can be either a physically enjoyable process or a painful and debilitating one. When training is largely pleasurable and rewarding, adherence to a program is usually high. When the opposite is true, adherence declines. Following are some of the major factors that underlie the positive training and motivational environment:

1. Clearly defining your goals—what you hope to get out of participation in multisport racing, mentally and physically.

2. Clearly defining success for yourself and understanding the degree to which that success will be based on meeting ego needs (beating other people in sport), accomplishing tasks that you define for yourself (simply finishing a race feeling good about what you have done), or some combination of both.

3. Developing a physical and psychological training environment that allows for objective measurement of training and racing progress without

introducing the need to achieve a new personal best or beat others as the only measures of improvement. Ideally such a training program also leads to the perception that training is an enjoyable and liberating process rather than one marked by drudgery and pain, and provides both physical release and psychological satisfaction.

Level of Involvement

People become involved in multisport racing for many reasons: enjoyment of physical activity, love of the outdoors, good health, and self-actualization at a level ranging from crossing the finish line happily and healthily to winning the race overall through competitive athleticism. In some instances the motivation may even extend to making a living as a professional competitor. While all of these expectations may exist in a single person, quite often people enter the sport with a simpler focus.

The most appropriate approach to training, the one that will make it more fun and less drudgery, should reflect these basic expectations. Thus it is helpful to periodically examine them. In particular, awareness of personal tolerance for regimentation in and planning of activities versus the spontaneous approach is also very helpful. As expectations begin to include performance excellence, the need for regimentation tends to increase. This is because physical adaptation to training works best when done in a gradual, controlled, and systematic manner. However, even the most successful professional triathletes still value the freedom and enjoyment of the outdoors that triathlon training can provide. Thus, if you are to sustain involvement in the sport, you need to strike an appropriate balance. This balance can and should change throughout the year as well as across the span of a career in the sport. This book targets those who seek to enhance their performance level, so a reasonable degree of tolerance for regimentation and planning is assumed. The motivational concepts suggested in this text reflect what has been observed in many other athletes.

Success Orientation

Success is often defined in terms of winning and losing, or how close you came to the winner. Thus the first question friends, parents, and co-workers typically ask after a triathlon competition is "How did you do?" They usually mean "Where did you finish?" or "What was your time?" How you answer that question says a lot about how you have defined success for yourself.

Certainly you learned early that winning or beating others is what appears to matter most to those around you. However, if you consider this definition of success relative to triathlon, are you really in control of the outcome? Even if you have the fastest race possible, can you stop someone else from having an even faster one? Are you not successful if you race to the best of your ability and accomplish your own goals for that race yet not beat anybody else?

The difficulty in trying to mobilize your motivation through the filter of ego orientation is that you are not in control of the overall outcome of the race. You can control only your own performance; and on any given day, even that is subject to outside factors such as environment, course measurements and type, and chance occurrences such as a flat tire. Consequently, a pure ego orientation to evaluating success sets up the majority of people for failure. This is particularly true if winning is your only definition of a successful outcome, even when you have raced to the best of your ability and training. In any given triathlon only one person can be the overall winner, even if you divide up the prizes into many categories so that there are many categorical winners (as is the case in any age-group multisport race). If you believe that successful performance can be defined only by beating other people, you dramatically reduce your potential to perform at your best by creating anxiety about an outcome you cannot control.

A more complete way to define success is to include elements of the racing and training process that are more within your control. Developing such a task orientation to success improves your ability to see competition in a less stressful way, which allows you to fully realize your abilities as well. Athletes who are successful on their own terms—those who have remained in the sport for a long time and perform consistently near their capability—evaluate their races in a multitude of ways. They go beyond their placings to discuss more controllable outcomes, such as their finishing time relative to conditions. They also consider process- and task-related goals, such as how they felt; how successful they were in implementing technique, strategies, and other race behaviors; whether they had fun that day; and whether they reached another milestone in terms of total number of races they have finished, regardless of speed. They create a task orientation to counterbalance their ego orientation, thereby offsetting the effect that society, and indeed certain other triathletes, have on how they interpret their own achievements in triathlon. Doing all of those things results in more enjoyable training and racing. It gives control over how you view the success of the process and reduces the anxiety associated with it. This process can help you release yourself from performance pressure and expectations that cannot be controlled or, for many, achieved. Much more often than not, the result is that you tend to perform more easily, to the best of your ability, on race day.

The most common examples of task-related goals that reflect reality encompass areas such as having fun, finishing races, and completing personal-best times. At various points in your triathlon development, each of these will carry more or less importance. At a minimum, task-related goals are those to be achieved in training: health improvements, skill development, strategy and pacing, family involvement, creating new relationships, traveling, and having new experiences. By using a variety of interpretations of your performance, you increase the possibility for an enjoyable experience in both training and racing. The specific application of the goal-setting process is discussed later in this chapter.

Performing Your Best by *Not* Thinking About Winning

Six-time Hawaii Ironman champion Mark Allen offers an inside view of the concept of counterbalancing ego and task orientations when he tells the story of his last Ironman victory. Focused on the idea of equaling the achievement of his great rival, Dave Scott, winner of six Hawaii Ironman races, as a culminating accomplishment in his own storied triathlon career, Allen entered the 1995 Ironman with his thoughts (and those of nearly everyone around him) focused on winning. That year saw the first signs of the coming domination of Ironman racing by German athletes, as newcomer Thomas Hellriegel took a 13-minute lead on the bike leg. As Mark Allen recounts the tale in his motivational speeches, he could see with each passing mile of the run that his thoughts of winning were becoming more and more unlikely as the split differentials between him and Hellriegel were not coming down quickly enough. Well into the marathon, he made a decision to forget about his outcome for the day and instead focus only on his own performance and live in the experience. With that change in focus, he began to run with less effort and faster, rapidly gaining ground on his rival. Of course he ultimately won that race and his sixth Hawaii Ironman title, solidifying him as one of the greatest athletes in the sport.

Mark Allen

Icon Sports Media Inc.

Pleasure and Pain

Unfortunately, the adage "no pain, no gain" remains the dominant approach to physical training. The majority of people perceive sustained physical exertion as painful and boring but necessary for achieving a successful outcome. For these reasons and others, less than 25 percent of adults engage in formal physical training on any regular basis. This fact represents a failure of both physical education and athletic institutions to teach a model for training and exercise that extends the inherent need for pleasure in movement. It also reflects a society that often provides neither time nor convenient and affordable places in which to engage in regular exercise. In fact, quite often institutions teach just the opposite: Exercise is punishment and must be punishing to be effective. Nothing could be further from the truth. To witness this, watch children playing, unrestrained by social institutions or adult expectations. They will run for hours playing tag, cover long distances like swimming dolphins while playing at the pool, and ride their bikes seemingly endlessly while exploring their neighborhood.

In this approach to multisport training and racing, substitute a new adage for the no pain, no gain philosophy: Train to do progressively harder work, not to progressively work harder. The difference between these concepts is subtle yet supremely important in developing a positive outlook on training and in the long-term maintenance of motivation, not to mention its positive effect on physical adaptation and long-term performance outcomes.

When asked what the most important variable is in the training process, people often think of things such as intensity or volume. But here is a different answer: consistency and regularity. The hallmark of successful multisport performance is consistent training over a long period, rather than through the short-term application of any specific type or amount of training. Pleasure and training go hand in hand. In application, this concept is both different from the traditional approach yet nearly universal in those who have trained consistently and regularly for long periods.

In triathlon training, this concept can be applied through the selection of appropriate intensities and length of work bouts that reflect individual ability, regardless of whether you're training in the weight room, in the swimming pool, or on the road. So that training can always be relatively comfortable, you need to evaluate the physiological difficulty of performance rather than the improved outcome of performance. Improvement is evaluated and adjustments are made as you adapt to training at tolerable intensities rather than achieve a particular improved performance outcome by maximal effort. By doing so, you remove the primary barrier to consistent training—unreasonable levels of pain. This approach also reduces the potential for injury and overtraining and allows you to focus on the naturally positive elements of the training process: freedom, the feeling of movement, physical and psychological release through exertion, experiencing the meditative state, and consistent task accomplishment. You might add external stimuli, such as pleasant conversation, scenery, music, or (indoors, of course) video images. By placing these elements of training above considerations such as with whom you train or, worse, whom you defeat in training, or how far or fast you can go on a given day regardless of what your training program calls for, you can create your own realistic expectations, meet them, and be successful.

Does this mean that all training should be easy? Not at all. You should train at a variety of intensities and modes, all depending on your own goals and definition of success. However, through planning, organization, and the improved ability to accept relative discomfort, you can implement the "do hard work but don't work hard" philosophy and create a training environment that keeps motivation mobilized.

Psychological Skills

Many areas of life can produce psychoemotional difficulty or anxiety. Whether it be flying in an airplane or speaking in front of a crowd, people admire those who can perform without apparent difficulty. It's often assumed that demonstrating such skill and enjoyment in a task must be a God-given talent and not something you can achieve for yourself. Yet a large body of scientific evidence suggests that this is not the case. Those who do things with less anxiety and more pleasure than others often have certain psychological skills specific to the situation. These are skills you can set out to systematically develop and apply in a given situation—often drawing on your own experiences in other areas of life in which you have been successful. Typically these skills include the ability to see potential outcomes with realistic optimism, to create sustained positive behavioral change, to control and use positive self-talk in times of difficulty or unexpected change, to enter a meditative state that can allow movement to occur most effectively, to be able to produce physical relaxation and the full expression of abilities, to develop a high level of self-efficacy regarding tasks associated with sport, to deal with physical discomfort when desired, and to be adaptive and able to change your perception of initially difficult situations as you experience them.

You can develop psychological skills by employing a systematic process very similar to that used in developing physical skills. You begin by isolating the skill and practicing it in an environment free of distractions and in which you have maximum control, just as you might learn to hit a forehand shot in tennis by banging a ball against a wall by yourself. If feedback on your performance can be provided, the learning process progresses much more quickly. The frequency of errors can be reduced and that of successful repetitions increased. Hence you can focus on positive outcomes. In the example of the tennis forehand, you are able to increase the number of hits and keep the ball in play longer against the wall by making adjustments to your stroke and seeing the immediate impact. As you strive to do better, the process becomes its own game.

The same development process can be brought into play in the psychological realm once you have defined the application of a skill and created measurable outcomes that provide feedback. You can then extend the use of those skills into progressively more challenging situations, ultimately extending them to real-world applications. As you intertwine this psychological skill practice into triathlon training, you will achieve the dual benefit of enhanced physical and psychological responsiveness. For example, consider achieving physical and psychological relaxation using a breathing technique, taking a slow nasal breath over five seconds of inhalation and five seconds of exhalation. Feedback on outcomes could be provided by measuring your heart rate in response and creating an awareness of your self-talk. You could start the practice by performing the breathing in a comfortable environment with few distractions, with the intent of lowering your stress level, using your heart rate as the measure. You could then use the technique in more distracting environments, such as during work, and then apply the technique to your movement during training and ultimately to racing.

Examples of specific psychological techniques that are useful to triathletes include realistic optimism as an approach to goal setting, performance visualization and imagery to learn and refine movement skills, nasal and "belly" breathing patterns combined with imagery to induce more effective respiration and relaxation, desensitization to overcome anxiety-related aspects of training and performance, belief systems and positive self-talk, and meditation to deal with performance discomfort.

Realistic and Optimistic Goals

It's easy to be optimistic when things are going well and within your control. It becomes more difficult when things are not going well. However, multisport racing and training do not always go well because, as in all life, some variables cannot be anticipated. The *realistic* optimist in a given situation not only focuses on a positive outcome but also immedi-
ately sets out to determine what factors he or she can control to get that outcome to occur. (Note that realism is essential to this total approach to training and racing. Thus, it is referred to repeatedly in this book.) This mind-set allows you to constructively respond to even very difficult situations. It also helps in determining the specific nature of goals you might set for training and competition. The mind-set can be created by planning for the accomplishment of challenging tasks associated with triathlon. Examples might include the completion of specific training efforts or challenging races.

AP Photo/Bill Ross

Developing a task orientation to success, in which you focus on the factors you can control, will help you meet your goal—whether it's simply to finish a race or to beat your personal-best time.

Creating Performance Expectations and Behavioral Change

Let's say that you want to run a faster 10K race segment. You might determine that to achieve that goal in training, you will need to achieve a faster 400-meter time. Thus you will need to engage in a new or additional training process or behavior, such as running some 400-meter target velocity intervals. Further, you need to run those intervals regularly for a period of time before your target race, thereby incorporating a series of short task goals in training that are likely to help you achieve your long-term outcome goals. If you have positive experiences in running intervals, making the change at this time will be quite easy because you already have experienced the value of doing so. However, if you have never run them before or have had negative experiences or beliefs associated with pain, injury, embarrassment, or lack of effectiveness in running, the task will be more challenging. Two things will be required: a stimulus for the task and something to immediately reinforce the behavior. A location, training time, and partner or coach make for excellent stimuli. The latter can also be reinforcers if you choose the right people—those who can help you see the positives in the process and who have value to you. But to continue to perform the task over time, you must get intrinsic value from it in a way that offsets potential negatives or drawbacks.

In a typical scenario, you might choose to run as fast as possible for 400 meters several times until fatigue causes you to stop. While there may be an immediate feeling of satisfaction in completing a difficult task, that is often offset by the fatigue that occurs either immediately after the bout or later in the day and the memory of the pain felt during the session. In later sessions of this unplanned, unregulated type of training, cumulative fatigue will often prevent successful duplication of the task. You end up failing on one or more levels again.

An alternative approach is to establish a realistic expectation of target times or velocity for a realistic number of intervals. This should be based on abilities or recent accomplishments in training rather than on the expectations of others. Performance testing and a knowledgeable coach are helpful in identifying realistic expectations. In this scenario it is also better to be conservative initially. It's much easier to set progressively higher goals in a training session (at the microlevel—"Gee, I feel good today; let's go a little faster than planned") and over the course of a training program (at the macrolevel—"Gee, I think that I can set a lower time goal for the upcoming race than I did a month ago"). Going backward—lowering expectations and reducing goals—is more difficult and might have very negative long-term effects.

Run the intervals at the projected target velocity and distance and within your current comfort zone, thereby meeting your basic training goal for the session. Doing so provides the first significant intrinsic reinforcement. A key will also be to reduce the inherent punishment of the situation—to accomplish this kind of work without creating unacceptable pain, injury, or fatigue.

Objectively measure your efforts with a heart rate monitor and sense of exertion to provide feedback. (Chapter 5 contains details on this.) In future sessions, either increase the pace or run more intervals, but only as doing so becomes easier to achieve. Make adjustments in small increments. An important aphorism here, and actually for training in general, is "Gradual change leads to permanent changes."

The refinement inherent in training this way allows a high level of training pleasure and is also a more effective approach physiologically, as discussed in chapter 1. A strong coach or training partner can further the process by providing external encouragement of your ability to meet the goal of running a given pace and time rather than running as hard as you can. With appropriate timing and recovery you will see progress in the successive sessions in the form of lower effort and heart rate, improved recovery between work bouts, and less fatigue as you perform the work. That way, you create numerous intrinsic reinforcers in the process. You can further this reinforcement by reviewing the outcomes in your training records. Finally, adapting to the training will lead to improved race performance, possibly the strongest reinforcing factor of all.

Periodically, however, issues you cannot control may interfere with your ability to complete a task. Maybe one day the temperature is extremely high and your heart rate is elevated. At that point you should be flexible in evaluating your progress in your goal. If you do not modify expectations to match changed environmental conditions, you may view such a session as a failure, which can lead to a downward spiral of lack of motivation and the perception that you are therefore a failure as an athlete. This can lead to the plan-disruption effect: If you drop out of a planned workout just once, you consider the plan and yourself to be failures. The program is broken and no longer exists for you. Consequently, you give up on the new behavior.

To deal with this problem, outside assistance and technical expertise can be very useful. An informed coach, for instance, will be able to reinforce the idea that a given performance in more difficult conditions may be the equivalent of actual improvement. Or you might conclude that you failed to get a good night's sleep the night before. Giving up in a hurry would be both a training mistake and a missed opportunity to improve by developing a new skill. For instance, you might need to focus on developing improved consistency in sleep and recovery by modifying the sleep environment so that you can adapt to similar training in the future. Of course, that would require additional behavioral change. Once mistakes or failures are viewed optimistically as opportunities for improvement through change rather than as failures, motivation can remain high. Another way to put it is "When something that seems to be bad happens, try to use it for good." Alternatively, if you can see the "mistake" coming, by realizing early that you are not ready for the set or session as it occurs, then you can also end or modify the session, essentially making a midstream adjustment that will be a more successful use of your efforts in the long run.

Developing the skills for making positive behavior changes requires the systematic undertaking of new challenges, which you can do by using two techniques: systematically listing the pros and cons of a given change in training approach and applying a problem-solving technique when a new training element is not working optimally. The first technique helps you overcome ambivalence about something new while you simultaneously create an optimistic focus. The second technique allows you to overcome obstacles in the training process by finding new and creative solutions to the problem. To do this, first list as many potential solutions to the problem as you can without limitations (think "out of the box"). Then evaluate those ideas for merit and consider which solutions are practical. Finally, test the approach using both objective and subjective criteria to evaluate response. Over time you both add and reject aspects of an approach to athletic preparation, gradually refining it and always striving to improve it. This process may be difficult for those whose belief systems exclude novel and creative concepts out of hand. (You will consider methods for influencing your belief systems later in this chapter.)

Modifying Goals

Once you begin to use a feedback-based approach to creating motivation (as discussed in chapter 1), goal setting becomes a natural extension of the process. Your goals will generally be of two types: process-oriented goals and outcome-oriented goals.

Process-oriented goals reflect activities that occur in the process of achieving the long-term goal. For instance, using the 400-meter speed session discussed previously, you might create specific goals for the application of targeted velocity training, weight training, and plyometrics in your training sessions. More specifically, a process goal might set the number of repetitions in each training session. These goals are controllable and provide a frequent basis for measurement of success.

Outcome goals represent the result of the process. In this example an outcome goal might be related to the eventual improvement in 400-meter speed or its impact on race performance. In many cases, typical outcome goals are less controllable and may often be affected by factors beyond your control, such as the rate at which your body responds to training or the performance of others in a race.

Organizing goal setting with the use of short-term process goals that lead to a few largely controllable long-term outcome goals improves your performance and assists in creating optimism and motivation for the process. Even with specific goals, you can still be flexible with the process. For instance, if you determine that a training session must be canceled because of fatigue, you might also be stimulated to create additional goals relating to recovery processes, such as sleep or eating habits. In this way, even the inability to achieve a goal helps with improvement if you view it as an opportunity for progress.

Applying Goals to Training and Racing Plans

Goal-setting skills are developed first by creating or deciding to adapt given plans for both training and racing. The training plan can focus on process goals that can be measured and can represent short-term points in the process. (Chapters 4 to 6 address training process goals; chapter 7 addresses specific examples of training plans.)

The race plan covers key behavioral aspects of the day, including prerace prep, final cool-down, and nutrition. It identifies specific process-related tasks and behaviors you would like to accomplish. An example of such a plan appears in the sidebar on pages 22 to 23. As with other elements of goal evaluation and achievement, you should evaluate your performance after the race, preferably with the aid of a coach or other objective observer. The emphasis should be on identifying what you were successful at and why, which reinforces the positive behaviors you engaged in during both training and racing. You use a problem-solving approach to identify areas that you can improve on. As noted previously, in some cases you must modify goals to fit a more realistic assessment of abilities and skills.

Performance Visualization and Imagery

The systematic practice of visualization—actually seeing yourself in your mind's eye performing a given task successfully—has been shown to enhance actual performance of the task. On the surface, this approach seems to be of little value when you can often relentlessly train in a purely physical environment, but it is a nearly universal practice among successful athletes. There are two likely reasons for this finding. First, it is apparent that visualization of a skill being carried out activates the neural network in the same way that the actual physical practice of the skill does, albeit to a lesser degree. This allows practice to occur even when the physical accomplishment of the skill is not possible. Some actions in triathlon cannot be duplicated easily enough in training to practice them consistently. For instance, re-creating a swim start with hundreds of people in your wave is likely to occur only in races; therefore you are severely limited in your ability to practice in a real-world situation. Visualization allows you an opportunity to practice that task otherwise.

Second, practicing in the visualized environment rather than the real one usually leads to a successful attempt. When teaching the nervous system to produce a given skill in a given set of conditions, successful attempts in balance with unsuccessful ones lead to learning. Unsuccessful attempts create confusion in hardwiring the new synaptic connections that are thought to represent learning, thereby slowing the learning process. In fact, when unsuccessful attempts become dominant, they enhance the learning of a skill that leads to failure, not success. For instance, if each time you do a triathlon swim start, you hyperventilate and have a panic attack, that quickly will become your learned response for that situation. Using visualization as an adjunct method

Sample Race Plan

Prerace Evening

1. Prepare cycle equipment: Lube drive train, mount race wheels, check tire true, mount race flat kit.
2. Pack race bag:
   - Swim cap, race suit, wet suit, goggles, optional beach shoes
   - Cycle helmet and shoes, additional cycle clothing as necessary, antichafing product, flat repair tools, spare tubes or tubular tires, tire pump
   - Running race flats, number belt, hat, sunglasses, other running clothing as necessary
   - Transition-area towel, antibacterial cream, other equipment as necessary
   - Cleanup supplies, clothing as desired
3. Arrive in time for cycle course preview as able.

Race Morning

1. Set wake-up time, dress, eat breakfast.
2. Arrive early: Check in and get markings completed, secure transition spot, place equipment.
3. If not done previously, take opportunity to review the cycle course by car.
4. Check cycle equipment and air in tires.
5. Complete cycle and run warm-up; use opportunity on bike to review the run course if possible.
6. Do final tire-pressure check, set up cycle shoes with pedals, place cycle helmet, set up run shoes and race belt.
7. Go to the swim area for wave check-in and swim warm-up. Top off prerace fluids.

Race Start

1. Complete the swim leg.
   - Get out quickly for first 20 strokes to get in position, then settle.
   - Focus on any key stroke elements that are currently helpful or try to relax at the pace.
   - Build pace at midway if feeling strong.
   - Begin thinking through the transition as you approach the finish.
2. Complete the swim-to-cycle transition.
   - Move forward quickly but in control.

- Execute planned transition sequence: Put on helmet and glasses, run with bike to mount line, straddle bike, and ride on top of shoes.
- Anticipate problems—dropped shoes, struggle with wet suit—and remain calm.

3. Complete the cycle leg.
   - Find your way into mounted shoes when you have momentum, pedal on top of them until then.
   - Build cadence first in lighter gear; focus on relaxing.
   - Build gear as you warm up and feel stronger.
   - In draft-legal races, be aware of opportunities to work with other riders and move into a group quickly.
   - Find a steady, controlled effort; avoid surging. In draft-legal races, share the effort evenly, spin your effort, and be aerodynamic at the front.
   - Lighten gear as you approach the finish to bring up cadence. Stretch your back on the bike to prepare for the run.
   - Think through your transition as you approach it.
   - In draft-legal races, try to establish forward position in the group—particularly if it's a large one—as you approach transition.

4. Complete the cycle-to-run transition.
   - Maintain controlled speed into the dismount line and then dismount running—controlled but quick.
   - Rack bike, remove helmet, and put on shoes while standing.
   - Put on race belt and hat while moving out of transition.

5. Complete the run leg.
   - Focus on increasing stride rate and relaxing initially.
   - Build pace over the first half mile.
   - Run conservatively to midpoint; use tangents and draft as able.
   - Build run if able over last half; finish strongly over last half mile.

6. Complete the immediate postrace tasks.
   - Take initial refeeding and rehydration as soon as possible, then complete the planned cool-down.
   - Refeed and rehydrate more extensively at race site.
   - Collect equipment and clear the transition area.
   - Seek out a full meal within two to three hours from race finish.

Of course, the specifics of the plan should reflect your own and your coach's thought process about what you need to emphasize.

of practicing your swim starts allows you to maximize successful attempts because you can completely control what you choose to see, thereby enhancing appropriate, positive, useful learning.

Visualization practice can follow a progressive application as described previously. After identifying appropriate tasks you want to enhance, such as your newly developed swim stroke or the ability to traverse a twisting, high-speed descent on your bicycle, you could use an isolated environment in order to "watch yourself" perform the task successfully, using your mind's eye. You could augment this by using sensory inputs that enhance the realism of the task, such as thinking about the feeling of the water in the swim or the feeling of the wind rushing past you on your bicycle. Eventually you want to transfer this technique to increasingly real and challenging environments, using enhancements such as video and audio. Ultimately it can be used as a prelude to practice in the real-world environment. An example of this is stopping briefly by the side of the road before descending a steep pass on your bicycle to quickly review the descent in your mind.

You may also choose to use imagery to enhance your self-perception as a physically capable triathlete. For instance, many athletes enter triathlon from backgrounds in competitive swimming, in which a higher body weight and percentage of fat may have contributed to their success. They tend to see themselves as sleek and powerful, like sharks or dolphins. It's common for those athletes to struggle to see themselves as runners, who are linear, lean, and springy. The practice of imagery can assist them in making the transition psychologically—also leading to improvements in performance. In this example, athletes can create powerful images of themselves as runners by using concepts such as lightness and quickness associated with images such as a gazelle running lightly or a racehorse running powerfully.

Relaxation Breathing

You can reduce physical and emotional anxiety through controlled breathing combined with visualization and imagery, or you can use each technique independently. The portability of this technique is valuable in prerace situations, during training and racing, and at any time you have undue stress.

The classic method of slow, deep breathing uses the contrasting effects of muscular tension and release as well as activation of the parasympathetic nervous system to induce relaxation. You can accomplish this by taking slow, deep breaths, but several additional technique points may also be helpful:

1. Breathe in through the nasal passage and out through the mouth. This promotes a deeper inhalation and a relaxed exhalation.

2. Focus on the rising abdominal wall—this is evidence of a sufficiently deep breath and full use of the lungs.

3. Breathe slowly on a fixed in-and-out count, generally two to four seconds. This again encourages deeper, more complete breaths and avoids muscular action for exhalation.

4. Focus on both the tension in your respiratory muscles during inhalation and the relaxation as those muscles release during exhalation. This helps you to learn the process of relaxation through contrast.

5. During exercise, consider using only nasal breathing because it automatically slows and deepens your respiration, thereby creating both relaxation and improved lung function.

Desensitization

Certain responses to situations you might experience in triathlon represent behavior acquired by the process referred to as *respondent conditioning*. In these cases you respond reflexively to a stimulus even without any apparent reinforcement. Often this response will transfer to other related experiences. For instance, you might have had fear in an earlier swimming bout and then gradually associated that with all swimming experiences and even with water itself. This shows up in triathlon competition as anxiety or fear before the swim leg. Cycling close to others, swimming while wearing a wet suit that might feel confining, swimming in open water, and descending at high speeds on the bike are all typical experiences that can elicit a negative response reflexively.

The process used in overcoming negative responses to potentially negative stimuli is called *progressive desensitization*. You first need to develop a behavioral skill that replaces an ordinarily negative response with a positive response. An example is to consciously engage in relaxation breathing, as described previously, when you experience a stimulus that ordinarily produces the fear or anxiety. You then expose yourself to a level of the stimulus that you can tolerate by using the new behavior to replace the old one. For example, you might overcome a fear of swimming in a wet suit by first visualizing swimming in a wet suit while engaging in relaxation breathing. You could then gradually increase the specificity and intensity of the stimulus as you are able to control your response. In the example given, you might try visualizing swimming while wearing your wet suit, then doing the same in the bathtub, then swimming in your suit in a pool, then swimming in it in a lake.

Belief-System Evaluation and Self-Talk

On occasion, what you say to yourself comes out in speech, particularly when you are under great stress. Think of someone in a ropes-challenge course, scared nearly to a frenzy, repeating, "I can't do this." That person is unaware of anything but the challenge that awaits her. In virtually all cases, performing the task in the controlled environment of the ropes course is well within her physical capability. All the safety elements to prevent injury are in place. Yet she firmly *believes* that she cannot do the task. Consequently, she does not try. An experienced instructor will try to help by saying such things as "You can try" (not "You can do it" because in reality the person might not be able to), "I'm here to catch you," and "Failing is OK; you can also try again another time." In many cases, if the student can bring herself to say, "OK, I'll give it a try (even though I might not succeed)," she will then be able to complete the task.

Experiences like this reinforce the effect that both beliefs and self-talk based on those beliefs have on your ability to perform physical tasks. Triathlon often creates similar scenarios in your ability to deal with the physical discomfort and sometimes the pain associated with repetitive and power-demanding exercise, the anxiety associated with a given situation, and the fatigue that comes with completing a race or bout of training.

Belief systems are the mind-set you have in approaching any given situation. Rational belief systems are those based on factual information and prior experience. Irrational belief systems, which everyone has to some degree, are generally based on ideas passed on by others without significant experience or factual information. For example, many people believe that exercise must be difficult and painful in order to be effective. This belief is perpetuated by teachers, coaches, parents, and friends as well as the media. In other cases, the belief may arise from a single negative experience and is then perpetuated in the culture.

As an example, you might trace this belief back to the common use of an all-out 1.5-mile run to test the fitness of untrained high school students. For most, this experience is physically uncomfortable, anxiety producing, and demoralizing because they enter it unprepared to pace themselves properly and without having experienced this type of exercise. The common dynamic is to run as hard as possible for as long as possible and then dramatically slow to a walk. The students are often compared to each other to evaluate their performances with the use of "norms" for the event. Consequently, at least half of the participants "fail" because they fall at or below the average, regardless of how fast the group is overall. This is just one cause of the common belief that exercise must be painful.

Triathletes, by virtue of having chosen to participate in an endurance sport, have often garnered enough experience to have moved past this basic irrational belief to some degree. However, many other related irrational beliefs continue to be perpetuated in endurance athletics. These include ideas such as exercise is the best punishment, expensive and heavily cushioned running shoes prevent injuries, static stretching before exercise prevents injuries, training more is always training better, weightlifting is counterproductive for endurance athletes, speed work is not useful for endurance athletes, and it is necessary to drink as much as possible during exercise. Virtually all of these ideas have been debunked by both scientific studies reported in the literature as well as the documented experiences of many athletes. Yet they are still widely practiced and perpetuated culturally by experienced and inexperienced athletes alike as well as by certain coaches and other "authorities."

You must always examine your beliefs regarding any given training concept, situation, or outcome in terms of scientific and experiential evidence. Improvement can be limited if those beliefs are not addressed. Beliefs that you hold simply because family, friends, and coaches have told you they are true may be less rationally based than those you hold because you have tried and objectively evaluated something through your own experience.

Further, beliefs that you hold that can be supported by strong science may be more rational than those that are perpetuated because that's the way it's most commonly done in a given culture. Resistance to alternative ideas, seemingly unrelated anxiety about the topic or a situation, and an overzealous nature regarding current views are all warning signs that your beliefs may not be rational—that is, not based in fact or real experience. A classic example of this is the belief that static stretching has value in preventing injury. While this belief is commonly held by coaches, athletic trainers, and physicians, the available scientific evidence, collected over many years, clearly demonstrates little or no relationship between the two. Many athletes believe that stretching is useful in preventing injury only because they have been told to do so by someone in authority.

Of course, the best route to go in first examining and then changing belief systems as appropriate lies in both accumulating real experience and acquiring objective, factual information. Typically, scientific information is the best source regarding athletic competition and training, although you must also consider that not all science is methodologically valid. Generally it is best to look for a large weight of evidence, meaning that ideas have been demonstrated in multiple studies over time. You should then examine those ideas objectively in yourself before accepting them.

The ability to deal with situations or approaches to triathlon preparation and competition that may be limiting your performance can be developed both by changing belief systems and by using appropriate, positive self-talk. The use of specific, realistic phrases that can lead you toward a positive rather than negative outcome has a direct bearing on your ability to perform that task. The utility of this approach is apparent in trained athletes responding to stressful situations as well as in those new to a task who use self-talk to guide themselves through it. A familiar example is young children who are learning new tasks and are unfettered by extreme self-awareness. They talk to themselves out loud frequently, generally unaware of what they are doing.

The positive effect may occur as much by eliminating the action associated with the negative self-talk by blocking it as by creating any new or previously undeveloped ability associated with the positive thought. You can learn and practice self-talk within the context of your overall training approach. You need to identify given situations in training in which you feel hindered by your perception.

Effective self-talk involves the use of realistic and simple phrases. For example, when using self-talk to handle discomfort, "I can handle this for now" is far more believable to you than "I feel no pain." Consequently, that grounding in reality allows the phrase to guide your behavior (in this case, to tolerate the training intensity longer) as a result. Of course, self-talk should be practiced in training situations in order to be more useful in racing situations. Let's say you have decided to introduce a higher level of intensity in a given cycling workout focused on increasing your $\dot{V}O_2$max speed. You will work at the intensity for the amount of time that you can handle without reaching unreasonable discomfort. During this interval session, you plan to use a specific phrase, such as "This is tolerable for 15 seconds" at 15-second intervals throughout the interval. You write down the phrase and post it on your handlebars and then repeat it to yourself throughout the interval. This serves to block out the inevitable negative self-talk that would arise otherwise, such as "This hurts." It also tunes you in to your ability to handle discomfort, making it less likely that you will overextend yourself on the first interval and reduce your ability to perform later intervals.

Meditative State

Eventually, as you learn new skills and "hardwire" your nervous system to perform them, self-talk goes underground, meaning you lose awareness of it and then it ultimately goes away. Then you are essentially running on "autopilot," meaning the cerebellum is in control of physical skills. This is the meditative state that occurs when you are relaxed, with all cylinders firing in perfect coordination. Psychologists have also referred to this as the flow state. It is achieved both through repetition and relaxation of the mind, an absence of thoughts. As a result, you are more efficient, more relaxed, and capable of doing more work. It also allows you either to focus your concentration elsewhere, like being aware of the rider beside you getting too close, or to focus internally and be in the moment. Of course, for safety reasons, swimming, cycling, and running all require some degree of external awareness. However, when you reintroduce consciousness of your automatic activity, things tend to go wrong. This happens because you are no longer relying solely on the portion of the brain (the cerebellum) that regulates the movement automatically. The coach who reminds a basketball player about his technique just before shooting a free throw in the big game is setting him up for failure in this way. Exerting your consciousness to change how you do something is unlikely to be helpful unless you are struggling or learning in a given situation, as described previously.

Achieving the Flow State

1. Seek out races and training scenarios that challenge your skills and current development without overwhelming them.
2. Direct your attention as exclusively as possible to the task at hand. Avoid disassociating by using distractions such as television.
3. Prepare for every aspect of competition so that as little as possible is completely "new" in the experience.
4. Create a competitive plan as previously described.
5. Create special circumstances for important training sessions.
6. Create goals for training and racing that you can reasonably achieve. Ideally, most of them will be of a behavioral nature rather than outcomes.

Summary

Developing and training a set of mental skills is essential to success in multisport racing, however you define success for yourself. (Doing so is a skill in itself.) Sustained improvement in triathlon performance involves consistent training and preparation. Vital to training consistency is the nature of the motivational environment that you use for training. Performance can be further enhanced through the development of psychological skills such as realistic and flexible optimism, goal setting, behavior change, relaxation breathing, imagery and visualization, belief-system evaluation and positive self-talk, meditation, and receptiveness to new ideas. These skills can be enhanced through the use of specific techniques and through their systematic practice and incorporation into the training process.

3

Assessing and Improving Technique

Many triathletes presume that improvement in triathlon is simply a matter of training. Nothing could be further from the truth. You can realize tremendous improvements in swimming, cycling, and running almost immediately upon learning and being able to implement some of the basic concepts of effective technique for each discipline. This process happens every weekend in Total Immersion swim clinics and pose method running clinics around the United States.

What seems to prevent many athletes from improving technique is the mistaken belief that even if they want to, old dogs (that is, adult athletes) cannot learn new tricks. Again, nothing could be further from the truth. Even athletes who are at the top of one of the sports do not realize that changing to a "triathlon-centric" technique, even in the sport they have been really good at, might be just what the doctor ordered for the "trifecta." While those with well-established movement patterns will certainly require more time and repetition to create new movement patterns than those who are learning for the first time, everyone, regardless of age, can learn new physical skills—and mental ones as well.

Many older athletes do not want to go through this process because they have not had success with previous attempts. They have been unable to make changes in their techniques that last. But you *can* make sustainable changes by using a few basic neuromuscular learning techniques. Even more important for success is having a clear biomechanical model for the movement pattern you are trying to incorporate. The clinics mentioned previously work very well for most participants because they present a biomechanically sound model for learning. Some specific practice methods are mentioned later in this chapter. But first is a discussion of breathing techniques, followed by the biomechanical model on which the optimal technique for each sport is based.

Efficient Breathing

There is one element of technique that is common to all three sports—the method of breathing. Many multisport athletes have breathing-related problems, such as the tendency to pant or hyperventilate when running, and then suffer debilitating abdominal stitches; coughing and discomfort in the lungs, especially after hard training or racing in the cold; frequent colds, bronchitis, pneumonia, and sinus infections; or even exercise-induced asthma. The use of nasal breathing rather than the oral route for both exercise and normal breathing can help with these problems. The nasal passage is designed to humidify and warm the incoming air so that the lungs receive warm, moist air rather than cold, dry air. The nose is also designed to trap and remove pathogens, such as viruses, bacteria, and mold, along with other pollutants in the air. Nasal breathing also requires a greater inspiratory pressure than oral breathing because the passageway is longer and narrower. As a result, you automatically take deeper, slower abdominal breaths when you breathe through the nose. This is what can stop you in your tracks when you first try it.

When you start breathing through your nose at exercise levels at which you are accustomed to breathing orally, you feel as if you are not getting enough air—as if you're oxygen deprived. This feeling creates anxiety, which in turn stimulates an even greater need to breathe—through the mouth. Before you know it, you're moving to a pattern of shallow, rapid oral breathing. But in fact, you had been taking in plenty of oxygen with deeper, slower nasal breathing—likely more than when breathing orally. It takes longer for oxygen to move across the lung tissues to the blood than for carbon dioxide to move from the blood into the lung. Slower, deeper breaths allow more alveoli (the tiny sacs in the lung through which oxygen passes into the bloodstream and carbon dioxide passes out) to be exposed to blood flow. This allows for more efficient absorption of oxygen.

Why the urgency to breathe when you try to breathe through your nose when exercising, then? It occurs because the primary factor driving breathing sense is not the blood-oxygen (O_2) level; it is the blood-carbon dioxide (CO_2) level. CO_2 diffuses very rapidly on its way out of the lungs. With deep breaths in, even while the amount of available oxygen in the alveolar sacs is increasing, the CO_2 is diffusing out more quickly than the O_2 is coming in. So it equalizes across the alveolar linings of the lung more quickly. The CO_2 level then begins to rise in the bloodstream. That's also why "panting," or rapid shallow breathing, causes CO_2 levels to drop; the rapid breaths allow full expulsion of CO_2 without, however, achieving the full intake of O_2. As a result, with rapid breathing, both blood CO_2 and O_2 levels drop and you become dizzy.

Given time and patience, the body can learn to respond differently to increases in blood CO_2 levels resulting from slower, deeper breathing patterns. Breathing urgency can diminish. This is why you can train yourself to hold your breath longer—you adapt to higher levels of carbon dioxide in the blood. Ideally this process allows for better oxygenation of the blood while also inducing relaxation, resulting in both a lower heart rate and lower blood pressure both during training and at rest.

Learning to consistently breathe through the nose not only can alleviate problems such as coughing, lung pain, high heart rate, high blood pressure, and sinus problems, it can also help you train more consistently because of the absence of those problems. Also keep in mind that there is little research examining the effects of nasal breathing during exercise. The observations presented previously are anecdotal, but several studies have demonstrated that nasal breathing can be as effective in the management of asthma in certain patients as the use of medication (Mangla and Menon 1981; Shturman-Ellstein, Zeballos, Buckley, and Souhrada 1978).

A problem you might have while adjusting to nasal breathing is the production of larger-than-normal amounts of mucus. This problem is largely resolved with the use of daily sinus irrigation (a technique discussed in chapter 9) and a capsaicin pepper spray before exercise. Over time, mucus production diminishes greatly and is noticeable only in very cold weather. Another problem is that dehydration can make nasal breathing more difficult because your nasal tissues dry out. You can resolve this by improving hydration habits and by using nasal strips while training. It can take a few months to a year to realize the full adjustment of your CO_2 receptors' response at all levels of work intensity. You can accomplish this by initially reducing all training intensities to those at which you can comfortably breathe nasally and then gradually increasing intensity again over time. Alternatively, you can begin by breathing nasally only during the lowest intensities of your current training program and then gradually increase the proportion of workout time during which you breathe this way until you can do so across the full spectrum of workout intensities.

The switch to nasal breathing is most easily done for cycling and running. During swimming, it can be achieved between efforts but not necessarily within the stroke. This may be due to the fear of inhaling water and the fact that the inspiratory breath has to occur very quickly in the freestyle stroke cycle. The aquatic environment is already warm and moist, so you are not as likely to experience any of the problems caused by oral breathing while running and cycling. Also, you are already forced to adopt a slower, deeper breathing cycle to meet the requirements of freestyle technique, which is discussed later in this chapter.

A consistent nasal breathing pattern requires an ongoing, conscious effort. In this case, it may prove helpful to look to an ancient tradition of the Apache Native Americans as a state-of-the-art method for learning the new behavior. The Apache taught their young warriors to run long distances by doing so with water in their mouths. This allows you to breathe only nasally, and there is no need to concentrate on it—you just need to concentrate on not swallowing the water. When you do swallow, you just replace the water again. Do not use sport drink for this purpose—holding a sugary substance in the mouth is a sure way to accelerate tooth decay!

Biomechanical Models for the Three Sports

The application of biomechanics to triathlon is the application of principles developed by the study of human movement in swimming, cycling, running, and making transitions. The biomechanical models for each sport in triathlon consist of a set of general observations about how the movement should occur. Four elements are common to all self-propelled movement techniques: balance, application of force for propulsion, limb recovery, and drag reduction. In applying the models to a given athlete, variations can occur, but the principles remain the same. The variations reflect differences in factors such as strength, limb length, and joint range of motion. A general understanding and application of these models in triathlon training is useful for three main purposes:

1. To reduce the potential for injury associated with constant repetition of the movement pattern

2. To improve the effectiveness of the movement pattern in creating maximal speed and power

3. To improve the efficiency (the energy cost) of the movement in order to be able to move at the same speed more easily and with less fatigue while covering longer distances

If you are not accomplishing these objectives with a given change in technique, you should reevaluate it—and sooner rather than later.

For triathlon athletes and coaches interested in improving performance, the task is to understand the principles that guide swimming, cycling, and running movements and apply them on a daily basis. Many triathletes have basic technique deficiencies in one or more of the three sports. Given that most triathletes have come to the event as adults, generally with any degree of expertise in only one of the three sports, this is not surprising. It is a reasonable conclusion that triathletes are well served by emphasizing technique development, particularly for the sports in which they have the least experience. Even for the most elite triathletes, consistent work on technique has resulted in improvements in the basic measures of efficiency: distance per stroke and stroke rate in swimming; average pedal force applied per rotation and cadence (revolutions per minute, or rpm) in cycling; and stride rate, distance, and body posture in running. The following, of course, is the ultimate litmus test for technique development: Does it improve your race performance while at the same time not increase your injury risk?

Physics of Human Movement

Before you learn of the specific technique models for swimming, cycling, and running, you must understand the physics that governs human movement: the force of gravity, the body's center of mass, elasticity, inertia, momentum, drag, lift, summation of force, and transfer of momentum. The discussion of technique begins here with a review of these concepts and their applications to movements used in triathlon.

Gravity

Movements like swimming, cycling, and running are thought to result entirely from muscular force applications to the medium or the machine. To some extent they do—but of course, not entirely. Because the creation of muscular force requires the expenditure of energy, any given technique that relies entirely on muscular force is limited in terms of the level of efficiency and the peak work level that can be achieved. Gravity is an ever-present and freely available force generated by the Earth, which pulls all things toward its center. Through the use of proper technique, it can be harnessed to contribute to forward motion in swimming, cycling, and running. Limitations on forward motion resulting from the force of gravity can be minimized, in particular through the achievement of appropriate balance. Remember that whenever anything with mass, including your body or any part of it, or any piece of equipment such as the bicycle, is moving downward in relation to the Earth's surface, you can allow gravity to do some or all of the work to achieve forward motion.

Center of Mass

The center of mass of an object refers to its balance point, that point in space where the mass of the object is equally distributed around it in order to achieve a static equilibrium. Your body, then, has a center of mass, although it moves as you move and reposition your limbs and alter the distribution of mass. When the center of mass is vertically aligned with the base of support for the object, balance is achieved. In that state, the power of gravity to move you forward or backward, away from the balance point, or base of support, is minimized. As the center of mass moves outside of the body's base of support, movement occurs. Forward movement can be either assisted or inhibited by gravity without undue muscular energy cost. The simplest example of this in triathlon is what happens when you go downhill on a bicycle. At some critical downward degree of slope, where your center of

AP Photo/Michael Probst

Gravity assists forward movement when the center of mass is shifted, such as with a slight forward lean in running.

mass is displaced forward, you actually need to stop pedaling and focus only on reducing drag, because gravity will move you faster than you could move yourself using muscular effort. In a more complicated example, when you displace your center of mass slightly forward in running, it allows you to fall into each subsequent step.

Elasticity

Gravity can obviously do work that involves downward movement. You can also capture gravitational energy and use it for both upward and forward movements. This is accomplished with the use of the elasticity of your muscles and soft tissues. Elasticity is the capacity of a material, such as muscle or tendon, to absorb and return force applied to it that results in stretching. Gravity, in pulling your body back to the ground, also stretches your muscles and tendons as you land, allowing them to store energy. If this energy is not allowed to dissipate, it can then be used to create forward movement in running in much the same way that a stretched trampoline can be used to throw the body back into the air. If done properly, this reduces the amount of energy you must otherwise create metabolically to accomplish the same movement.

Inertia and Momentum

Inertia is the tendency of an object in motion to remain in motion once it has been initiated, or remain at rest if the object is not currently in motion. The forces necessary for overcoming the current state of inertia in an object (such as your moving body or stationary body) are referred to as the object's momentum. In physics, momentum is the mass of the object multiplied by its velocity at a given inertial state. As the inertial state of your body changes, its momentum also changes. It increases as you accelerate to higher velocities and lowers as you decelerate to lower velocities, ultimately reaching its lowest state at rest. When in your movement patterns you decelerate and then accelerate, your momentum fluctuates up and down. When you move through air or water, your forward movement velocity and resulting momentum are decreased by drag (discussed later), an external force that works to change your inertial state by resisting movement. Inertial movements, those in which a constant velocity is maintained without undue acceleration and deceleration, are more efficient than movements in which the state of inertia is constantly changing.

An example of this concept is the playground merry-go-round. To get the merry-go-round going initially (that is, to overcome its inertia at rest), you have to apply large forces to it through long pushes on it. This is necessary for overcoming its fairly large stationary inertia and creating momentum for movement and for the establishment of moving inertia. However, once the merry-go-round is going, or has achieved some state of movement inertia, you can maintain the latter easily by using frequent but small pushes. As long as you keep pushing at the same rate and pressure, you reduce both the tendency of the merry-go-round to decelerate

Going Faster by Pushing Less, Not More

Consider Amanda Stevens, a top triathlete who had competed at the NCAA Division I level as a swimmer for Texas Tech University. She was a lifetime swim star and hoped to transfer those abilities to elite triathlon. A typical assumption for someone with such a background is that there is no need to consider making adjustments in the swim stroke and that all energies should be focused on improving technique in cycling and running. In Colorado Springs for an altitude-training period, Amanda asked for an evaluation of her swim stroke. Of course, all the elements were there, but it became apparent pretty quickly that her stroke was not as "inertial" as one would like because she persisted in pushing during the last phase

Amanda Stevens

Photo povided by OU Medical Center, Oklahoma City

of her stroke before the recovery. This allowed her a small measure of increased distance per stroke, yet it caused her to decelerate more than necessary between strokes. It also created muscle fatigue in her triceps, which is typical for someone with her stroke pattern. Then she tried applying the inertial concept: She stopped pushing and brought her hand out rapidly after each rolling phase. Although it slightly reduced her distance per stroke, it allowed her to comfortably increase her stroke rate.

She came back just a few days later, excited about how easily she had swum a target set using the new stroke, an almost immediate indication that the stroke modification was effective for her.

and the possibility of acceleration. You thus create an efficient movement inertia that can be sustained over time without fatigue. Raising the force or frequency increases the momentum, settling in at a higher state of movement inertia.

An inexperienced merry-go-rounder will stop pushing for several turns after getting the machine going. Then as it begins to slow down, the pusher will give long and hard pushes in an attempt to keep it going. The resulting large accelerations and decelerations of the merry-go-round can cause rapid fatigue in the pusher. You can apply the same concept to creating efficiency in swimming, cycling, and running. You want to find ways of applying minimal forces quickly and frequently in order to achieve an inertial state of rapid forward movement. This helps you to go faster over time and reduce fatigue. You'll notice the high stroke rates in the swim, the high cadences on the bike, and the high stride rates on the run of the most efficient athletes. In practice, the most efficient rates vary from athlete to athlete based on such factors as body weight and the "drag values" that each creates. Higher frequencies are not always better when the distance covered per pedal stroke, run stride, or swim stroke is disproportionately reduced.

Drag

Drag refers to the tendency of a gaseous or fluid environment (air or water) to impede a body's movement through it. When some level of force is not being applied to propel the body forward, then drag causes deceleration. By reducing drag, you reduce the level of force required to overcome that deceleration and maintain movement inertia. The more dense the environment (water is more dense than air, for example), the greater the drag level for a given speed. The negative effect of drag in either medium increases exponentially as speed is increased.

The faster you go, the more important a factor drag becomes in inhibiting forward motion. The degree to which this occurs depends on such factors as the amount of frontal surface you present to the medium in which you are moving and how smooth or rough that surface is. By presenting a frontal surface area that is small and smooth, the body is able to more easily slice through air or water molecules much the way a knife slices through a watermelon more easily than a hammer does. Although the hammer will still get the job done, it does so less efficiently and at a greater energy cost.

The easy movement of air or water molecules around your body as you slice through them is referred to as laminar flow. The biomechanical means of improving laminar flow, thereby reducing drag, are more applicable in swimming and cycling than in running. However, they cannot be totally ignored in running and have greater significance both as you run faster and when you run into a headwind. You can also reduce drag by following behind another mass going in the same direction as you are. This is known as drafting. Drafting can substantially reduce the energy needed to move forward in swimming, cycling, and running—again as a function of speed and the nature of the environment.

Lift to Overcome Drag

In swimming you do not have a stable medium to apply forces against, as you do in running and cycling. (Roads are, of course, stable. Water, however, is not.) So when you push directly backward on the water, the force that you hope will propel your body forward is minimal, because the water moves as well. Swimming by pulling the hands and arms straight backward is referred to as using drag for propulsion. This is because the drag created by the hand moving backward becomes the anchoring force in the water that you have to push against. An illustration of this type of swim stroke is the paddle wheel as the method of propulsion for steamboats. (They do not move with great speed.) The paddle wheel pushes backward as the boat goes forward. The wheel anchors itself—that is, creates a base against which it pushes—by virtue of the drag it creates in the water. That force can then be transferred, albeit inefficiently, to push the boat forward. By using a stroke in which they push their hands directly backward under the body, many inexperienced swimmers do the same thing.

Efficient swimmers are defined primarily, although not entirely, by their long distance per stroke. This means that they travel farther for each force application, all other things being equal (which they usually aren't). They achieve this by creating lift rather than drag with their hands and arms, particularly through the first two-thirds of the stroke (see figure 3.1). This allows them to create a better anchor in the water against which they can apply pressure to propel themselves forward. Just as an airplane propeller creates a forward-acting force by sliding sideways, or perpendicular to

Figure 3.1 The proper position of the arms and hands to create lift instead of drag.

the intended direction of movement through the air, efficient swimmers move their forearms and hands laterally rather than backward. Lift refers to the force created by an object (the hand and forearm) moving perpendicularly to its line of travel. Thus, pulling with the core muscles is translated more efficiently into forward movement.

Summation of Forces

When you require the creation of large forces, as when lifting a heavy weight, you generally attempt to use as many muscles as is feasible at one time. This is the summation of forces. It is best accomplished by the simultaneous movement of all the joints that are involved in a particular muscular action. This is epitomized by a powerlift in weightlifting competition. In endurance sports, the peak forces you need for forward propulsion are usually not high, in comparison with the forces needed for lifting weights. Thus, instead of force maximization, you tend to favor the use of the transfer of momentum (discussed in the next section). One exception is during running. When each foot hits the ground, your body has to absorb as much as three times your body weight. So for this motion the summation of forces comes into play. With each step you simultaneously flex all of your joints from ankle to knee to hip in an effort to absorb the tremendous force through muscle contraction. Ideally, you will be able to retain the force through the elasticity of your muscles to assist in creating the next step forward.

Transfer of Momentum

In running, cycling, and swimming, the degree of force you need to create is relatively low. The main objective is to move the joint systems of your arms and legs in swimming and running, and your legs in cycling, quickly over and over again to create and maintain forward motion. This requires the transfer of momentum, which refers to the idea of maximizing the speed of limb movement (your hands and forearms) rather than maximizing the force applied.

The principle is illustrated by the action of a pitcher throwing a baseball, a light object. When you observe it in slow motion, you can see that the throwing action begins in the legs and trunk, gradually extending to the shoulder, then the elbow, and finally the wrist, each joint engaging in its action in turn. This creates a whiplike effect, transferring the initial momentum created by the trunk motion to the ball, with each successive joint movement adding velocity to the system as a whole. This is why every good pitching coach will say that it all begins with the legs.

The principle of transfer of momentum is applied in most human movements by the initiation of those movements from the core muscles and then the transfer of the movements to each successive joint in a kinetic chain sequentially. The velocity achieved in the final joint motion is the cumulative velocity of all the preceding joint motions. This transfer of momentum is how you connect your hips upward to your hands in swimming and your hips downward to your ankles in running and cycling. It is also the primary reason that traditional weight training movements (which are slow and use simultaneous joint actions) offer less-than-ideal carryover to sport movements like swimming and running because swimming and running rely on limb *velocity* more than limb *force*.

In swimming and running, the creation of force, even when sprinting, is low in comparison to maximum muscle capacity. In running it is applicable as you recover the leg after each landing on the ground. Transfer of momentum does not mean that physical strength is not important in producing these movement patterns. But understanding the principle will help you learn more efficient methods for developing the strength you need to employ each movement pattern and efficiently use its initiating core elements.

Effective Technique in Swimming, Cycling, and Running

The understanding and use of the principles described previously are the basis for creating a model of technique in swimming, cycling, and running. The translation of the various elements of this model into actual forward motion in each of the three sports produces many differences in the appearance of technique among athletes. This is due to differences in individual factors, such as muscular strength, joint flexibility, neuromuscular control, body type and weight, buoyancy, reaction time, level of fatigue, and environmental conditions. If you are to develop efficient techniques in the three sports, you need to use a set of technique elements effectively, regardless of the factors just mentioned.

Balance

All technique begins with either the static or dynamic balance position you use when either applying a force or gliding forward between force applications. When appropriately learned and developed, your dynamic balance in swimming will help you to minimize the use of energy to fight gravity and stay horizontal in the water. This allows you to devote more muscular energy to moving forward. In seated cycling, appropriate balance will allow you to achieve a more comfortable and relaxed aerodynamic position for both power generation and control of the bicycle. When standing on the bike, appropriate balance allows you to use gravity and reduce your muscular efforts as well. In running, the appropriate dynamic balance allows you to use gravity to fall forward into each ground contact and minimize the use of muscular energy.

Streamlining

When you move through water and air, they resist your movements forward by producing drag. As discussed previously, effective technique in both swimming and cycling relies heavily on the use of body positions that reduce drag by creating smooth laminar flow, otherwise known as streamlining or becoming aerodynamic or hydrodynamic. Especially on the bike, the design of the machine and its components can be made aerodynamic as well (see the various discussions of equipment). The dramatic improvements in time-trial cycling (racing against the clock) that occurred once the aerobar position on the bike was adopted by top athletes during the 1980s are a classic example of this concept. But in running, technique is not influenced by the need to reduce drag other than by an athlete's choice to run behind and draft on another athlete or by the selection of clothing.

Force Production

Effective swimming, cycling, and running techniques all require specific points of force production. These must be optimized to allow the largest muscles to be used effectively (thereby reducing fatigue and increasing power), to allow the force to be applied quickly (to maintain the forward motion inertia), to allow the force to be applied in a way that captures gravitational energy when possible (to improve efficiency), and to reduce the potential for injury through proper joint alignment and proper muscular contraction patterns. In general, effective joint alignment is achieved through the use of the joints in a way that allows them to create force with the direction of movement and use the involved joints in the neutral position. In running, the hip, knee, and foot should all be pointed forward during ground support. In swimming, the need to create lateral movements to achieve lift further complicates the question of optimal joint alignment.

Recovery

Once force is applied in swimming, cycling, and running, effective technique allows the limbs to apply the force and then return easily to a position where the force can be applied again. As with force application, recovery should occur in a way that allows for the use of large-muscle groups, rapid return, minimal resistance created by the returning limb, maximal assistance from gravity, and maintenance of optimal joint alignment.

Evaluating Efficiency of Technique

You can evaluate efficiency of technique in swimming, cycling, and running easily by measuring distance per stroke and stroke rate as they affect speed in swimming, cadence and application of force as they influence power and speed in cycling, and stride frequency and length as they influence speed in running. Adjustments in technique that alter these factors should allow for greater short-term speed or other direct measures of performance. Short-term speed often improves first because, when not fatigued, you can more easily maintain the mental focus necessary in order to produce a given technique. In swimming, you sometimes fail to recognize positive change because you misapply other markers of effectiveness of technique, such as distance per stroke, in evaluating the effect of a technique change.

In the study of technique change in sport science, people sometimes get confused on this point by measuring economy or aerobic energy cost. Virtually all studies that examine aerobic energy cost in relation to changes in technique find that energy cost is increased over the short term. This makes sense because if the new technique requires your conscious attention in order to produce it, the nervous system has not yet learned it. However, if the technique allows you to produce work at higher rates or in a way that you perceive as easier, as measured directly through performance, then any temporary increase in aerobic energy cost seems to you less important. It is also likely that if the technique is mechanically more efficient (more work can be produced per unit time), then the body will eventually become physiologically more efficient (less energy or oxygen is used) over time. The only question is how rapidly that process will take place. Basic methods of enhancing neuromuscular learning rates are discussed toward the end of this chapter.

With appropriate application, you can use several other measures of mechanical effectiveness. In swimming, coaches examine both distance per stroke and stroke rate. If, at a given effort, you see distance per stroke improved without sacrificing stroke rate, that generally indicates an improvement. For instance, if a swimmer achieves better distance per stroke by lowering his head to achieve better balance at the same stroke rate, then he will swim a length faster at the same effort. However, if in achieving a greater distance per stroke, the stroke rate is reduced and the times are slower, this is often a nonproductive stroke change. An example here is the outcome when you emphasize pushing at the end of the force-production phase of your stroke cycle: Even though distance per stroke can be improved this way, stroke rate is reduced and greater muscular fatigue is created for the same swimming velocity.

You can easily evaluate distance per stroke by counting strokes per pool length. You can determine stroke rate afterward by dividing the time it takes to swim a length by the number of strokes it took to get there. A coach can quickly check stroke rate by timing several stroke cycles, averaging them, and then converting to strokes per time unit. The model of stroke development advocated here focuses on improving distance per stroke at a given rate, using both stroke development and strengthening exercises that mimic the swimming movements and then using more general conditioning methods to achieve higher stroke rates with minimal or even no sacrifice in distance per stroke.

In cycling the most fundamental measure of technique is cadence, the number of pedal revolutions per minute. Cadence must be measured with an odometer. As a general rule, if you can achieve a given power output by increasing cadence without increasing energy cost (which can be roughly measured by perception of effort), you will likely have improved your pedaling technique. Doing so should also result in at least a short-term increase in speed, as discussed previously. A second basic measure lies in the inertial application of force to the pedals. Improved technique will result in a steadier application of force with less acceleration and deceleration. You can readily examine this by using stationary equipment that creates noise. You simply seek to reduce fluctuations in the noise level to incur steadier force applications. The Computrainer stationary trainer offers the spin scan, a graphic representation of power output during the pedal stroke. This offers an even clearer method of feedback regarding cycling efficiency.

In running, as in swimming, the frequency and length of strides give you basic feedback about effectiveness of technique. You can measure stride frequency by placing foot sensors on the shoe or by counting the number of steps taken over a fixed time. You can measure stride similarly while running by using foot-sensor technology or calculating it based on the number of steps you take to complete a fixed distance. As discussed earlier relative to swimming, an increase in stride length at a given frequency and effort is a productive change. However, increasing stride length with a decrease in frequency often leads to the most common error in technique: overstriding. And at a given speed, improved technique often, though not always, leads to an increased stride rate and reduced stride length. You are moving your legs faster, but you are running more efficiently. If your technique is correct, you will eventually be able to achieve a longer stride length at higher stride rates, thereby achieving a higher high-end running speed without overstriding and risking injury.

Because you increase speed by increasing stride length, developing a technique that allows you to easily achieve a high stride rate without limiting the potential for adjustments in stride length as you run faster is advantageous. Again, any technique improvements along these lines should occur quickly with short-distance performance improvements.

Measuring Technique Efficiency

Swimming

Distance per stroke: Distance swum divided by the number of strokes taken in that distance.

Stroke rate: Time taken to swim a distance divided by the number of strokes taken in that distance.

Cycling

Cadence: Measured with an odometer.

Inertial force applied to pedals: Evaluated with a stationary cycle that creates noise.

Running

Stride frequency: Number of steps taken over a certain time.

Stride length: Distance run divided by the number of strides taken in that distance.

Technique Model for Swimming

An assumption made by many competitive triathletes is that the stroke of choice for competition will always be the crawl stroke, or freestyle (as it is commonly, although inaccurately, referred to in the United States), because this stroke is generally the fastest. The term *freestyle* actually refers to the use of any style in competition; however, the term is used here in place of the crawl stroke. For some athletes with inefficient technique or poor conditioning, it might not be possible to sustain the freestyle stroke through a complete race. For such athletes, a combination of strokes, particularly backstroke or breaststroke, provides the best opportunity to finish the swim safely and in comfort. Numerous texts address the principles associated with those strokes, so the focus here is on the freestyle. Most people learn most easily by using the part–whole method. This means that you break the movement down into logical parts and learn those parts progressively, eventually merging the parts into the whole.

Balance

By creating and maintaining a balanced horizontal body position, you expose a smaller surface area to the water as well as reduce the kicking energy necessary to keep the legs up. Many swim coaches and teachers consider this the most fundamental aspect of swimming skill to develop first. Optimal body balance in freestyle swimming creates a position as close to horizontal as possible. You achieve this by balancing the body across its central rotation point, or center of buoyancy; in this case the center of buoyancy is the lungs because you are floating in water. You can picture this by imagining the way a teeter-totter is balanced by creating equal forces on each end and placing the fulcrum, or rotation point, in the center. However, in swimming, the teeter-totter is inherently unbalanced because one lever is longer than the other. Because your center of buoyancy is in the chest, your legs are a longer and heavier lever; this is why they tend to sink. In freestyle swimming you can offset this with the position of your head and an extended arm. By keeping your head down and an extended arm forward at all times, you tend to balance the system and stay horizontal in the water more easily. Some coaches and athletes refer to this as creating pressure forward, or "pressing the T."

➤ BASIC BALANCE

You can test balance easily by first attempting to float facedown with your arms at your sides. You'll notice that your legs tend to sink unless you kick. Then experiment with pressing forward with your head to offset the sinking effect. You can then extend this concept to achieve the same floating ability as you roll from side to side. Increase the difficulty of this drill as you become better at it by placing a successively greater number of kickboards under the chest. This creates an inherently less stable situation, further developing your balancing skills.

➤ SIDE BALANCE

You'll move to the classic extended arm position on your side, which is used as a basic drill for balance. You make approximately a quarter turn from a flat position in the water to achieve the correct alignment (see figure 3.2). Note that your head should maintain its neutral alignment except when you are breathing. You can easily evaluate the effectiveness of your balance by your ability to minimize kicking while maintaining your body position in the drill. It's easiest to do this drill with flippers on. It becomes progressively more challenging when you remove the flippers and then when you reduce the kicking frequency.

Figure 3.2   Side balance.

The most common error in balancing is to lift the head too much, which forces your legs down, increases the work required of kicking, and increases drag. These things in turn increase the rate of fatigue. If you exhibit this error, improved balance will immediately increase distance per stroke and reduce stroke count at a given effort. Even very effective swimmers often lose balance somewhat while breathing. You must seek to maintain your balance throughout the complete stroke cycle. Further, in a race, when lifting the head to sight the next buoy (or other mark) in open water, teach yourself to rebalance quickly by dropping the head again immediately.

Another related error is to use a stroke in which the arm movements are always in opposition to each other. This creates a substantial period in each stroke cycle during which no arm is extended forward and tends to inhibit body roll during the stroke. Many swimmers achieve their best short-sprint times this way because it allows for a very rapid stroke rate, which is easy to learn. However, drag is greatly increased, and so many of the great freestyle sprinters use the optimal mechanics described earlier in the chapter, albeit at a very high stroke rate and with less rolling range of motion than when swimming longer distances.

In open-water triathlons, these errors begin to surface, even in those with well-developed balance otherwise. If you do not learn to deal with this in training, you will gradually lose balance and lose stroke effectiveness. The use of a wet suit might further aggravate this process by improving buoyancy (so the head can be held up too long too easily) and inhibiting the natural roll.

Streamlining

In the freestyle stroke, you can achieve effective streamlining by using the side balance body position described previously. The extended arm, lowered head, and quarter-turn position create both a horizontal position and a long, tapered alignment that reduces drag by presenting a smaller and smoother surface for water molecules to move past, encouraging smooth laminar flow. Imagine the long, sleek lines of a speed boat to visualize this concept.

Competitive triathletes also use both wet suits and body shaving to improve laminar flow. Each allows the surface of the skin to create less turbulence in the water molecules moving past. The wet suit also enhances buoyancy, making it easier to sustain a horizontal position in the water.

➤ SIDE BALANCE WITH FLIPPERS

The side balance drill is also effective for practicing streamlining. You can further augment it by using flippers to move through the water rapidly in the position—this enhances the sensation of drag when inappropriate body positions occur. You then learn to move from side to side, rolling between opposite-side streamline positions and spending as little time as possible in the less streamlined, flat position in the water. If the drill works in transferring the streamlining skill to your stroke mechanics, you should notice a reduction in your stroke count for a given distance.

Force Production

Forward motion in swimming results from effective applications of the force you create to the water. This works best when you create force using the powerful trunk muscles and then transfer that force to lateral movements of your hands and forearms, which are your paddles. However, the rotational movements involved must also be counterbalanced by an efficient kick. Each of these aspects of force production is discussed in greater detail in the following sections.

Transfer of Momentum From the Core Muscles

This concept can be described by relating it to the use of a hand saw. When you begin to make a cut in wood, you use small movements coming largely from your shoulder. But this fatigues the small muscles of the arm and forearm, so you quickly adopt a technique that allows you to move the saw by rotating the torso. The larger muscles of the torso doing the work do not fatigue as easily, and you become more relaxed in your movements. The torso begins moving first. Then the movement is transferred sequentially into each of the joints leading out to your hand, which is holding the saw. When possible, you also brace your legs by holding on to something with the opposite arm, allowing you to apply more force to the saw more easily through stabilization.

This analogy can be extended further for those familiar with kayaking. In kayaking you create each stroke by placing the paddle in the water in the best alignment and then sweeping it laterally by using a sequential movement that begins in the torso. This allows you to create stroke after stroke at increasingly higher rates with minimal fatigue in the arm or local muscle. In freestyle swimming, the same principle can be applied. By initiating movements in your powerful torso muscles and then transferring them to the arms, which act as paddles in the water, you can achieve a powerful and nonfatiguing swimming stroke that resembles what a skilled kayaker achieves. The key to success is linking the hips and torso to the arms in stroke-power production as a means of lengthening the kinetic chain (that series of interconnected muscles and bones that extend the trunk movements out to the limbs) from which each stroke's hand speed and power are derived. You do this by placing the hand forward in the water with the fingertips pointing down and then rolling laterally to move the hand laterally. This causes the elbow to rise and creates an effective lift position whereby the hand and forearm act as a propeller as they are swept sideways. When moving from the starting position (the quarter-rotation balance position described earlier) to the midpoint of the roll (a flat position in the water), the shoulder is moving out from the midline of the body (see figure 3.3*a*).

As a result, the hand is also sweeping out from the midline of the body because the arm and hand are moving with the torso rather than independently of it. This is often called the outsweep or downsweep. It is achieved not by moving the arm laterally but by rolling and maintaining the current orientation of the arm to the torso, which sweeps the arm, forearm, and hand (the paddle) laterally as the body rolls. As this sweep occurs, you create a propeller by pointing the fingers down, keeping the underwater elbow high or forward, and angling the little-finger side of the hand forward. As you pass the midpoint of rotation, your shoulder begins to move back toward the midline of the body. This allows you to naturally reverse the direction of your arm, forearm, and hand to create an inward sweeping motion most often referred to as the insweep or upsweep (see figure 3.3b). This inward motion is achieved without the need for conscious thought because the shoulder

Figure 3.3   In the freestyle stroke, (a) moving to the midpoint of the roll, (b) the insweep, and (c) creating a propeller with the hand and arm.

continues to follow the torso rotation with the forearm and hand following in turn. The only necessary adjustment is a repositioning of the hand and forearm to create a propeller. This is done by angling the thumb side of the hand forward (see figure 3.3c). These sweeping motions provide for effective anchoring of the paddle (your hand and forearm) so that the large muscles of the back can be used to flex the shoulder simultaneously to pull the body forward over and past the anchoring point.

However, as you complete the trunk rotation, you must achieve further lateral motion of the hand outward or movement backward by using the smaller muscles of the arm, particularly the triceps. Because pushing backward at this point relies primarily on drag to anchor the hand, to do so you would use lots of muscular effort for very little payback in forward impulse. In addition, this wasted movement reduces your potential stroke rate and results in deceleration and loss of your current inertial state. Consequently, you want to rapidly remove the hand from the water at this point without fully extending the elbow to quickly initiate your recovery.

You recover the arm by drawing it forward in a high elbow position while on your side and then allow it to fall easily into the extended arm position forward of the body. This falling, if done by relaxing the arm rather than by forcing it into the water, allows you to use the elevated part of your body to capture gravity and help in initiating the next consecutive rolling action of the body. If the opposing extended hand is allowed to relax and sink slightly into an ideal catch position (fingers and forearm down, elbow high and forward) while you're recovering your opposite arm, then the next roll also initiates the next insweep and outsweep in a well-timed stroke.

The timing concept of one arm or the other always extending in front of the body is referred to as front-quadrant swimming. Done correctly (body roll and sweeps created from the trunk and not the arms), it results in the most rapid movement of the sculling hands and forearm (to create lift) for the least expenditure of energy by the arms, which are more subject to fatigue than the larger muscles of the trunk and upper back. These movements are further facilitated by a relaxed high elbow return of the pulling arm to reduce efforts for recovery and maintain a neutral joint posi-

Figure 3.4   The high elbow position during recovery.

tion in the shoulder (see figure 3.4). Basic drills for learning and practicing this concept are simple extensions of the side balance drill on page 45.

➤ SIDE BALANCE EXCHANGE

Begin from a side balance position, recover the trailing hand, and make an exchange to the opposite side balance position. The exchange is initiated when the recovering arm begins to fall. The extended arm should be allowed to relax and sink with fingers down before the recovery arm falls. You then balance on the opposite side for a few breaths so that each exchange is discrete and you are able to give your full attention to it. This drill is easiest to do while using flippers and paddles, and it becomes progressively more challenging as you do the drill without them.

➤ SINGLE-ARM SWIMMING

This force-production and timing drill is more advanced. Begin in the side balance position and then complete a full stroke by initiating rotation from the hips, rolling to the opposite side during the pulling phase, and then rerolling in return during the recovery phase to return to the original side balance position (see figure 3.5). This is all done with the opposite arm held back at the hip and not used. It is important to both initiate and return to the side balance position rather than initiate and return from a flat position in the water.

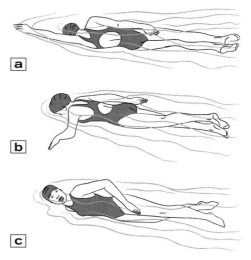

Figure 3.5   Single-arm swimming.

Effective Lift With Sculling Movements

The ability to feel the water is often attributed to great swimmers. As you come to understand the concept of lift forces allowing you to anchor the hand in the water as it slides laterally, the concept of feel for the water becomes more comprehensible. The use of effective sculling movements to create lift through the hands and forearm results in improved efficiency in propelling yourself through the water. Rather than relying on muscle strength to pull water back, you use the trunk-initiated stroke to allow the power of the hips to be translated to hand and forearm lateral velocity in a way that anchors the hand in the water relative to the line of travel (as it moves rapidly sideways, perpendicular to the line of travel, with each sculling stroke). This approach allows the body to be pulled past each stroke point with minimal wasted muscle force and reduced fatigue in the arms.

The arm muscles are used only to maintain a lift position, which allows the more powerful upper-body muscles to pull the body forward. This results in the classic outward and inward sculling pull pattern seen in all proficient swimmers. The most significant aspects of this principle of technique are a well-timed catch with fingertips pointing toward the bottom of the pool before initiating hip roll, the hand angled properly, and a high elbow throughout the outsweep and insweep of the stroke to keep the hand and forearm in the vertical lift-generating position.

It is important to reiterate that the sculling motions seen in the hand are merely extensions of the rotation of the trunk, not the results of deliberate attempts to create an S-shaped pulling pattern. Consequently, you learn this not by trying to create a pattern of hand movement in the water but by positioning the hand and forearm correctly and then allowing the trunk to move it. If you've already achieved proper stroke timing, this can be as simple as trying to drop the fingers downward as you begin each roll. This idea is what constitutes feel for the water. Australian swimming coach Cecil Colwin (2002) describes the sculling concept as one that "interprets and uses flow." You might come to understand how lift forces work in practice by placing your hand in moving water, a stream for instance, and noting the effect as you reposition it. When held parallel with the current, your hand can be maintained easily in alignment with the flow; however, once you angle the hand in one direction or the other relative to that alignment, it begins to deflect laterally from the direction of flow. This deflection results from a lift force generated by the water molecules moving past the upper and lower surfaces of your hand at unequal speeds and with greater or lesser turbulence. You can discover this feel in the pool by using a combination of sculling drills, swim paddle exercises, and closed-fist swimming.

➤ BASIC SCULLING

This drill consists of floating flat and facedown in the water, similar to the position used in the basic balance drill described previously. In this case, both hands are projected forward with fingers pointing down to the bottom of the pool and elbows high (see figure 3.6). You then sweep the hands back and forth laterally to your forward line of movement, altering the pitch of the hand to place the little finger forward on outsweep and thumb forward on insweep. While doing so, remember that this drill is used primarily for learning how to position and angle your hands to create pressure. In actual freestyle swimming, you should avoid using your arm and shoulder muscles to create lateral sweeps; instead, rely on your torso movements to do so.

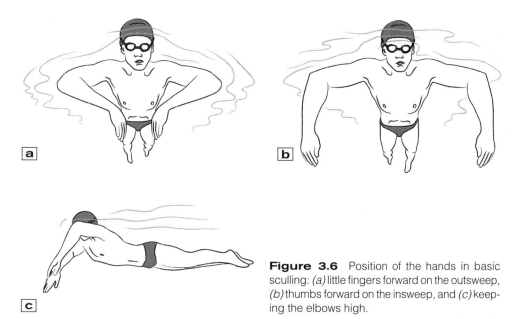

Figure 3.6   Position of the hands in basic sculling: *(a)* little fingers forward on the outsweep, *(b)* thumbs forward on the insweep, and *(c)* keeping the elbows high.

➤ SIDE BALANCE SCULLING

You can modify the basic sculling drill so that you scull with a single hand forward while in the fundamental balance position (with body in a quarter turn and a single arm extended forward) described on page 45.

When swimming the freestyle, focus on allowing the fingers to drop and the forearm to sink in a relaxed way and concentrating on the roll itself—the rest will tend to flow if the arm is positioned properly before the roll and then allowed to follow with it in a relaxed way. A common stroke error that interferes with this approach is attempting to extend the arm as far forward as possible with fingers extended upon entering the water. This inhibits your ability to make an effective catch at the stroke-entry point by placing the hand and forearm in a poor sculling position when the next roll is initiated, and it creates unnecessary tension in the hand and forearm.

➤ PADDLE SWIMMING

You can increase the effectiveness of your sculling actions in practices by using paddles to provide a larger surface area for creating lift. Paddles provide the further benefit of penalizing you when you fail to position your hands properly at various points in the stroke cycle. If you use paddles incorrectly, you will find yourself "catching" them in the water.

➤ FIST SWIMMING

To heighten sensitivity once you begin to experience the elements consistently, you can also try swimming freestyle or completing the other drills with your hands held in fists or wearing fist gloves. Fist swimming increases the need for proper forearm positioning before the roll, which helps in keeping the elbow high and forward.

Kicking

In the well-balanced stroke of an elite freestyle swimmer moving at aerobic-effort level, the kick primarily serves to counterbalance torso rotation. Because the ankles are supple and the feet can be easily extended in a relaxed way, at this level of swimming it is common to see a two-beat kick per complete stroke cycle. Each kick offsets the two opposing torso rotations that are created by the complete stroke cycle. However, even in efficient swimmers, the kicking tempo will naturally increase as the stroke rate is increased toward sprinting speeds. Some coaches emphasize the kick as the driving mechanism to bring up stroke rate when sprinting, for instance. This allows the kick to provide propulsion as well as balance, particularly through the gliding phase of each stroke cycle. Sprinting swimmers will often use four or even six kicks per stroke cycle. Some highly conditioned swimmers can achieve this kicking rate over distances longer than the sprints as well.

In poorly balanced swimmers, however, a high kick rate even at low stroke rates is an indication that the kick is the primary force being used to balance the body. This is extremely fatiguing and ultimately results in loss of efficient body position over time. In some extreme examples, often seen among triathletes without a competitive swimming background, the kick actually creates a drag force pulling the body backward. This is because many runners have difficulty allowing the lower-leg muscles to relax, in turn allowing an extended toe (plantarflexed) position to be created naturally by the downward action of the kick. Rather, they hold their ankles in a dorsiflexed (toes-toward-shins) position throughout the kick cycle. This dominance of toe position, which inhibits the development of an effective swim kick, probably results from the practice by some runners of holding the foot in a dorsiflexed position before foot strike, a common running error discussed later.

As with effective arm technique, effective kicking technique first and foremost is initiated from movements of the hips. The rest of the upper- and lower-leg musculature then responds in a relaxed, whiplike fashion to create the final forceful flexing motion of the ankle. You can learn this type of motion both by using vertical kicking and by using flippers.

➤ VERTICAL KICKING

Assume a vertical position in the water and use the flutter kick to support yourself with your head out of the water. Use your arms to scull initially and then increase the difficulty of the drill by using your arms less and eventually even lifting them out of the water so that you become increasingly reliant on your kick. Doing the flutter kick in a vertical position in the water allows you to more easily relax and create the extended foot and ankle position necessary for effective kicking.

➤ FLIPPER KICKING

Flipper kicking increases the forces on the kicking musculature, allowing for improved muscular control and relaxation as well as an improved rate of neuromuscular learning. In addition, flippers so heavily compromise the dorsiflexed kicking position described earlier as to make it impossible to achieve. You can use flippers to improve your kicking in combination with your full stroke and with many other drills.

You should allow the timing of the kick to develop naturally as improved kicking mechanics are created and improved body balance in general develops in the stroke. Higher-tempo kicking will then evolve naturally as you swim faster in training.

Recovery

Many great freestyle swimmers are noted for relaxed high elbow stroke recoveries. The high elbow allows the arm to be drawn forward quickly with minimal effort by shortening the arm's length. A less obvious but equally important observation concerns the positioning of the recovering arm in relation to the middle upper back. When the middle upper-body musculature is weaker than the propelling muscles, the scapula (shoulder blade) is often rotated outwardly during the recovery. This creates some pressure on the shoulder's rotator cuff (especially the part of the muscle group that makes up the rotator cuff, known as the supraspinatus) and is a likely cause of shoulder pain. This forward rotation of the scapula is usually seen in a relaxed standing posture as well.

To rectify this problem, you want to engage in scapular setting, or the pulling of the scapula back to the midline of the back during the high elbow recovery. You can learn this in the gym (as discussed in chapter 4) and then emphasize it in the stroke.

➤ FINGER TOUCH

This is a classic drill for developing the high elbow recovery. In this drill you try to exaggerate the high elbow position by touching the thumb on the armpit while recovering the arm either while swimming freestyle or while doing the other drills described. This encourages both the high elbow position and scapular setting. Scapular setting is also encouraged by angling the palm of your hand toward your face while recovering the arm.

A second aspect of the recovery is the need to allow the recovering arm to fall to the water rather than be placed in it with undue muscular control. With proper timing, this allows you to use the recovering arm to initiate the next roll and reduces the efforts necessary for recovery. You can practice this by focusing on the idea while performing the previously described force-production drills.

Putting It All Together

All of these stroke elements may be easily observed in the strokes of the great Australian distance swimmers of the first decade of the 21st century, including Kieren Perkins, Ian Thorpe, and Grant Hackett. Although each looks a little different and has a stroke rate that varies based on height, strength, flexibility, and buoyancy, they all use the same stroke elements described previously. What's most interesting is how these great swimmers retain those elements even when swimming the 100-meter freestyle at very high stroke rates.

To achieve your best possible results in the swim, you are best served by beginning your technique work by focusing on the balance concept, then progressively adding the other elements as you build and rebuild your stroke. Table 3.1 provides a sequential set of drills that can be used for this purpose.

Table 3.1 Freestyle Drill Element and Drill Progression

Technique element	Drill
Balance	Basic balance
	Side balance
Streamlining	Side balance with flippers
Force production	Side balance exchange
	Single-arm swimming
	Basic sculling
	Side balance sculling
	Paddle swimming
	Fist swimming
Kicking	Vertical kicking
	Flipper kicking
Recovery	Finger touch

Technique Model for Cycling

In cycling it is commonly presumed that motor skill is of little consequence to the outcome. After all, many think, you are connected to the pedals and forced to follow the route the pedals' circular motion creates. But even in cycling, movement skill development offers some potential for performance improvement and injury reduction. Most triathletes ride an upright rather than recumbent bicycle because the latter is currently outlawed in competition. Beyond this presumption, the same basic movement model discussed previously for swimming can be applied to upright cycling as well.

Balance

Effective body positioning on the bicycle produces an optimal blend of comfort, control, power output, and aerodynamics. What is optimal in this case takes into account that in triathlon an athlete must run after cycling. This consideration also influences the balance of comfort and aerodynamics that you choose for any given type of bicycle and the body position you attempt to create on it. How you prioritize these factors in creating a position on the bike may vary based on event length, power requirements, and the flexibility and skill of the rider. For instance, an athlete training for an Ironman-length event might choose a less aerodynamic position that will also allow for less muscular fatigue over a long ride. Thus for cycling, the riding position must be individually developed.

To maximize control and comfort, it is normally presumed that a rider will distribute body weight equally across the bicycle's ground contact points or wheel centers. Normally, riders will put slightly more weight on the back wheel than on the front, leading to a 55 to 60 percent weight distribution on the rear wheel and a 40 to 45 percent weight distribution on the front wheel. This allows the seat to accommodate a larger proportion of the body weight while still providing for control through the front wheel.

In terms of weight distribution, the most common problem in triathlon is that when aerobars are used on conventional-frame-geometry road bicycles, there is more weight on the front wheel than on the back. Most of the commercially available clip-on aerobars place the rider too far forward on the conventional road bicycle. This reduces control by creating an unstable platform, which can be a problem when the rider encounters road irregularities and sharp turns. There are a variety of ways to remedy this problem without sacrificing aerodynamics, such as modifying stem length and height, selecting aerobars that have the pads behind rather than in front of the handlebar–stem intersection, or selecting a triathlon bike with a steeper seat tube. The most efficient approach to this problem, once you settle on a frame and handlebar setup, is to use an adjustable stem for the time necessary to establish your best position and then replace it with a fixed stem later. You can achieve proper positioning and weight distribution on the bike by making corrections for frame size, seat position, and stem, handlebar, and tribar adjustments. However, bike fitting and positioning are not an exact science. The best advice is to find a bike professional who can assist you in selecting the type and frame size of racing bicycle and the ancillary equipment (aerobars, stem, seat) that will work for you, and then make the adjustments that will lead to the most effective and comfortable position on the bike.

Once you have created an effective position on the bike, developing your dynamic balance occurs normally through riding. You can use a specific form of practice called roller riding to move this process along more quickly.

➤ ROLLER RIDING

Riding stationary rollers improves your balance by narrowing the possibilities for both lateral movement and backward-and-forward movement on the bike. You can also use this approach to create a controlled training environment for the development of speed, endurance, and heat acclimation, as discussed in chapter 5. You should begin by riding in your most comfortable upright position with your hands on the top of the handlebars for maximum control; you can progress to positions in the drops and on your aerobars, standing, and performing the other drills described later in this section.

Streamlining

Another consideration in creating an effective body position on the bicycle is the need to reduce drag. To do this, you need to streamline the body as much as possible (see figure 3.7). This is important in cycling because the higher speeds achieved while riding, in comparison to running, increase the effect of drag. Further, when air is moving toward you, opposite your line of travel, the perceived wind speed is increased even more so. If, for example, you are riding into a 10 mile-per-hour (mph) headwind at 20 mph, the perceived wind speed is 30 mph. The faster you go, in fact, the higher the wind speed you need to overcome. Thus the importance of streamlining your body increases as your power output (and resulting speed) improves.

You'll want to create as narrow an aerodynamic profile to the perceived wind as you can without substantially sacrificing your ability to create power or run later. You do this by leaning forward and placing your forearms over the handlebars in a forward and parallel position, similar to that seen in downhill ski racing. This position is achieved with the help of aerobars, which create a "cockpit." Your aerodynamic position is then enhanced by lowering the stem, handlebars, and aerobar in the head tube. However, you can go only so far in doing this, because dropping your upper body more and more toward the horizontal position has a direct effect on the range of motion of the hip.

As the bars are lowered and your forward lean is increased, the angle between your torso and upper thigh decreases. There is also a point in the process of lowering your position over the bars, thereby reducing drag, at which the benefits will be offset by a reduction in the ability to pedal effectively and produce optimal power.

Figure 3.7 Appropriate positioning allows the athlete to create an approximately 90-degree angle between the upper torso and the extended leg and between the upper torso and the upper arm. The cyclist in the foreground has created an effective and relaxed aerobar position using the principles described above. The cyclist in the rearground is overstretched, forcing an overly tight hip angle and shallow shoulder angle, and placing greater strain on the low back as a result of poorly designed aerobars and a saddle that is too low and too far back.

A related concern is identifying the point in lowering at which significant rounding of the back occurs. As you lower your position, you will instinctively seek to preserve an effective working angle in the hip by rotating your pelvis backward. When excessive, this position creates undue stress on the lumbar muscles and leads to difficulty in running after cycling. The idea is to find the lowest point for setting the bars such that power is not compromised significantly and where you may maintain your back in a reasonably comfortable position. Finally, with lowering, you place more weight on the perineal area between your legs. This can increase nerve compression and disrupt blood flow, resulting in temporary penile numbness and potentially long-term damage in males (Leibovitch and Mor 2005; Mellion 1991). While documented negative health outcomes are not yet apparent in females, for many multisport athletes an extreme aero position is uncomfortable and difficult to maintain. You can reduce this effect by angling the saddle forward and using a saddle that minimizes pressure on the perineum.

The point at which any or all of these problems begin to occur must be found through experimentation and may change with changes in dynamic flexibility (flexibility during movement) while pedaling. Start with a comfortable position: back not overly rounded, seat pressure rearward on the ischial tuberosities (sit bones), legs able to pedal easily. Gradually examine the utility (effects on power output, comfort level, and back position) as the aerobars are lowered on the head tube incrementally. The same basic concept for positioning applies to both mountain bikes and traditional road bikes, except that with mountain bikes you do not use aerobars in competition.

As you develop your aerodynamic position on the bike, you can examine the effectiveness of your position in the following ways. Each of these methods is based on the concept that reducing drag will increase speed at a given power output.

➤ CONSTANT POWER TEST

If you are able to measure power while you ride, you can examine the effect of your aerodynamic position by riding at a constant power output on a level road blocked from the wind over a fixed distance. An ideal situation is to conduct the test in a velodrome, if available. Improved aerodynamics will allow you to complete the distance in a faster time if wind conditions are not a factor. You should use a sustainable level of power that is close to what you use for racing.

➤ ROLL-DOWN TEST

If you don't have access to a power meter, you can examine the aerodynamics of your position by using a roll-down test. For this you need to find an unobstructed hill. You then time your ability to roll down a fixed distance without pedaling while using various positions or equipment. If you have an odometer on your bike, you can begin the test by passing the starting line at a fixed rate of speed. Otherwise you should begin from a standing start with the same minimal number of pedal strokes to get some initial momentum.

Force Production and Recovery

The single characteristic that best defines efficient pedaling mechanics is the ability to minimize disruption to the inertial state of the drive train (pedals, chain, chain rings to which the pedals are attached, and cogs on the rear wheel) as it is in motion. This means that forces, whether from gravity or muscle action, applied to the pedal will be applied in such a way as to minimize both acceleration and deceleration in each pedal stroke, aiming to maintain a steady rate of power output. A common interpretation of this idea is that forces should be applied over long applications or impulses that cover a large portion of the circular pedal stroke. It has been suggested that you should push both across the top of the stroke and down through it, and then pull the pedals across the bottom of the stroke (much the way you might scrape mud off your shoe) and up. But that's not effective.

Effective pedaling is the application of very brief force impulses at the point in the stroke where gravity is least likely to either assist or resist the process—that is, during the pedal's travel across the top of its circular path (see figure 3.8). You must also consider that you are applying force to a single drive train from two legs on opposite sides of it. This brief application of muscular force occurs once during each complete pedal stroke for each leg. However, because the force applications occur in tandem with each other, two muscular force inputs are applied to the drive train for each complete revolution of the chain ring.

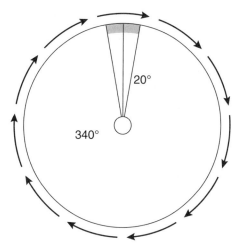

Figure 3.8 The segment of the pedal's path from about 340 degrees to 20 degrees is the optimal place to apply muscular force.

Once you apply the force briefly through the top of the pedal stroke (between about 340 degrees and 20 degrees with the top center established at 0 degrees), you should allow the descending leg to relax and leave the ascending leg unweighted from the pedal as you bring it into position for the next application of force. Pedaling in this way, you can rely on gravity to maintain the inertial state as the pedal falls forward during each revolution (with the weight of the leg attached). When the descending leg has reached the bottom of the circular pathway, the opposite leg will be in position to apply a brief force impulse in turn. During the upstroke, if the weight on the pedal of the recovering leg can be diminished, the downward-moving weight of the opposite driving leg will be able to maintain momentum and inertial motion of the drive train without undue muscular effort.

This analysis leads to a simple approach to pedaling the bike. You need only to create a rapid kicking force across the top of the pedal stroke and then relax the leg as the pedal moves downward. This phase of the stroke constitutes the force production during pedaling. Relaxing the leg as it descends allows it to be carried down by the effect of gravity on the pedal system. You then lift the foot as the pedal comes up, in anticipation of the next kick forward at the top of the cycle. The unweighting of the ascending pedal maintains the current momentum of the inertial system. This phase of the pedal cycle constitutes the recovery portion of the movement.

What's interesting is that this method of pedaling seems to occur naturally as pedal cadence is increased. At very high cadences (100 rpm and more), it is virtually impossible to do anything other than apply force quickly across the top of the stroke. A forward seat position relative to the crank set further exaggerates this response. This is supported by observations of pedal-force profiles at high cadence, which reveal that when you pedal at a higher cadence, there is a more constant force on the system, most likely resulting from the engagement of gravitational force during the downward stroke and lift-up during the upward stroke.

The exception to this is when you are forced to pedal at very low cadences, which sometimes occurs on very steep climbs in dirt, as in an off-road, mountain-bike triathlon. Deliberate application of force through the bottom of the pedal stroke to maintain the inertial state of the drive train becomes necessary when using very low cadences (sometimes 40 rpm and lower) and cycling in poor rolling conditions. Doing so in these conditions allows a more consistent application of muscular force to the movement when the inertial state is likely to change rapidly due to extreme resistance to the forward-rolling wheels. By creating a more constant power output to the wheel in conditions where you cannot rely as heavily on gravity, this pedaling modification prevents the tire from breaking free as easily and you can use it deliberately in loose-dirt, steep conditions. However, when gearing and course conditions allow for it, even seated hill climbing on a bicycle at a higher pedaling rate using the technique previously described will allow for the reduction of leg fatigue and greater efficiency of pedaling over the entire race course. There are two basic methods for improving pedaling efficiency: using cadence drills and using single-leg pedaling.

➤ LOW-GEAR, HIGH-CADENCE CYCLING

This drill involves lowering your gear for any given stretch of the course—up, down, or flat—and pedaling at higher cadences. To do this, you can just get the feel of it, count your strokes, or (best choice) have a bike computer that constantly records your cadence (along with speed and elapsed time). You should make such adjustments in small increments of 5 rpm or less and use a cadence-output odometer to provide feedback on your work. You will gradually increase your cadence by recording your baseline (present) rate and then make incremental increases over time. This approach helps you to pedal faster and learn the pedaling technique described previously.

➤ HIGH-CADENCE INTERVALS

The process of learning higher pedal cadences will be aided by using high-cadence drills of a minute or less whereby you try making larger adjustments (about 10 rpm to start) over your normal cycling cadence. During these drills you increase your pedaling rate to a level just below that at which you begin to bounce in the saddle for somewhere between 30 seconds and a minute. Generally, you do this for intervals, using a low gear that allows a comfortable aerobic effort. You should do this drill using the various positions in which you will race rather than just sitting upright. If you're a beginning triathlete, you'll set the first target for achieving a constant, comfortable cadence at approximately 80 rpm, possibly going up to 100 rpm for brief periods. Over time you might achieve a constant cadence of up to 100 rpm during steady efforts while racing and training and up to 130 rpm or more in a shorter, high-revolution effort. Downhill cycling also provides an excellent natural opportunity for high-cadence pedaling practice because the high state of momentum inherent in that situation facilitates the use of a higher-than-normal cadence as well.

➤ SINGLE-LEG PEDALING

Single-leg pedaling is customarily done on a stationary trainer where the nonpedaling leg can be supported. But with practice it can actually be done while in the aerobar position on the road and even on stationary rollers. The most common method is to pedal for short periods using one leg while propping up the opposite leg on an external support or the rear chain stays of the bicycle. You attempt to create an even stroke (as judged by changes in the associated noise of the trainer or surging when on the road) while creating force through the kicking action on the pedal previously described. Because the opposing leg is no longer a part of the pedaling equation, some acceleration and deceleration will occur. But you will attempt to minimize this to the degree possible. As mentioned previously, to achieve maximum effect, you should do this drill in the various positions used in racing.

The most common error is to pedal at too high a gear and mash the pedals, meaning applying a large force as the pedal begins to descend. This is analogous to pushing the merry-go-round with one big effort and then waiting for it to noticeably decelerate before pushing it again. Doing so increases disruption of the inertial state and is ultimately more fatiguing than using more frequent and rapid force applications at high cadence. A natural cadence is 50 to 60 rpm. You readily mash the pedals when you pedal at that cadence and then attempt to go faster by increasing the gear and not the cadence. In this case, you quickly sense that the easiest place to apply force to the pedal is when it is descending, and since the forces required are higher at slow cadences, indeed you do so. This pattern is also observed in otherwise effective riders when they climb and are "overgeared," meaning they have not selected a gear low enough to allow for a more effective higher cadence.

Putting It All Together

In watching Lance Armstrong win seven Tour de France stage races, two dominant themes were apparent. First is that he had spent considerable time both developing and training in the aerodynamic position he used to win or place highly in the time-trial events. Second is that he had also spent considerable time in developing the ability to ride time trials at cadences in excess of 100 rpm. Those with a longer memory of his career might remember that he illustrated neither characteristic in his time-trial style before developing cancer; his tour-winning style appears to have been the result of conscientious effort to change. The same application of effort to the development of riding technique holds potential for triathletes as well.

As with swimming, this process should begin with bike position and balance and progress to gradually increasing relaxation at greater cadences as cycle-specific strength and peak power output develop. Table 3.2 presents a progression of the cycling drills described in this section.

Table 3.2   Cycling Drill Element and Drill Progression

Technique element	Drill
Balance	Roller riding
Streamlining	Constant power test
	Roll-down test
Force production and recovery	Single-leg pedaling
	Low-gear, high-cadence cycling
	High-cadence intervals

Technique Model for Running

Most athletes, many running coaches, and many sport scientists assume that running is a natural human activity. This means that the method of running tends to develop without instruction and uses basic neuromuscular reflexes for which you are hardwired. However, one element of modern running changes the natural progression of running technique: the use of running shoes—in particular, the use of high-technology, highly cushioned, gait-altering competitive running shoes. In wearing these kinds of shoes, you too often change your method of running.

The East Africans, particularly runners from Kenya and Ethiopia, are the best distance runners in the world. Their degree of superiority is so compelling as to have become the subject of scientific scrutiny. While a variety of elements that may produce this superiority have been studied, possibly the simplest and most important has not: East Africans learn to run without wearing shoes. As a result, they develop a very natural running technique. Elite East African runners land on the ground on the balls of their feet, then pick them up quickly. Compared with less skilled runners, they have a high stride rate with long stride distances. Most also have a forward lean as they run and appear incredibly relaxed. While little published data exist, they do not have the incredibly high rate of either acute or chronic injuries that recreational runners in the United States do—plantar fasciitis, inversion sprains, tibial pain, iliotibial band syndrome, stress fractures.

Try this experiment: Run in your normal shoes over a hard surface and examine how you run—thinking about how you land, how you create each stride, and how you hold your body. Then take off your shoes and run briefly over the same hard surface, examining the same factors. Most who try this experiment observe a difference ranging from the subtle to the dramatic. They find that when running in their bare feet, to protect themselves from injury they land naturally on the balls of their feet, then lift that foot quickly before their weight shifts to their toes. They find that they lean forward slightly to ensure landing properly. They also find that their stride most often quickens and that almost immediately they feel more fluid and relaxed.

When you wear shoes, you deprive yourself of much of the neuromuscular information collected as you touch the ground—sort of like driving a car while wearing thick goggles smeared with grease. As a result, you lose your way quite easily, particularly when others are giving you misguided advice, such as "Lengthen your stride" and "Lift your knees." With shoes removed, you quickly relearn how to land properly on the ground. When you land properly, using the foot as a natural lever, the force of gravity is then transmitted into the muscles rather than into your skeletal structure. This has two basic effects: You use the force you retain elastically in your muscles and tendons to help create the next step, and you can reduce the forces that you need to dissipate from your skeletal system. Your body becomes a series of springs, capturing and returning energy with each step while minimizing harm to your skeletal and soft-tissue structure.

This gait requires you to pick up the foot quickly and to avoid applying excessive forces to the toes, which, collectively, are weak extensions of the foot as a lever. Doing this often creates a higher stride rate at a given velocity with rapid force impulses allowing for a sustained inertial state and better speed and efficiency. You also quickly learn to lean forward slightly, much the way you need to lean forward on skis. Virtually everyone experiences almost immediate improvement with this technique—the ability to run faster and more easily. This likely happens because you quickly return to something that is hardwired in you, a method of locomotion that uses your innate reflexes to their greatest degree.

In running this way, very little thinking is required. But here is a major note of caution: In a body weakened by a lifetime of using highly supportive shoes, you must proceed very gradually. You are asking your muscles to work in ways they may not have worked since you were a very young child. With a slow progression in the amount of running you do this way, however, you readily adapt to the process in a very natural way. Such a model can also be learned through the use of drills and imagery. These approaches, as evidenced in pose method and ChiRunning, can augment or intertwine with a more natural approach as well. We favor the emphasis on a natural approach using minimalist shoes or bare feet because it removes the need to continually monitor the process for success by creating conditions that require it to occur.

Balance

When you land with each running stride in a balanced, efficient body posture, as noted earlier, you can maximize your ability to absorb energy and reduce your likelihood of injury. This position, sometimes described as the running pose, should resemble a spring, allowing you to use your joints and vertebral curves to absorb the force of gravity (Romanov and Fletcher 2007). The position should allow for vertical joint alignment by placing all the joint centers of the hip, shoulder, and head in a straight line, beginning with the ball-of-foot contact point (see figure 3.9). This straight line should also have a slight forward inclination from the vertical, translating the gravitational forces absorbed into forward movement. This slight forward lean places the center of your body mass slightly forward of the contact point on the ground once you begin to leave the ground, encouraging forward movement, or falling into the next step.

More specifically, the ground contact should occur through the ball of the foot, the knee should be bent, the pelvis should be neutral, and the back, shoulders, and head should be upright and centered to allow for normal vertebral curves. From the front view, the center of the patella (kneecap) and the foot on both the support and the recovery legs should be projected directly forward or very nearly so. The pelvis should be parallel with the ground and the arms should be relaxed and minimally cross over the body. These positions are optimal functional alignments of the involved joints, resulting in improved efficiency and ease of joint movement.

Figure 3.9   The running pose allows for vertical alignment of the hip, shoulder, and head.

➤ RUNNING POSE

Stand, balancing in the running pose described previously. Your ability to refine this skill involves moving the stationary pose to increasingly unstable environments, such as standing on a medicine ball or a BOSU ball. You can further augment your balancing abilities with the drill by closing your eyes. Create feedback by timing your attempts (count in slow, relaxed breaths).

➤ TRAIL RUNNING

As your stationary balance improves, you can increase your dynamic-running balance by running in increasingly complex environments such as trail systems, where the ground is less even. However, you should approach this progressively, beginning with trails that are less technically challenging.

Streamlining

Unfortunately, the optimal body positions during support in running preclude optimal streamlining. Anything you might gain by trying to make your body contours smoother, you lose in running efficiency. You can positively influence the effect of drag by running behind another athlete (ideally someone who's slightly faster) or by wearing close-fitting clothing. You should put these tactics into practice to improve running splits. Running closely with other runners is a skill that requires practice.

➤ PACELINE RUNNING

As in cycling, practice running in closely packed groups by looking forward through the lead runner and using your peripheral vision to judge the distance between you and others. In this way you anticipate any change in direction or speed as the lead runner does so. Ideally you will come as close as possible without interfering with the lead runner's stride. You can practice this by running in pace lines; each runner takes a turn in the lead and the other runners line up behind.

Force Production

The most efficient form of overland movement makes use of the wheel. A central characteristic of a wheel's movement is that the center of mass of the wheel always remains over the point of ground contact and does not oscillate (move up and down). You can achieve running efficiency by making ground contact directly below your body. This approach will minimize vertical oscillation with each stride. This is accomplished through the use of a body position at the time of foot contact with the ground and leg mechanics between foot contacts that allow the foot to make contact with the ground as little forward of the center of mass as necessary. While running, your center of mass will be roughly in the middle of your torso front-to-back and about mid-chest height vertically.

The recommended leg mechanics are characterized by the rapid removal of the foot from the ground in a vertical direction with minimal ankle flexion and equal flexion of the hip and knee joints. In other words, the lifted foot should stay under the torso rather than extend in front of the body (as when the hip is flexed excessively) or fall behind the body (as when the knee is flexed excessively). In addition, you should allow the foot to hang loosely rather than hold it in a rigid flexed position. Barefoot running creates conditions whereby rapid foot removal by lifting occurs naturally to avoid transferring weight to the toes. You can also use a variety of drills to practice the concept.

➤ HOPPING

You can use hopping drills to practice removing the feet from the ground as quickly as possible. Do these drills first with both legs and later with one leg at a time. The focus should be on landing on the balls of the feet and removing the feet as vertically from the ground as possible. Repetitive hops can be forward, backward, or side to side. As you become more relaxed, you should also attempt to touch the lower buttocks with the heels during each hop, as in the butt kick drill described on page 67.

➤ JUMPING

The natural extension of hopping drills is jumping drills. In this case you jump for maximum distance or height using the same basic technique used for hopping. With the addition of weight and repetition, these drills can also be used for conditioning, as described in chapter 4.

Hopping and jumping drills ultimately progress into other conditioning techniques such as bounding and plyometric jumps, which are discussed in greater detail in chapter 4 as well. Although it might seem counterintuitive, you should do these kinds of drills in shoes that are only lightly cushioned and allow for maximal sensory input. This allows the body to properly absorb these high forces and prevent injury.

Recovery

In efficient running, you rapidly contract the hamstrings to lift the support foot vertically, after which the muscles should be completely relaxed. You lift the foot and ankle only as high as necessary to prepare them to fall into the next step so that minimal energy is expended. The ankle should remain in a relaxed posture with toes downward slightly even as it falls to the ground again. This allows the calf muscles to respond reflexively to the next ground contact with perfect efficiency. Holding the muscles in contraction (seen in the dorsiflexed ankle of the overstriding runner) invites injury and reduces efficiency by inhibiting a reflexive response. This is analogous to tensing your body before a car crash. The drunken driver who remains relaxed always seems to experience fewer injuries.

➤ PONY

This is a basic shifting of body weight from one foot to the other. You stand in a relaxed running pose with the nonsupport leg slightly elevated. You then allow your weight to shift to the nonsupport leg easily by lifting the support foot and letting the nonsupport leg fall. When you do it properly, you should land on the new support foot without sliding. You progress through this drill by adding a small degree of forward lean and a quicker, more forceful foot removal, ultimately falling into a larger step without sliding on landing. The key concept is to shift your weight by lifting your support foot rather than by pushing off it. In this way you fall onto the other leg.

➤ TAPPING

Stand in a relaxed running pose and let your nonsupport leg fall to the ground without lifting your support leg. When your foot touches the ground, briefly tapping it, you quickly pull it up again, allowing it to float between taps. You can easily evaluate your leg's relaxation state during recovery by observing how easily you can get your heel to touch the lower portion of your buttocks. When the leg is relaxed, you will achieve it with minimal effort and the leg will naturally decelerate when going up and accelerate while falling into the next tap. Practice this in front of a mirror to get feedback.

➤ BUTT KICK

Once relaxation is achieved, you can practice further by using single-leg pulls while striding normally or alternating pulls on both legs. To be accurate, however, you really try to kick your lower buttocks by using equal hip and knee flexion so the feet are removed vertically. Finally you can combine the two concepts—rapid foot removal and complete relaxation—by doing double-foot hops (and later single-foot hops) where you maximize height or distance while still touching your heel to your lower buttock with each jump. You must withdraw the feet vertically in these drills when touching your lower buttocks (see figure 3.10), as opposed to the high knee drills and rear kick drills used by many coaches. The traditional drills begin to develop over- or understriding movements in your nervous system, which compete with the optimal stride movements you hope to produce while actually running.

a   b   c

Figure 3.10 Butt kick drill.

Putting It All Together

You need only watch images of phenomenal runners such as Haile Gebrselassie to see the concepts described previously in full display. Notable for his seemingly effortless running style, rapid stride rate, and exceptional stride length at his size, Gebrselassie epitomizes these running principles. Some may question the utility of this approach in heavyweight recreational athletes who, it is assumed, require highly cushioned and gait-controlling shoes. However, you must consider two facts when making that judgment for yourself. First, the rate of injury among recreational runners has only risen since the advent of increasingly "high-tech" shoes. Second, the existing data comparing barefoot runners with those who run with a more conventional approach illustrate a lower rate of injury among the barefoot populations (Warburton 2001). While those facts are far from definitive proof of the value of using a more natural technique, they do certainly raise questions.

Should you then take off your shoes and start doing all of your running barefoot, assuming you live where that is possible? Absolutely not. What you should do involves a gradual progression to less supportive and less cushioned shoes that allow for the development of more efficient and injury-sparing running technique. This technique can be further developed with regular barefoot running and the use of running drills such as those described in this chapter and listed in table 3.3.

Table 3.3 Running Drill Element and Drill Progression

Technique element	Drill
Balance	Running pose
	Trail running
Streamlining	Paceline running
Force production	Hopping (double-leg hop, single-leg hop, lateral hopping)
	Jumping (long jumping, vertical jumping)
Recovery	Pony
	Tapping
	Butt kick

Methods for Learning New Technique

When you learn a new way to move, you initially organize that activity consciously, meaning that you have to constantly think about what you are doing to achieve it. When your thought process goes elsewhere, say to how much that effort costs or how you are doing in the race, then the old way of moving often resurfaces. However, with enough repetition of the new pattern, it will eventually become dominant and appear without conscious control. At this point the brain's autonomic regulation system in the cerebellum is taking over control. In theory, this process happens as a result of new synaptic or neuronal (nerve) connections that build a "program" to control the new way of swimming, cycling, or running.

This process occurs most rapidly if there is no old competing program or set of neuronal connections. For instance, this means that experienced swimmers have a harder time building a new stroke pattern than beginners, particularly if the pattern is very similar to one they used previously. It may take advanced athletes months to years to automate a new movement pattern depending on the efficiency of their learning process.

In the case of learning new patterns to replace old ones, the neuronal hardwiring process appears to be confused by switching back and forth between the old movement pattern and the new. This slows the development of the unconsciously regulated movement stage that you seek. Avoidance of this dilemma comes largely by creating conditions that minimize the occurrence of the old pattern and maximize the occurrence of the new pattern in practice. In this way the nervous system learns the fastest. The learning process also appears to be hastened if the movement pattern is performed against increased resistance or at increased speed or power output, thus providing a higher level of neural stimulation. This may be the reason fast running so significantly improves running economy—it probably helps your nervous system to hardwire the movement pattern even more effectively than the generally slower running you do more often.

An ideal scenario for development of new technique is as follows:

1. You must have a clear and simple idea of what you are trying to accomplish with the new technique. In most cases this process involves part–whole learning, whereby you break down the technique and practice it in manageable parts first and then practice it as a whole later. For example, you might work on developing balance in swimming by first practicing balancing in the water as in the first drill described for swimming. Later you can apply this balancing skill to your entire freestyle stroke. Initial practice then involves cueing and feedback from a second party. This is where the use of an experienced coach, particularly early in the learning process, is extremely useful.

2. Nearly immediately, practice should then include keeping your focus on the main ideas by using imagery or cue words with repetition. Examples are such things as seeing yourself as slippery like a shark when you swim, machinelike when you cycle, and light like a gazelle when you run. Examples of key words are *long and loose* for swimming, *kick and relax* for cycling, *quick and light* for running, and *quick and powerful* for lifting. Both you and a coach can use these images and words as cues to help you retain your focus.

3. Further practice should then occur in an environment that minimizes the need for conscious control by allowing the conditions to create the technique. Examples of this are learning new running technique in bare feet or by running uphill, learning to breathe nasally by placing water in the mouth, learning cycling technique on rollers, learning effective kicking technique with flippers or vertical kicking, and learning to pedal in a given body position by setting the bike up to create the position. Even when your cueing system or conscious monitoring process breaks down, the new technique is maintained by the environment itself.

4. Further practice should also incorporate a source of immediate feedback so that success or failure can be constantly evaluated and adjustments made. Examples of this are using counts of stride or stroke rate and distance when running or swimming, using a cadence device when cycling, using mirrors when learning weight-room techniques, and using video feedback when possible with all techniques.

5. Later practice should include replication of the technique with added resistance, speed, or power. This should occur only when you've developed the fundamental movement reasonably well and can maintain it for short and then increasingly longer distances. Examples of added resistance are paddles in swimming; high-gear, slow-cadence cycling; weighted running; movement-specific weight training and plyometric routines; and a variety of high-power-output, high-movement-speed forms of training discussed in the chapters on training. You must also consider that these higher-intensity training methods will often break down new technique if you incorporate them too early or if the objective is the outcome of the effort rather than correct development of technique.

6. Advanced practice may also include the removal of some sensory feedback to maximize the development of other sensory input. You would use these methods only when the technique is well established and you seek further improvements related to the more subtle elements of improved balance or relaxation. Examples of this are fist swimming, running in pose balance with your eyes closed, swimming with your eyes closed, riding on rollers in the dark, and running in the dark.

Summary

All effective movement technique originates with an effective breathing process. Although currently it is not in common use, there is reason to believe that the development of the nasal breathing approach can provide the basis for relaxed and well-oxygenated movements as well as superior health and consistency of training. Clear, easily developed models enhance basic speed, improve efficiency, and reduce injury potential in repetitive swimming, cycling, and running. The key principles are optimizing the blend of balance, understanding the concept of the inertial state and how to use it, and employing the force of gravity in your favor. These approaches provide the basis for superior performance in triathlon. New techniques are best learned with the use of practices that minimize incorrect attempts and maximize correct attempts so that the unconsciously regulated state is reached quickly, leading to an effective movement pattern that occurs under all conditions.

➤ 4

Training for Strength and Muscular Balance

Most people start training for distance running races, triathlons, or bike tours by simply increasing the amount of time or distance they run, cycle, or swim. This usually leads to a rapid initial improvement in speed over longer distances and becomes the dominant model for training. As people perceive that they are no longer simply trying to finish races and are now athletes, they may eventually add some short-distance speed work, some race-pace sessions, and longer endurance sessions. Further improvements in performance will usually ensue, leading many athletes to adopt the "a little of this and a little of that" approach to training as their permanent model. However, eventually almost everyone reaches a performance plateau sometime down the road. If the model is simply one of increased volume, you will reach that plateau in a few years. If it is some variant of the more sophisticated multi-intensity model, it may take six to eight years to reach a plateau. However, if you stay in one or another of these models indefinitely, after a time performance usually starts to decline, even when your total training time is maintained. This outcome is most often chalked up to aging and is considered inevitable.

You can break the cycle of plateau and decline by using weight training in your program. When you increase your strength for a movement related to loco-motion, either directly or indirectly (think core musculature), all other things being equal, you provide the platform for going faster—not only in sprints but at all distances for which you are otherwise prepared. This is particularly true when you strengthen the muscles in relation to the movement itself rather than strengthen the muscles without regard to the specific movements you are using them for in your distance racing. If the muscles that create a movement become stronger, then the movement itself becomes easier. As a result, you can do it more times before fatiguing (better endurance) or you can do it at a higher speed for the same energy cost (improved speed). In addition, as the research models examining this relationship between increasing movement-specific strength and performance have improved, by measuring more specific resistance movements, you can see this concept validated by science (Ebben et al. 2004; Girold et al. 2007; Jung 2003; Mikkola et al. 2007; Millet et al. 2002; Paavolainen, Hakkinen, et al. 1999; Paton and Hopkins 2005; Spurrs, Murphy, and Watsford 2003).

Why, then, do so many endurance athletes avoid the weight room like the plague? This goes to many of the most fundamental, yet irrational, beliefs: Lifting weights makes you slow and heavy, time spent lifting weights can't help performance as much as time spent cycling, running, or swimming; and it's always better to be outside training. This chapter presents some facts and experience that provide an empirical and rational basis for the use of this new training concept. It is a fundamentally new model for endurance sport preparation.

Resistance Training for Improved Performance

An increasing body of scientific literature now clearly illustrates the value of using movement-specific strength and power exercises to improve endurance and speed in longer-distance swimming, cycling, and running. Two of the more elegant studies illustrate that doing these exercises and reducing the amount of time on endurance training create a greater improvement in race performance than simply devoting more time to endurance training alone (Paavolainen, Hakkinen, et al. 1999; Paton and Hopkins 2005). It is true that the gym is a different environment than the trail, the lake or ocean, or the road. However, beyond the physiological benefits, using a mixture of training environments offers the positive aspects of variety, the opportunity to meet new people in what can be a rather lonely training experience, and the ability to train even when the weather is not good.

An alternative to the conventional view of training is that each person has a functional strength level in each movement (swim stroke, cycling pedal stroke, running step) that limits the power and work output that person will be able to sustain when repeating the movement over and over again. You can easily conceptualize this idea by considering that muscles consist of fibers, which in turn consist of individual contractile units called myofibrils. By strengthening a movement over time, you increase the number of myofibrils in each fiber and thus increase the resulting force produced by each fiber when it contracts. As long as you increase capillarization (blood flow) in the muscles at the same time, through endurance training, then greater strength means fewer fibers need to contract at a given power output, hence less effort. This development also provides for a higher power output at a given level of effort.

The next successive performance limitation in the movement pattern at any given level of peak strength is the ability to produce the force rapidly, therefore creating peak movement power (work per unit time). The peak power potential

Sport performance and technique can be improved by resistance training, especially if the exercises mimic the movements used in races.

of a muscle in any given person at any given time comes from a combination of a neural component (the ability to recruit a maximum percentage of the available muscle fibers to engage in the task at hand) and an anatomical component (fiber size and fiber-type distribution). Both components are fully developed only through resistance training specific to the movement (swimming, running, and cycling).

You might think of it this way: You first increase your movement speed to some upper limit using a given level of resistance in a movement. Most triathletes do this by using their body weight and running, swimming, or cycling faster. However, if you add resistance to the movement, initially slowing it down, over time you are then able to increase movement speed again. Your peak power improves as a result. The key to forward progression, then, lies in the use of progressive resistance. This is best accomplished through the use of a combination of training methods that encourage both high-end movement speed and a progressive increase in resistance at levels that promote strength, peak power, and short-term muscular endurance.

The ability to create power over increasing lengths of time is limited by the peak power you are able to produce at any given time. This endurance training approach is the model of successive limiters. A 100-meter speed is limited by movement strength and power, 200-meter speed is limited by 100-meter speed, 400-meter speed is limited by 200-meter speed, and so on up to any distance imaginable. Does this mean that you should spend as much time developing basic speed and strength as you do in developing endurance? Absolutely not. It means that you should devote a proportionate amount of time to each, as determined by your training and racing needs and goals. The relative proportions of each type of training that you will incorporate into your own program will shift as the length of the intended race distance increases. As you develop the ability to exert a given level of power over a lengthening period of time, you can also enhance the process by adding a small amount of additional resistance while actually doing the endurance training. This approach is strength endurance training, a concept discussed in chapter 5.

Consider all of this in light of your own experience. If you are a long-timer in any of the given sports that make up triathlon, or in triathlon itself, then you have probably experienced the phenomenon whereby you slowed down over time while using basically the same endurance training program month after month and season after season. Without a high-end stimulus to maintain or improve density of muscle fibers, your body naturally sheds over time extra myofibrils that may have been developed earlier in life. In other words, you lose functional muscle mass. This happens most quickly in those who do the least fast or high-power training, and progressively more slowly in those who maintain high-power training, and least in those who also maintain a true strength stimulus in their training. For athletes who have never used a high-end resistance stimulus, this addition to training (when used consistently and properly) offers a new avenue for improvement, regardless of age, that can sustain progressions over many years.

Strength and Power Training Model

In this model you improve overall endurance performance by developing movement strength and peak movement power (work per unit time) to your highest feasible levels. You also concurrently or cyclically build endurance over increasing distances—such as 400 meters to 10,000 meters in running—using target velocities based on your rate of fatigue, a concept discussed more fully in chapter 5. Each successively longer distance is a link in the chain that allows peak power to be linked more effectively to successively longer-duration power outputs. Once a full level and a range of endurance training are achieved, further improvement in movement strength becomes the primary limiter to performance improvement. By increasing strength, you are then able to increase peak power and each level of endurance power produced as the target race or training distance or time increases.

Interestingly, the time frame required for maximum development of an endurance-based performance is about six to eight years in athletes who have engaged in a typical training program. However, the time frame for fully developing your maximum strength in a movement may be much longer. Consequently, the use of a strength-based model for triathlon training may extend the time over which you might expect to continue improving your performance considerably.

A second element of the model is the focus on work rather than effort in planning and conducting workouts, as described in chapter 1. This allows physiological measures of exertion (heart rate, lactate production, or RPE) to be more appropriately used as measures of how hard the work is to accomplish rather than the guideline for the work itself. This leads to achievement of one of the principal goals for training, as set forth in chapter 1: Complete the best quality of work with the least physiological effort over a given time. By applying this principle, you make your training more enjoyable. You train more consistently, and most likely your race performance improves.

In resistance training you apply the principle by designing work sets that may approach but do not create "failure," which is the inability to complete another repetition. Say that you could lift 200 pounds in an exercise once and 140 pounds in that same exercise 12 times to failure. In this approach, if you do sets with 140 pounds, rather than try to do 12 repetitions, you would plan to do only 10. So you rather easily accomplish the set. And because there is a rapid recovery of the heart rate, you avoid a high level of acidosis, which is the lowering of pH or buildup of hydrogen ions in your tissues and blood. Although the basis for this is not completely understood, people commonly accept the idea that excessive acidity both reduces force of muscle contractions and stimulates the sensation of pain. By avoiding excessive acidity, the body adapts quite easily to the load and it becomes very easy to increase the number of sets (i.e., amount of work at that stimulus) you perform. The real-world result is that you can complete more work at the target stimulus with less effort and better adaptive capacity—meaning you are more likely to show improvement the next time you train. Further, the training is fun because it is not excessively painful. With each set, you succeed in completing your target number of repetitions.

Self-esteem is built by success in training, not by failure. In the conventional "failure set" approach, you might complete 12 repetitions with greater effort and acidosis the first set. However, your recovery would be slower and each successive set would become harder as well, resulting in fewer reps completed and the last set a failing effort by definition. The overall result is that you perform less work at the target stimulus, the sets are very painful, you experience failure in the process, and your adaptive capacity is likely to be lessened through excessive fatigue—meaning you are less likely to show improvement the next time you train. As if this were not enough, you also are more likely to experience delayed-onset muscle soreness in the days after the training. That's because it appears that pushing muscles to the point of failure is more likely to induce significant myofibril damage, inflammation, and pain.

The third aspect of the model is that training for strength and power should be continued throughout the racing season, rather than only during the off-season (winter, when it's harder for most people to go outside). In this way gains in basic movement strength can be maintained during competitive training periods and progressions made year to year in it. This provides the platform for ongoing improvements in endurance performance.

The final element of this model is that the strength and power movements need to be specific to swimming, cycling, and running and they need to address both power production and recovery phases of each. In this way the strength exerted for each movement increases over time and builds muscular balance and

Determining Individual Weight Loads

In weight training, the optimal way to establish your workload for sets is in reference to the maximum amount of weight you can lift in the movement one time. This amount of weight is referred to as the one-repetition maximum, or 1RM. Sets, meaning the completion of more than one repetition of the movement in succession, are then defined either by a higher RM level or by a percentage of the weight lifted for 1RM. For instance, if you could lift 100 pounds in a movement once (1RM = 100 pounds), then you might choose to do a 10RM set (the amount of weight you could lift 10 times) or a set using 80 percent of your 1RM (80 pounds, which you would likely lift about 10 to 12 times). The second is preferred because it allows a more precise definition of the load to use. To figure out your load, multiply your current 1RM weight by the percentage you choose to use for a set. If your 1RM load is currently 180 pounds and you want to do 10 repetitions at 80 percent of 1RM load, the calculation would be as follows:

$$180 \times 0.80 = 144 \text{ pounds}$$

You would then use the closest practical load below this based on the nature of the equipment used.

To establish the amount of weight you can lift once, you can start at some weight that you're confident you can lift once and then gradually add more weight in very small increments. Eventually you'll reach a weight you cannot lift succesfully, so your 1RM weight is defined by the last weight you did lift successfully. Another approach, for those who might not want to attempt a 1RM test, is to estimate the amount of weight you can lift once based on a formula. In this approach you use some lighter weight and see how many times you can lift it in succession before failure. You then use the weight and number of successful repetitions in the formula to predict your 1RM load for that movement. A calculator program for this process, as well as guidance on identifying relative loads, appears at the following exercise instruction Web site: www.exrx.net/Calculators/OneRepMax.html.

joint stability by maintaining appropriate levels of strength across the joint. In addition, they help to create functional muscular balance and improved posture. The set and weight structures of the exercises are then modified to help build short-term muscular endurance, strength, short-term power, and peak power. Short-term muscular endurance refers to endurance in the movement over approximately one minute, as when running 400 meters. This type of endurance is largely limited by increased acidity created through the production of lactic acid.

Resistance Training Program for Triathletes

There are four primary objectives of a movement-specific resistance training program for triathlon:

1. To develop basic functional strength, posture, and joint stability, thereby facilitating injury-free swimming, cycling, and running. This occurs by creating appropriate muscular balance in triathlon movements and by increasing the tolerance to stress in the muscles used for support during triathlon movements.

2. To build peak muscular strength for both force-producing and recovery phases of the swimming, cycling, and running movements without increasing body weight substantially. You accomplish this by combining movement-specific resistance exercises for triathlon with endurance training in the overall training program. This prepares the body to handle even higher-intensity peak power and plyometric training as well.

3. To increase the ability to apply high muscular forces at high rates of speed. In other words, you develop the ability to increase peak power in triathlon movements.

4. To minimize the loss of muscle mass and power associated with training at altitude and aging.

Following are the key characteristics of this recommended training program:

■   The resistance training exercises maximize the strength-to-power ratio in the force-producing movements used in swimming, cycling, and running.

■   Resistance training is generally done last in the training session, after higher-intensity workouts, which minimizes deleterious effects on the more specific swimming, cycling, and running training. This approach also provides a cool-down because the lifting program is not as metabolically taxing as the distance training. Specific forms of the resistance and plyometric exercises described later in the chapter can also be used as a warm-up technique (rather than a primary training stimulus) for the neuromuscular facilitation of the swimming, cycling, or running movement itself.

■ The resistance training program should reinforce swimming, cycling, and running technique rather than interfere with it. In this way it will lead to improvement in technique, not just additional power.

■ Strength improvements typically occur during base training periods. Strength maintenance occurs during more race-specific periods of training. You can drop resistance training from the program during short prerace peaking periods (two weeks or less), or you can taper this form of training, a topic discussed in chapter 7. But you should maintain resistance training throughout the training year if you hope to make improvements in strength and triathlon performance over many years.

■ Balance all exercises across any given joint or movement to maintain a balance of muscular tension, postural alignment, and dynamic range of motion. In other words, if you do three sets of a pulling exercise, you should also do three sets of the complementary pushing exercise with appropriate resistance. Do this by using exercises that develop both the force-producing phase of the movement and the recovery phase of the movement, as described in chapter 3.

■ In general, the strength exercises in a training session should proceed from compound (multijoint) to single-joint exercises and from legs to upper body. Complete core muscular strengthening movements last, or even in separate training sessions, in order to minimize deleterious effects on stabilization during the joint-specific force and recovery movements. You might also do some training sessions in race-specific order—swim movements, cycle movements, run movements—for greater specificity.

■ A thorough warm-up is required before resistance training. You can most easily manage this by doing the resistance training immediately after a swimming, cycling, or running training session. Also, each set progression for an individual exercise should begin with a relatively lighter and less challenging set to provide for the specific neuromuscular warm-up for that movement.

■ You develop basic strength over several months by gradually increasing resistance in the general set and repetition range of 8 to 12 reps at 12- to 15RM (repetition maximum) resistance range, or at 70 to 80 percent of the 1RM. As sets become easier to achieve at a given weight, you gradually increase the weight. During this early adaptation, if time allows, you should resistance-train three times a week. This period might last anywhere from a few months to a year. Once further progress becomes challenging, then a differentiation of training emphasis becomes important. This basically means that individual weight training sessions within a training cycle have differing emphases on strength development, peak power development, and short-term muscular endurance development.

■   Create training differentiation by including set variations throughout the short-term training cycle or microcycle. Variations in training sets should focus on increasing force (4- to 8-repetition sets in the 6- to 10RM range or about 80 to 90 percent of the 1RM), increasing the speed of force application or peak power (6 to 12 explosive repetitions in the 15- to 20RM range or about 50 to 70 percent of the 1RM), and increasing short-term endurance (15 to 20 repetitions in 20- to 25RM range or about 40 to 50 percent of the 1RM). This is analogous to first developing the tolerance or endurance to run a certain volume at aerobic speeds and then diversifying workouts to emphasize different points in the speed continuum. At this point in the adaptive process, many athletes find that less frequent sessions of resistance training allow for better adaptation. This might involve resistance training twice per week or every third day instead of every other day.

■   In most cases, you should not do resistance exercises to failure. Rather, you should do them only to the targeted number of reps at the targeted weight to avoid fatigue of the adrenal glands and overtraining.

■   During periods of strength and power maintenance (rather than development), you can continue to repeat the same sets and repetitions without increasing the resistance level. This allows more energy to be used in adapting to other forms of training without losing strength adaptations over time. You can also reduce training frequency if necessary. However, after any period of detraining exceeding more than a few weeks, you should not attempt to resume sessions at the same weight loads used previously.

■   You can easily judge success in resistance training by applying a subjective analysis of difficulty of the final few repetitions in the set. You can also wear a heart rate monitor and take note of the recovery heart rate between sets. When your heart rate drops more quickly and sets are noticeably easier to complete, then adaptation has occurred.

■   In weight training progression, you must also account for the relatively slower increases in the density of the skeleton and soft tissues, such as ligaments and tendons, particularly once the stimulus is relatively high after several months to a year of training. A very conservative approach to progression is always best. As a general rule, you might anticipate spending at least six weeks of training microcycles working at a given weight before making adjustments upward. Adjustments upward in resistance should then be less than 5 percent of the current weight. This extended time frame will allow for bone and soft-tissue remodeling, resulting in density increases in the skeletal system and connective tissues so that they are strong enough to handle the efforts created by increased muscular forces without injury.

■   You will achieve full adaptation to a new level of work in resistance training only in improved endurance performance over a period of months. This is largely due to hormonal fluctuations that occur once the initial adaptive work is completed (testosterone and growth hormone production may be suppressed) and the body has some time for relative recovery and new tissue development (testosterone and growth hormone production are again enhanced). In a very controlled approach to this adaptive process, as described, subsequent improvements in endurance performance may come in smaller increments, although they also appear more quickly. Sticking with the program while being patient in terms of outcomes is the key.

■ Both in initiating this kind of resistance training program and when attempting subsequent increases in load, the specificity of the work will lead to a carryover in fatigue to endurance training. In other words, when you increase your lifting load, you should expect to feel fatigue while swimming, cycling, and running in the following days. This can be viewed as positive, however, because it illuminates the specificity of the training and the likelihood of carryover effect once you have adapted to the new load. This fatigue disappears quickly, as you make the basic adaptation to the new load, and continues to work to allow for successful bone and soft-tissue response as well.

Resistance Training Exercises

Following are resistance training exercises that simulate force-producing and recovery movements in swimming, cycling, and running. They include both weight training exercises and plyometric training exercises as well as basic core stabilization exercises designed to compensate for muscular imbalances created through the triathlon movements themselves. Numerous elite and top-level age-group triathletes have used these exercises successfully.

The exercises are presented in a typical order used for training, which reflects several concepts described previously. They are grouped by their specific applications and paired based on the force-producing aspect of the movement and the recovery aspect of the movement. In this way, you can alternate sets of each companion set of exercises when your training situation allows for it. The exercises are also ordered progressively within application areas from compound movements to isolation movements. The application areas begin with lower-body movements and proceed to upper-body movements as might occur most typically if all the exercises were used in a single training session. It is certainly possible to modify this last ordering of application areas to reflect triathlon race specificity.

Running-Specific Movements

A standard quarter or half (parallel) squat provides the most basic and commonly used movement for force production in running. This movement also encourages complete body strengthening. However, the most running-specific movement is the single-leg squat. Complementary exercises follow.

➤ SINGLE-LEG SQUAT

Force production movement for running

Begin this exercise in the running pose position. As described in chapter 3, the running pose is defined by ground contact through the ball of the foot, the knee of the support leg bent slightly, the pelvis neutral, and the back, shoulders, and head upright and centered. From this starting point you then squat down farther, flexing the hip, knee, and ankle about 15 degrees, and then return to the starting position. This mimics the range of motion you go through as you land on the ground and absorb force while running. In the early development of the movement, you should face a mirror and hold a dumbbell on the training-leg side. Your nonsupport heel should be slightly elevated throughout. Focus on keeping a level pelvis while dipping into the squat and otherwise maintaining your body alignment in the neutral position. Your weight should be on the ball of your foot (as in the running pose), with your upper body upright and head balanced over your center of mass as you lower and raise yourself. Once you establish basic strength and balance, further strength increases require more specialized equipment to apply adequate resistance. As you get stronger, you should do the exercise using an Olympic bar supported across the shoulders, as in conventional squatting (see figure 4.1). However, because of the relative lack of stability, you should attempt this more advanced version of the exercise only in a

Figure 4.1 Single-leg squat.

Smith machine, a spotting rack found in most gyms. Again, ideally you will be able to use a mirror so that you have feedback. You should increase the weight only if you can maintain your basic running form.

You can also use this movement as a diagnostic test for basic strength imbalances. If the unsupported side of the pelvis dips during the downward movement, you should begin hip abduction exercises (see next section) before attempting this movement further. You can do the movement with or without added weight. If you do it with weight, the greater the weight necessary to create the pelvic displacement, the less "positive" the test is for strength imbalance. The dipping of the pelvis during support in running illustrates a fundamental mechanism leading to undue stresses at the hip, knee, ankle, and foot, as well as energy loss and less-than-optimal efficiency.

➤ HEEL-TO-BUTT LIFT

Recovery movement for running

Do this exercise while standing in the pose position, with a slight forward lean on the ball of the foot (as when running). Lift your heel toward your pelvis (underneath the buttocks) while simultaneously lifting your knee in front of your body (see figure 4.2a). Your ankle should remain relaxed with your foot hanging down. The focus is on relaxing the quadriceps and being explosive off each successive foot touch so that the heel floats up to touch under the pelvis with each repetition. The movement is diagnostic of both your state of relaxation in recovery and your tendency to dorsiflex the ankle unnecessarily.

You should achieve a relaxed movement, whereby you can easily touch your heel to your pelvis with a natural deceleration while lifting and acceleration while falling, before attempting to increase the challenge by adding extra weight. Apply added weight by using a wrap-around-the-ankle weight. Later use a low pulley and stand on a 12-inch (30 cm) or larger platform or box to add greater resistance and to create a relatively vertical movement (see figure 4.2b). This exercise trains the leg-recovery aspect of running and is complementary to the single-leg squat. It is a dynamic movement that requires you to create momentum.

Figure 4.2 Heel-to-butt lift *(a)* without weight and *(b)* using a low pulley and platform to add resistance.

Supplemental Running Exercises

➤ HIP ABDUCTION, OR LATERAL LEG RAISE

Do this exercise either by lying on the ground on your side or by using a low pulley and standing. When lying down, use a light ankle weight at first, and abduct the hip by lifting the top leg up and away from the body (see figure 4.3). By using circular movements in both directions, you will strengthen all the rotator muscles deep in the hip and stabilize the pelvis during support in running. High weight is not recommended or needed, although you can still make weight progressions. You should keep repetitions above 20 to keep the resistance level low enough to avoid injury. The lower force allows you to recruit the hip rotators rather than the more powerful external hip muscles. This exercise directly prevents various injuries

Figure 4.3 Hip abduction.

in the hip and throughout the leg and improves running efficiency by stabilizing the pelvis for improved support while running. If necessary, a standing version of the same movement using a low pulley and ankle cuff for cable attachment will allow for further progressions in resistance.

➤ HIP ADDUCTION, OR LEG SQUEEZE

You can do this exercise most easily using the standard gym machine that allows for the movement. In this case you sit in a machine designed with pads that allow you to open and then squeeze your legs together (see figure 4.4). It is awkward to access these muscles in a more natural setting other than as stabilizers in basic movements such as the single-leg squat described earlier. The adductors and internal rotators of the hip must be balanced in strength with the abductors and external rotators to avoid an externally rotated hip during support in running and cycling. Because many of the primary hip-extending propulsive muscles in running and cycling also externally rotate the hip, this imbalance develops naturally through running in training.

Figure 4.4 Hip adduction.

You can observe an externally rotated hip in a foot plant, made while standing or running, that angles the foot outward from the line of travel. This foot-plant position results from imbalanced muscles that lead to a misalignment of the hip joint. This creates undue rotary forces on the hip, knee, and ankle during running and cycling and also indicates inefficiency in force production as the foot creates a significant lateral component of force. The regular use of a hip adduction exercise will assist in offsetting this imbalance and create a more straight-ahead and efficient foot placement during running support.

➤ HIP FLEXION, OR LEG LIFT

Lie on your back on the floor, keeping your shoulders and legs off the ground. Lift the straight legs upward alternately overhead by flexing your hips (see figure 4.5). This creates improved hip flexor strength, core stabilization, and enhanced dynamic range of motion in the hips. You can progress the exercise by using ankle weights and a less stable surface, such as a stability ball. The stability ball also offers a greater range of motion than the same exercise

Figure 4.5   Hip flexion.

performed on the floor; it also requires holding onto an immoveable object. The alternate-leg action more closely duplicates the muscular demands of running.

➤ HIP EXTENSION, OR REAR LEG LIFT

Lie on a stability ball or other gym equipment, in this case on your front side. If needed for stability, hold some immovable object (such as a heavy piece of furniture or a weight rack) with your hands. Lift the straight legs upward alternately for running specificity (see figure 4.6). This exercise offsets the natural tendency to create dominance in the hip flexors and a resulting forward tilt of the pelvis, which also increases the lumbar (lower back) curvature, precipitating back problems.

Figure 4.6   Hip extension.

➤ ANKLE DORSIFLEXION, OR ANKLE CIRCLES

Sit or lie down on your back. Flex your toes up toward the shin using a strap-on weight over your metatarsals or a device specifically designed for the exercise. This exercise provides for critical muscular balance and injury resistance across the ankle. If you circle your toes in both directions, the exercise is also useful for rehabilitating inversion sprains, those turned ankles encountered so often in running. As you develop your running ability using the natural running mechanics described in chapter 3, the plantarflexor muscles (calf muscles) often get out of appropriate balance with the much smaller dorsiflexors (shin muscles). This exercise is critical for restoring and maintaining that balance to avoid injury. If you know how to do a breaststroke kick (eggbeater kick) in the water, you can accomplish much the same goal, although the addition of external resistance improves the process.

Core Stabilization Exercises

Core stabilization exercises allow your body to absorb energy efficiently while supporting you in running. They also create a more streamlined and stable body position in freestyle swimming.

➤ HIP STATIC FLEXION, OR FRONT PLANK

Assume a push-up position, but with your body weight resting on your elbows rather than your hands. Your body is in a straight alignment. To create resistance, you can add weights to the hips with a weighted belt or have a partner push the hips down. You can do this exercise both statically (hold position as described to create static control) and dynamically (move through a range of motion). For the dynamic version allow

Figure 4.7   Front plank with leg lifted.

the hips to drop and return to the initial position. You can modify this exercise by lifting one leg off the ground to increase resistance to the opposite hip (see figure 4.7).

➤ HIP STATIC EXTENSION, OR REAR PLANK

Assume the reverse of a push-up starting position in a faceup position, with your shoulders flexed (arms down) and body weight resting on your elbows or hands. Hold your body weight in a straight alignment, or move through flexion and extension at the hips. To create resistance, add weights to the hips or have a partner push them down. You can modify this exercise by lifting one leg off the ground (see figure 4.8).

Figure 4.8   Rear plank with leg lifted.

➤ HIP STATIC FLEXION TO THE RIGHT AND LEFT, OR SIDE PLANK

Assume a lateral position with your body aligned diagonally to the ground and your weight supported by the lower foot. Abduct the shoulder down and rest your weight on your elbow or hand with a fully extended lower arm. You can use the opposite arm to maintain your balance on a chair, although you should work toward not using a support. You can also abduct the hip so that the upper leg is raised to increase resistance (see figure 4.9). You

Figure 4.9   Side plank with leg lifted.

can add weight to your trunk for the same purpose. Reverse this position to work on each side of the body. You can do this exercise both statically (holding position) and dynamically (by moving your hips up and down).

Cycling-Specific Movements

These movements are specific to the seated cycling movement pattern. They use standard equipment found in most gyms, although you can modify range of motion and upper-body position somewhat to more closely simulate cycling positions. You can address the muscle-strengthening needs of cycling in the standing position by using the running-specific exercises.

➤ KNEE EXTENSION

Force production for cycling

This exercise uses the seated knee extension machine found in most conditioning rooms and gyms. You should sit in a comfortable position on the machine with the knees aligned with the machine's cam and directed straight ahead as they extend and flex (see figure 4.10). Extend the knee, pushing with the lower leg, mainly using your quadriceps. Try to find equipment that allows you to complete the exercise using one leg at a time—this will allow for greater specificity. Also focus on using a range of motion that allows you to achieve the same or a slightly greater degree of knee flexion and extension achieved while pedaling.

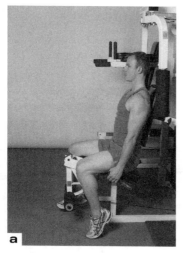
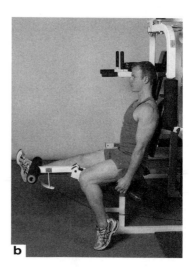
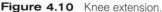

Figure 4.10   Knee extension.

➤ KNEE FLEXION, OR HAMSTRING CURL

Recovery movement for cycling

This exercise uses one of two hamstring curl machines found in most conditioning rooms and gyms. It's better to use the seated machine rather than the prone version of the machine because the seated version allows the more specific body position for cycling. You create a comfortable seated position by aligning your knees with the cam and adjusting the pads you pull down to create a range of motion that is at least comparable to that used while cycling. Adjust the back rest to accommodate the desired seated position. This exercise complements the knee extension to maintain muscular balance and is also helpful in creating general hamstring strength for both running and cycling.

➤ NARROW- AND WIDE-GRIP SEATED ROW

Upper-body stabilization

This exercise uses a standard seated rowing machine found in many gyms. In initiating the movement, the narrow-grip version of the exercise allows for a body position very similar to that used with aerobars. Set your lower back in neutral position and then use a deep starting position (comparable to the pulling position achieved during cycling on the aerobars) and a narrow grip, as used with your aerobars (see figure 4.11a). You use the movement to develop the musculature of the lower back and arms, which stabilizes the upper body as you pull on the bars when you create force by pedaling. You should both extend your hips somewhat and pull the bar to your torso when performing the movement for this purpose (see figure 4.11b). Maintain a neutral position of the pelvis. In other words, avoid letting the top of the pelvis rock back too far while beginning each pull, which can result in a loss of lumbar curvature.

Figure 4.11   Narrow-grip seated row.

To complement this exercise, perform additional sets using a wide-grip bar that allows for better activation of the upper-back muscles (see figure 4.16 on page 93). This is an important functional exercise that also aids shoulder balance in freestyle swimming. The exercise helps you to learn scapular setting, or the use of the upper-back muscles to position the scapulae closer to the middle of the back, when doing other shoulder movements, such as in freestyle swimming. This exercise will help you to reduce your risk of injury while making your shoulder movements more efficient by improving muscle balance across the shoulder. Perform this version of the exercise using the wide-grip bar while keeping your lower back relatively fixed and pulling the bar to the torso using the upper-back muscles. Focus on squeezing your shoulder blades together while doing so.

Swimming-Specific Movements

The swimming-specific movements are divided into two exercises each for force production and recovery, in order to deal with the fact that swimming mechanics require motion in two planes simultaneously, something that is very difficult to address in a conventional weight room with a single exercise. The single-plane exercises allow for the use of conventional equipment found in most gyms.

➤ FRONT LAT PUSH-DOWN

Force production for swimming

Do this exercise with the standard high pulley and straight lat bar found in most gyms. However, it is not the conventional lat pull-down exercise. Standing and facing the equipment, place the hands on the bar with the elbows high, as in the catch position at the beginning of the outsweep in the butterfly. Hold the hands on top of the bar about 12 inches (30 cm) apart with palms open. Position the elbows outside the hands and as high as possible (see figure 4.12a). Then press the bar down, keeping the elbows high (see figure 4.12b). It is not necessary or

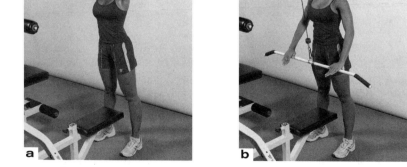

Figure 4.12   Front lat push-down.

even desirable to continue the movement to full extension of the elbows, which would encourage similar inefficiency in the swim stroke (see chapter 3). Press down until the elbows begin to extend and then allow the bar to return, controlling recovery. This exercise should simulate the body position as the hips initiate force through the arms during the catch, outsweep, and insweep in the freestyle. Generally it is necessary to stand and lean forward to complete the exercise on standard equipment.

Another way to do this exercise is by using the Vasa Trainer, although you must add resistance to bring it into the 6- to 20RM relative resistance range for efficient strength and short-term power development. This exercise and the three following exercises combine to create specific power through trunk rotation and a high elbow position in the water.

Use scapular setting (that is, hold the scapulae together) during the lift as best as you are able. Scapular setting should occur in virtually any lift using the shoulder joint as well as during the freestyle stroke. This reduces pressure on the supraspinatus (uppermost rotator cuff muscle) and helps to prevent injury. In the freestyle, scapular setting during recovery creates a high elbow, allowing for efficient and injury-free movement.

➤ LATERAL DUMBBELL LIFT WITH ARMS BENT
Recovery movement for swimming
Hold dumbbells in each hand and lift them from in front of the body directly upward toward the shoulders, simulating the high-elbow recovery motion in swimming (see figure 4.13). You can also accomplish this by using a bar and the upright row exercise. However, using the bar may cause you to rotate your shoulder girdle (scapula and shoulder) anteriorly too much, putting excessive strain on the rotator cuff muscle.

Figure 4.13 Lateral dumbbell lift with arms bent.

When performing the exercise, focus on setting the scapulae together while lifting the upper arms in the same frontal plane as your torso rather than creating the movement toward the perpendicular (sagittal) plane. This will help you develop the high-elbow recovery position when swimming the freestyle as well. This exercise simulates the arm's recovery in freestyle and complements the lat push-down previously described.

➤ BACK EXTENSION WITH CURL

Force production for swimming

Use either a Roman chair (found in gyms) or a stability ball (ideal) to complete standard back extensions, adding a twisting motion to elevate your shoulders alternately (as occurs when you roll your hips or shoulders to create power in your catch). If you use the stability ball, you'll need a partner or some other method of fixing your feet. Hold the extension for one count with each repetition—this increases your potential peak muscular force substantially. You should begin from a flexed position and extend fully while simultaneously rotating alternately to the left and right with successive repetitions (see figure 4.14). Hold your head in alignment with your torso, as occurs in the properly done freestyle. For added weight, hold either dumbbells or weight plates to your chest.

Figure 4.14 Back extension with curl.

➤ ABDOMINAL CRUNCH WITH CURL

Recovery movement for swimming

This exercise also uses a stability ball. It complements the back extension by assisting in recovery of the arm in freestyle and helps to create strength for flip turns. Assume a flat position with the stability ball under your lower back and your feet on the floor or extended and fixed in some way. Hold your arms and weight directly over your chest, with arms extended. Then complete a curling, or crunch, movement by flexing your torso. Add a rotary movement by alternately extending each arm higher in turn (see figure 4.15). Hold the full flexion for one count with each repetition—this increases muscular force substantially.

Figure 4.15 Abdominal crunch with curl.

Supplemental Swimming Exercises

➤ WIDE-GRIP SEATED ROW

This exercise, referred to previously in the cycling section, compensates for the development of the anterior muscles that occurs naturally through free-style swimming. A wide grip, unlike that used for the cycling exercise described previously, is necessary for maximally activating the upper-back muscles. This exercise helps to sustain the integrity of the upper-back muscles and prevents the winged scapula and forward-rotated posture that often predisposes an athlete to the rotator cuff injuries associated with swimming. The primary emphasis is on pulling the scapulae together (scapular setting).

Figure 4.16   Wide-grip seated row.

Sit in a comfortable position at a seated row machine with back upright. Use a handle designed to allow for a grip that is outside your shoulders, and pull the bar directly backward to your lower chest without significantly extending your hips (see figure 4.16). Focus on squeezing your shoulder blades together while maintaining your upright back posture.

➤ SHOULDER SHRUG

This exercise reduces chronic muscular imbalance associated with swimming and swimming-specific movement exercises. Stand with dumbbells in your hands and arms resting at your sides. Lift the dumbbells by elevating and pulling the scapulae together (see figure 4.17).

Figure 4.17   Shoulder shrug.

➤ ROTATOR CUFF EXERCISES

These exercises are essential for maintaining stabilization in your shoulder joint so that you prevent injury during movement-specific exercises and when you swim. The basic exercises involve internal and external rotation of your humerus (upper arm). You can perform them in both the standard position (arms at sides) and a swimming-specific position as described next. Use elastic tubing, a cable system, or light dumbbells for resistance. The resistance should be light enough to allow for 20 or more repetitions—this way muscle recruitment is focused on your internal and relatively weaker rotator cuff muscles and not on your larger external muscles.

- Internal rotation (standard position): Standing to the side of the cable or tubing base with the elbow of your working arm flexed 90 degrees, pull toward the midline of the body while keeping the upper arm close to the body (see figure 4.18).

Figure 4.18   Internal rotation, standard version.

■ External rotation (standard position): Standing to the side of the cable or tubing base with the elbow of your working arm flexed 90 degrees, pull away from the midline of the body while keeping the upper arm close to the body (see figure 4.19).

Figure 4.19   External rotation, standard version.

- Internal rotation (swimming-specific position): Facing away from the cable or tubing base standing with both arms abducted to approximately 90 degrees and your elbows flexed to 90 degrees, pull from overhead toward the ground by rotating your upper arms while maintaining their parallel alignment with the ground (see figure 4.20).

Figure 4.20   Internal rotation, swimming-specific version.

- External rotation (swimming-specific position): Facing the cable or tubing base standing with both arms abducted approximately 90 degrees, as in the recovery and force-production positions in swimming, and your elbows flexed 90 degrees, pull from the ground direction overhead by rotating your upper arms while maintaining their parallel alignment with the ground (see figure 4.21).

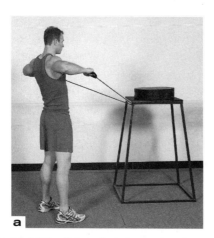 

Figure 4.21   External rotation, swimming-specific version.

➤ BEHIND-THE-NECK PRESS

This exercise allows you to create improved scapular setting while also moving the scapulae and shoulder joints through a full range of motion. Grip a bar slightly wider than shoulder width and lower it behind the head (see figure 4.22). Pull the shoulder blades together so that you can maintain an upright standing posture with your head in a normal balanced position. The exercise will assist in offsetting the negative effects of lots of freestyle swimming.

Figure 4.22 Behind-the-neck press.

Plyometric Training for Running

Running differs from swimming and cycling in that muscular forces are applied to the ground very rapidly using eccentric (lengthening) muscular contractions that allow the body to act as a spring. In swimming and cycling, force is applied with concentric (shortening) muscular contractions against the water and the pedals to create forward movement. Effective resistance training for running includes plyometrics, which are jumping exercises that duplicate the eccentric muscular contractions and springlike movement patterns of running. Plyometrics also maximize instantaneous power, the maximal rate of work you can achieve in a single repetition of a movement. An example is the ability to perform a vertical jump. This capability is the ultimate limiter to the short-term peak power described previously.

Plyometric movements create the highest forces the body will adapt to with training; therefore, you should approach plyometric work intelligently. Once you have developed a basic adaptation to strength and power training in the weight room—ideally over at least six weeks—you can incorporate the use of plyometric training.

Plyometric training allows you to maximize the ability of your muscles to create force in a given movement by using what is known as the stretch reflex. The stretch reflex in your muscles activates a higher contractile force in a given muscular response than is otherwise possible in "normal" conditions. The stretch reflex occurs when a muscle is stretched while being contracted eccentrically (it actually lengthens during contraction) just before creating the concentric contraction that produces movement force. This is also part of the process whereby you can store energy derived from the force of gravity, as described in chapter 3, through the natural elasticity of your muscles and soft tissues. An example is found in the squat you use before attempting a standing vertical jump. This crouch stretches out the muscles used in jumping upward and allows them to create great force. In plyometric training you intentionally create a rapid and forceful prestretch by jumping into power-production positions and then creating the propulsive power to come out of those positions as quickly as possible. You accomplish this by dropping down from a height, repeatedly jumping vertically, or catching and throwing an object in a single, rapid motion.

The plyometric training concept is most significant for running, where gravity, working through your entire body mass, loads large potential forces into your propulsive muscles as you land on the ground. By practicing plyometric techniques that use the running movements, you train your nervous system to use this force production more advantageously in running itself.

Many people fear plyometric training because it involves jumping. However, virtually all athletes can safely engage in this training once they develop basic strength, learn proper technique, and employ appropriate loading and progression.

Plyometric Technique

The most important aspects of plyometric technique for running are the same as the most important aspects of running technique in general. First and foremost, you must establish an effective loading posture for landing on the ground, just as when running. See chapter 3 to review this concept. Second, you must learn to land in a relaxed posture on the balls of the feet. The ankles should appear loose, with feet hanging downward before landing. This allows the muscles to respond reflexively to the ground conditions rather than be overly stiff. Finally, the entire focus of the technique, as in running, is to pick up your feet (or foot) as quickly as possible once you have made contact with the ground. You can enhance the movement by imagining the ground as being hot. You can further enhance it by using shoes that allow you to feel the ground on contact. You should not land, pause, and then jump from the ground, as is so often pictured in the media. This approach prevents the muscles from properly absorbing the forces created by gravity and is likely the reason that so many people perceive plyometric techniques as injurious.

Plyometric Exercises for Running

The following exercises are examples of the most fundamental plyometric training movements for running. You can augment these with dozens of variations on the same basic theme. An excellent resource for these kinds of training exercises is the pose method of running by esteemed running coach and sport scientist Nicholas Romanov.

➤ DOUBLE-LEG HOP

These hops are a series of quick foot removals on a double support (both feet) in the pose position. Keep your ankles relaxed and attempt to lift the feet from the ground without pushing—rather, lift your ankles, as if you were trying to keep yourself off a hot plate. To understand this conceptually and to visualize the activity, you might watch the way a rabbit or deer hops. A good starting point is 5 to 10 hops for a beginner. As you become more adept at relaxing and removing the feet quickly without elevating your center of mass excessively, you will be able to touch your heels to your pelvis in the air during each hop. You can progress this exercise later by doing more jumps, adding a horizontal (or forward) movement component to the jump, and adding weight (in the form of a weight vest).

➤ SINGLE-LEG HOP

These are a series of quick foot removals on a single support leg (one foot) in the running pose position. This is an excellent drill for coordination and power development. Keep your ankle relaxed and hold up the nonsupport leg slightly. You can use these jumps as a general running warm-up and technique drill by using very low heel lifts with rapid turnover. A good starting point is 5 to 10 hops in sets, with 1 to 2 sets per leg initially. Focus on keeping your center of mass as low as possible with each hop.

With increased skill and relaxation, you will be able to touch your heel to your pelvis in the air during each hop. When you increase your range of motion in the hop to this extent, the forces involved become much greater. Consequently, the exercise becomes suitable to use as a training method for power rather than simply a warm-up or skill development technique. In this context it should be done only a few times per week as previously described. You can make the exercise even more demanding by adding horizontal distance and wearing a weighted vest.

➤ VERTICAL BOX HOP

This exercise is a variation on the previously described double-leg hop using a plyometric box. Place the box where you can touch something for balance, and then drop off the box with a short hop, falling as vertically as possible to the ground. Bounce off the ground as quickly as possible on contact by lifting your feet up and returning to your original position on the box.

There are innumerable versions of this basic exercise. The simplest is to hop up onto and back off the box and then back onto it. This requires a focus on landing in the running pose position; you should attempt it with a small box first (2 to 4 in., or 5 to 10 cm). Apply progressive stress by adding repetitions, increasing the height of the box, and adding weight. Do 1 or 2 sets initially with 5 to 10 contacts. You can progress the exercise initially by increasing the height of the box by 2 inches or less. If you add weight, use small increments, such as 1 to 2 pounds. Maintain any progression in the basic force of the movement for 6 to 8 weeks to allow for soft-tissue adaptations.

Ultimately you will want to add single-leg hops to this exercise, but do not do so until you can complete double-leg hops easily from at least 6 inches of height. The starting height for single-leg hops should be no more than 2 inches and should not later exceed half of the current height of the box you are using for double-leg hops. Try to minimize foot contact time by picking up the relaxed foot as quickly as possible on contact, both on the ground and on the box. It is also useful to perform these exercises with either a side-view or front-view mirror so that you can easily evaluate your form on landing. You can find this setup in a gym that has a spotting rack for squats. Try to avoid leaning forward to support yourself on whatever surface you use for balancing. Maintain your upright running posture throughout the exercise.

➤ BOUNDING

This exercise is a series of exaggerated strides achieved by rapidly picking up your feet while running uphill. Imagine the way a deer springs into the air while running. Try to maintain the same form (vertical ankle pickup), but relax and exaggerate the up motion of the ankle, which increases the vertical element in the stride. Do not attempt to lengthen the stride by reaching the foot forward on contact. Use uphills to reduce landing impact and increase muscular tension. Approximately 20 steps in 2 to 4 sets with recovery is a good starting point.

➤ STAIR RUNNING

You can do this type of running using quick, vertical heel-lift strides quite effectively on steps of relatively low height, such as are found in many stadiums. This drill is a low-impact way of increasing neuromuscular speed. Repetitions of 10 to 20 seconds are ideal. Musculoskeletal stress is relatively low.

Design of Resistance
Training Sessions

Resistance training sessions should either follow a metabolic training session in swimming, cycling, or running or include a metabolic warm-up before the weight training. Metabolic training is endurance-oriented training that enhances energy delivery over time. Such training doesn't negatively affect a weight training session after it unless the metabolic training is exhausting. This is probably because weight training sessions are limited by neuromuscular fatigue rather than low energy status. In addition, weight training sessions that substantially reduce peak muscular force through neuromuscular fatigue do inhibit metabolic training sessions in the same movement pattern. This is particularly true when adding new loads in weight training as previously discussed.

Once you have warmed up before a resistance training session, you should normally proceed to do the exercises in the order indicated. First you will do the single-leg squat followed by heel lift, knee extension, leg curl, seated row, lat push-down, lateral dumbbell lift, back extension, and abdominal curl. This order is based on the principles of moving from large-muscle group, compound movements to small-muscle group, isolated-joint movements as well as starting training with lower-body movements and finishing with upper-body movements. Ideally, when using this order, either running or cycling should precede the resistance training as a general warm-up.

You can also subdivide the exercises into separate workouts by movement pattern and pair them with a prior metabolic workout. For example, you can do the swimming exercises after a swim training session. But if you have time limitations, you can quickly complete a combined training session with 1 to 3 sets of all the movement-specific exercises. Finally, it might be useful to do the exercises in race order on occasion. In this case, swimming should ideally precede the resistance training session as your warm-up activity.

You can do the supplemental exercises in a separate training session at home, because most require minimal resistance. Where feasible, do the complementary exercises (such as single-leg squat and heel lift) in alternating sets. This reduces recovery time somewhat and provides a natural stimulus to your muscles similar to that used in the movement pattern itself; therefore, you create greater specificity. When this is not possible, do the force-production movement first and the recovery movement next.

To the extent possible, do the exercises as alternating unilateral (one side at a time in alternating fashion) or isolated unilateral (all reps of one side followed by all reps of the other side) movements as they occur in the related whole-body movements of swimming, cycling, and running. For example, in the knee extension, an alternating unilateral movement would allow one leg to extend while the other is flexing. Not all equipment will accommodate this, however. In an isolated unilateral movement, you would do one repetition of the complete movement at a time with one leg only. In a bilateral movement, you would use both legs together. The last is the least specific approach. Using alternating unilateral movements creates movement-specific strength and the transfer between body sides so essential to the actual movement patterns in each sport that you are training to improve. However, it is sometimes necessary to perform less specific versions of the exercises because of equipment or time limitations. This approach is still effective in building up your strength for the whole-body movement, although transfer is less than ideal.

Initiate each new set in a workout session once your heart rate drops to approximately 70 percent of your running peak heart rate. This should happen within 1 to 2 minutes when working at an appropriate weight and number of repetitions. If not, consider that you may be too fatigued to benefit from your training or that the loads are inappropriate.

You can see the application of many of these concepts and a few of the exercises in the following example of a running-specific and strength-oriented resistance training session complemented with plyometrics for power development. The sample program shown in table 4.1 presumes a running training session as a warm-up.

Table 4.1   Sample Running-Specific Resistance Training Session

Exercise	Set	Repetitions and weight
Single-leg squat (current 1RM = 195 pounds)	Set 1 (warm-up set)	12 repetitions at 70% of 1RM or 136.5 pounds. Use 135 pounds.*
	Set 2	12 repetitions at 75% of 1RM or 146.25 pounds. Use 145 pounds.*
	Set 3	8 repetitions at 85% of 1RM or 165.75 pounds. Use 165 pounds.*
Heel-to-butt lift (current 1RM = 50 pounds)	Set 1 (warm-up set)	12 repetitions at 70% of 1RM or 35 pounds. Use 35 pounds.
	Set 2	12 repetitions at 75% of 1RM or 37.5 pounds. Use 37.5 pounds.**
	Set 3	8 repetitions at 85% of 1RM or 42.5 pounds. Use 42.5 pounds.**
Double-leg vertical box hop	Set 1	20 repetitions using a 6-inch box
	Set 2	15 repetitions using an 8-inch box
	Set 3	10 repetitions using a 10-inch box
Double-leg hop	Set 1	10 successive jumps emphasizing full range of motion to buttocks with comfortable forward movement
	Sets 2 and 3	6 successive jumps emphasizing maximum horizontal distance

*This is the weight you can feasibly use with an Olympic-style bar (45 pounds) and typically available weight plates.
**This presumes the use of a low-pulley machine and available 2.5-pound half plates.

A complete discussion of the practical development of a resistance training program is addressed in chapter 7; sample programs appear in chapter 8.

Summary

A model for endurance sport development that focuses on developing movement-specific strength and peak power using resistance training for all three sports and plyometrics for running provides the basis for sustained progression in triathlon performance, injury prevention, and a varied and motivational approach to training. These characteristics are fundamental to endurance performance. Once you include all the elements in a training program, you should use the methods throughout the training year in conjunction with the endurance and speed training methods described in chapter 5.

Complex Speed and Endurance Training

Basic speed is how fast you can swim, cycle, or run for short distances that take 10 to 15 seconds to complete. Endurance training is simply extending that basic speed over longer distances. As you extend your basic speed in swimming, cycling, and running by completing longer distances in triathlons, you also have to reduce your average velocity (slow down) to do so. The relative amount that you have to slow down as distances increase is your fatigue rate, and the ability to complete a given distance is your endurance level. Fatigue rate and the simple ability to complete longer distances are the main elements athletes try to improve with endurance training.

As discussed in chapter 4, the training model advocated in this book is based on the concept that the basic speed that you can develop at any distance is first and foremost a function of peak power and strength in the movement. Because both strength and peak power in a movement are trainable, you can improve your basic speed by using the process described in chapter 4. However, extending your capability for basic speed (creating endurance) is the objective of the majority of your training time in triathlon. You create endurance and reduce fatigue rate most efficiently by simply establishing a target work level or velocity for a training session and performing an amount of that work that you can complete without undue fatigue or effort. Then when you repeat that same work sometime later in the training process; if it has become easier, you extend it in some way, meaning that you have adapted to it. When that happens, you can add some work (make a progression) without working harder. Over time this process allows you to complete longer distances at faster velocities, which is the primary point of endurance training, without constantly having to train at greater efforts. The same basic process applies regardless of the level of intensity of work you choose to use when training.

The answers to several key questions govern this process. The first question concerns the power outputs or velocities at which you should train to create endurance. Often this is thought of as how hard you should train, most often referred to as training intensity. The classic approaches to determining your training intensity are to use your heart rate or sense of effort and to respond to conditions—that is, to train according to how hard everyone around you is training. The second question is how often you should train at any given power output (work level). This is referred to as training frequency. Typically the emphasis is on the idea that the more often you can train, the better. A third question is how much you should train in a given session or overall. This concept is referred to as the duration of training when applied to a given session and the volume of training when considering the overall view. Again, in many athletes' minds, more is better. Finally, the question of how to organize your training is important. The most common view is to be spontaneous and "train how you feel." Various approaches to training organization are defined by using training systems and implemented according to training plans. As you'll see in the next section, the most common approaches to these issues aren't necessarily advocated.

Endurance Training Model

This approach to training is based on several premises that address the basic questions. The first premise is that training for a targeted velocity or power output over a given meaningful distance (an event distance, for instance) is a more useful approach for establishing training intensities than attempting to simply train at given efforts or heart rates. This is true even when you are targeting a specific

AP Photo/CP, Jeff McIntosh

The distances that you race will determine your training distances and velocities, thus creating specificity in your training.

physiological response (such as your lactate threshold) to determine your levels of intensity. Your ability to finish any given distance as quickly as possible affects your ability to complete both longer and shorter distances as quickly as possible. In addition, by training for relevant distances (those at which you often race), you apply the greatest specificity to your training. You do not sacrifice the ability to tax various specific aspects of your energy systems because efforts at given distances are also closely associated with physiological variables, such as the lactate threshold or $\dot{V}O_2$max, as illustrated later in the chapter. This concept allows you to identify appropriate training intensities either by using direct performance outcomes or by using physiological measures. Regardless of which approach you use, it's not recommended that you create training intensities primarily by feel, heart rate, or rating of perceived exertion. Rather, you should use these kinds of measures to gauge adaptation to work as described next.

Training at specific velocities or power outputs also means that you can test yourself readily, ideally every time you train. The information you obtain about the effort required to complete a given level of work guides your ability to objectively judge your state of adaptation to that level of work. This helps you to know when to add additional work or to increase the intensity of the work to create the basis for further adaptation, a process referred to as training progression.

The second premise is that specific training sessions should be repeated, but not until an adaptive response has occurred to the previous training session. When adaptation occurs, you can add more work with each specific training session, at least over two progressions. This allows you to apply an adaptation model of training, as described in earlier chapters and explained further in this chapter, whereby you progress work as a function of adapting to your current levels of work rather than by simply trying to work harder or do more because you think you should. It also lets you know when you should not attempt to progress your work level, in some cases even allowing you to take a recovery day instead.

The third premise is that targeting the specific velocities and power outputs you are capable of performing for specific event distances also defines the training volume for that level of work. In other words, the training duration you hope to achieve for any given training intensity is the distance over which you hope to maintain that intensity. For example, if you are working at a projected 40-kilometer cycling power output or velocity, then you should strive to complete the amount of work necessary in order to ride 40 kilometers but not more. At the point you can complete this amount of work at the projected intensity, it becomes appropriate to implement progression by increasing the intensity (power output or velocity) of the work rather than further increasing duration. The overall volume of training is of secondary importance to the concept of targeting the correct duration for any given intensity.

The fourth premise is that a variety of training sessions should occur at distances and velocities or power outputs that are in turn shorter and higher than the target event distance (to build speed), longer and lower than the event distance (to build endurance), and specific to the event distance (to build speed at that endurance level). This is known as complex or multiple-intensity training. It allows you to build your greatest speed at any target distance for the least total work volume.

The fifth premise is that training should be both planned and cyclical. This approach is often referred to as periodization. It prevents boredom, reduces the likelihood of injury, and progresses and addresses the cyclical nature of both hormonal production and your adaptations to exercise.

Measuring Work on the Bike

With the advent of reasonably valid and reliable methods of measuring work directly on the bicycle, you can apply the concepts described in this chapter with even greater precision to ensure an optimal adaptive process. While the great swimming and running coaches of the past have long relied on the constant conditions of the running track and the swimming pool and the measurement of times and distances to directly prescribe training loads, this approach was not previously very achievable for cyclists outside of the velodrome. However, through the ability to measure work on the bike directly at all times, the concepts described in this book can be applied in virtually any setting, thereby elevating the effectiveness of the training process in cycling beyond that of its previously more esteemed cousins, swimming and running. Not exploiting this opportunity means giving your competitors a serious advantage in cycling development.

Creating Training Intensity

When implementing the kind of training systems described here, the first requirement is to have a method for identifying appropriate training intensities for any given training session and focus. Athletes accomplish this goal in three basic ways: experimentation, physiological testing, and creating projections based on performance tests using a fatigue curve.

Experimentation

The most common way for athletes to develop their optimal intensity levels is simply by experimenting. For example, assume that you want to improve your swimming speed. You might go to the pool and, after warming up, simply attempt a set of short intervals and swim them as fast as you can. As previously discussed, this approach often can create a variety of problems over time, such as unacceptable exertional pain, failure to achieve a set objective with repeated attempts, gradual overtraining response, perpetuation of bad technique, and lack of consistency of application.

Motivated athletes will often surmount these problems over time and become very adept at performing appropriate work that is within their pain tolerance and that allows for progressive adaptation. Many world records have been set and will continue to be set with the use of the simple experimentation approach. But for every athlete who is successful learning this way, a long line of athletes behind him or her have dropped out of their sport or out of higher-velocity training as a consequence of using this shotgun approach.

Physiological Testing

A second approach that is becoming more common in triathlon training is to undergo physiological testing in order to establish optimal training intensities. In this approach an athlete completes a variety of performance tests for each sport and then uses that information in developing specific training plans. Examples of the tests used most often are the $\dot{V}O_2$max test to establish the power or velocity at which the highest utilization of oxygen by the muscle cells occurs; a progressive lactate test to establish the power or velocity at which lactate accumulation in the blood first occurs (the aerobic, or first lactate, threshold) and later reaches its highest stabilization point (the anaerobic, or second lactate, threshold); and a peak anaerobic power test, such as the Wingate protocol for cycling, to establish short-term and long-term anaerobic capacities.

Because each of the triathlon sports differs in the relationships between work and physiological response, such as heart rate or lactate accumulation, triathletes should complete these tests for all three sports. Many coaches have also developed simplified performance tests that reflect these same parameters. For instance, running a 200- to 400-meter time trial provides information about an athlete's anaerobic capacity because of the time frame of the exertion. A talk test helps to establish the velocity or power at which an athlete reaches the first lactate threshold or aerobic threshold. In this approach you simply monitor the difficulty of talking and rate of ventilation with progressive increases in intensity until you reach the point where breathing is noticeably quicker and talking begins to be impaired. A 30- to 60-minute time trial provides a basic evaluation of the second lactate (anaerobic) threshold. A time trial of 1,600 to 3,200 meters provides a basis for establishing information about the aerobic capacity, or $\dot{V}O_2$max. However, a performance-based approach to testing is very demanding and requires a significant break from the training process.

Based on the current understanding of how physiological factors relate to endurance sport performance, sport scientists and coaches commonly use the following model for the development of endurance sport capacity:

$$\dot{V}O_2\text{max} + \text{Fractional utilization of oxygen} + \text{Anaerobic energy production} + \text{Sport economy} = \text{Performance}$$

The components of the model are defined as follows:

$\dot{V}O_2$max is a person's peak oxygen utilization capacity. The fractional utilization of oxygen is the relative percentage of $\dot{V}O_2$max at which an athlete can sustain work for a given distance or time. The higher, the better.

The anaerobic energy production capacity is the maximum rate at which an athlete can produce energy anaerobically (without oxygen present). The higher, the better.

Economy refers to the oxygen cost of moving at a specific work rate. The lower, the better.

This model is widely accepted. Each variable is viewed as a piece of a puzzle. When the pieces are put together, they contribute to an increase in speed over race distances from 5K upward in running. Training sessions are then developed to maximize each of these energy variables in concert with each other and in balance with the specific nature of the event of interest. In application, this means identifying appropriate velocities or power outputs using physiological testing. Here is an example:

A triathlete in training at the Olympic Training Center in Colorado Springs performed a standard United States Olympic Committee lactate threshold protocol and a $\dot{V}O_2$max protocol. After these tests, velocities and heart rates at each of the points previously discussed were identified for training purposes; these are shown in figure 5.1.

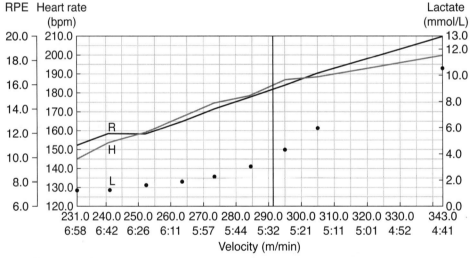

Max HR (bpm):	200.0	HR at threshold (bpm):	181.0
Max lactate (mmol/L):	10.6	Lactate at threshold (mmol/L):	3.4
Max RPE:	20.0	RPE at threshold:	15.0
Max pace (mi/min):	4:41 (20 sec)	Mile pace at threshold:	5:31
Max $\dot{V}O_2$:	5.02 L/min		
	67.8 mL/kg/min		

Treadmill lactate/$\dot{V}O_2$max

Figure 5.1 Rating of perceived exertion, heart rate, and lactate measured at various velocities during lactate threshold and $\dot{V}O_2$max testing.

Armed with the information thus gained, the athlete attempts to train for reasonable periods at identified intensities representing the maximal activation of various elements of physiological energy metabolism. While this training approach is a vast improvement over the experimentation-with-maximal-effort approach, it still presents basic difficulties. Physiological testing is cumbersome, expensive, and difficult to carry out on a consistent basis, even for elite athletes (unless they are working in specialized training facilities with the necessary labs). The simplified performance tests that many coaches use are still demanding and often detract from the training process.

Fatigue Curve

A third approach that has been used is to establish training intensity targets for each training session by using short performance tests and creating a fatigue curve. A fatigue curve is simply a projection of an athlete's current capability over a variety of distances based on ability to perform at least two shorter distances. By comparing two shorter-distance time trials (such as a 200-meter and 400-meter run) and determining the rate of fatigue (percentage of drop in velocity with each doubling in distance), performance times can be projected for any longer distance using natural log equations. The application of such an approach is explained in greater detail next as well as in chapter 6.

This approach provides target velocities or power outputs for any specific training distance. It can also be reevaluated easily. Finally, it makes testing part of the training and racing process.

The rate at which velocity or power output drops as race distances increase can be expressed as a consistent percentage of reduction in velocity or power each time the length of performance is doubled. For example, if your velocity in a 1-mile race is 6 minutes per mile and it then slows to 6 minutes 18 seconds per mile over 2 miles (you run 12:36), you have reduced it by 5 percent. This percentage of loss in velocity or power will be relatively constant each time you double the distance covered. This is because the relationship between the velocity or power you can sustain and the distance covered can be described by a natural log function that is specific to each person. This concept has often been expressed in a simpler way by running coaches as the 4-second rule. This rule states that you can add about 4 seconds per 400-meter pace each time you double the target distance for racing. However, the 4-second rule presumes that all athletes have the same fatigue rate, or loss in velocity, each time distance is doubled—about 5 to 6 percent. This assumption covers many but not all well-trained endurance athletes. You can measure the current fatigue rate by performing two short time trials such as a 200-meter and 400-meter run on the track.

A person's rate of fatigue is very likely related to basic muscle fiber composition and training status. It can be used to identify the athlete's best performance distances. Based on an examination of best performances of world-record holders running at multiple distances, the rates of fatigue appear to vary from approximately 3 percent in elite endurance athletes to 12 percent in elite sprinters. An average triathlete might expect to have a fatigue rate of 8 to 10 percent, whereas elite triathletes might approach 4 to 5 percent. Beginning athletes might have fatigue rates as high as 20 percent.

This concept is very likely specific to each sport in triathlon as well. The relationship between power and distance can be more simply expressed as consistent rate of fatigue for any athlete in any sport at any time. This rate of fatigue and the mathematical function that produces it can then be used to project velocities or power outputs at various levels across the spectrum of power output once performances are measured for shorter distances. In turn, the level of strength and peak power in a related movement will then be related to the short end of this velocity curve. This is illustrated by the following theoretical data based on a 6.5 percent fatigue rate typical of a well-trained subelite runner.

1RM quarter-squat strength	400 pounds (181 kg)
Peak squat power	1,200 foot pounds/second (166 meter kilograms/second)
6.5 percent fatigue rate	
400-meter time	1:10 (4:40 minutes/mile)
800-meter time	2:29 (4:58 minutes/mile)
1,600-meter time	5:18 (5:18 minutes/mile)
3,200-meter time	11:16 (5:38 minutes/mile)
5,000-meter time	18:16 (5:53 minutes/mile)
10,000-meter time	38:54 (6:16 minutes/mile)
42,195-meter time (marathon)	3:07:42 (7:10 minutes/mile)

Once you have estimated your potential ability to complete various distances by establishing your fatigue rate, as in the example on page 111, you have the basis for creating specific training session targets that you are likely to achieve. By combining training sessions at both ends of the power and velocity curve, along with all elements along the chain in appropriate balance, you will develop your ability to perform your best at any given distance. The art of applying the multiple-velocity training concept comes in finding the appropriate blend of all elements for any given time. There are two basic observations in this regard. First, as stated previously, a complex training program should include a session targeting distances and work rates that are shorter and higher than the target event, the same as the target event, and longer and lower than the target event. Second, the longer the target event,

Calculating Target Velocities
Using the Fatigue Curve

Begin this process by measuring your performance across two distances. For example, you might measure your time swimming 50 yards and 100 yards. You can then project your time for additional distances, such as 200 yards, 400 yards, 800 yards, and 1,600 yards using the following equations:

$$t(x) = T1 \times (T2/T1)^{[LN(x/D1)/LN(D2/D1)]}$$

where

t(x) = predicted time for distance $\times$ (distance for which you want to predict a time)

T1 = time for test 1 (the shorter test, or 50 yards in this case)

T2 = time for test 2 (the longer test, or 100 yards in this case)

D1 = distance for test 1 (50 yards in this case)

D2 = distance for test 2 (100 yards in this case)

LN = the natural log

You can use the same calculations for power by substituting average power over a given distance for time. The calculations use the natural log because velocity and power decay in an exponential function. To complete them rapidly, you would need to either use a calculator that performs natural log calculations or design a spreadsheet to do so. The Excel spreadsheet will manage this quite nicely.

In a natural log function, the percentage of reduction in velocity or power for each doubling in race distance can be expressed as a constant, which is referred to as the fatigue rate. It is calculated using the following equation, assuming distance 2 is twice as long as distance 1:

$$T2 - [T1 \times (D2/D1)] / T1 \times 100$$

---

the more heavily weighted (the greater the volume of work) the velocities or powers at the low, or endurance, end of the range should be in the training program. However, all elements should be included in the program regardless of weighting.

Your basic strength and peak power output in the movement relate to the fatigue curve concept in that they represent the upper limit of the curve. As small increases in strength and peak power occur with training, short-term speed will increase and the same rate of fatigue will produce improvements across longer performances with similar endurance-oriented training, as illustrated:

1RM squat strength	425 pounds (193 kg)
Peak squat power	1,275 foot pounds/second (176 meter kilograms/second)
6.5 percent fatigue rate	
400-meter time	1:08 (4:36 minutes/mile)
800-meter time	2:25 (4:50 minutes/mile)
1,600-meter time	5:08 (5:08 minutes/mile)
3,200-meter time	10:57 (5:29 minutes/mile)
5,000-meter time	17:44 (5:43 minutes/mile)
10,000-meter time	37:47 (6:06 minutes/mile)
42,195-meter time (marathon)	3:02:20 (6:58 minutes/mile)

Alternatively, in developing greater endurance without sacrificing basic speed (referring to the first example), a lower fatigue rate will result and produce faster endurance performance times as well. In the following example, an athlete with lower peak strength, power, and speed than the athlete in the second example might still exceed the performance of the previous athlete at longer distances by virtue of a lower rate of fatigue, a fairly common scenario.

1RM quarter-squat strength	400 pounds (181 kg)
Peak squat power	1,200 foot pounds/second (166 meter kilograms/second)
5.4 percent fatigue rate	
400-meter time	1:10 (4:40 minutes/mile)
800-meter time	2:27 (4:55 minutes/mile)
1,600-meter time	5:11 (5:11 minutes/mile)
3,200-meter time	10:57 (5:28 minutes/mile)
5,000-meter time	17:38 (5:41 minutes/mile)
10,000-meter time	37:12 (6:00 minutes/mile)
42,195-meter time (marathon)	2:55:53 (6:43 minutes/mile)

By concurrently developing both peak power and endurance at a variety of speeds across your complete range of speeds in the appropriate balance, you can then optimize your performance at a given target distance by improving through both mechanisms: speed and endurance.

Integration of Physiology and Performance-Based Training Intensities

The integration of the physiological testing approach to establishing target training intensities using the fatigue curve to project specific velocities or power outputs for distances is illustrated by the following complete range of physiological capacities and specific distance capabilities you should strive to develop in a complex training approach:

1. Movement strength refers to your ability to produce force in your swimming, cycling, and running movements. You develop this by using a movement-specific resistance training program that allows for at least 85 percent of your 1RM force. In this case, speed of execution is not a factor, only the development of maximum force.

2. Movement peak power refers to your greatest ability to produce power (work rate) over a very short period in the swimming, cycling, and running movements. Full development of peak power requires the use of a movement-specific resistance program using approximately 50 to 70 percent of your 1RM resistance. This allows you to create your highest power outputs (work over time) by using a level of external resistance that allows you to move quickly. Peak power is further augmented by the use of plyometric (jumping) training methods applied at maximal speed.

This technique allows you to engage the stretch reflex to increase muscular force to its highest levels. You accomplish this by dropping from a height into a landing position on the ground that allows your muscles to prestretch before you contract them as rapidly as possible while jumping up again (see chapter 4 for more details on performing plyometrics). The prestretch increases the peak force your muscles can produce reflexively. This training technique is applicable to running, where force must be applied in milliseconds at a very high level.

3. Alactate, or short, power refers to the peak-level energy production you can create for very short periods (generally less than 15 seconds) in swimming, cycling, and running. It is referred to as alactate power because you don't work long enough to develop high levels of blood lactate and the resulting acidity (hydrogen ion concentration). This makes high-level work relatively comfortable to complete. You develop this type of power by focusing on 50- to 100-meter run speed, 12.5- to 25-yard (or meter) swim speed, and 0.125- to 0.25-mile cycle power or speed.

4. Anaerobic power is the development of peak power over periods of about 45 seconds to 2 minutes. During this time, the production of lactate and acidity is maximal, making the work extremely uncomfortable to perform. Many athletes avoid work in this range because of the discomfort. Others sometimes overuse this range of power unintentionally by overexerting themselves to keep up in group-training situations in a nonsystematic way. You develop this level of power by performing work at your 200- to 800-meter projected run speed, 50- to 200-yard swim speed, and 1-kilometer to 3-kilometer cycle power or speed.

>> continued

5. Aerobic power ($\dot{V}O_2$max) maximizes your ability to use oxygen. It focuses on the level of power or speed you can maintain over approximately 3 to 7 minutes. In physiological testing, it is often defined by the work rate you achieve in the final stage of a $\dot{V}O_2$max (aerobic capacity) test. This level of work is also extremely uncomfortable to perform over extended time. You develop it by focusing on your 1,600- to 3,200-meter run speed, 400- to 800-yard swim speed, and 4- to 8-kilometer cycle power or speed.

6. Second, or anaerobic, lactate threshold is the highest level of work you can sustain over an extended time (between 30 and 60 minutes). During the progressively increasing work intensities of a physiological test, it is often defined by speed or power at which blood lactate no longer stabilizes within several minutes but continues to rise. This intensity of training is sometimes referred to as red-line effort. It also requires significant exertion to maintain over time. This work level is most representative of and specific to your race pace in typical triathlons at the sprint and Olympic distances. You develop this capacity by focusing on the 5-kilometer to 10-kilometer run speed; 2,000-yard to 4,000-yard swim speed, and 20-kilometer to 40-kilometer cycle power or speed.

7. First, or aerobic, lactate threshold is also identifiable in a progressive work test by the intensity at which your blood lactate begins to rise over its baseline with successive increases in work intensity. It represents the workload at which your anaerobic and aerobic energy systems begin to become unbalanced. This is significant because as these energy systems become unbalanced, you use proportionately more carbohydrate for energy and reach exhaustion much more quickly.

This intensity provides a level of work you can complete comfortably and with minimum fatigue for long periods, yet with maximum benefit in terms of aerobic development. It can be thought of as a ceiling for the relatively comfortable aerobic work that makes up the majority of endurance athletes' training programs. This level of work is most often associated with swimming, cycling, and running training sessions lasting from 30 minutes to more than a few hours, although well-trained athletes can sustain this level of intensity over many hours. This capacity is associated with the currently projected 40-kilometer run power or speed; 13,200-yard swim speed, and 80-kilometer cycle power or speed.

8. Strength endurance refers to performing swimming, biking, and running work at aerobic intensity with small amounts of external resistance (as in item 7) that do not alter movement mechanics. Adding such resistance slows swim stroke rate, cadence, and stride rate proportionately.

You may be thinking that this seems like an awful lot to do. But if approached properly, in fact it is not. The first consideration in combining all these speeds in one training program is how much to do of each. One easy way to think about that is to consider the effect of each if you add the times for all the distances together. The shortest distances would require the least amount of your training time and the longest distances the most. Say your running times were as follows:

Type of training	Percentage of total training time	Distance	Time
Alactic speed work	~0.04%	10 meters	1.6
		100 meters	18.0
Mixed anaerobic and aerobic speed work	~0.50%	200 meters	37.9
		400 meters	1:30.0
		800 meters	2:48.7
Aerobic capacity speed work	~2.00%	1,600 meters	5:55.6
		3,200 meters	12:29.6
Race-pace work	~8.00%	5,000 meters	20:11.6
		10,000 meters	42:34.3
Tempo work	~12.00%	13.1 miles (half marathon)	1:35:10.1
Long endurance work	~25.00%	26.2 miles (marathon)	3:20:38.0
General endurance work	~50.00%*	52.4 miles	7:02:58.4

*This percentage will drop considerably in those athletes who work best at or are restricted to lower total training volumes and potentially increase in those who are able to find time for and can benefit from higher total training volumes.

This approach precludes doing a good deal of steady aerobic training every day, particularly in a training schedule in which you must train for three sports simultaneously. Rather, you would typically have three separate targeted training sessions for each sport in a normal weeklong training cycle, each focused on one or more of the key velocities combined with more general aerobic work.

A single-sport example for an athlete at full training tolerance for all the velocities currently being used might look like the following, in this case for swimming:

Tuesday

Short speed—100-yard through 500-yard velocities combined with 20 minutes of aerobic swimming

Specific sets—4 × 25 yards at 100-yard velocity, 4 × 50 yards at 200-yard velocity, 5 × 100 yards at 500-yard velocity

Thursday

Race pace—1,500 yards combined with 20 minutes of aerobic swimming

Specific sets—3 × 500 yards at 1,650-yard velocity

Saturday

　　Overdistance—4,000-yard speed for an extended aerobic swim

　　Specific sets—4 × 10:00 minutes at 4,000-yard velocity

For highly adapted professional triathletes and single-sport athletes, additional sessions in a weeklong cycle would focus largely on recovery. In a longer training cycle, you could include more purely aerobic-velocity sessions between higher-velocity key sessions.

A more evolved program for an advanced athlete might also further subdivide key training velocities into more sessions (as illustrated in the sidebar on pages 113 to 114) as the ability to perform each improves. However, this requires a longer training cycle for adaptation—quite often 10 to 14 days is useful. The 10-day training cycle might appear as follows:

　　Day 1: Short speed—50 to 200 yards

　　Day 3: Aerobic-capacity speed—500 yards

　　Day 5: Race-pace speed—1,650 yards

　　Day 7: Tempo speed—3,000 yards

　　Day 9: Overdistance speed—6,000 yards

Additional training sessions would then focus on general aerobic work and recovery. Based on this simple approach to organizing training, what follows is a more detailed discussion of the methods of applying these ideas to a training process. Specific examples of training plans using these concepts appear in chapter 8.

Determining How and When to Progress

Regardless of how it was determined, the target rate of work performed in a given training session can be tied to physiological effort by measuring the rating of perceived exertion (RPE) and heart rate. Progressions in work should occur when physiological effort at a given workload is reduced. This approach maximizes the rate of adaptation and makes training more tolerable and fun. You quickly learn how to create appropriate training efforts that you'll be able to repeat and adapt to more quickly. To implement this approach, you must have a means of measuring both the work and the physiological outcome of the work.

Measuring Work Rate and Its Outcomes

For the physiological response training model, you must be able to either measure the work rate or power directly or measure a related performance outcome, such as velocity or time for a given distance. This is essential for determining the relationship between work accomplished and the physiological strain on the body. You accomplish this in the swimming pool and on the track by measuring times and distances for work intervals, a model that can also be extended to cycling with the use of odometers. You can also carry out run training on the treadmill and measure the work-related outcome even more precisely by evaluating both treadmill speed and grade. An additional advantage is that the prescribed work-load can be set, removing the need for you to create the pace. This allows you to focus on relaxing at the pace rather than struggling to achieve it.

With the advent of portable power-measuring devices in cycling, you can immediately determine wattage (a measure of power or work rate—work divided by time) while riding. You can even extend the model to stationary bike trainers and even bike rollers by using an odometer. Another advantage of this approach lies in the ability to control environmental conditions for more valid comparisons between work efforts. A stationary approach allows you to more easily create the specific heat and humidity levels for which you are preparing to race. With the recent advent of miniaturized and portable global position-ing system devices for civilians, you can extend this concept to riding outdoors and to virtually any form of human locomotion. In the sidebar below are the primary ways in which you can measure work rate or its direct result in each sport that makes up triathlon along with concerns for each method. When you are not measuring work output directly, such as with a power meter, then you must consider how other factors may have influenced the work you needed to do to get a particular performance result.

Methods for Measuring Work Rate and Its Outcomes

Swimming

- In the pool, swim a predetermined distance and get your time. You must consider the effects of changes in turbulence on your work rate to achieve a given time.

- In open-water courses, you can also swim a set distance. You must also consider the effect of wave action and currents on work rate.

Cycling

- Ride with an onboard power meter on an open course. This is the opti-mal approach. A hub-integrated power meter, such as the Power Tap, or a crank arm–integrated model, such as the SRM, will provide reliable comparisons in power regardless of external conditions or tire pressure. The newer models, which calculate power based on a range of predic-tor variables, are not as reliable with changing conditions. You can also transfer hub-integrated power meters to stationary training.

- Ride rollers at a fixed resistance level using an odometer. This approach is preferred for flat training, but it doesn't allow for climbing-specific conditions except through the manipulation of gear selection. The main concern in evaluating work outcome is the effect of variations in tire pressure.

- Perform stationary training with devices that measure either velocity or power output. The main consideration is calibration of the device, which

>> continued

normally reflects variations in tire pressure. This approach allows for a greater variety of cycling positions than rollers do, although it does not allow for natural bike movements.

■ Ride on a premeasured road or trail using an onboard odometer or by simply timing yourself. The main concerns in evaluating response are temperature, humidity, wind conditions, and tire pressure.

Running

■ Run on the treadmill using velocity and grade to determine work level. This is preferred for most higher-velocity training if a full range of velocities and grades can be accessed. Consider that treadmill running at a given velocity will require a slightly lower work level than equivalent-velocity overland running. The addition of a 1 to 2 percent grade or an adjustment upward in speed of approximately 10 to 20 seconds per mile will offset this difference.

■ Run on the track and time yourself for set distances. Consider the effect of wind on work rate. This approach does not allow for the use of hills or descents.

■ Run on premeasured road- or trail-course distances and times. You must also consider wind conditions in this approach.

■ Run on an open course using velocity determined by GPS units or foot pod units. This doesn't account for hills or wind in relationship to work rate.

Measuring Physiological Effort

Once you have established a means of measuring work and its outcome, you also need a means of measuring your physiological efforts, or strain, to perform at that work level. The primary value in understanding the physiological systems of energy production and oxygen delivery lies in the ability to evaluate the progress of the adaptive process. You can use the physiological response to specific training workloads to make intelligent decisions about the progression of those workloads you should undertake in order to achieve greater fitness for racing. When physiological response to a training load improves, you can then increase workloads with a high probability of further adaptation and better fitness. When physiological strain (effort) increases for a given workload attempted a second time, you must consider whether it is productive to continue with the planned training load at that time as well as consider methods of augmenting the recovery processes to increase adaptation. You are often better served by taking that day off for recovery and either skipping the planned session entirely or postponing it. This approach allows for a training plan that involves doing progressively harder levels of work only as you adapt, rather than trying to work harder each time you train.

The distinction can be illustrated in this way: Assume that you are attempting to improve your running speed for 1,600 meters or your $\dot{V}O_2$max with a specific training session. The traditional approach to this type of training is to complete a series of efforts at the fastest possible pace you can sustain in that specific training session. Success would typically be evaluated by virtue of the outcome alone: If you complete more work—such as a faster-interval set—than previously, you are successful. The physiological and psychological costs of the work would play minimal roles in determining the value of the session or the overall training process. The following is an example:

Run 3 × 1,600 meters at the best pace possible
with full recovery in between each set.

Quite often this will result in a first effort at or close to the target velocity (the velocity at which you hope to race that distance) with declining outcomes at greater effort for the second and third intervals. In attempting this training session at a later point, you find value when you can do the same runs faster than the last time you tried it. Quite often this does not happen, because you have not fully adapted to the first session. You must try to be up for a training session of this sort because it will always be exceptionally demanding. You must also be willing to accept the physiological and psychological pain of completing the session at a higher effort each time if you are not adapting.

In a model driven by improvement in physiological response rather than performance outcome, you would complete a series of intervals that elicit the $\dot{V}O_2$max improvements but are tolerable. You do this by working only at the desired intensity long enough in a given interval effort to stay within your reasonable pain tolerance. The primary goal is to complete the prescribed work at the prescribed power output with the least effort necessary, rather than to maximize effort to complete the work. You would be judged successful if you could complete the work with a lower physiological and psychological strain. If so, you would add more work as the training session proceeds or in a future training session addressing the same physiological variable or performance distance. A description of this approach applied to the previous example is as follows:

Run 3 × 400 meters at your current projected 1,600-meter pace
with a 100-meter jog between intervals and a full recovery between sets.

The first difference in this approach is that the session should not be exceptionally demanding to complete initially. Second, by running only 400 meters at the target velocity, you are far more likely to spend more time overall in the training session at that target velocity as fatigue is reduced by using the shorter segments of work. When you reapply the session in the next microcycle, you would then make progress based on response to the work. Assuming the first 400s (run at the same velocity in the second session) elicited improvements in either training or recovery heart rates, you could do additional training (an additional 400, for instance) without making the training exceptionally difficult to complete.

In this approach your nervous system and muscles experience more of the target work velocity with significantly less physiological discomfort. As a result, adaptation is likely to occur more quickly, and psychological and physiological distress is reduced. You are also likely to use training of this type more consistently. This question has been examined scientifically by comparing the response to training at the $\dot{V}O_2$max pace using both shorter intervals (60 percent of the time an athlete could run at $\dot{V}O_2$max velocity) and longer intervals (70 percent of the time an athlete could run at $\dot{V}O_2$max velocity). The study examining this concept demonstrated a more favorable response in the subjects whose training was organized around a shorter work interval and a greater number of efforts, because that type of training allowed for work at the target velocity to be completed more easily and allowed for a more successful adaptive process (Smith, Coombes, and Geraghty 2003).

While the maximal-effort approach is time honored and has proven effective in the short term in highly motivated people, it is problematic in the long run. Among the problems encountered are loss of motivation for extremely difficult training, greater likelihood of injury, and overtraining. Consistency of training application is diminished in favor of short-term gains in conditioning after very difficult training sessions. The physiological response model, used intuitively by some of the greatest coaches of our time, allows for a more appropriate pattern of adaptation by keeping training load tolerable and guiding the creation of progressions in load after adaptation rather than simply motivating athletes to their best performance through exhortation. The training itself becomes motivational because improvement occurs with less discomfort; the coach does not have to create motivation in order for the athlete to tolerate the training. With the advent of tools for measuring both workload and the physiological response to it, decisions on training progression previously made according to the coach's "feel" can now be made objectively by anyone who understands the basic process.

Physiological strain can be measured in a variety of ways, including heart rate monitoring, rating of perceived exertion (RPE), blood lactate level, and measurement of oxygen consumption. While metabolic analysis methods such as blood lactates and $\dot{V}O_2$ analysis are technical and inaccessible to the average athlete and coach on a regular basis, heart rate monitors are now quite inexpensive and available to virtually all athletes. Rating of perceived exertion (RPE) using the Borg scale is also available to anyone and can be found in figure 5.2. Both athletes

6	No exertion at all
7	
8	Extremely light
9	Very light
10	
11	Light
12	
13	Somewhat hard
14	
15	Hard (heavy)
16	
17	Very hard
18	
19	Extremely hard
20	Maximal exertion

Borg RPE scale
© Gunnar Borg, 1970, 1985, 1994, 1998

Figure 5.2 Borg's rating of perceived exertion scale.

Reprinted, by permission, from G. Borg, 1998, *Borg's perceived exertion and pain scales* (Champaign, IL: Human Kinetics), 47.
© Gunnar Borg, 1970, 1985, 1994, 1998

and coaches can accomplish this measurement task with great objectivity and sensitivity by rating efforts as they make progressive increases in work intensity, as might happen during the warm-up period on a stationary trainer or treadmill.

Combining Work Output With Physiological Effort to Progress Training

The concept of progressing training by adaptation is very simple, although it is often seen as very complex. In any given training session, you simply begin moving at your target power output or velocity and continue doing so within your current limits for discomfort or until you complete your target distance or time for a given effort. Then you stop or slow to recover. If you're equipped to do so, note your heart rate just before finishing and after a fixed amount of recovery time. You then complete the number of repetitions of this work that you can do without becoming unduly fatigued or until you reach your current target for work. You then stop and recover for the next set or cool-down.

When first working at a new velocity or power level, generally three or fewer efforts at the new intensity is a good starting point. Sometime in the future (usually on a cycle of 7 to 10 days) you repeat the same session. If you find yourself expending less effort to achieve that power level or speed, you then add some small amount of work (more intervals, longer intervals, or once you've reached the desired distances, more speed or power). You should employ the 10 percent progression rule—that is, you never add more than 10 percent in distance, power, or speed when progressing toward a training session target. In fact, the smaller the amount of planned increase in work, the more likely you are to adapt to it easily. Thus 5 percent is actually a better target in most cases. Logically you should first progress the total duration of the work until you reach the target distance. This can be defined by a specific event distance. For example, 1,600 total meters of work is the best target duration for work at your projected 1,600-meter pace. You should then increase the length and reduce the number of repetitions to reach the target distance. Finally, once you are completing the target distance using four or fewer repetitions, you should increase the velocity or power. At this point you can either retest yourself to reestablish your current fatigue rate and projected distance targets or make a reasonable progression of 5 to 10 percent increase in velocity.

An example might be as follows: You've completed 21 minutes or 7 miles on your bike at a power output of 250 watts (or speed of 20 mph) and heart rate average of about 150 bpm (beats per minute) in training. When you repeat this session with less effort, your heart rate is now about 145 bpm after several minutes. You then decide to make a progression in the next session where you target this work, so you increase your intensity over the last 5 minutes of the next session to 260 watts (a little less than 5 percent increase). Later you will gradually increase the intensity over the entire interval.

You can generally succeed in repeating this kind of training cycle with adaptation and progression two or three times. Then you should deliberately plan on a reduced cycle of work, usually about half of what you had been doing previously, although at the same target work rates. This is the three-to-one rule of progression: For every three progressive adjustments upward in work, you should include one planned reduction in work. A simple approach is to reduce work to 50 percent of the last progressive increase.

An example applying both concepts is illustrated by the runner increasing training volume week to week:

Week 1: 180 minutes (3 hours)

Week 2: 189 minutes (3 hours 9 minutes or ~5 percent increase)

Week 3: 198 minutes (3 hours 18 minutes or ~5 percent increase)

Week 4: 99 minutes (1 hour 39 minutes or ~50 percent reduction from last week's sessions)

Evaluating Physiological Response

Both the exertional heart rate during the work and the capacity of the heart rate to recover after the work are important in evaluating the difficulty of a training session. In general, when the exertional heart rate is elevated beyond the level reached in previous attempts, this indicates greater strain and no adaptation in the current session, regardless of the reason. This may be caused by dehydration, accumulating fatigue, increased temperature, or the use of stimulants. A reduced heart rate for a work level indicates lower strain and adaptation.

A widely held notion (although not scientifically validated) concerns the evaluation of recovery state. It holds that a decline in heart rate to approximately 70 percent of its peak, a rate in the 120s for many healthy younger athletes, within one to two minutes from when training is stopped and a walking recovery is initiated is a standard that indicates the given effort was completed with acceptable levels of physiological strain. When the recovery is considerably poorer than this, it is suggested that strain has been unacceptable and the athlete will take significantly longer to adapt. When recovery is better, then the training challenge is considered an insignificant stimulus for improvement and may enhance recovery from previous training.

After brief periods of reduced training, as might occur in restoration or tapering periods, heart rates at given workloads tend to elevate over normal. This very likely reflects the return of the adrenal gland to a state of hyperfunction. In this case it does not indicate greater strain and is not accompanied by either increased sense of effort (it may actually be lower) or a worsened recovery response. This phenomenon allows you to work at even higher heart rates than normal yet with improved recovery.

Creating a Training Environment and Volume of Training

By never overextending yourself in any training session and by planning for periods of restoration before the time you would normally plateau in your ability to progress, you create a training environment that encourages the maximum rate of adaptation and improved ability for racing. By learning to manage your efforts appropriately, you also learn to enjoy training at all levels of power or speed. Doing so leads to greater training consistency—the most important element in achieving long-term improvement.

This same approach then applies to all the speeds or powers you use in training, including your longest endurance sessions. Ideally, when preparing specifically to race, at a minimum your overall race-specific training program will include sessions that target speeds and distances shorter than those of your target races, at your target race distance, and longer than your target race distance. To the degree that your training program encompasses an even wider variety of speeds, you create a more complete link between your peak power or speed and your various endurance speeds. In other words, when you improve your 200-meter running speed, by training at that intensity, it links automatically to your longer run performance (say 10K) and improves your speed over that distance as well without further increases in the more specific training for the velocity associated with that distance. In practical application, you become faster at the longer distance by becoming faster at a shorter distance, all other things being equal. If you then work to improve your 400-meter speed, this has the effect of creating an even better link between your 200 speed and your 10K speed. That is, you get even faster at 10K without getting faster at 200 meters or doing more specific training for 10K. The effect of each additional link in speed that you create is synergistic. With each additional increase in speed at longer distances, the link becomes more complete and all your performances benefit.

This approach advocates creating the most complete link across your current range of speeds that is practical for you using all the various links from basic speed to endurance speed. This concept is supported by various reports of research that have linked training at virtually every intensity with a given athlete's improved racing performance in endurance events (Esfarjani and Laursen 2007; Esteve-Lanao et al. 2005; Faria, Parker, and Faria 2005a, b; Laursen et al. 2005; Paavolainen, Hakkinen, et al. 1999; Paton and Hopkins 2004). For many athletes, this approach means training less rather than more. As noted earlier, many endurance athletes view the volume of training that they complete as the most important variable leading to success. Thus they try to train as often and as much as possible. However, when this volume and frequency exceed individual capacity to adapt, it leads to a reduction in work outputs—running, swimming, or cycling more slowly or with greater efforts at the same work rate. This type of training limits the ability to recover from and adapt to training. Ultimately it results in most training occurring at less than the specific speed or power necessary for successful racing. Another way to say this is that you become well trained to go slow every day but less effectively trained to go fast on any given day. If triathlons were multiday events, this approach might be effective, but very few triathlons are multiday events. To race at a given velocity, you must adapt to training (perform the work) at that velocity—no other factor in training is more important.

The value of increasing your overall training volume by training more frequently and more slowly is often extolled based on the high training volumes of elite athletes. Higher training volumes in elite athletes actually represent their genetically preordained greater capacity to perform additional aerobic work and still allow for adaptation. This often reflects differences in muscle fiber type and basic musculoskeletal structure. Those with high work volume adaptability are very likely also equipped with higher percentages of slow-twitch muscle fiber, a lighter frame, and lower body weight. For those with less than exceptional ability, attempting to duplicate this approach is usually counterproductive. A general rule is that the current total training volume is appropriate for any given athlete if adaptation is occurring but should be reduced when it is not.

Adaptation to a racing velocity occurs more easily if you are also adapting to velocities greater than race velocity. Adaptation is even further enhanced when you are also adapting to longer, slower velocities. However, each of these specific adaptations is more the function of a given individual training session than the cumulative effect of many training sessions within a training cycle. To do this, you must allow for recovery in between the focused training sessions. Trying to increase total training volume by increasing the number of training sessions in each sport weekly often inhibits this process. In other words, more training overall is not better if it does not lead to an improved ability to complete each specific training session targeting a specific velocity and distance. This is especially true in those with less than exceptional ability for endurance sport. Once you view training as an adaptive process, the value of recovering between focused training sessions rather than trying to increase total training volume between them becomes apparent almost immediately.

Of course, it is always useful to build training tolerance before involving yourself in the race-specific approach described here. Training tolerance refers to the total volume of training that you can respond to. This concept is known as base training. It involves adapting your body to progressively higher amounts of easily tolerable aerobic training and building movement strength so that you will ultimately respond better to the race-specific forms of training (sessions at faster than race pace, at race pace, and longer and slower than race pace). It is useful to return to this type of training systematically throughout the year because it offers you more freedom in how and where you train, reduces the physical and mental stress of more specific race-preparation training, and creates a natural variation in the process that keeps it fun and interesting. For example, rather than riding your bicycle on a trainer with some specific interval work in mind, during base training you are more likely to simply go out on a ride that you enjoy with the simple goal of sustaining a given power, speed, or heart rate throughout. By varying base and race-preparation training cycles throughout the year, you stay fresher and more enthusiastic, and you make greater improvements in race speed over time.

Training Aerobically Rather Than Anaerobically

At this point it is useful to discuss the value of training aerobically rather than anaerobically at virtually all times. This is the idea that training should rarely or never stress the anaerobic capacities of the body significantly. This does not mean that you should not do work at the power outputs that would create an anaerobic response. Rather, it means that you should organize that work to avoid an excessively stressful training session. When you push as hard as possible for as long as possible, you do several things that are counterproductive to the adaptive process. First you experience great physical pain, which makes it less likely that you will want to repeat the experience. This inhibits training consistency. Second, you stimulate the body to an overproduction of adrenal-gland hormones epinephrine and cortisol—the stress-response hormones. The ability to produce these hormones is essential to performing physical work and then recovering from it. By forcing sustained overproduction, you exhaust the adrenal gland for a time, causing the phenomenon referred to as parasympathetic overtraining. This state both inhibits your adaptive ability and removes all joy from the training process.

Through both experience and testing, however, you can learn the heart rate limits at which you begin to rely too heavily on the anaerobic energy systems. By using these heart rates as monitors to establish the upper limits for training efforts, regardless of velocity, you can sustain an aerobic training environment yet still train at the full range of powers and velocities you are capable of performing. For example, an athlete might choose to train at his current 1-mile target velocity—let's say it is a 6-minute-per-mile pace. This athlete has determined that efforts begin to get very uncomfortable at a heart rate of about 150. That is his aerobic heart rate ceiling for efforts. He would train to improve his target mile velocity by running at the 6-minute-per-mile pace until his heart rate reaches that aerobic limit and then he would slow and recover. If recovery were adequate, he would then repeat the same work again using the same process. He would continue to do so as long as his heart rate is able to recover similarly between efforts or he could stay within his reasonable limits for heart rate during the interval.

Training this way would be classically defined as anaerobic work because of the velocities he is running. Yet he would be completing the work within an aerobic range of effort without producing extreme acidosis and discomfort. In all likelihood he would then adapt to this work easily and be able to add more work in the next training cycle because he would not be overproducing adrenaline or cortisol when performing the training session and recovering from it. The question of greatest interest is whether the amount of time he spent running at the target velocity is more important than how hard the efforts were for him to complete. The former is the most important measure of an effective training stimulus. In this model the athlete will both accomplish more work at the target velocity and produce less adrenaline and resultant fatigue for the given effort.

By working concurrently within a training cycle at a variety of velocities and force ranges, across your own personal range, you then create the most effective overall response to the training and increase your speed for any given distance. Again, for example, to train to run 10 kilometers as fast as possible, you might work on your running movement strength and power as well as your ability to sustain speed at 10 meters, 100 meters, 200 meters, 400 meters, 800 meters, 1,600 meters, 3,200 meters, 5,000 meters, 10,000 meters, half marathon, marathon, and beyond, all concurrently.

Organizing a Training Plan

One hallmark of successful competitive triathletes is the presence of a long-term training plan. The method used to create such a plan usually involves one of three general training approaches: random training, mixed training, or periodization.

Random Training

A random training approach refers to a philosophy of training by feel. In other words, the athlete or coach makes a decision on a session-by-session basis to do a specific workout that reflects both the desire for diversity and the athlete's capability or mood on that day. For example, on one day you might arrive at a swimming workout to find that you are working on race-pace speed and on another day you are working on endurance without reference to any overall training plan. The primary advantages of this approach, which is so often used by recreational athletes in group training programs (such as masters swimming or group training rides), is that the athletes are never bored by doing repetitious work or compelled to train hard when they feel tired. The primary disadvantage of this approach is that athletes are less likely to achieve their potential because all elements of training and development are rarely addressed systematically to allow for ongoing progression. This tends to occur in unorganized group training programs.

The drive to train is often fueled by the desire to be part of a group more than the desire for individual achievement. Consequently, athletes often train in a less-than-efficient manner as dictated by the group dynamic. While this might seem to lead to greater enjoyment, it often leads to an overtrained state and loss of training interest when individual athletes place more value on staying with the group than on allowing themselves to adapt before adding a higher training stressor. It can also lead to an undertrained state if the group performs only at levels lower than what some athletes are capable of. Most training groups come and go and their compositions vary from year to year—a fact that illustrates the paradigm described previously.

Mixed Training

A mixed training approach uses a complex training model in which the key components are included systematically in a cycle of training that is repeated throughout much of the training year. The most notable advocate of this approach—Robert de Castella, Australia's former world-record holder in the marathon—used this training approach with great success. The primary advantage is found in the regular use of a variety of training intensities to create the most favorable overall development for competition. This approach allows an athlete to be race ready through much of the year. It is favored by many successful age-group and professional triathletes. The most notable drawback of this approach—a concept that is emerging in the published research on this topic—is the comparatively diminished potential for achieving full development over extended periods in comparison with a periodization approach (Kraemer et al. 2000; Marx et al. 2001; Stewart and Hopkins 2000). However, at least one short-term study using resistance training illustrates that a mixed training approach offers an improved response in comparison to a traditional phased periodization. In the phased periodization, various training intensities were isolated in early mesocycles and then not specifically maintained in later mesocycles (Rhea et al. 2002). This illustrates the importance of maintaining the full spectrum of training intensity in some way at all times. It is also worth noting that a mixed training approach may be used more often when employing an adaptive training model as described in this book. In a more conventional training approach that emphasizes progression by improved performance outcomes in training and is consequently more fatiguing, the need for regular change in training emphasis may be greater in order to maintain physical and psychological "freshness." Regardless of training approach, people still seem to adapt in a cyclical way (ebbing forward in surges) rather than in a consistent, linear way (constantly improving). Planned periods of reduced or altered training stress appear to allow this natural process to happen more successfully.

Periodization

Periodization refers to the application of a long-term plan using cyclical phases in the training process. It is really a method of organizing training systems as opposed to being a system in and of itself. As in the mixed training system described earlier, it is common to include a variety of types of training in the short-term training cycles, which are referred to as the microcycles. A periodized training plan emphasizes specific training themes in blocks of several microcycles, which are linked together and referred to as mesocycles. The mesocycles vary systematically throughout the year. Each consists of several microcycles, typically three or four. Successive mesocycles reflect a succession of themes culminating in the highest performance state. The mesocycles and their component microcycles are then combined to create a macrocycle, or overall progression of training toward a key race or racing period. The most common overall theme, when applied to endurance sports like triathlon, is a progression from very generalized forms of training for basic biomotor capacities (such as aerobic endurance, movement strength, and technique) to very race-specific forms of training that prepare athletes more specifically for the demands of multisport racing. Traditionally athletes would perform one extended macrocycle per year. However, in modern triathlon it is common to complete two or even three shorter macrocycles per year in order to peak for several important competitions. This approach creates tremendous diversity in the training program, ensuring long-term consistency and development.

A common application of the variation of microcycles within a mesocycle uses the three-to-one rule. Under this theme, workload progression is made over three microcycles while a fourth is used for restoration. Once certain aspects of fitness are developed with a given mesocycle (such as your training capacity or general aerobic endurance), they are often maintained in successive mesocycles while other aspects of more race-specific fitness are further emphasized (such as your tolerance for race-specific training velocity). This is often accomplished by reducing the frequency or amount of a given training stimulus without reducing its intensity. The same three-to-one concept can be applied to the use of successive macrocycles within a year. Following three progressive macrocycles, it would then be prudent to include a shorter macrocycle of restoration training at greatly reduced volumes and intensities.

Within the overall periodization plan, the mesocycles are combined to create an overall training macrocycle that progresses the athlete from more general to more race-specific fitness. This formulation provides the opportunity for peak performance in a given race or group of races, usually one to three times in a training year. There is emerging research in the scientific literature on this topic (Zaryski and Smith 2005) coupled with the long experience of former Soviet and Eastern Bloc athletic programs. Together this evidence supports the view that this approach allows athletes an improved opportunity to reach their highest performance level at specific times during a given year, although possibly on a less consistent basis throughout the competitive year.

Elite athletes and coaches are attracted to the periodization approach because it offers an improved opportunity to create peak performances on demand, such as at major competitions. A growing number of age-group triathletes as well use this approach for the same reasons, along with the benefits of reduced risk of overtraining, injury, and loss of motivation inherent in a steadily more intense program of training without periodization. Traditionally some professional triathletes have avoided such an approach when they perceive their income potential to be based more on consistent race performance throughout their season rather than their success in a few key races.

The practical application of a periodization approach requires an athlete or coach to establish specific goals for specific races during the upcoming racing year. From these goal races and dates, the athlete simply works backward to develop progressive cycles of training leading up to the key race or racing period. A simple approach to this process is to combine two primary training-emphasis types of mesocycles known as base training and race-specific preparation training. You can find practical examples of this concept in the training programs in chapter 8.

Base Training Mesocycles

During the base training mesocycles, the focus is on four factors: developing training capacity or general aerobic endurance; developing peak movement strength and power; increasing aerobic speed; and improving technique in swimming, cycling, and running. Unless a period of detraining has occurred, you also seek to maintain both short-distance speed (in running 200 to 400 meters) and aerobic capacity speed (1,600 to 3,200 meters) developed in preceding race-preparation mesocycles by using minimally stressful sets of very short alactate effort several times per microcycle. More advanced athletes may also seek to maintain race-pace speed by using short-tempo training sessions. These training periods should allow for more spontaneity in selecting training routes and training partners. They also become a mental break from the more focused race-preparation training cycles.

A variation on base training that you should use at least once yearly is restoration training. In it you reduce your current training loads considerably (50 percent or more) and engage in alternative training (different from your usual activities). Examples include substituting trail running for road, treadmill, or track workouts; mountain biking for road cycling or stationary trainer or bike-roller workouts; and multistroke general swimming workouts or water polo for more specific freestyle-preparation swim training. You could also incorporate other less specific activities such as Nordic skiing, snowshoeing, team sports (soccer or basketball), or any other activities that help to maintain basic cardiorespiratory fitness but offer a variation from the customary training routine. These restoration base periods can range from a few weeks to a few months depending on your interests, motivation, and setting.

Race-Specific Preparation Mesocycles

The second form of mesocycle in this approach to periodization is race-specific preparation. During these periods, the focus is on the use of a full range of training velocities in a more complex training approach. So you focus on developing your ability to exert your peak power potential at short distances, race distances, and longer distances. The specific combination of target velocities and power level varies depending on developmental level and target race distances. During these training periods, you also seek to maintain basic training tolerance, peak strength and power, aerobic speed, and general technique.

An example of a short periodization plan macrocycle with two mesocycles is as follows:

Week 1: Base 1

Week 2: Base 2

Week 3: Base 3

Week 4: Restoration

Week 5: Race prep 1

Week 6: Race prep 2

Week 7: Race prep 3

Week 8: Restoration or taper and race

Scheduling Training Sessions

Once you become involved in a complex training approach, you must make a decision about how to schedule training sessions of different intensities. Because certain sessions are perceived as hard, implying greater need for recovery to ensure adaptation, the planning usually centers on the appropriate placement of these sessions. These are often referred to as key training sessions. A traditional approach to this problem, popularized in the United States by Bill Bowerman at the University of Oregon, is referred to as the hard–easy scheduling of training. In this scheme, harder sessions are alternated with one or more easier sessions to allow for recovery and adaptation before training hard again.

The hard–easy concept has not been widely studied using a scientific approach, in spite of the fact that it is a cornerstone of current training plan models used widely today. Based on experiential evidence, its primary value lies in the allowance for adequate recovery and adaptation, thereby minimizing the number of training sessions where progress is not seen or felt.

A newer approach is the concept of block training. In this approach, multiple harder sessions are grouped together in a training plan to produce a greater total training stimulus, resulting (theoretically at least) in a greater total adaptive response. In other words, the total work an athlete is able to do at a given intensity is increased by coupling multiple sessions together. This type of training approach requires extended periods of two or more days of sequential hard training followed by extended periods of easier training. Some elite cycling coaches claim that athletes can reach a higher level of adaptation more quickly using this approach. However, few would claim this mode of training organization as a means of making training more enjoyable, a vital element to the maintenance of training consistency.

Practical experience illustrates the greater difficulty, both physically and psychologically, in completing successive hard training sessions as an athlete becomes progressively more fatigued. The regular use of the multiple hard sessions also seems to be more likely to induce injury, overtraining states, and loss of motivation. As they become progressively harder to accomplish, training sessions produce degenerating performance outcomes in a training block. However, note that this approach has been used by some elite athletes in cycling with great success, an occurrence that might also reflect a high degree of psychological and physical pain tolerance and self-motivation methods that center on punishment rather than enjoyment. This approach illustrates the concept of winning the battle but losing the war. Immediate success is far less valuable than sustained success and enjoyment in the process for most athletes.

As noted, in triathlon the problem of organizing training sessions is further complicated by the need to train for the three sports simultaneously. While not clearly demonstrated scientifically, it would appear that cycling and running, through their similarity in movement pattern and muscle activation, each produce crossover fatigue that interferes with training sessions in the other. This phenomenon does not appear as much with swimming, however, unless the leg muscles are so fatigued by cycling and running that push-off force on the turns in the pool is greatly reduced.

One strategy to combat the problem of crossover fatigue is to schedule harder cycling and running sessions close together (on the same day, often in normal race sequence), then provide for a recovery period from both over one or more days. Harder swimming sessions can then be scheduled on offsetting days with a minimal concern for creating an additional stimulus that might prevent leg recovery.

Block training in triathlon appears to offer less potential for success than in cycling or swimming alone because the need to accommodate running training into the overall schedule greatly reduces an athlete's ability to respond to successive hard training sessions without substantial recovery. In the triathlon resident team program at the Olympic Training Center in 1996, a significant number of athletes reported that using block training caused them to become overtrained and lose motivation, and in general the approach turned training into a chore rather than a labor of love. The hard–easy approach, with coupled key sessions in running and cycling offset by key swimming sessions, offers more benefits.

Application of the Fatigue Curve Training Model

In the women's cross country program at Colorado State University at Pueblo, a small number of prospective team members had indicated the desire to run, although no formal practices or team meetings had yet been held. With some rapid recruiting in classes, the group of interested athletes quickly expanded. A training process was immediately started based on the principles described previously, which were adapted to the realities the young women faced. Rather than use a conventional approach, they followed these procedures:

1. Each person established her current training tolerance. Many of the candidates were not currently running.

2. Each athlete did 100-meter and 400-meter time trials at the track.

3. With an Excel spreadsheet of equations previously described, their fatigue curves and projected velocities were calculated at 400 meters, 800 meters, 1,600 meters, 5K, half marathon, and marathon.

4. An individualized training program was created in which they ran a progressively longer effort at half-marathon velocity on Mondays; a speed session with work at 400-, 800- and 1,600-meter velocities on Wednesdays; and a race-pace session on a golf-course measured loop at 5K velocity on Fridays. For strength endurance, they also did additional aerobic work on these days at a comfortable intensity using a treadmill at about 2 to 4 percent grade. In the weeks in which they had a meet, they simply ran that effort on Saturdays, and the Friday race-pace session was canceled, providing an additional recovery day.

The number or length of repetitions at each target work level was increased only if they showed adaptation week to week. Depending on their prior training load, they either ran recovery workouts on Tuesdays and Thursdays or engaged in some form of cross-training. On Saturdays when no race was scheduled, they did enjoyable team runs in natural mountain settings using the comfortable pace of the slowest runner in the group that day. Sunday was a rest day. After three weeks the team took a restoration week and reset loads by retesting at 100 meters and 400 meters. All had improved considerably. The eighth week before the regional meet, they took a taper week.

The young women all ran in Nike Frees or other similar lightweight shoes, using spikes for the race-pace intervals. They ran their strides two or three times weekly in bare feet on grass when possible. Most learned to breathe through their noses when training. There were no significant injuries, and each team member made progress throughout the season, averaging a 14 percent improvement in performance for the team for the season.

Every team member who ran the regional meet ran her personal record (PR) at that point. This allowed the team to place ahead of several established teams and place one athlete very close to the NCAA individual qualifying levels—all with a team largely recruited out of classes eight weeks prior. One scoring member of that regional team had never run competitively and had not even been running recreationally when she began.

Strength Endurance Training

The use of resistance training described in chapter 4 will help you optimize peak strength and power levels. You can also use resistance training separately from that process as a variable for progressing through your endurance training. This concept is strength endurance training. Those familiar with the rapid drops in the cycling hour record times achieved by Francesco Moser in the 1980s may also be familiar with his application of interval work using an extremely high gear on the bicycle and very low cadences in the range of 40 to 60 rpm. This approach has since become time honored and widely practiced by elite cyclists, and recent research has supported its application (Taylor-Mason 2005). A plausible explanation for the effectiveness of this type of training centers on the idea that the slightly increased resistance level and lower cadence may allow an athlete to recruit additional muscle fibers not normally trained except at higher intensity.

By engaging in this practice, you can build endurance in muscle fibers, allowing for a broader base of muscle fibers that can work primarily aerobically. Of course, the downside of too much training in this mode will be a decline in your pedaling rate if you allow the slower rate to become dominant. You should deliberately and judiciously apply the approach in the training program, as opposed to having it occur spontaneously through fatigue or overgearing. The main concern expressed by coaches and athletes unfamiliar with this approach involves possible injury to the joint structures resulting from higher sustained force applications. Any potential for injury is likely to be related more to the pedaling technique than to the pedaling forces used. As with all forms of training, the method is used with reasonable tolerance and progression.

The same concept for developing triathlon-specific strength can be applied to the individual training methods for swimming and running. In swimming, you can use paddles of progressive sizes or towing systems. In running, you can use hill training or running with weights. In both cases the amount of resistance should allow for effective application of technique as described in chapter 3. In particular, swimmers who persist in using a contralateral, arm-based stroke with flat recovery, as well as runners who persist in overstriding and heel striking, should avoid these methods. For those who employ them, these forms of training have the additional benefit of providing a more rapid neuromuscular learning rate as well as increasing movement-specific strength. If you use such an approach once you have learned the elements of stroke and stride, the application of additional resistance will augment that learning process.

Finally, here are a few key recommendations. To build leg strength in cycling, use a gear that targets between 40 and 60 rpm and maintain your common racing positions while performing this kind of training at aerobic intensities. Never incorporate strength endurance training more than every other training session, which generally means no more than twice per week.

In swimming, you might choose to use the newer profile paddles that claim to reduce the forces applied to the shoulder. You can also consider a towing-system approach, although there is a concern for altering mechanics. The newest state-of-the-art towing systems do not alter mechanics substantially. However, more primitive methods, such as wearing T-shirts while swimming, directly deteriorate your swimming mechanics and should not be used at all.

In running, carry the additional weight in a weighted vest and proceed cautiously within the following framework. Begin with a load that is less than 2 percent of your body weight. Make any upward adjustments in weight after a minimum of eight weeks of training at the current level. Make adjustments in small increments of one to two pounds (0.5 to 1 kg). Never exceed approximately 10 percent of body weight in total load. Treadmill applications for hill training also offer a controllable means of creating progressions in strength endurance work as well as reducing the need for extended downhill running except as desired. Begin with small amounts of such training (5 to 10 minutes) and never exceed race times or distances by large amounts.

Overtraining and Overreaching

Effective training involves the achievement of adaptation producing the greatest progress over time. Overtraining is then defined by a too-frequent stress application (the same stress is reapplied too soon) or a too-excessive stress application (the amount or intensity of the stress is too great). In either case, maladaptation (loss in ability) occurs rather than adaptation. Overreaching is a movement in the direction of overtraining. In other words, it is the application of a training stimulus somewhat beyond that to which you can readily adapt. Some coaches advocate overreaching in highly trained athletes so that they achieve even greater fitness—a view embodied in the block training organization discussed previously.

If an athlete and coach adopt a physiological response training model, they can eliminate overtraining because they create training progressions only when adaptation occurs. The need for overreaching becomes less useful as well. The primary virtues are patience and a focus on organizing training and recovery to improve adaptation and train consistently rather than simply to train hard in the periods before competition.

You should proceed with organizing your training program around the principles described in chapter 1. You can monitor adaptation both at training sessions by measuring heart rate, RPE, blood lactates, and even submaximal $\dot{V}O_2$ (running economy) as available and at systematic points in the training cycle. Measurements at the end of each training cycle might include such elements as resting heart rate, orthostatic heart rate response (response upon standing), blood pressure, body weight, grip strength, and a variety of blood parameters as available. In addition, simple Likert scale ratings of lifestyle factors such as quality of sleep, mood, desire to train, and general and muscle-specific fatigue level can be very useful in tracking change in adaptability to training. An example is provided in table 5.1. Finally, coaches and athletes should take a proactive approach to enhancing the recovery process between and during training sessions.

Table 5.1   Overtraining Assessment Scale

Factor	Rating (circle appropriate number)				
Sleep quality	1 very poor	2 poor	3 typical	4 good	5 very good
Desire to train	1 very low	2 low	3 typical	4 high	5 very high
Appetite	1 very poor	2 poor	3 typical	4 good	5 very good
Muscle soreness	1 very high	2 high	3 typical	4 low	5 very low
General fatigue	1 very high	2 high	3 typical	4 low	5 very low

Enhancing Recovery

You can use a variety of techniques to enhance the recovery process between training sessions, thereby improving the adaptive process over the long term. Unfortunately, there is a lack of scientific evidence concerning most of the recovery techniques used. What is available is somewhat equivocal and often the product of poorly designed studies. However, the anecdotal evidence supporting the use of a variety of modalities is strong enough to have convinced the United States Olympic Committee to fund a new recovery center at the Olympic Training Center in Colorado Springs. This center uses many of the following methods to assist athletes in improving their adaptability to training programs through active recovery interventions:

- Optimal sleep environment
- Massage
- Hot or cold total-body immersions, such as cold-water baths and warm-water whirlpools
- Hyperbaric chambers
- Recovery training and stretching
- Pretraining, during-training, and posttraining feedings

Most of these techniques focus on creating increased blood flow to the muscles between training sessions so that inflammatory metabolites and damaged proteins can be removed and carbohydrates and amino acids can be delivered. Other techniques focus on enhancing the quality of rest so that the body's more general recovery processes, such as hormone production and secretion, can progress in an unimpeded fashion. Much can also be made of using appropriate nutritional practices to resupply fuels, water, minerals, vitamins, and muscle proteins, a more complex topic addressed in chapter 9. To the extent that you can incorporate such activities, they are likely to be most beneficial after races and the most demanding training sessions.

Creating Regulation of the Nervous System

A topic not yet addressed in the scientific literature regarding recovery and adaptation is the idea that virtually all training for endurance sports (excluding races) should be conducted in an aerobic environment in which a balance of the parasympathetic and sympathetic nervous systems is maintained. The sympathetic branch of the peripheral nervous system is responsible for creating an elevated energy state, or sympathetic activation. This is accomplished both through the activation of sympathetic nerves and through the release of sympathetic hormones, such as epinephrine (adrenaline) and cortisol. By contrast, the parasympathetic side of the system is responsible for returning the body to its normal resting state. When the two systems are in balance, you can create the additional energy production necessary for exercise training and competition and return to normal resting functions within a reasonable time.

When the sympathetic system becomes dominant, you overreact to the exercise stressors and struggle to return to a resting level. Between training sessions, a continual elevation of the sympathetic response, which is generally referred to as stress, indicates that recovery and adaptation are not occurring. When the sympathetic–parasympathetic relationship is still unbalanced in subsequent training sessions, it indicates overreaching, or failure to fully adapt to the stimulus; therefore, more rest is required. In a training model that promotes a regulated nervous system, training efforts will not require you to become excessively stimulated sympathetically. You can evaluate the extent of nervous system regulation by measuring heart rate during and after load applications. In this model, you would alter or postpone training sessions if you could not recover your heart rate to an aerobic level during recovery periods in training, indicating sympathetic overstimulation and dominance. The purpose of training is to increase loads without inducing overactivation of the sympathetic system.

This approach does not preclude training at a full range of work intensities. Rather, anaerobic work and neuromuscular work are allocated in amounts that allow for recovery to aerobic heart rates within 1 to 2 minutes between work sets and within shorter periods within work sets. An example is swimming 5 ×100 yards at a projected 500-yard race pace with 30 seconds of recovery. During the 30-second recovery, heart rate should recover to an aerobic level of approximately 80 percent of the maximum heart rate. Between sets, heart rate should recover within 1 to 2 minutes to 70 percent or less of the maximum heart rate. Consider in this example that the heart rates should be compared to the swimming-specific maximal heart rate, because it will be considerably lower than a running or cycling maximal heart rate due to the horizontal body position and more efficient cooling environment. Further, the highest-intensity work occurs in the general training schedule to allow for adaptation between sessions, generally a minimum of two days apart.

When completing aerobic work that is continuous in nature, you can evaluate nervous system regulation by measuring the working heart rate to determine whether the effort is remaining aerobic and by stopping periodically to measure the recovery heart rate. You can also use this type of work more frequently; it becomes the foundation of an endurance athlete's training program, largely because adaptations can be made quickly.

Another novel approach to evaluating the nervous system regulation during training is in the pattern of breathing you choose to use. As described in chapter 3, the use of deliberate nasal breathing will limit exercise intensity to one that is largely aerobic in nature and is less likely to create sympathetic overstimulation. This may also create the additional benefit of allowing you to more successfully filter pathogens as well as cold, dry air and develop a deeper abdominal breathing pattern. The deeper breathing pattern is further associated with parasympathetic nerve stimulation resulting in a relaxation effect and reductions in heart rate at a given work level once you fully adapt to the nasal breathing method.

However, as noted previously, nasal breathing is a learned skill. For most people, mouth breathing is dominant during exercise. With nasal breathing, initially carbon dioxide levels in the blood will rise slightly, creating the potential for anxiety as the drive to breathe more deeply is stimulated. With progressive application, however, your breathing sense returns to normal as you learn to tolerate higher carbon dioxide levels through gradual adaptation. This is analogous to the experience of learning a slower, deeper breathing pattern in swimming due to the inability to breathe freely throughout the stroke cycle.

This approach augments both training recovery and the general training process of adaptation without undermining work capacity or racing performances. This model helps in creating the kind of long-term development and more consistent use of all training intensities so you can reach your potential in triathlon.

A further application of this concept helps you to understand how to develop an individualized training schedule. Once you have decided on the focus of specific training sessions and can evaluate your state of adaptation during each, you are in a position to create optimal timing for your training cycle. Over time it will become apparent how often you can afford to perform each kind of session in your training program based on the time frame necessary for adaptation.

The runner attempting to use the 400- to 800-meter speed emphasis training session described previously might find that he has to wait several days in his general training program before reapplying that specific training session if he hopes to adapt. More general aerobic training sessions might show adaptation more quickly and be reapplied more often. Numerous factors influence your rate of adaptation: age, the number of sports you are training in, the effectiveness of your recovery process, and the occurrence of additional stressors such as work, emotional issues, altitude of residence, and current heat or humidity level. Chapter 8 contains target training programs that allow for adaptation in most athletes. Each athlete responds differently, so an effective training cycle can be worked out only through trial and error. Also, the optimal timing of training sessions within a training cycle will change over time as well as with varying conditions.

Adapting to Different Environments

Exposure to variations in the environment, such as increased or decreased altitude, temperature, and relative humidity, adds a set of stressors to which the body must adapt in order to maintain homeostasis. When applied appropriately, these environmental stressors can create physiological adaptations that improve performance in triathlon. Failure to account for the additional stress can result in poor performances or overtraining.

Using Higher Altitudes

By reducing the availability of oxygen carried in any one breath that can be supplied to the tissues, training or living at higher altitudes than you are accustomed to creates a stressor on the body. This occurs as a result of a reduced barometric pressure on a given volume of air, thereby allowing the air to occupy a larger space. Because the lungs do not increase in size at altitude, the same lungful of air contains less oxygen even though the concentration of oxygen in the air remains constant. This results in a reduced arterial concentration of oxygen, essentially depriving the tissues of oxygen. The result is an increased production of lactic acid (lactate and hydrogen ion) as well as increased carbon dioxide production. The need to clear excess hydrogen ions and carbon dioxide from the body stimulates an increased rate of both ventilation (breathing) and diuresis (production of urine).

The short-term result of this initial acclimatization is dehydration and fatigue. The long-term adaptation is an increase in the number of red blood cells and thus an enhanced oxygen-carrying capacity in the blood. Exposure to increased altitude results in improved oxygen delivery. However, continuous exposure to increased altitude may also reduce the physical work capacity of the muscles because the training stimulus to local muscular development is typically reduced over time when training in higher-altitude conditions. In other words, you simply cannot train at the same intensities at higher altitudes as easily, so you lose muscular capability over time. The resulting loss in muscular function may offset the improvements in oxygen delivery when returning to sea level to compete, resulting in no meaningful improvement in performance.

The historical research addressing the value of living at altitude for training purposes to improve sea-level performance has not been conclusive, although more recent work considering this problem has illustrated greater potential (Stray-Gunderson, Chapman, and Levine 2001; Wilber 2001). It is indisputable that altitude acclimatization is absolutely essential in maximizing performance in events occurring at altitude, as occurs in numerous Xterra triathlon events. The optimal short-exposure time course for this adaptation is likely a minimum of three weeks. When that is not possible, you should arrive at the increased altitude of the event site as close as possible to the occurrence of the event to avoid the initial fatigue created by early efforts of the body to acclimatize. The worst-case scenario is to arrive several days to a week before the event because most athletes will experience the fatigue caused by the acclimatization process by the time the race occurs.

Regarding the use of altitude residence to improve sea-level performance, the most current model for altitude-stressor application, referred to as high–low training, resolves the problem of lost muscular function by using exposure to altitude to increase oxygen delivery in combination with training in conditions that allow work output to reach or even exceed what can be completed at sea level. The result is a meaningful improvement in sea-level performance beyond what might be attained otherwise. Sometimes you can accomplish this by driving to lower altitudes for training, although that is uncommon.

Another version of the model practiced by numerous elite triathletes training at the Olympic Training Center uses increased oxygen-concentration gas mixtures (hyperoxia) to allow for higher-intensity training. Because the gas is administered through a gas mask from a stationary set of tanks, this model limits hyperoxic (high oxygen concentration) applications to training that can be conducted on stationary ergometers, such as the treadmill and cycle trainer. It also allows an athlete to live in virtually any moderate-altitude location. Finally, the most popular application of the model relies on hypoxic (low oxygen availability) tents or chambers to create a nighttime altitude simulation for sleeping, allowing for living and training at sea level. This last approach, although popular, has not been clearly established as effective in scientific literature, potentially because of the problem of insufficient exposure to low oxygen levels possible in the typical eight hours of sleeping.

The optimal altitude for training exposure for the high–low approach appears to be in the range of 2,100 to 2,500 meters. Altitudes lower than this provide a less-than-optimal stimulus for red blood cell production, and higher altitudes often result in a deteriorated ability to recover and adapt to training. In addition, the response is variable: Some athletes are largely nonresponsive. To have a significant effect on red blood cell mass, the minimal exposure necessary for a short-term camp approach using this model appears to be greater than 12 hours of exposure per day over a stay of at least three weeks. In addition, a 12- to 14-day reacclimatization period at sea level after altitude exposure is considered essential before anticipating improved training or racing. This is based on the time course for mature red blood cell development (4 to 6 weeks) and the initial fatigue created by reacclimatization upon return to sea level. After this reacclimatization period, a window of approximately 1 to 2 weeks allows for enhanced training or race performance; any performance-boosting adaptations are likely to recede after that.

For those who choose to live the majority of the year at moderate altitudes, the need for a significant advance period at sea level before competing is less important. A late arrival to the sea-level race site will minimize the inevitable acclimatization process likely to cause fatigue, particularly when heat acclimatization and time-zone transition fatigue are not significant issues. When long travel for races is required, such as to Europe or Australia from the United States, it is a good idea to arrive early—12 to 14 days early if possible. Doing so will allow for the maximum adjustment to the new time zone while also maintaining the increased oxygen delivery associated with altitude residence. This period also allows for a significant acclimatization to heat and humidity to occur at the race site.

Dealing With Increased Heat and Humidity

Increased environmental temperature and relative humidity also create a significant stressor to training and competing triathletes. This occurs because the blood flow must be used not only to deliver oxygen to working muscles but also to remove heat through the peripheral circulation in the skin. Further, as evaporative cooling through sweating becomes the primary mechanism for releasing heat from the skin, significant increases in water loss occur as well, ultimately reducing the volume of the blood and cardiac efficiency. This phenomenon explains why your heart rate increases in heat and humidity at the same absolute work level, as well as why heart rate begins to drift upward sooner in these conditions.

Fortunately, the primary mechanism by which you adapt to hot, humid conditions occurs through an increase in the sweat output during training. In preparation for hot, humid events, you can make significant adjustments quickly. A well-trained person is already somewhat heat acclimatized, although not fully if training does not occur in hot conditions. Two avenues are commonly recommended for the purpose of developing a more complete heat and humidity adaptation: natural acclimatization and artificial acclimation.

In natural acclimatization, an athlete arrives in a hot, humid location and adapts to the conditions through natural exposure. This is considered to take 12 to 14 days for full acclimatization and coincides with the time frame previously discussed when traveling from altitude over long distances. This has obvious disadvantages in that it does not allow for a typical arrival at an event site one to two days before the event. A less obvious disadvantage may be a reduction in training quality, particularly when acclimatization is carried out over long periods and conditions inhibit training intensity.

In an artificial acclimation approach, an athlete uses training in artificially hot and humid conditions to produce a maximum sweat rate and body-water turnover. This may provide a significant adaptation in four to six days. You can accomplish this by using stationary training in conjunction with heaters and humidifiers as well as by wearing extra clothing while training outside and seeking the hottest times of the day for acclimation training. To optimize work and power output, conduct high-quality key training sessions in optimal environmental conditions. You should use lower-intensity aerobic sessions to develop heat acclimation where a sacrifice in power is less meaningful for future race performance.

During these sessions, measure body weight before and after with the dual objectives of maximizing sweat rate and minimizing weight lost to dehydration by the generous replacement of fluids while training. Hydration will also minimize the increase in body temperature during the session and any threat of heat illness. You should never wear heat-retaining clothing because it increases body temperature and the likelihood of heat illness. In addition, you should apply this stress in a gradually progressive manner, just as with any other adjustments in the training stressors. This form of heat adaptation results in a rapid retention of increased body water and an increase in blood plasma volume that provides the basis for earlier and heavier sweating in hot conditions. It can be thought of as event-specific preparation and may not entirely extend your ability to tolerate 24-hour exposure to hot conditions. You should minimize total exposure to a hot environment at the race site when arriving close to the date of the event. The obvious advantages of this approach lie in the ability to adapt to the heat and humidity stressors and use the method regardless of living location or time of year. Effects of heat acclimatization or acclimation are also lost very quickly if conditions change abruptly. You must consider that spending much of the day in an air-conditioned hotel room at the race site when you are not otherwise used to the cooler temperature will often result in increased diuresis so that you literally pee away a substantial portion of your increased body water.

Summary

The triathlon training program should make use of a physiological response training model that fits your psychology and lifestyle and allows for adaptation. While no universal approach is best, several basic concepts apply. The program should use a range of powers and velocities below, at, and above the target-event requirements that are specific to your abilities. The program should increase work levels as a result of adaptation rather than as a result of harder work. The program should use a cyclical training plan to allow for adaptation and to introduce variety. You can also emphasize several recovery considerations as part of the training process, including optimal nutrition, sleep, and training schedule. An optimal training environment will then be one in which you make consistent adaptations to small adjustments in training load and minimize the physiological pain associated with the process. By using this set of approaches to training, you will make the entire process fun rather than laborious, and, assuming that the approaches are within your basic physical capabilities, you will be able to achieve the outcomes you desire.

➤ 6

Race-Specific Training and Strategy

Triathlon is unique as a competitive event in relation to its component sports. That is, of course, because the sports are done consecutively in a race. First, your time is your total elapsed time, including the time spent in transition from one sport to the next. Second, while each sport requires the use of a distinct set of muscles and a distinct mental approach, you go right from one to the next without any pauses. The problems that can occur because of this reality can affect triathletes from their first race through their 200th.

Many athletes initially prepare for triathlons by simply training in swimming, cycling, and running separately. But in that first race, the deficiencies of this isolated training approach become apparent, particularly as you experience your first run after a bike ride. The sensation of fatigue in the run in your first race, after a hard bike ride, is nearly indescribable. Common thoughts during a first triathlon are *If I finish this run, I'm never doing another triathlon* and *I wonder how I'll ever make it through the run.*

With time and experience, this problem diminishes and you become better able to swim, cycle, and run during a triathlon, as if you were doing each segment first in the race. In the early days of the sport, many triathletes adapted to making the changes efficiently with a minimum of discomfort on the next leg simply by racing. However, working on effective transitioning only in races, it took several years to become good at this even when racing fairly frequently. Now, however, long-established experience with elite training programs and the available research have pointed to the utility of using more race-specific training methods focused on transitioning (Bentley et al. 2007; Hue et al. 2002).

Today's elite triathletes are able to come off the bike and do the run for 10 kilometers within 45 seconds of their best capability. It is clear that combination training (combining two or more sports in a single training session) and transition training (practicing transitions as a separate skill at race speed), including specific skill training in bike mounts and dismounts, provide benefits on race day. This chapter addresses those methods, along with other issues specific to racing, including tapering training for peak performance, racing strategies, race pacing, and prerace preparations.

Combination Training

The bike–run transition is addressed first because it is much more difficult than the swim–bike transition and thus the most practiced. Often referred to by many longtime triathletes simply as bricks, combination bike–run training is more than simply following a bike ride with a run. In the modern application of the method, a variety of combinations of two or even all three sports are used in training, primarily to help the body adapt quickly to the stress resulting from rapid changes in movement patterns. When you stop doing one activity and begin doing another very soon afterward, your body must make adjustments in blood flow, nervous system regulation, and muscular tension. For example, while the majority of blood flow has been directed toward your upper body during the swim, it must be redirected to your legs for the bike ride. During the ride, you hold your back muscles in an elongated, flat position with tension. For the run, those muscles must rapidly readjust and shorten to hold you in a more upright posture.

Your leg muscles may have grown accustomed to a slower turnover pace (cadence) during an extended period of cycling at 80 to 90 rpm. In the run they will need to adjust quickly upward to a stride rate of 90 or more per minute. Your ability to make each of these basic physiological adjustments improves with training that is specific to the demands of transitioning between sports rapidly. It stands to reason that just as performance in each sport improves with better training, as you practice and train for the changeovers and related adjustments between the sports, they will go more smoothly too. By learning to make the physiological adjustments in training, you are also training to be more successful psychologically by building realistic self-talk and a positive mind-set regarding the same transitions in racing situations.

The modern approach to combination training for successful transitions uses short training bouts in each sport while focusing on moving through the transitions to the next sport at race speed. This allows for more transition-specific practice, and it creates better overall

AP Photo/Kai-Uwe Knoth

Practicing transitions as a separate skill can shave minutes off your total race time.

quality in the swimming, cycling, and running segments of the session. It also makes the training more varied and more interesting. For this approach you set up physical locations specifically for practicing transitioning and plan routes that make such transition practice convenient. Practice for efficiently switching from one sport to the next simply becomes part of the training process in a way that adds a unique element to multisport training and increases enjoyment.

As noted, in triathlon and duathlon for most athletes, the bike-to-run transition is the most demanding one. This is probably due to the relatively high levels of fatigue and dehydration that occur as the race progresses and the change from a relatively static and crouched position on the bike to an upright and dynamic one on the run. Thus the most commonly emphasized combination training element is the bike-to-run transition. However, at the elite amateur and professional levels, the swim-to-bike transition, while not as difficult, is still extremely important in keeping overall times down. At these levels of competition, the bike speed of the racers is very high, at times more than an average of 25 mph. Thus the need to stay close to the other competitors, even in nondrafting events, is critical for successful performance. Of course, in draft-legal elite racing, how you do in the swim–bike transition can completely make or break your race. Losing just a few seconds in the transition process can easily lead to riding on your own rather than in a pack. Losing the advantages of drafting usually means that you have to work much harder on the bike. That will often lead to an increased split time in cycling. Then you will have the same problem on the run because you will be more tired when you get to it than you would have been if you had been in a draft pack on the bike.

Transition-focused training sessions require more preparation to organize and conduct than typical one-sport workouts. Thus their use is emphasized for race-specific intensities and endurance along with course-specific preparation in order to get the most out of the training. You should use a generic training setting that is similar to most triathlon courses (rolling hills) or a race-specific practice course to prepare for specific events. Ideally this will include a closed loop for the bike and a loop or out-and-back course for the run. For the swim-to-bike transition training, an available lake or outdoor pool with a nearby cycling loop is ideal. To do either one, you will need a safe place to leave your bicycle and other equipment in a transition zone.

A typical combination training session includes two to four repeats of cycling and running or swimming and cycling at a speed endurance effort. This level of effort is a little lower than full racing effort yet faster than typical aerobic training. It is also definable as a tempo-effort, comfortable-speed intensity, or a specific level of work that represents your current projected speed for approximately twice your race distance. In other words, if you project a 7-minute-per-mile pace for 10K and a 7:30-per-mile pace for the half marathon, you would run this kind of effort at a 7:30-per-mile pace. Essentially these are miniduathlons or triathlons done at just below race speed.

Before completing the target combination sets, you should do a full warm-up for both sports and for all three when you are doing triple combinations. This should include all the elements of the warm-ups described in chapter 5, including a progressive warm-up in each sport followed by skill sets and a set of progressive alactate efforts.

You begin each bike-to-run work interval by running to the bike at race speed as if you had come out of the swim. After mounting the bike at full speed, you ride the bike segment at tempo effort as described previously. Then you move through the transition to the run at speed and complete the run at tempo effort. The same scenario would occur in a swim-to-bike session. You begin the swim at speed, ideally using a start method similar to what you will use racing, then exit the water and proceed through a transition at speed, followed by the mount and your bike segment at tempo effort. You should use any equipment (such as a wet suit) that you anticipate using in the racing environment.

By breaking this training session into multiple efforts in an interval format, you will improve your performance quality while overlearning the transition skills and physiological adjustment processes. The primary goal of this training is to achieve a total training effort somewhat in excess of race distance at a power output that is similar, although less, than race effort when preparing for Olympic or sprint-distance races. If you are going for a longer race, you may not be able to do the full race distance in training on a regular basis. Note that this training can also be done at aerobic intensities. A lower-intensity approach to combination training is useful during base training periods (when most training is in an aerobic range of intensity) as described in chapter 5. A cool-down for the session should include both cycling and running, or swimming and cycling, or all three depending on the number of individual sports involved. The typical training session follows:

Warm-Up

45-minute cycling at progressive aerobic effort with 10 × 30-second single-leg pedaling drill (see chapter 3) and 6 × 15-second alactates

15-minute run at progressive aerobic effort with 6 × 60-step butt kicks followed by 6 × 15-second alactates

Main Set

3 × 9-mile (14 km) ride and 2.5-mile (4 km) run with transition at speed, several minutes of recovery between each set

15-minute run cool-down

30-minute cycle cool-down

You can modify the length, number of repetitions, and targeted intensity of training to create various physiological effects yet retain the basic emphasis on combining sports. As noted, this type of training requires you to set up a transition area where you can leave the bike and other equipment while you run. Therefore, it becomes a great opportunity for a coached workout. A coach or helper can take splits, evaluate and provide feedback on transition skills, and take care of nutritional needs as well as provide security for equipment. For International Triathlon Union (ITU) racing (that is, draft-legal racing), training with a group adds specificity to the transition-practice environment. This focus could become the basis for a very enjoyable age-group training session as well. To reduce concerns about bike theft, in solo training you could use a trainer for the cycling and then do the run workout from home, although this option reduces transition specificity considerably. Some athletes bring a trainer to a track and do their bike–run combinations there so that their equipment stays within easy view for security.

Transition Training

It is useful, particularly early in an athlete's development, to engage in training sessions that focus solely on transition skills, although it is still helpful to have a ride-in and run-out section and a swim-in and bike-out section for specificity. The USA Triathlon (USAT) coaching certification program has distinguished this training method by referring to it as transition training. This kind of training is quite fun to do in groups and prepares you to refine the skills that allow you to move through transitions quickly. Consider that in a typical ITU World Cup event, the athletes move from cycling to running in 15 to 20 seconds. At a typical age-group event, the elite amateurs take approximately 30 to 45 seconds, although often the transition areas are physically longer but less congested. Less experienced athletes will often take upward of 2 minutes to complete a transition. Imagine if you could reduce your 10K running time by more than 1 minute. You can accomplish this without expending any extra energy by simply learning to make the transitions more efficiently. Following is a description of the fundamental skills that allow for rapid transitions.

Swim-to-Bike Transition Skills

The swim-to-bike transition requires the following easy-to-master skills:

1. Remove cap, goggles, and wet suit as you run from the water to transition.
2. Minimize equipment you will need to put on in the transition area for the bike ride (that is, put on only your helmet and glasses in this area).
3. Learn to run with your bicycle and then mount your bicycle with shoes premounted in the pedals. By premounting your shoes, you avoid stationary time, which is lost time in the race.
4. Learn to place your feet in the premounted racing shoes while pedaling early in the bike leg.

For the first skill, you practice by simply removing your cap and goggles as you run. You can drop those pieces onto a transition-area towel as you reach your first transition point. Remove your wet suit by drawing down the zipper string and pulling the top of the suit to waist level as you run. This is easier to accomplish using a farmer john–style wet suit without sleeves. Once you reach transition, you then pull the suit off your hips and ankles from a standing position and leave in it your transition zone. This process is facilitated if you use a nonstick coating on your ankles. However, consider the effect of any product you use on the neoprene material from which your suit is constructed.

Consult the manufacturer's instructions for your wet suit. Also consider the need to remove any material from your hands before beginning the swim.

Ideally the only bike equipment you will need to put on while standing at your transition area are your helmet and glasses. Although socks, gloves, and additional clothing may seem necessary, they also dramatically slow your transition and add to your race time. To be able to cycle and run without socks in a race, you will have to do so in training so that you know you will not develop blisters. You can eliminate the need for additional clothing by purchasing and regularly training in triathlon race–specific clothing that you wear under your wet suit and then for both the bike and the run. Some competitors will, however, choose to do the entire race wearing only a swimsuit, when the weather allows. Some triathletes always wear a triathlon-specific one- or two-piece outfit for the whole race.

Place your helmet on your bicycle handlebars upside down with the straps on the outside so that you can easily pick it up and put it on. Place your cycling shoes in the pedals. Arrange to stabilize the crank arms parallel to the ground by putting a rubber band over the rearward crank arm and the tip of the rear wheel stay. Do this by looping the rubber band over the pedal and pulling it around the stay and then back over the pedal before placing your shoes in the cleats. The rubber band will break when you begin pedaling.

Once you arrive at your bike, first put on your glasses or sunglasses (if you use them) and then immediately pick up and put on your helmet. Fasten the chin strap in the transition area, as required by USAT. Then lift your bike off the rack and begin to run with it (depending on traffic in the transition area) toward the transition exit and mount line. If you can support your bike on the bike rack by the seat rather than the handlebars, then do so. This will make it easier to begin moving your bike efficiently out of the transition area.

There are several methods of running through the transition area while pushing your bicycle. Without some practice, athletes often choose to run while holding the bicycle at two points—the handlebars and the seat, particularly when wearing cycling cleats (as opposed to having previously clipped them into the pedals). With more experience, athletes learn that they can run more naturally with the bike by placing one hand on the saddle only. Assuming that your headset is properly adjusted so that the front wheel will keep going in a straight line, you can steer the bike with your hand from the seat the same way you should steer the bike while riding—by using your hips through the seat. This allows for freedom of movement while running with the bicycle. Also, once you get used to it, it is easier and faster to run through transition in your bare feet rather than in your cleats. This is another advantage of having your shoes already clipped into your pedals.

An alternative method for one-hand steering is to place a single hand on the handlebars, ideally on the stem. However, this method, while seemingly more stable, makes running with your bicycle more awkward. Obviously, it is easier to use the hand-on-the-saddle running method in paved transition areas than it is in grassy areas. You can further facilitate running with your bike through transition by fixing your bicycle crank arms parallel to the ground with rubber bands, as previously described. In this way your premounted shoes will not bang into the ground. As noted, the rubber bands will break easily once you mount the bike and start pedaling. Some extremists even fix the shoes parallel with the ground by using additional rubber bands—this assists in hitting the cyclocross mount described next.

Once you pass the bike-mount line, you can get on your bicycle while still moving by using a cyclocross mounting technique. Athletes in cyclocross races (in which road-style bikes are ridden on off-road courses with barriers and other obstacles) have to constantly mount and dismount to go around and over barriers. They complete running mounts by putting both hands on the handlebars and then pushing off from the outside leg (relative to the bicycle) while running, swinging the inside leg over the saddle and landing squarely on the seat. Both feet then come down on the pedals simultaneously, effortlessly engaging them and allowing pedal action to begin immediately.

In the recommended triathlon mounting technique, you bring both feet down on the tops of your premounted shoes and begin pedaling from that position. Continue to do so until you find a level, or ideally downsloping, area where with a minimal loss in momentum you can reach down to put your feet inside the shoes. Some professionals are able accomplish this by forcing their feet into the preopened shoes while pausing in the pedal stroke and without using their hands. If your shoes do not allow for such an entry, it is necessary to stop pedaling and then reach down to hold the circle loop on the back of a triathlon cycling shoe so that you can slide your foot in. For more control, hold the center of your handlebars while doing so. A quick adjustment of the shoe-tensioning strap and you are set to put your foot in the opposite shoe and start pedaling again. Of course, you can facilitate this maneuver by using a triathlon-specific cycling shoe with a rear loop and single tensioning strap. It is also easiest to place your foot in the shoe when you've rotated your pedal back to its most rearward position. It is also tempting to look down while performing this maneuver, but train yourself to avoid it, and you'll be less likely to have an accident on the course.

Bike-to-Run Transition Skills

The bike-to-run transition requires the following easy-to-master skills:

1. Prepare for the bike-to-run transition by flexing and extending your back on the bike and maintaining or increasing cadence to run-stride rate or above.
2. Pull your feet out of your shoes while riding and then dismount at speed, leaving your shoes clipped into your pedals.
3. Run with your bike as described previously.
4. Minimize equipment you will need to put on in the transition area for the run (that is, put on only your shoes in this area).
5. Put on your running shoes while standing.
6. Put on any other equipment—hat, glasses, and race belt—while running.

As you approach the bike-to-run transition, it's likely that you've been cycling either in an aerobar position or on the drops of a conventional bar. In either case, your lower-back muscles have been in a state of contraction while being overextended for a long period. This often results in back tightness or even spasm as you attempt to stand up straight for the run. The degree to which you will experience this certainly relates to your level of back fitness and nature of the cycling position you use (see chapter 3). Nevertheless, to avoid unwanted muscular responses when you make the next transition, perform some simple neuromuscular facilitation movements in the last few minutes as you come in on the bike. Do these exercises before removing your feet from your shoes so that you have a more stable platform on which to continue pedaling. These movements cause the muscular tension in the lower back and abdomen to rebalance, allowing for more normal posture when running. You can rebalance the tension by flexing and extending your pelvis and spine while seated on the bike. Move in both directions by alternately arching and then flattening your back, as cats do when they stretch out upon rising from a nap.

As you enter the last half mile or so of the bike ride, look for a flat or downhill section so that you can pull your feet out of your cycling shoes, leaving the shoes clipped into the pedals. This will allow you to pedal on the tops of your shoes right up to the dismount line, ready for a rapid dismount from your moving bicycle just before reaching the line. Do this by reaching down with one hand at a time and releasing your Velcro shoe straps, then holding the rear loop as you pull your foot out of the shoe and place it on top of the shoe. Once you have done this for both shoes, pedal to about 15 to 20 feet from the dismount line (or earlier if that area is backed up with competitors) and then execute the cyclocross-style running dismount.

Execute the cyclocross-style dismount by lifting the leg you want to start running with over the saddle while standing on the opposite-side pedal. The leg lifted over the saddle is now the inside leg and will be the one you put down first. As you slow to running speed, place this free inside leg on the ground. You then step quickly from the balanced leg still on the pedal into the next stride right after your inside leg has hit the ground.

As the saying goes, hit the ground running. During this time support your upper body using both hands on the tops of the handlebars. Once you are into the run to your bike-rack spot, you can quickly switch to a single-hand position in the center of the top of the bars to guide your bike and run more effectively. For a long run in the transition area back to your bike rack, you may even want to shift your hand-control point back to the saddle for greater running effectiveness, as previously described.

A word regarding the relative importance of such a skill here: Even in World Cup racing, you will see athletes using a stop-and-mount approach, or "botching" their running mount or dismount, resulting in a lost shoe, dropped water bottle, or other delaying factor. For these maneuvers to be useful for you, you will have to practice all of them. Again, the advantages of using them are to get free speed in the race. Any time saved in transition obviously reduces your overall finishing time. In high-level racing (both age group and professional), four to five seconds lost in mounting your bicycle can be more than enough to separate you from other athletes who had been right in front of you. This can result in much greater time losses over the course of that segment. In World Cup racing with draft-legal cycling legs and large running packs, such losses often can total several minutes.

Again, you want to keep the amount of equipment you need to put on for the run to a minimum. In an ideal world, all you need is a pair of shoes. These will be your racing flats chosen both for the ease of putting them on as well as for their other more typically valued characteristics. You simply stand and put on each shoe. Do not sit down; that adds considerable time to the transition process. This is yet another skill that you should practice, particularly if you are older and challenged in balance and flexibility.

The ideal shoe for quick bike–run transitions has a stretchy upper that allows you to pull on the shoe and go. In the 1980s Nike made such a shoe, called the sock racer. The current Nike Free has a similar construction. If you favor a more typical racing flat, you can use elastic laces that accomplish the same thing as the stretchy upper. For heavier, stiffer shoes you can also use lace locks fixed to the original laces. Stopping to tie shoes in transition will often add 30 seconds to a minute to your final race time. As discussed previously, you need to train regularly in the shoes and socks (or lack thereof) that you will use while racing. If you know that you develop minor hot spots, use either a dry baby powder (to absorb moisture) or a lube in your shoe, helping to reduce the risk. Just as you should not use a new or unfamiliar bike for the first time in a race, do not wear racing shoes of any type for the first time in a race. Be sure to practice in them first.

The other primary concern is that you need to have your race number on and in the front as you finish the run. In World Cup racing, the athlete's required uniform has the name and country on it. Before the start of the swim you will have your race number stenciled on your skin with Magic Marker in one or more places. In age-group racing, paper numbers (along with the stenciled numbers) are used. Under most federations' rules, the paper number needs to be worn only for the run leg because you will have attached a separate number to your bike before the start, either with a self-stick system or safety pins. The stenciled number is for the swim.

The ultimate solution is to have the paper number already attached to you in some way that has also not introduced drag on the bicycle. The most common approach is to use a race belt with the number attached that you simply pick up in the bike-to-run transition and then clip on while running. Some innovative athletes also stash a number inside the swim or triathlon suit (if two-piece) or shorts and then pull it out, already attached to the clothing, while running. You can also pull on other clothing, such as a singlet or hat, while running. In cold-weather racing, however, you will have to take the time in transition to dress appropriately.

Transition Training Sessions

Once you have established the basic skills, it is both fun and effective to establish specific transition training sessions to continue to improve them in a race-specific environment. This works nicely in a park or similar space where you can set up a rack for your bicycle and in which you can conveniently practice the run-in-from-the-swim, cycle-out and cycle-in, run-out segments. You can then time these sessions as intervals from entry to exit (using only a minimal actual riding or running component) and use the sessions as a baseline for improving your performance. Because this aspect of racing is largely skill based and not metabolically challenging, it makes for a fun and competitive group training situation without much concern for the downside of overextending yourself in group training swims, rides, or runs. You can further develop the skills in the combination training sessions described previously by creating a similar transition zone between segments and some method of timing the process.

Race Strategy

Triathlon performances are generally best when the actual work of swimming, cycling, and running is performed at a relatively even or slightly ascending rate. This is referred to as even or negative splitting or pacing. This pacing approach actually translates into starting out with a very low sense of effort and increasing that sense of effort over time. This seemingly contradictory state occurs because progressive fatigue increases the perception of effort to produce the same work.

In addition, by starting conservatively, you are less likely to create an anaerobic debt in your body that you must repay by slowing down disproportionately later. This approach also makes racing more comfortable and successful, and you will go faster overall. It is an almost universally agreed-on premise that great endurance performances are marked primarily by what happens at the end of the race rather than by what happens at the beginning.

All that being said, in high-level racing the opportunity to draft other competitors (within the context of the rules) exists in the swim, on the bike (even in draft-illegal racing), and in the run. The benefits of drafting are substantial and offer a great potential for improving performance, particularly when multiple competitors work together for the benefit of all. Now, before those of you with a misplaced moral interpretation of that statement put down the book and head out the door in disgust, an explanation of some basic physics is in order. First and foremost, drafting in swimming and running creates meaningful reductions in workload for drafting competitors, and drafting is legal in all forms of triathlon racing. You can see as much as a 3 percent improvement in your time for a given distance depending on speed, wind conditions, and water movements. The basic moral issue, as is the case in all sports, concerns competing within the rules of triathlon, not whether you are cheating by working with another competitor. And again, drafting in the swim and on the run is perfectly legal at all levels of multisport racing.

The physics of cycling is another matter. When you're moving at higher speeds in bike racing, the effect of drafting another competitor can reduce work output by 100 percent in certain settings. For instance, an athlete sitting in a large group traveling downhill at 30 mph can often do so without even pedaling and might even need to apply the brakes frequently to avoid overrunning the leading riders. Consequently the amateur federations (and some so-called nondrafting professional events) create arbitrary positioning rules for the bike segment of the race that reduce the potential effect of drafting to something similar to that encountered in swimming and running.

The proof that a load reduction (drafting) is still occurring in spite of the positioning rules is found in professional racing (even in Ironman-length events with proportionately slower speeds) whereby packs of athletes form, all riding legally (usually) within the positioning limits of the rules, yet still working together to race at higher speeds. This has occurred over the 25 years or so in which the sport has had a significant professional presence and will always occur as a result of the physics involved. The positioning rules create a scenario in which the effect of drafting (particularly uphill) is minimized enough to allow a clearly superior athlete to break away from a lesser athlete.

The positioning rules do not eliminate the drafting effect, however; they simply reduce it. It is not by coincidence that most passing moves between closely matched competitors occur while going uphill. Within the current set of rules requiring positioning at 10 meters apart and allowing for staggering of riders on the road, both observation and the laws of physics indicate that significant drafting still occurs among higher-level athletes at typical race speeds, even on the flats and particularly on any downhills. The ITU long recognized this reality and made the decision in the 1990s to simply allow drafting to occur. By doing so they changed the nature of racing substantially yet also eliminated the perceived moral dilemmas by simplifying the rules and the need for draft marshals. Not coincidentally, this rule change also made elite triathlon a more spectator-friendly sport with less opportunity for the outcome to be influenced by the subjective interpretation of drafting by referees. This rule change very likely also influenced the rapid inclusion of triathlon into the program of the 2000 Sydney Olympic Games.

For age-group athletes (and professionals riding classic non-drafting events, a misnomer), this

AP Photo/Polfoto, Jens Panduro

The lack of positioning rules in World Cup racing creates typical bike racing strategies.

means that an athlete must develop the availability to judge placement relative to the current positioning rules in order to race within the rules. A deliberate choice to not do so is then the moral issue. All triathletes are "drafters" at one point or another in races. Even those who are passing or are being passed by other athletes in a time-trial race are temporarily drafting. Those who choose to break the positioning rules (or any other rules of the sport) can then more accurately be referred to as cheaters.

This is a long-winded way to get to the next point regarding pacing. Sometimes the need for even pacing may be offset by the need to create position among the other athletes or the opportunity to legally draft in the swim, bike, and run. To move well beyond your basic pace is always a judgment call. For instance, virtually every endurance athlete has watched a talented beginner overrun the first 1 to 1.5K of a 10K in an attempt to run with the leaders. Even though they may have benefited from the opportunity to draft faster athletes early, the benefit is nearly always greatly overshadowed by a significant reduction in pace once they "blow up." This means that once their muscles become so acidic from excessive anaerobic energy production, they are forced to slow down. Recovering rapidly from the excessive acidosis while still moving at a reasonable pace is virtually impossible, so the result is inevitably a slower time overall. On the other hand, the well-conditioned triathlete coming out of the bike-to-run transition with a group going at a little over their optimal starting pace may still recover well enough (as the group slows after the initial surge) to run a better overall split than by running alone otherwise. It's always a gamble, but the odds improve if you prepare for that scenario in training.

Finally, there is the issue of hills and pace. Some recent research points to the fact that cyclists may benefit by working slightly harder going uphill or into the wind than when going downhill or with a tailwind during cycle time trials. This is a natural outcome of the conditions in that a small increase in power going uphill or into the wind at slow speeds minimizes the penalty created by increased drag. When moving downhill or with a tailwind at much greater speeds, the relative increase in drag for the same increase in power output is much greater and so it carries a much larger penalty. Most riders adopt this strategy to some degree naturally, but it is optimal to keep power output as consistent as possible.

Preparing to Race

As in all facets of sport, training for triathlons and competing in triathlons are two completely different things. Training is routine, systematic, sometimes relaxing, sometimes demanding, and forever modifiable. Racing is unique, energizing, fixed, and unyielding. Some people love to train and hate to race; others hate to train but love to race. Ideally you will be able to enjoy both.

For those who hate to race, it is an opportunity to fail. Racing can be painful, it can produce performance stress, and it can create a sense of dread. But racing is an opportunity to express for yourself and others what you have done in the training process. It is the icing on the cake. It is the opportunity to have a higher energy state than you would have otherwise in order to demonstrate your innate and developed abilities. It is an opportunity to compete with others of the same mind-set and synergistically provide for your best performance as a result. It may be the reason you train, and you would not do so or would not do as much if you didn't race.

To enjoy racing, to look forward to it, and to get yourself ready to do your best in it, you need both psychological and physical training. You need to do both to do well. The first, discussed in depth in chapter 2, requires the creation of appropriate process and controllable outcome goals, a developed focus on the positive elements of the experience, the development of rational beliefs in and for yourself, and the ability to evaluate your performance in a race relative to a task orientation in appropriate balance with ego orientation. In other words, did you achieve the task-oriented goals over which you had control (what you thought about, how you chose to breathe) in balance with the ego-oriented goals (the competitors you beat) over which you had little control? The second type of training, obviously, is physical training, and that may include strategies such as tapering and other prerace preparations.

Tapering

The physical aspects that make racing a positive experience are at least as controllable as the mechanical aspects, such as the nature and condition of your equipment. If you have followed a systematic and progressive training program, such as the one suggested in this book, leading to a particular triathlon or group of triathlons, you've done 90 percent of what is necessary to race to your capability. However, such a program builds up both your triathlon racing fitness and your fatigue level. If you are able to reduce your accumulated fatigue in the period just before the race, you open a window of opportunity to race at an even higher level of performance than you might have done otherwise—that last 10 percent of what you are capable of accomplishing. You do this by reducing your training load for a time. This practice is called tapering your training. This contradicts much of the common (although largely irrational) wisdom that more is always better. In this case, less (for a time) is much better. This concept alone is an important factor separating those who finish farther ahead in the race from those (with similar ability and training) who finish farther back.

Tapering occurs by reducing training load in a planned manner. The available science would suggest that a reduction of 50 percent or more over one or more weeks is the amount necessary for creating a fully rested state. It is also clear that you should retain all or most of the elements of your prerace training, but do them in reduced amounts. Some scientific work with triathletes suggests that an exponential taper, one where the work volume is dropped rapidly at first and then more slowly later, is the most effective in triathletes, although all forms of tapering appear to offer some positive effect (Banister et al. 1999). You should experiment with various approaches and find what works best for you.

While tapering, continuing to do the parts of your training that you normally do at a higher-quality level but at a lower volume will allow you to retain your feel for the faster and more powerful movements you will use when racing yet still unload your fatigue. This also minimizes the dull, tired feeling many athletes feel in tapering programs that largely dispense with higher-quality work.

Another gray area in the science on tapering concerns the time frame necessary for a successful taper. The length of tapering should reflect the degree of accumulated fatigue you have developed in the training process. In training programs that more heavily emphasize anaerobic levels of training and high training frequency (such as is typical in swimming), taper periods of several weeks or more often appear to be necessary to allow athletes to lose accumulated fatigue. In more aerobically based training programs, typical for triathlon preparation, this period may be substantially shorter, on the order of one to two weeks. When using a controlled training approach based solely on adaptation (such as described in this book), athletes are often only a week of rest away from a top-level performance and only a few days of rest away from a high-quality one. Also note that substantial tapering can occur only a limited number of times (generally one to three) each season. To do so more often is to detrain. It's useful to identify the most important races for the season and plan accordingly.

A measurable sign of the fully rested state is a relative sympathetic imbalance. This means that both resting and training heart rates (during the taper) may become higher than normal. This is indicative of a restored and then overshooting sympathetic activation system. However, this higher energy state can also be easily interpreted as prerace stress. It is productive to find ways to combat this feeling of stress and create relaxation (particularly for sleeping) during this time frame. You might accomplish this by using alternative physical activities (such as stretching and relaxation breathing) or other pursuits that you find enjoyable and relaxing.

Regarding the nature of work reduction in the traditional approach, tapering involves gradually reducing your work over time. Linear tapers may offer you the slight psychological benefit of not allowing the sympathetic overshoot described previously (with its resulting anxiety) to occur too early. In this approach, you reduce the total load (50 percent, for example) by dropping training loads gradually. Over the course of a week, you might reduce loads from 70 to 30 percent as illustrated in the following example. However, recent research also suggests that a rapid and stable load reduction is equally effective in improving performance. In this example, you might drop the load immediately to 50 percent of normal and hold it there throughout the week.

It is also possible to create significant rest using what might be called a minitaper. In this approach, you would take a day of nearly complete rest (generally two days before an event) and then do a complete warm-up the day before the event. This approach is often combined with a more extended taper. It allows for travel the two days before as well as a full warm-up on the course. The warm-up on the day before the race should always include some high-end work so that the neuromuscular system is stimulated for the next day. However, you must control the volume of this work to avoid fatigue. This is a function of your normal training loads and training microcycle. A safe approach for many age-group athletes is to do several alactates (10- to 15-second high-power efforts) in each sport as a part of the general warm-up. For elite athletes, some kind of miniset based on prior training may be needed.

Here is an example of a taper for an athlete doing about 6,000 yards of swimming, 6 hours of cycling, and 3.5 hours of running in three weekly training sessions, along with two weekly weight training sessions:

Recent Training Weeks

Monday: No training

Tuesday: Run speed focus 1 hour, bike speed focus 1.5 hours

Wednesday: Swim speed focus 1,500 meters, weight training (strength) 30 sets at average 12 reps

Thursday: Bike race-pace focus 2 hours, run race-pace focus 1 hour

Friday: Swim race-pace focus 2,000 meters

Saturday: Bike endurance focus 2.5 hours, weight training (power and muscular endurance) 20 sets at average 8 reps

Sunday: Swim endurance focus 2,500 meters, run endurance focus 1.5 hours

Taper and Race Training Week

Monday: No training

Tuesday: Run speed focus 0.5 hour with 4 alactates, bike speed focus 0.75 hour with 4 alactates

Wednesday: Swim speed focus 750 meters—speed work 4 alactates, weight training (strength) 15 sets at average 6 reps

Thursday: Bike race-pace focus 0.75 hour—2 × 1 minute at race pace, run race-pace focus 0.33 hour—2 × 1 minute at race pace

Friday: No training or just very short loosening up

Saturday: Swim 500 meters with 4 alactates, bike 30 minutes with 4 alactates, no weight training or running

Sunday: Warm-up and race

One temptation during tapering is to increase the quality of work. However, you must consider that increasing the intensity of training has a large impact on total training load, and doing so might actually prevent you from overcoming accumulated fatigue. Athletes often describe the application of this idea as "leaving their race" in a particular training session, often a week or so before the race. When feeling somewhat rested, they find it easy to overrun during a high-quality session and then suffer from the lingering fatigue even a week later. This problem is less likely to occur when training loads are applied in controlled ways as described in chapter 5.

By using a taper, you can ensure a relatively rested racing state. This contributes to the positive racing experience—racing becomes easier to accomplish and you perform to your highest ability. So often athletes say that they could have raced much harder after their best performances. This is because racing while well rested feels easier than training hard, even though they go faster. Racing experiences can be truly special only when the frequency of racing is not overdone. If your intent is to race every weekend, then you might review your interpretation of what you are doing. In that case, racing is really training and should be interpreted in that light. Tapers can be expected to create special races only a few times per season.

Previewing the Course

Once you've picked a triathlon (or triathlons) you want to do, it is useful to find out as much about the course as possible. In an ideal world, you will have the opportunity to preswim, preride, and prerun the course, possibly even train on it. This can be critical of mountain bike–style courses such as in the Xterra series. You must be able to do this in a time frame before the race that is reasonable for you, within the context of your overall training volume and taper. One common way that less experienced triathletes "leave their race in training," as described previously, is to preride and prerun a triathlon course the day before the competition at fairly high speeds. Even very few pros can afford to completely preride a race course the day before the event, depending on race distance and how much they are tapering their training.

The majority of triathletes do not have a sufficient training base to enable them to preride the race course without experiencing some residual fatigue on race day. But it is often useful to drive the bike course by car just before the race as well as to preride some of the more technical (particularly downhill) sections, within the context of your taper training volumes. You can often preview a run course by bicycle. This gives you some confidence when following the course on race day and prepares you to handle technical sections.

You can also use this information to create specificity in your training program, particularly if the event is important to you. For instance, before most World Championship and Olympic Games events, Hunter Kemper has used course information to create course simulations for race-pace training. This may be as detailed as having power profiles for various elements of the bike course from prior World Cup events. Failure to address the specific nature of the course for a particular event can be harmful to performance on race day. For example, if a course includes multiple U-turns at cones and you fail to address that in your training program, you will find yourself fatiguing on event day as you struggle to deal with the accelerations required for completing each of the turns.

Assessing Transition Spaces

Transition areas for most races open on the morning of the race. It is often useful to secure a transition space early by arriving early. Many races still operate on a first-come, first-served basis in regard to transition spaces (even when bike-rack placements are determined, usually in groups of 10, by your age group or race number), although it is becoming more common to have the spaces preassigned by race number. This is most likely to occur in larger and more prestigious events. In World Cup races, the transition spaces are assigned before the event, so this is not an issue. In that environment, a real issue may be securing your equipment while warming up. It is not unheard of for an athlete to have equipment stolen or altered at this level, including having substances placed in fluid bottles. A properly credentialed team helper or coach can be useful in this regard.

Obviously when racing in a first-come, first-served setting, whether overall or even by rack, you should come by early to secure an optimal rack space. An optimal space is one that allows for easy access to your bike and minimizes the distances you will have to cover during transitions. In a well-designed transition area, there is no advantage to be found in any given space over another. However, the majority of transition areas are designed within the confines of a parking lot, field, or other accessible area. This often creates significant limitations. With some quick observation of the area and the pattern of traffic flow, it is often possible to find spaces that provide for significant advantages in transition.

One strategy is to stop by first thing to drop off your bicycle and then proceed with other check-in duties and warm-up activities once you have secured your space. Assuming that you already have identified your race number from the race Web site or the competitors' list that is sometimes posted adjacent to the transition area, this approach is advantageous even when you are assigned by number to a rack. The end spaces on each rack are almost always the more desirable ones.

Planning Prerace Warm-Ups

Prerace warm-ups should be progressive and include some short high-end alactate efforts in order to fully engage the nervous system. The length of the warm-up should be proportionate to the duration of your typical training session—normally from 5 to 15 minutes in each sport. It is useful to warm up in all three sports and allow for a last-minute check on equipment for each. It is usually possible to warm up on the course, providing another opportunity to review the approach to transition. With the increasing use of multiloop courses (such as occur in ITU World Cup events), the warm-up may even allow for a full review of the course under controlled traffic conditions.

In very hot conditions, minimize warm-up time to avoid elevating body temperature significantly before the race. Use this tactic when the temperature and humidity are relatively high even at the start. In this case the on-land warm-ups might consist of dynamic movements that simulate running and cycling rather than actual running or cycling. In some extreme conditions, elite athletes now use cooling techniques before a very hot race. This might be as simple as taking a cool shower just before the swim if facilities allow, although the state-of-the-art approach now involves use of a cooling vest. Before very cold races, bring body temperature up as much as possible without relying only on an excessive physical warm-up. You can do this through the active warm-up process and externally by taking a hot shower (if available) or wearing heavy, warm clothing just before the start. The need for this varies and depends on the actual water temperature, your body type and composition, the time from warm-ups to start, and whether you are wearing a wet suit.

The warm-up period is also an opportunity to prepare psychologically. You can spend this time reviewing your basic race objectives: what you want to accomplish in this particular race, how you are planning to pace yourself, the elements of technique you may be working on, and the self-talk you plan to use during the race. Later on in your racing career, warm-up time may become an opportunity to relax, say hello to friends, and focus on the positive elements of the situation.

Accommodating Travel

Reaching your potential often means traveling to compete against others with similar inclinations and abilities. Prospective World Cup triathletes can ultimately only test themselves by racing World Cup events, which involves traveling around the entire globe. This adds a level of complexity to the competition process. It is not by accident that U.S. elite athletes have had their greatest successes competing in World Cup events in North America. The shorter travel time and less dramatic change in time zones along with similar weather patterns allow them to more easily perform without undue fatigue caused by travel stress and the required acclimatization to a new locale. For age-group athletes, major competitions nearly always involve travel on the order of a day or more.

Although there is little definitive science examining the most effective ways to reduce the negative impact of travel on performance, travel, time-zone change, and change in weather patterns are clearly stressors. With this understanding, you can use the basic stress-management principles described earlier to both deal with travel stress and minimize its negative effects on performance. There are two basic strategies for dealing with this problem. The first is to travel well before the event to allow for an extended period at the race site to acclimatize to the new location. Unfortunately, even for professional athletes, it is not always possible to do this. In addition, you must consider the loss of potential benefits you might have accrued by being at home, including altitude exposure, ease of training, familiar food, and the presence of support systems such as family. An early arrival (one that allows 10 to 12 days at the race site) is optimal. This allows for significant accommodations to heat and time-zone changes and minimizes loss of altitude acclimatization. This approach works best when training facilities, housing, and appropriate meals can be prearranged. At the same time, it can be problematic when those concerns are not accounted for beforehand—two weeks of living in uncertain and possibly uncomfortable conditions is fatiguing to anybody. A useful variation on this is to arrive at a nearby location that offers a more optimal environment (such as a place at altitude and with training facilities). Then you can move to a living space as close as possible to the race site. This approach is common for major events such as the Olympic Games or World Championships, which are often held in urban areas that may be polluted, at sea level, and inadequate for triathlon training.

The other basic approach is to arrive as late as possible before the event. This minimizes fatigue caused by acclimatization, accumulating time-zone change, or poor living or training conditions. Optimally this late arrival will be within 48 hours of the event. It is generally between 2 and 3 days after arrival that you begin to feel the fatigue of acclimatization or accumulated travel stress. Over the next week or so, you can make basic adjustments—hence the 10- to 12-day window. As described in chapter 5, altitude benefits will then often begin to diminish once 12 to 14 days have passed. Further, if going to an environment that is much different than your current training environment (hotter, more humid), you should acclimate before getting there, as described in chapter 5. However, on a pragmatic level, a late arrival also increases the risk that your bike will not arrive on time when you're traveling by air. You can minimize this problem by shipping your bicycle well beforehand. In some cases doing so will be cheaper as well if you are paying current air-carrier fees for transporting your bike.

These considerations of time, climate, and altitude change as well as practical bike-arrival problems can also mean that the common approach of arriving three to four days before an important event is often the worst approach, but you can manage that if you control your training. A significant source of fatigue upon going to sea level from a higher altitude results from training at higher work outputs than you're accustomed to. Over several days this creates local muscular fatigue. You can control this by training based on workload rather than perception of effort or heart rate. Plan for training at workloads that are appropriate for your current state of fitness, and avoid the temptation to go faster because it feels easy.

When traveling by car, train, or plane, you are forced to sit for extended periods. This is an ineffective way to prepare your body for the rigors of a peak race, and it increases your risk of developing blood clots in your legs. To offset these negative consequences to the degree possible, employ a driving strategy that allows for regular stops where you can move around, or get up and move around at regular intervals when flying and traveling by train. As with all things behavioral, this is most likely to occur if you create a specific plan and cueing mechanism. You might set your watch timer to beep every hour to remind you to get up and move around.

Air travel is dehydrating. You should use a similar strategy to increase your drinking behavior as well. In addition, extended drives cross-country seem to work better before a race if you allow time each day for some basic training activity, ideally in accordance with a tapering plan or restoration week as discussed in chapter 5.

Endurance athletes are subject to the increased possibility of infection, particularly in airplanes. With a large number of travelers breathing the same recirculated air and sharing enclosed space, the basic health behaviors of covering your mouth and nose when sneezing and washing your hands frequently become critical. This may be even more important when returning from a race, because your higher-than-normal fatigue level is likely to compromise your immunity, particularly when flying within several hours of finishing the race. Of course, traveling the next day is the preferred approach. In some cases athletes will seek to minimize this possibility by wearing a face mask. Try to use relaxed nasal breathing while traveling; this is useful not only in preventing infection but in creating relaxation as well.

When changing time zones, the most commonly suggested strategy is to place yourself physiologically and behaviorally in the new time zone as early as feasible. Typically this occurs at the beginning of travel, but depending on the differences and the importance of the competition, you might choose to do so even earlier. What this means is that you begin to eat, sleep, and act as if you are in the new time zone. You can accentuate this process by resetting your watch; engaging in behaviors associated with meaningful points in time, such as awakening, eating meals, and going to sleep; and training in time frames that match the new time zone or race time.

You can further encourage sleeping at the appropriate time by taking a melatonin supplement. You should also try to get full light exposure on the morning of arrival. This approach allows your body to reset its internal clock (circadian rhythms), allowing for a more successful adaptation to time-zone change. Keep this approach in mind when traveling across more than two time zones. Also, eastward travel is more problematic than westward travel in terms of time-zone adjustments.

For age-group athletes traveling to local or regional events within a few hours' drive, the more complex concepts of time zone, altitude, and climate changes are not significant. However, athletes must always make the decision to either drive in the morning before the race or to get a hotel room near the race site sometime beforehand. Sometimes an earlier arrival is dictated by check-in procedures. Most major and many minor events require day-before-the-race check-in. But in any case, a primary consideration is getting the best night's sleep. Some people sleep well in hotels and prefer not to drive before racing. You should consider the improved opportunity to preview the course, get an optimal transition space (when it is not preassigned), and feel less rushed. For others a poor night's sleep in a hotel and increased travel costs may more than offset any benefit to be derived by not having to drive in the morning.

Summary

Multisports such as triathlon and duathlon are unique in that they combine multiple endurance sports completed in continuous fashion, including the transition time between each event. Effective training for triathlon addresses this by making use of multisport-specific training methods such as combination training, or bricks, transition training, and the development of a skill base for the transition aspect of the race.

The racing experience in triathlon and duathlon is fundamentally different from training, and the best result occurs when you address that in your preparations. To create the best opportunity for a successful racing experience, you should taper training, secure an effective transition space, thoroughly review the course, create an appropriate warm-up, apply the use of even pacing or drafting within the context of the rules, and develop effective travel strategies.

Creating a Long-Term Training Program

Once you are familiar with the training principles described in chapter 1 and the more specific training methods described in chapters 4 and 5, the development of a training program that will be effective, motivational, and fun to do is well within your grasp. If you have fully digested those principles you'll also realize that training must be individualized. The right program for you is one based on your own adaptive response, basic physiological and psychological capabilities, performance aspirations, and goals in the sport. The information in this chapter is an outline for developing training programs that you can individualize by testing yourself and applying your own values to the approach. In the following sections, resistance, speed, and endurance elements of program development are addressed.

Outline of the Process for an Experienced Athlete

1. Establish racing goals for the upcoming competitive year.
2. Before the season begins, make any upgrades in equipment, facilities, or coaching you will use.
3. Establish a periodization training plan for completion of a key race or racing period during the competitive year. Your program should combine both base and race-preparation training periods.
4. Use performance testing to establish your target workloads.
5. Cycle through your training plan and make planned progressions as you adapt; periodically retest yourself.
6. Incorporate your training for psychological skills into your physiological training.
7. Complete each season with a period of active rest or restoration.

Developing a Progressive Resistance Training Plan

Just as in any other form of training, before being able to fully exploit resistance training you must go through a developmental period in which you learn and become comfortable with the movements and increase the density of your soft tissues (muscles, tendons, and ligaments) and skeleton before taking on heavier loads. You also want to condition your mind and body for the more diversified training to come without creating either undue soreness or a sense of extraordinary effort. The parallel to this is that you should begin intensive interval training only after having increased your time and distance in aerobic training. This is referred to as creating training tolerance before developing the ability to train more specifically.

When beginning this process in weight training the first hurdle is to identify an appropriate starting weight for each exercise. As with running, you can never start *too* easily. You can, on the other hand, start out too hard, trying to lift too much weight. There is no more effective way to start this process than with a given weight for each given exercise that you feel you will be able to move easily. In other words, begin light!

Here are some conservative suggestions for weights to try as you begin working on common exercises:

Single-leg squat: One-third body weight or less

Heel lift: 2.5- to 5-pound ankle weights or weightless until you develop solid technique

Knee extension: One-third body weight or less

Leg curl: One-fourth body weight or less

Seated row: One-fourth body weight or less

Lat push-down: One-fourth body weight or less or lightest available weight until you develop solid technique

Lateral dumbbell lift: Lightest weight available until you develop solid technique

Back extension: Body weight on equipment or on the ground initially

Abdominal curl: Body weight on equipment or on the ground initially

Over the first six to eight microcycles of the program described in the following list, you should follow a conservative schedule of advancement, always working well short of failure sets. For most people, a microcycle of training is 7 to 10 days. Perform the sets described here one to three times per week depending on how much time you are able to allocate for weight training. You should progress microcycle to microcycle as follows:

Microcycle 1: 1 × 20RM weight or roughly 50 to 60 percent of the 1RM for each movement-specific exercise you choose to include in your program. Supplemental exercises may use lighter weights or body weight initially. Ideally you will be able to complete 10 to 15 reps at this weight without reaching failure.

Microcycle 2: 1 × 15 to 18 reps at 20RM

Microcycle 3: 2 × 10 to 15 reps at 20RM

Microcycle 4: 2 × 15 to 18 reps at 20RM

Microcycle 5: 3 × 10 to 15 reps at 20RM

Microcycle 6: 3 × 15 to 18 reps at 20RM

Microcycle 7: 3 × 6 to 8 reps at 20RM. Restoration or recovery microcycle— reduced loading allows for full adaptation to the previous work completed.

During this time you would simultaneously make progress in your swimming, cycling, and running training in separate training sessions. These may occur independently or be linked with the weight training sessions for greater efficiency, as described later.

Diversifying Your Strength and Power Development

Once you've developed basic strength and training tolerance over the first seven microcycles, you can develop a more sophisticated microcycle that emphasizes strength, short-term muscular endurance, and power in separate training sessions. Given a training tolerance of three high-repetition sets developed before the training sessions, a set structure would be as follows.

Strength

In this type of training session, starting with relatively lighter weights than the optimum for strength development, you complete sets using progressively heavier weights for progressively fewer repetitions to reach your target set for strength development. If you have more time and adaptive energy, you can expand the number of target sets over time. The workout would appear as follows for each exercise:

1 × 12 reps at 20RM

1 × 12 reps at 15RM

1, 2, or 3 sets × 6 to 12 reps without a failure rep at 12RM

Once you complete 12 reps relatively easily without failure and a reasonable time has passed, you should increase the weight.

Short-Term Muscular Endurance

In this type of training session you do a warm-up set and then one or more target sets that each last for about one minute. You can increase the weight as your muscular endurance levels increase. The following is the set structure for this objective:

1 × 12 repetitions at 20RM

1, 2, or 3 sets × 15 to 20 reps without a failure rep at 20RM

Once you can do 20 reps relatively easily without failure, you should increase the weight.

Peak Power

To achieve this objective, do a warm-up set and then one or more target sets designed to develop maximum power. Use a relatively light weight (50 to 70 percent of the 1RM) and limited number of repetitions, but do them as explosively as possible in the lifting, pushing, or pulling phase of the movement, with a controlled recovery. A general rule is to use a weight you can move for just a few repetitions as fast as you would normally perform the movement in the whole-body activity without external resistance. Here is the set structure for this objective:

1 × 12 reps at 20RM

1 to 3 sets × 6 to 12 reps without a failure rep and with explosive movements at 15- to 20RM

Once you complete 12 reps without failure and with sustained, high speed, you can increase the weight. Generally this will happen once you have also increased weight in your strength-focused training session.

Using Plyometrics for Peak Instantaneous Power in Running

You should not start training with running plyometrics until you have established a general foundation in strength through several months of weight training. In addition, plyometric technique is very critical to reducing impact forces on the skeletal system—you must use an extended learning period before using a taxing level. You can accomplish this by using a double-leg box hop, as described in chapter 4, with a height of no more than a few inches. Precede any single-leg jumps from boxes with multiple relaxed single-leg hops from the ground.

The loading measure used for plyometric exercises is the combination of your body weight (and anything you add to it) and the height from which you drop during the exercise. Duration is defined by the number of contacts you make while performing the exercise. As you become more skilled and are able to drop from greater heights, the peak forces your body is absorbing exceed that of any other exercise you will perform, including strength and peak power training with weights. Consequently you should progress slowly using a six- to eight-week period before adding loads. A typical starting point for a plyometric set is approximately 30 contacts from a relatively low height (2 to 4 inches, or 5 to 10 cm) carrying only your body weight. Complete the plyometric exercises once and no more than twice per microcycle to allow for adequate recovery. Ideally they will follow the running-specific strength and power exercises with resistance in the same training session. This allows the weight work to prepare your nervous system for rapid and powerful peak forces and serves as the warm-up for the plyometrics. You can also use less taxing plyometric movements (those without significant drop height or added weight), such as single-leg quick hops, as skill-reinforcement drills, and you can apply those movements more regularly.

Periodization of Resistance Training and Plyometrics

Once you have completed the basic adaptive period and begun the more diversified approach to resistance training, continue with the weights throughout your training year or season. Doing weight training only in the winter—the common practice for many endurance athletes—reduces your potential for progressive improvement in strength and peak power year to year. While it is often stated that strength gained in the weight room is transferred to the activity itself during the competitive season, the reality is that the endurance training stimulus does not produce force levels high enough to optimize and then maintain increased strength levels in movement.

The result of a partial-year approach to resistance training is that during the competitive season, you will lose most of what you gain in strength and power each winter and simply start back at the same point the following winter. This off-season approach is better than doing no resistance training at all, but if you maintain strength and power during the competitive season, then you can make new strength and power gains year to year. Obviously, the movement-specific strength and peak power you have attained and then maintain are the ultimate limiters to movement speed and endurance performance in your training and racing. To reiterate, doing resistance training year-round is vital if you want to make progressive improvements in triathlon performance over long periods. Further, the strength and peak power you develop in any given year will translate more effectively to improved performance in the later stages of that competitive season if you maintain it appropriately.

Now, the traditional approach to this problem is to use periodization, in which you cycle through the various elements of a training program several times during the training year. This topic is also discussed in chapters 4 and 5. However, the traditional periodization approach specifically for strength and power development uses the following scheme.

- Nonspecific exercises (such as the standard squat) proceed to more specific exercises (such as the modified squat described earlier) in successive training phases or cycles. This follows the periodization principle of moving from more general work to more specific work as you prepare for racing.

- General strength and muscular endurance development proceeds to high-level strength development, then proceeds to peak power development, in successive phases called mesocycles. This again follows the principle of general to specific.

A training plan developed using this kind of periodization would look like this:

Base Period

Cycles 1 to 4: General strength and muscular endurance development using general movements

Cycles 5 to 8: General strength and muscular endurance development using more specific movements

Race Preparation

Cycles 9 to 12: Peak strength development using specific movements

Cycles 13 to 16: Peak power development using specific movements

An alternative approach to periodization that is useful for busy triathletes involves varying the nature of the work (but not the weight training exercises) within the microcycle. You then periodize in phases by emphasizing the development of strength and power during the base or general preparation phases of your training in swimming, cycling, and running. Follow with maintenance workouts for strength and peak power during periods of more race-specific training in the three sports. In this way, overall energy use is more constant, and higher levels of strength and peak power create the platform for improved ability to work at a high power output over various periods. Given the multiple sports and levels of training stimuli necessary for preparing yourself for racing, this is a simpler approach to training.

Once you begin the specific race-preparation training periods in swimming, cycling, and running, you should move into a maintenance phase for your strength training—continuing to do the weight training workouts at the weight levels previously reached without attempting further increases. This approach maintains strength and peak power while allowing you to respond to the additional key sport workouts that extend that new power level over time. Base training periods then become your opportunity to increase your primary performance limiter, movement-specific strength. Race-preparation periods extend the capacity over race distances and beyond. Variations in the training focus of each training session occur across a given microcycle rather than across successive training periods or mesocycles as in the traditional approach.

Once you begin using running plyometrics in conjunction with resistance training, you can do the indoor plyometric exercises throughout the training year for the reasons previously described. You can also use the nontraditional periodization approach described earlier by focusing on progressions in the plyometrics during base training periods and maintenance of current work levels during race-specific preparation periods.

Training Frequency for Resistance Training and Plyometrics

Initially you should do the weight training three times per week on alternating days as you begin to increase strength. Once you develop strength and use a more sophisticated approach to the microcycle, the three training sessions will allow you to focus one individual training session each on strength, power, and short-term muscular endurance. Eventually, however, you should decrease your resistance training workout frequency to twice per week. This might occur after several years of weight training as you begin to approach your limits for strength development.

If in one of the two sessions you emphasize strength and in the other peak power and short-term endurance, a lower frequency of training will allow for greater progress. This is because greater recovery time becomes necessary between training sessions as they become more demanding (in work performed, not sense of effort). Doing so requires a relatively higher and more specific stimulus for more improvement in each area—peak strength and peak power. You can use a similar frequency for plyometric training in conjunction with your resistance training, ideally immediately after the running-specific resistance movements.

When doing maintenance training during more race-specific training periods, keep resistance and plyometric training frequency at two per microcycle if weight and repetitions are stabilized at a level at which you were previously well adapted. If possible, continue such training for a minimum of once per week.

Making Progressions in Resistance Training and Plyometrics

During base period resistance training, increase weight for a given set by approximately 5 to 10 percent once you have reached your target reps easily or with improved recovery heart rate between sets. The three-to-one, or planned restoration, principle (described in chapters 1 and 5) is also applicable here with three microcycles of increased load followed by one of a reduced load. You can accomplish this restoration cycle by performing approximately 50 percent of your total reps in each set with normal resistance levels. You must also consider development of your underlying soft-tissue structure, so it is best to be conservative in making progressions. After your first six months of training, it would not be unusual to spend six to eight weeks at one strength level, even when nervous system regulation (lower heart rates) adaptation has occurred, to ensure that your soft tissues have time to develop. This period of training necessary for complete physiological adaptation at a given level of weight continues to increase the closer you come to reaching your physiological limits of strength. Experienced triathletes who have been training efficiently in the weight room for several years might make only a single progression once or twice per year.

You should approach progression in plyometrics using similar principles. Initially you gradually increase the number of contacts until you reach the volume of work you anticipate continuing over time. You can then increase the height from which you jump progressively. You will reach some practical limit here as well, which is often dictated by your ability to retain running-specific technique in your jumps or the availability of appropriate plyometric training boxes. You can continue to progress plyometrics through the addition of a weighted vest. In this case you should begin with no more than 2 percent of your body weight and slowly increase that amount using the considerations previously described for progressing your levels in resistance training.

Developing Speed and Endurance With Complex Training

In conjunction with your development of functional and movement-specific strength and peak power, you will extend your ability to move faster and longer in swimming, cycling, and running using complex speed and endurance training, as described in chapter 5. Your top-end movement speed is a function of technique, strength, and peak power in that movement. You then develop speed by swimming, cycling, and running at high velocities. Your endurance in these movements is definable by your current rate of fatigue, as discussed in chapters 4 and 5. You reduce your rate of fatigue by extending the time you can sustain less-than-maximal speeds though endurance training.

To create speed and endurance simultaneously, you will use a complex training program. The program consists of a variety of training sessions targeting velocities or power outputs in swimming, cycling, and running. You establish these targets by using physiological testing, performance testing to create a fatigue curve, or your sense of feel, as discussed in chapter 5. Simple performance tests that evaluate your speed directly over given distances will most likely improve your results.

The application of this approach to training program design is based on three premises. The first is that training for a targeted velocity (rather than heart rate or level of effort) over a given distance is a more useful approach for race preparation than attempting to train at given efforts. This is true even when you are targeting a specific physiological response, such as your peak oxygen uptake, to determine your levels of exertion. The second premise is that you should train and test yourself using performance outcomes that you can measure readily every time you train. This allows you to apply an adaptation model of training, as described in chapter 5. Further, this approach presumes that targeting the specific velocities and power outputs you are capable of performing for specific event distances or work time frames directly develops the key physiological variables necessary for success. To review this concept, see the sidebar on pages 113 to 114 of chapter 5.

By using a combination of training at each of these velocities in tolerable amounts, combined with basic aerobic endurance training at powers or speeds below the aerobic lactate threshold, you create an overall training approach that can maximize performance. You can establish the specific training velocities or power outputs by using complex physiological testing or performance testing. In the second approach, establish the determination of target training workloads across your full spectrum of ability by using your fatigue rate based on time-trial performances over two or more different distances. You can then use 1RM testing or estimation to establish loads in the weight room.

The performance approach to testing occurs naturally in the training environment. For example, in cycling you can use a cycle trainer, rollers, or an outside ride for a measured distance and perform a half-mile and 1-mile cycling time trial to provide a projection of fatigue rate and the corresponding estimates of projected race-pace effort at corresponding longer distances. You will need the equipment to measure time and distance, power and distance, or velocity (miles or kilometers per hour) directly in any case.

Here is a simple version of the mathematics of that process:

Time-Trial Test Data

0.25-mile time trial completed in 26.2 seconds at an average of 320 watts and 34.35 mph

1-mile time trial completed in 2:00 at an average of 274 watts and 30.00 mph

You must use time-trial distances that are doubles of each other, such as 1, 2, 4, 8, and 16.

$$\text{Fatigue rate} = \{[(TT1L \times TT2T)/(TT2L \times TT1T \times D)] - (1/D)\} \times 100$$

where

TT1 = shorter time trial

TT2 = longer time trial

TT1L = length of TT1

TT2L = length of TT2

TT1T = time of TT1

TT2T = Time of TT2

D = number of times that TT1L must be doubled to equal TT2L

In this case, 0.25 mile must be doubled two times to equal 1 mile as follows:

$$2 \times 0.25 = 0.50,\ 2 \times 0.50 = 1.0$$

Therefore,

$$\text{Fatigue rate} = \{[(.25 \times 120)/(1 \times 26.2 \times 2)] - 0.5\} \times 100$$

$$= [(30/52.4) - 0.5] \times 100$$

$$= (0.5725 - 0.5) \times 100$$

$$= 0.0725 \times 100 = 7.25\%$$

You can also calculate the fatigue rate using average time-trial measures such as power in watts or miles per hour by using a modified equation as shown in the following example:

$$\text{Fatigue rate} = \{[(\text{TT1w or TT1mph} - \text{TT2w or TT2mph})/D]/ \\ \text{TT1w or TT1mph}\} \times 100$$

where

TT1w = watts for TT1

TT2w = watts for TT2

TT1mph = miles per hour for TT1

TT2mph = miles per hour for TT2

D = number of times that TT1L must be doubled to equal TT2L

From the previous example,

$$[(320 - 274)/2]/320 \times 100 = (46/2)/320 \times 100$$
$$= 23/320 \times 100 = 0.0719 \times 100 = 7.2\%$$

Your rate of fatigue is likely related to your basic muscle fiber composition and endurance training status; consequently, using it to create training intensities individualizes your training loads appropriately. One of the objectives of your training is to reduce fatigue rate over time. As you should periodically redo the basic time trials to establish your various training intensities, you can reevaluate your fatigue rate in the same process. It is not necessary to do long time trials for testing purposes. You can use time trials as short as 100 meters and 400 meters in running. The equivalents to these distances in cycling would be 0.25 mile and 1 mile, and in swimming they would be 25 yards or meters and 100 yards or meters. However, the shorter the time trial the greater the need for accuracy of timing to accurately predict rate of fatigue.

Here is an example that applies the previous cycling data, along with some related strength data:

Athlete Performance Profile

Knee extension 1RM	160 pounds
Strength training load at 85% 1RM	6 reps × 136 pounds

Peak power training load at 50% 1RM   6 reps × 80 pounds

Leg curl 1RM   100 pounds

Strength training load at 85% 1RM   6 reps × 85 pounds

Peak power training load at 50% 1RM   6 reps × 50 pounds

0.25-mile time trial   0:26.2 seconds (34.35 mph or 320 average watts)

1-mile time trial   2:00 minutes (30.0 mph or 274 average watts)

Fatigue rate   7.25%

Projected Target Velocities

The rest of the target velocities are calculated using the natural log equations described in chapter 5 and would appear this way:

Distance	Predicted finish time	Average power	Average velocity
1 mile	2:00	297.3 watts	30.00 mph
2 miles	4:17	253.0 watts	28.04 mph
4 miles	9:09	234.0 watts	26.20 mph
12 miles	30:35	207.0 watts	23.53 mph
25 miles	1:08:29	190.0 watts	21.91 mph
56 miles	2:45:58	174.0 watts	20.25 mph
112 miles	5:55:11	160.5 watts	18.92 mph

You can apply the same kind of model to swim and run training by using movement-specific resistance exercises and time trials or average power sustained over key time periods in each sport to establish training intensities.

Creating a Speed Endurance Training Session

You would next create training sessions to develop capabilities for specific distances using the predicted velocities. Each of these training sessions should include a progressive or steady warm-up period, a set that emphasizes skill or general neuromuscular development, and then a set targeting distances and velocities or power. This might be followed by additional aerobic work, depending on your tolerance, and a cool-down period.

Extending the previous example, you might create a stationary trainer–based or roller-based session to develop speed at 1 mile and 2 miles using the following training session model.

1. Do a progressive warm-up of 4 × 4 minutes at increasing workloads that begin at a comfortable level and reach the aerobic threshold (marathon pace in this example):

   4 min × 14 mph or 110 watts

   4 min × 16 mph or 130 watts

   4 min × 18 mph or 150 watts

   4 min × 20 mph or 170 watts

2. A series of cycling drills to increase movement speed and reinforce cycling technique might include short sets of single-leg pedaling (see chapter 3) and high-cadence intervals while cycling at a comfortable power output on the trainer or rollers.

3. A progressive set of 6 to 8 alactates builds to or beyond the fastest target velocity or power for the session. In this case that would be 28 mph or 253 watts, the 1-mile targets. The alactate set would then appear as follows:

   2 × 20 seconds at 27 mph or 240 watts

   2 × 20 seconds at 28 mph or 250 watts

   2 × 20 seconds at 29 mph or 260 watts

   You would complete these with an easy cycling (in this case 100 watts or less) recovery between each. Recovery should generally be less than 1 minute or the amount of time necessary for heart rate to return to a comfortable aerobic level at 70 percent of the maximum heart rate or below.

4. Do a main set targeting projected 1-mile and 2-mile velocities. The efforts should represent no more than 25 percent of the actual target distance or time initially. Alternatively, you could simply cycle at the target velocity or power as long as you're able to stay comfortable. This would appear as follows:

   4 × 20 seconds at 1-mile target velocity or power (30 mph or 274 watts) with 40 seconds easy cycling recovery between each

   1 to 2 minutes easy cycling recovery between sets

   4 × 40 seconds at 2-mile target velocity or power (28 mph or 253 watts) with 50 seconds easy cycling recovery between each

5. Depending on your current training tolerance and time, you might also include some additional aerobic training. This could be either straightforward aerobic work at your aerobic threshold (56-mile to 112-mile target velocity or power) or strength endurance work at the same range of power but using a high enough gear to produce 40 to 60 rpm comfortably. The following is an example of strength endurance work:

   20 minutes at 20 mph or 170 watts using a gear that produces 40 to 60 rpm

6. The session should always finish with a cool-down or transition directly into a weight training session (as described in chapter 4). The cool-down before lifting might be 5 minutes at 14 to 16 mph or a power range of 110 to 130 watts.

7. Immediately after this, you could do the following resistance training for power:

Knee extension: 1 × 12 reps at 50% 1RM (80 pounds); 2 × 6 reps at 50% 1RM (80 pounds) as explosively as possible

Leg curl: 1 × 12 reps at 50% 1RM (50 pounds); 2 × 6 reps at 50% 1RM (50 pounds) as explosively as possible

The total time for this training session is 45 to 65 minutes, depending on the inclusion of the extra aerobic work (item 5). Chapter 8 contains more specific examples of training sessions and training plans using these concepts for swimming, cycling, and running.

Organizing the Frequency and Placement of Training Sessions

In the early training phases of a competitive year, assuming there has been a break from previous training, the focus should be on gradually expanding endurance and general strength at whatever speeds you are capable of completing with reasonable comfort. This is referred to as base training. This period should also be focused on developing a basis in technique. Once this basic developmental period of 8 to 12 weeks passes, you can begin diversifying training sessions within the microcycle to target various points on your velocity curve or specific physiological response thresholds. This is referred to as race-preparation training.

Following are examples of race-preparation microcycles. They are based on the hard–easy training approach described in chapter 5. Note that your own microcycle of training must address elements such as work schedule and your other general life commitments. This presumes you are an experienced age-group athlete training at least three times per week in each sport who can organize the microcycle around 7 (three key sessions) or 14 days (four key sessions) as follows:

7-Day Microcycle

Day 1: Complete recovery day

Day 2: Speed swim

Day 3: Speed run, speed bike, weights strength

Day 4: Race-pace swim

Day 5: Race-pace combination bike and run

Day 6: Endurance swim, weights power

Day 7: Endurance run, endurance bike

14-Day Microcycle

Day 1: Complete recovery day

Day 2: Speed swim

Day 3: Speed run, weights strength

Day 4: Speed bike, aerobic swim

Day 5: Recovery swim, recovery run or bike

Day 6: Race-pace swim, weights power

Day 7: Race-pace run

Day 8: Race-pace bike

Day 9: Tempo swim

Day 10: Tempo bike and run combination, weights strength

Day 11: Recovery swim, recovery run or bike

Day 12: Endurance swim, aerobic run

Day 13: Endurance bike

Day 14: Endurance run, weights power

With this setup, you can accomplish longer endurance and race-pace sessions on weekends (when many working athletes have more time). In the 14-day cycle a greater emphasis is also placed on general aerobic endurance, allowing for the development of a lower rate of fatigue.

If you are a professional athlete or elite age-grouper with greater schedule flexibility, you might organize 4 to 6 days per week training in each sport around a 10-day microcycle that emphasizes four key training sessions in each sport. This approach presumes greater recovery time and a higher level of general development.

10-Day Microcycle

Day 1: Complete recovery day

Day 2: Speed run

Day 3: Speed swim, speed bike, recovery run, weights strength

Day 4: Aerobic run, recovery bike, aerobic run

Day 5: Race-pace swim, race-pace bike and run, weights general

Day 6: Recovery swim, bike, and run

Day 7: Tempo bike and run combination, aerobic swim, weights power

Day 8: Tempo swim, recovery bike and run

Day 9: Endurance run, aerobic bike, recovery swim

Day 10: Endurance bike, recovery run, aerobic swim, weights general

Periodization of the Training Program

Speed and endurance training should cycle back and forth between base training periods (in which you focus on expanding general swimming, cycling, and running endurance, movement strength, and peak power) and race-preparation periods (in which you maintain the aforementioned qualities and focus on expanding speed and endurance over the full range of distances and power or velocities).

An extended base training period of 8 to 16 weeks is recommended in the early part of the training year. This creates the basic training tolerance and peak force-producing capacity for the next period. You should follow this with a race-preparation period whereby peak speed is then extended across the full range of velocities. This period might encompass 8 or more weeks. Traditionally some athletes carry this training out over the full course of a triathlon season that might encompass many months. If you are training using a conventional approach to progression by achieving personal-best efforts, you should return to base training for shorter periods of 4 weeks, especially after periods of extensive or peak racing. This allows for both physiological and psychological recovery as well as further progress in basic limiters. This period would again be followed by a race-preparation period of 8 to 12 weeks. If you are an elite or age-group athlete competing 6 to 11 months per year, you might go through two or even three complete macrocycles in a year. Alternating between base periods and race-preparation periods is vital for maintaining training enthusiasm and allowing for more sustained training progress.

If you follow a more conservative adaptive approach to training, such as advocated in this book, it may be very possible to spend more of the training year in race-preparation mesocycles, because the accumulation of physical and psychological fatigue is generally lower than with more typical "hard" training methods.

Making Progressions in Speed and Endurance Training

If you use an adaptive model for training and target specific velocities and power outputs, then you make progressions when lower physiological effort occurs. You can plan these progressions, but you should not implement them unless evidence of adaptation occurs. This might mean a lower training or recovery heart rate or rating of perceived exertion when performing the effort. Planned progressions should be approximately 5 to 10 percent of the current workload, whether they are increases in length, power, or velocity of the effort. The resulting workload should then still be tolerable if you have adapted to the previous load. When adaptations are not occurring, you must reorganize the training plan to provide more or improved recovery between key targeted training sessions.

Putting It All Together

Combining weight training with swimming, cycling, and running requires that you integrate the use of the gymnasium into your training approach. This is often easier than it might seem because YMCAs, city recreation facilities, and private health clubs commonly have pools, resistance training facilities, and an assortment of treadmills, stationary bikes, and other aerobic training equipment all in the same place. To combine these efficiently, you have to open your mind to new ways of organizing your training. This becomes possible when you begin to see individual training sessions as consisting of blocks of various activities rather than seeing each swim, bike, run, and weightlifting session as a separate training session. For example, on a day when your schedule calls for cycling, running, and weight training in a typical prework period, you might organize it this way:

6:00 a.m. Arrive at the YMCA having warmed up by commuting by bicycle.

6:05 a.m. Finish warm-up by doing alactates on a stationary bike and then complete the main body of your cycling training sets.

6:30 a.m. Move to the treadmill or an outdoor run to complete your target sets for running.

7:00 a.m. Move directly from a short running cool-down to your cycling and running-specific weight training. Follow the running-based weight training movements immediately with your plyometric exercises for running.

7:30 a.m. Ride your bicycle home or to work, completing any additional aerobic training or a cool-down process.

Effective training sessions for multisports can be combined in a myriad of ways. By moving from one training emphasis to another, you also reduce the need for the time-consuming preparation and clean-up processes that go into separate training sessions while replicating the conditions of multisport racing. By training both inside and out with ergometers and in natural conditions, and in various combinations, you can gain the benefits of each type of approach synergistically. The diversification associated with such a complex approach can also add tremendously to your motivation and enjoyment in the training process.

Summary

You create the training program for a triathlon first by assessing your physiological abilities (through the use of performance tests, physiological tests, or instinct) and then planning specific training sessions to develop each of those abilities. You organize the training sessions within a microcycle that emphasizes the full spectrum of your abilities across various training sessions. You then combine the microcycles to create mesocycles, or training blocks, in an extended plan preparing you for specific races or racing periods. In mesocycles, emphasis on base training and race-preparation training alternates throughout the training year. You plan and make training progressions as you adapt. Year-to-year progress occurs through a variable but consistent training approach in which you remain active throughout the year by using a periodization plan and following an adaptive process.

8

Race-Specific Training Programs

The training programs are organized by an increasing level of training experience as target race distance increases. They follow a common process in which you might begin with a shorter race and progress to longer races over the course of a season. This is not always the case, so consider that methods introduced in the programs targeting the longer distances might be used in shorter-distance programs as well. The programs address physical and psychological skill development and reflect the types of goals that are most common among triathletes, based on the considerations that are typical at each level. The approach is simple in application yet uses sophisticated training concepts. It's presumed that you have read the preceding chapters before using programs; there is also a glossary of terms at the end of the book to further your understanding.

The most effective use of the programs requires the use of a heart rate monitor and a training environment where you will be able to measure your work outcomes over a long term. The programs presume a balanced approach to training in all three sports—something you should strive for even if you have considerable competitive experience in one of the three triathlon sports. They include a brief description of the approach and provide targets for training progression along with specifics on training session organization. These training volume targets represent the low end of the scale for a "racing" approach at each distance. Many athletes benefit by gradually adapting to greater aerobic training volumes, although you should increase the velocity or power, rather than volume, of the distance target sets once you achieve the basic target distance. The best indicators of the value of adding more aerobic training volume are monitoring adaptation to the various key training sets that make up the program and your fatigue rate. If adding more aerobic training volume inhibits adaptation or results in performance tests that predict slower velocities at your target race distances, then it has become nonproductive.

The most basic types of sets are used in creating response at each target velocity or power. There are a multitude of combinations, using varying distances and gradients and other course-specific considerations, you can use to achieve the same purpose once you understand the principle.

The programs provide a periodization and details of the main sets for each focused training session. Review the description of training session organization in chapter 7 to remind yourself of how these main sets will fit into a specific training session that you create. You should use the fatigue curve process described in chapter 5 for determining specific training velocities or power outputs, at least initially. Consider that even during base training it is productive to incorporate all the elements of the typical training session described in chapter 7, recognizing that the main set might be nothing more complicated than steady aerobic-intensity training at a specific velocity or power output during base-preparation periods. Following is a detailed description of each program.

- Sprint distance
- Olympic distance (page 196)
- Half-Ironman distance (page 222)
- Ironman distance (page 240)

Sprint Distance

Term

Minimum 8 weeks to race a sprint-distance triathlon in the 500-yard swim, 20K bicycle, 5K run range.

Training Periodization

This presumes an 8-week block of time and an initial buildup in volume from an existing basic program. If this were the first base period of the year, you might extend it over 8 to 16 weeks. What follows is an example of a typical beginning base mesocycle combined with a race-preparation mesocycle.

Mesocycle 1: Base Phase

Week 1: Base 1

Week 2: Base 2

Week 3: Base 3

Week 4: Base 4

Mesocycle 2: Race-Preparation Phase

Week 5: Race prep 1

Week 6: Race prep 2

Week 7: Race prep 3

Week 8: Race prep 4 (taper) with target race

Base Phase

In the base-preparation mesocycle, swim, cycle, and run three times per week each with one session longer and slower and two sessions shorter and slightly faster. Add in one or two weight training sessions per week. All sessions should be at comfortable exertion levels. If you're a more experienced athlete, you might use a greater frequency of training, although you should always consider adaptation when extending total training volume. Work intensity can progress as training adaptation becomes apparent (HR and RPE drop during the exercise and in recovery). Each session should begin with a warm-up, drill set, and progressive alactates in the applicable sport (swim, bike, or run). See tables on pages 186 and 187 for base phase training details. Review chapter 6 for a specific training session format.

Race-Preparation Phase

During race-preparation training, hold training volume constant (after reducing it by about 10 to 20 percent) and use each of three training sessions per week in each sport for a specific training focus or key workout. The key workouts include focus on speed, race pace, and endurance. Details are given in the tables on pages 188 through 195. Aerobic sets are not described and can be in a variety of formats. Precede each session with a warm-up, drill set, and progressive alactates in the applicable sport (swim, bike, or run). Ride all bike sessions in your race position. Do run and bike race-pace sessions on a measured course. Do run and bike endurance sessions on a race-specific course (hills, turns) on a road or dirt trail (depending on type of race). The sets are presented in a week-by-week or microcycle-by-microcycle format so that you can see the anticipated progressions. Make progressions only if adaptation has occurred (see chapters 1 and 5).

Mesocycle 1: Base Phase Week 1

Day	Training session	Specific session details
Monday	No training	
Tuesday	Run intermediate length	3 miles at 12 to 14 RPE
	Bike intermediate length	10 miles at 12 to 14 RPE
Wednesday	Swim intermediate length	1,000 yards at 12 to 14 RPE
	Weight training (strength), all swim-, bike-, and run-specific and supplemental movements	1 × 12 reps at 50% 1RM 2 × 6 to 8 reps at 85% 1RM
Thursday	Run intermediate length	3 miles at 12 to 14 RPE
	Bike intermediate length	10 miles at 12 to 14 RPE
Friday	Swim intermediate length	1,000 yards at 12 to 14 RPE
Saturday	Bike long	15 miles at <12 RPE
	Weight training (power and muscular endurance); all swim-, bike-, and run-specific and supplemental movements; plyometrics	1 × 20 reps at 50% 1RM 2 × 6 reps at 50% 1RM explosive
Sunday	Swim long	1,500 yards at <12 RPE
	Run long	5 miles at <12 RPE

Mesocycle 1: Base Phase Week 2

Day	Training session	Specific session details
Monday	No training	
Tuesday	Run intermediate length	3.25 miles at 12 to 14 RPE
	Bike intermediate length	11 miles at 12 to 14 RPE
Wednesday	Swim intermediate length	1,100 yards at 12 to 14 RPE
	Weight training (strength), all swim-, bike-, and run-specific and supplemental movements	1 × 12 reps at 50% 1RM 2 × 6 to 8 reps at 85% 1RM
Thursday	Run intermediate length	3.25 miles at 12 to 14 RPE
	Bike intermediate length	11 miles at 12 to 14 RPE
Friday	Swim intermediate length	1,100 yards at 12 to 14 RPE
Saturday	Bike long	16.5 miles at <12 RPE
	Weight training (power and muscular endurance); all swim-, bike-, and run-specific and supplemental movements; plyometrics	1 × 20 reps at 50% 1RM 2 × 6 reps at 50% 1RM explosive
Sunday	Swim long	1,650 yards at <12 RPE
	Run long	5.5 miles at <12 RPE

Mesocycle 1: Base Phase Week 3

Day	Training session	Specific session details
Monday	No training	
Tuesday	Run intermediate length	3.5 miles at 12 to 14 RPE
	Bike intermediate length	12 miles at 12 to 14 RPE
Wednesday	Swim intermediate length	1,200 yards at 12 to 14 RPE
	Weight training (strength), all swim-, bike-, and run-specific and supplemental movements	1 × 12 reps at 50% 1RM 2 × 6 to 8 reps at 85% 1RM
Thursday	Run intermediate length	3.5 miles at 12 to 14 RPE
	Bike intermediate length	12 miles at 12 to 14 RPE
Friday	Swim intermediate length	1,200 yards at 12 to 14 RPE
Saturday	Bike long	18 miles at <12 RPE
	Weight training (power and muscular endurance); all swim-, bike-, and run-specific and supplemental movements; plyometrics	1 × 20 reps at 50% 1RM 2 × 6 reps at 50% 1RM explosive
Sunday	Swim long	1,800 yards at <12 RPE
	Run long	6 miles at <12 RPE

Mesocycle 1: Base Phase Week 4 (Restoration)

Day	Training session	Specific session details
Monday	No training	
Tuesday	Run intermediate length	1.75 miles at 12 to 14 RPE
	Bike intermediate length	6 miles at 12 to 14 RPE
Wednesday	Swim intermediate length	600 yards at 12 to 14 RPE
	Weight training (strength), all swim-, bike-, and run-specific and supplemental movements	1 × 6 reps at 50% 1RM 2 × 3 or 4 reps at 85% 1RM
Thursday	Run intermediate length	1.75 miles at 12 to 14 RPE
	Bike intermediate length	6 miles at 12 to 14 RPE
Friday	Swim intermediate length	600 yards at 12 to 14 RPE
Saturday	Bike long	9 miles at <12 RPE
	Weight training (power and muscular endurance); all swim-, bike-, and run-specific and supplemental movements; plyometrics	1 × 10 reps at 50% 1RM 1 × 6 reps at 50% 1RM explosive
Sunday	Swim long	900 yards at <12 RPE
	Run long	3 miles at <12 RPE

Mesocycle 2: Race-Preparation Phase Week 5

Day	Training sessions	Specific session details
Monday	No training	
Tuesday	Run speed focus	**Total-session target volume = 3.5 miles.** Set 1: 2 × 100 meters (track) or 2 × 20 seconds (treadmill) at target 400-meter velocity with 100-meter walk or jog (track) or 30-second recovery walk off treadmill. Set 2: 400-meter recovery walk or jog (track) or 1- to 2-minute easy jog (treadmill). Set 3: 2 × 200 meters (track) or 2 × 40 seconds (treadmill) at 800-meter target velocity with 100-meter walk or jog (track) or 40-second recovery walk off treadmill. Set 4: 400-meter recovery walk or jog (track) or 1- to 2-minute easy jog (treadmill). Set 5: 2 × 400 meters (track) or 2 × 1:30 (treadmill) at 1,600-meter target velocity with 100-meter walk or jog (track) or 30-second recovery walk off treadmill. Set 6: 400-meter recovery walk or jog (track) or 1- to 2-minute easy jog (treadmill). Set 7: Additional aerobic running to achieve target volume.
	Bike speed focus	**Total-session target volume = 11 miles.** Set 1: 2 × 0.125 mile at target 0.5-mile velocity or power with equal rest (easy spin recovery). Set 2: 1- to 2-minute easy spin. Set 3: 2 × 0.25 mile at 1-mile target velocity with 30-second spin recovery. Set 4: 1- to 2-minute easy spin. Set 5: 2 × 0.5 mile at 2-mile target velocity with 40-second spin recovery. Set 6: 1- to 2-minute easy spin. Set 7: Additional aerobic cycling to achieve target cycle volume.
Wednesday	Swim speed focus	**Total-session target volume = 1,100 yards.** Set 1: 2 × 25 yards at target 100-yard velocity with equal rest. Set 2: 50-yard easy swim. Set 3: 2 × 50 yards at 200-yard target velocity with 30-second rest. Set 4: 50-yard easy swim. Set 5: 2 × 100 yards at 500-yard target velocity with 40-second rest. Set 6: 100-yard easy swim. Set 7: Aerobic swim or set to achieve target swim volume.
	Weight training (strength)	1 × 12 reps at 50% 1RM. 2 × 6 to 8 reps at 85% 1RM. No weight progression—same reps and weight maintained as during the base period. Complete all swim-, bike-, and run-specific and supplemental movements.

Day	Training sessions	Specific session details
Thursday	Bike race-pace focus*	**Total-session target volume = 11 miles.** Set 1: 2 × 3 miles at target 12.4-mile velocity with 1-minute easy spin. Set 2: 1- to 2-minute easy spin. Use an appropriate cadence target to help select your gears (see chapter 3). Set 3: Additional aerobic cycling to achieve target cycle volume.
	Run race-pace focus*	**Total-session target volume = 3.5 miles.** Set 1: 3 × 1,000 meters at 5,000-meter target velocity with 400-meter recovery walk or jog. Set 2: Additional aerobic running to achieve target volume.
Friday	Swim race-pace focus	**Total-session target volume = 1,100 yards.** Set 1: 3 × 200 yards at target 1,600-yard velocity with 30-second rest. Set 2: 100-yard easy swim. Set 3: Aerobic swim or set to achieve target swim volume.
Saturday	Bike endurance focus	**Total-session target volume = 17 miles.** Set 1: 12 miles or 35 to 50 minutes continuously at target cadence and 56-mile target velocity (you can do this comfortably for these distances). Ride on your race bike and in race position with a focus on taking in fluids and nutrition as you will in the target race. Set 2: Additional aerobic cycling to achieve target cycle volume.
	Weight training (power and muscular endurance)	1 × 20 reps at 50% 1RM. 2 × 6 reps at 50% 1RM explosive. No weight progression—same reps and weight maintained as during the base period. Complete all swim-, bike-, and run-specific and supplemental movements and plyometrics.
Sunday	Swim endurance focus	**Total-session target volume = 1,600 yards.** Set 1: 12 to 15 minutes or 800 yards continuously using at least one head lift per 25 yards or every 12 to 20 strokes at target 3,200-yard velocity. Wear the equipment (goggles, wet suit, race suit) you will wear in the race. Set 2: Aerobic swim or set to achieve target swim volume.
	Run endurance focus	**Total-session target volume = 5.5 miles.** Set 1: 3 miles or 20 to 25 minutes continuously at half-marathon-mile target velocity. Set 2: Additional aerobic running to achieve target run volume.

*It is optimal to combine these sessions (see chapter 6).

Mesocycle 2: Race-Preparation Phase Week 6

Day	Training sessions	Specific session details
Monday	No training	
Tuesday	Run speed focus	**Total-session target volume = 3.5 miles.** Set 1: 3 × 100 meters (track) or 3 × 20 seconds (treadmill) at target 400-meter velocity with 100-meter walk or jog (track) or 30-second recovery walk off treadmill. Set 2: 400-meter recovery walk or jog (track) or 1- to 2-minute easy jog (treadmill). Set 3: 3 × 200 meters (track) or 3 × 40 seconds (treadmill) at 800-meter target velocity with 100-meter walk or jog (track) or 40-second recovery walk off treadmill. Set 4: 400-meter recovery walk or jog (track) or 1- to 2-minute easy jog (treadmill). Set 5: 3 × 400 meters (track) or 3 × 1:30 (treadmill) at 1,600-meter target velocity with 100-meter walk or jog (track) or 30-second recovery walk off treadmill. Set 6: 400-meter recovery walk or jog (track) or 1- to 2-minute easy jog (treadmill). Set 7: Additional aerobic running to achieve target volume.
	Bike speed focus	**Total-session target volume = 11 miles.** Set 1: 3 × 0.125 mile at target 0.5-mile velocity or power with equal rest (easy spin recovery). Set 2: 1- to 2-minute easy spin. Set 3: 3 × 0.25 mile at 1-mile target velocity with 30-second spin recovery. Set 4: 1- to 2-minute easy spin. Set 5: 3 × 0.5 mile at 2-mile target velocity with 40-second spin recovery. Set 6: 1- to 2-minute easy spin. Set 7: Additional aerobic cycling to achieve target cycle volume.
Wednesday	Swim speed focus	**Total-session target volume = 1,100 yards.** Set 1: 3 × 25 yards at target 100-yard velocity with equal rest. Set 2: 50-yard easy swim. Set 3: 3 × 50 yards at 200-yard target velocity with 30-second rest. Set 4: 50-yard easy swim. Set 5: 3 × 100 yards at 500-yard target velocity with 40-second rest. Set 6: 100-yard easy swim. Set 7: Aerobic swim or set to achieve target swim volume.
	Weight training (strength)	1 × 12 reps at 50% 1RM. 2 × 6 to 8 reps at 85% 1RM. No weight progression—same reps and weight maintained as during the base period. Complete all swim-, bike-, and run-specific and supplemental movements.

Day	Training sessions	Specific session details
Thursday	Bike race-pace focus*	**Total-session target volume = 11 miles.** Set 1: 3 × 3 miles at target 12.4-mile velocity with 1-minute easy spin. Set 2: 1- to 2-minute easy spin. Use an appropriate cadence target to help select your gears (see chapter 3). Set 3: Additional aerobic cycling to achieve target cycle volume.
	Run race-pace focus*	**Total-session target volume = 3.5 miles.** Set 1: 4 × 1,000 meters at 5,000-meter target velocity with 400-meter recovery walk or jog. Set 2: Additional aerobic running to achieve target volume.
Friday	Swim race-pace focus	**Total-session target volume = 1,100 yards.** Set 1: 4 × 200 yards at target 1,600-yard velocity with 30-second rest. Set 2: 100-yard easy swim. Set 3: Aerobic swim or set to achieve target swim volume.
Saturday	Bike endurance focus	**Total-session target volume = 17 miles.** Set 1: 14 miles or 45 to 60 minutes continuously at target cadence and 56-mile target velocity. Ride on your race bike and in race position with a focus on taking in fluids and nutrition as you will in the target race. Set 2: Additional aerobic cycling to achieve target cycle volume.
	Weight training (power and muscular endurance)	1 × 20 reps at 50% 1RM. 2 × 6 reps at 50% 1RM explosive. No weight progression—same reps and weight maintained as during the base period. Complete all swim-, bike-, and run-specific and supplemental movements and plyometrics.
Sunday	Swim endurance focus	**Total-session target volume = 1,600 yards.** Set 1: 14 to 17 minutes or 900 yards continuously using at least one head lift per 25 yards or every 12 to 20 strokes at target 3,200-yard velocity. Wear the equipment (goggles, wet suit, race suit) you will wear in the race. Set 2: Aerobic swim or set to achieve target swim volume.
	Run endurance focus	**Total-session target volume = 5.5 miles.** Set 1: 3.5 miles or 25 to 30 minutes continuously at half-marathon-mile target velocity. Set 2: Additional aerobic running to achieve target run volume.

*It is optimal to combine these sessions (see chapter 6).

Mesocycle 2: Race-Preparation Phase Week 7

Day	Training sessions	Specific session details
Monday	No training	
Tuesday	Run speed focus	**Total-session target volume = 3.5 miles.** Set 1: 4 × 100 meters (track) or 4 × 20 seconds (treadmill) at target 400-meter velocity with 100-meter walk or jog (track) or 30-second recovery walk off treadmill. Set 2: 400-meter recovery walk or jog (track) or 1- to 2-minute easy jog (treadmill). Set 3: 4 × 200 meters (track) or 4 × 40 seconds (treadmill) at 800-meter target velocity with 100-meter walk or jog (track) or 40-second recovery walk off treadmill. Set 4: 400-meter recovery walk or jog (track) or 1- to 2-minute easy jog (treadmill). Set 5: 4 × 400 meters (track) or 4 × 1:30 (treadmill) at 1,600-meter target velocity with 100-meter walk or jog (track) or 30-second recovery walk off treadmill. Set 6: 400-meter recovery walk or jog (track) or 1- to 2-minute easy jog (treadmill). Set 7: Additional aerobic running to achieve target volume.
	Bike speed focus	**Total-session target volume = 11 miles.** Set 1: 4 × 0.125 mile at target 0.5-mile velocity or power with equal rest (easy spin recovery). Set 2: 1- to 2-minute easy spin. Set 3: 4 × 0.25 mile at 1-mile target velocity with 30-second spin recovery. Set 4: 1- to 2-minute easy spin. Set 5: 4 × 0.5 mile at 2-mile target velocity with 40-second spin recovery. Set 6: 1- to 2-minute easy spin. Set 7: Additional aerobic cycling to achieve target cycle volume.
Wednesday	Swim speed focus	**Total-session target volume = 1,100 yards.** Set 1: 4 × 25 yards at target 100-yard velocity with equal rest. Set 2: 50-yard easy swim. Set 3: 4 × 50 yards at 200-yard target velocity with 30-second rest. Set 4: 50-yard easy swim. Set 5: 4 × 100 yards at 500-yard target velocity with 40-second rest. Set 6: 100-yard easy swim. Set 7: Aerobic swim or set to achieve target swim volume.
	Weight training (strength)	1 × 12 reps at 50% 1RM. 2 × 6 to 8 reps at 85% 1RM. No weight progression—same reps and weight maintained as during the base period. Complete all swim-, bike-, and run-specific and supplemental movements.

Day	Training sessions	Specific session details
Thursday	Bike race-pace focus*	**Total-session target volume = 11 miles.** Set 1: 4 × 3 miles at target 12.4-mile velocity with 1-minute easy spin. Set 2: 1- to 2-minute easy spin. Use an appropriate cadence target to help select your gears (see chapter 3). Set 3: Additional aerobic cycling to achieve target cycle volume.
	Run race-pace focus*	**Total-session target volume = 3.5 miles.** Set 1: 5 × 1,000 meters at 5,000-meter target velocity with 400-meter recovery walk or jog. Set 2: Additional aerobic running to achieve target volume.
Friday	Swim race-pace focus	**Total-session target volume = 1,100 yards.** Set 1: 5 × 200 yards at target 1,600-yard velocity with 30-second rest. Set 2: 100-yard easy swim. Set 3: Aerobic swim or set to achieve target swim volume.
Saturday	Bike endurance focus	**Total-session target volume = 17 miles.** Set 1: 16 miles or 55 to 70 minutes continuously at target cadence and 56-mile target velocity. Ride on your race bike and in race position with a focus on taking in fluids and nutrition as you will in the target race. Set 2: Additional aerobic cycling to achieve target cycle volume.
	Weight training (power and muscular endurance)	1 × 20 reps at 50% 1RM. 2 × 6 reps at 50% 1RM explosive. No weight progression—same reps and weight maintained as during the base period. Complete all swim-, bike-, and run-specific and supplemental movements and plyometrics.
Sunday	Swim endurance focus	**Total-session target volume = 1,600 yards.** Set 1: 16 to 20 minutes or 1,000 yards continuously using at least one head lift per 25 yards or every 12 to 20 strokes at target 3,200-yard velocity. Wear equipment (goggles, wet suit, race suit) you will wear in the race. Set 2: Aerobic swim or set to achieve target swim volume.
	Run endurance focus	**Total-session target volume = 5.5 miles.** Set 1: 4 miles or 30 to 35 minutes continuously at half-marathon-mile target velocity. Set 2: Additional aerobic running to achieve target run volume.

*It is optimal to combine these sessions (see chapter 6).

Mesocycle 2: Race-Preparation Phase Week 8 (Taper)

Day	Training sessions	Specific session details
Monday	No training	
Tuesday	Run speed focus	**Total-session target volume = 1.75 miles.** Set 1: 2 × 100 meters (track) or 2 × 20 seconds (treadmill) at target 400-meter velocity with 100-meter walk or jog (track) or 30-second recovery walk off treadmill. Set 2: 400-meter recovery walk or jog (track) or 1- to 2-minute easy jog (treadmill). Set 3: 2 × 200 meters (track) or 2 × 40 seconds (treadmill) at 800-meter target velocity with 100-meter walk or jog (track) or 40-second recovery walk off treadmill. Set 4: 400-meter recovery walk or jog (track) or 1- to 2-minute easy jog (treadmill). Set 5: 2 × 400 meters (track) or 2 × 1:30 (treadmill) at 1,600-meter target velocity with 100-meter walk or jog (track) or 30-second recovery walk off treadmill. Set 6: 400-meter recovery walk or jog (track) or 1- to 2-minute easy jog (treadmill). Set 7: Additional aerobic running to achieve target volume. This volume is 50% of previous week's training session.
	Bike speed focus	**Total-session target volume = 5.5 miles.** Set 1: 2 × 0.125 mile at target 0.5-mile velocity or power with equal rest (easy spin recovery). Set 2: 1- to 2-minute easy spin. Set 3: 2 × 0.25 mile at 1-mile target velocity with 30-second spin recovery. Set 4: 1- to 2-minute easy spin. Set 5: 2 × 0.5 mile at 2-mile target velocity with 40-second spin recovery. Set 6: 1- to 2-minute easy spin. Set 7: Additional aerobic cycling to achieve target cycle volume. This volume is 50% of the previous 3 weeks' training sessions.
Wednesday	Swim speed focus	**Total-session target volume = 550 yards.** Set 1: 2 × 25 yards at target 100-yard velocity with equal rest. Set 2: 50-yard easy swim. Set 3: 2 × 50 yards at 200-yard target velocity with 30-second rest. Set 4: 50-yard easy swim. Set 5: 2 × 100 yards at 500-yard target velocity with 40-second rest. Set 6: 100-yard easy swim. Set 7: Aerobic swim or set to achieve target swim volume. This volume is 50% of previous week's training session.
	Weight training (strength)	1 × 6 reps at 50% 1RM. 1 × 3 or 4 reps at 85% 1RM. No weight progression—same reps and weight maintained as during the base period. Complete all swim-, bike-, and run-specific and supplemental movements.

Day	Training sessions	Specific session details
Thursday	Bike race-pace focus*	**Total-session target volume = 3 miles.** This work is replaced by the race at the end of the week. Do aerobic cycling with one or two 1-minute efforts at race pace to reach target volume, which is 50% of previous 3 weeks' training sessions.
	Run race-pace focus*	**Total-session target volume = 1 mile.** This work is replaced by the race at the end of the week. Include aerobic work and one or two 400-meter efforts at race pace only. Volume is 50% or less of the previous week's training sessions.
Friday	Swim race-pace focus	**Total-session target volume = 300 yards.** This work is replaced by the race at the end of the week. Include aerobic work and one or two 50-yard efforts at race pace only. Volume is 50% or less of the previous week's training sessions.
Saturday	Bike endurance focus	This is replaced by the target race.
	Weight training (power and muscular endurance)	Eliminate weight training and plyometric exercises before race.
Sunday	Swim endurance focus	This is replaced by the target race.
	Run endurance focus	This is replaced by the target race.

*It is optimal to combine these sessions (see chapter 6).

Olympic Distance

Term

Minimum 16 weeks to compete at the Olympic distance in triathlon in the 1,500-meter swim, 40K bicycle, 10K run range.

Training Periodization

This presumes a 16-week block of time and previous completion of the age-group sprint program or comparable training as well as further increases in tolerance of total training volume. This program first increases the general endurance necessary for completing the longer Olympic-distance race and then further develops race-specific training levels. If you have already completed a base period reaching volumes comparable to those outlined here, you might move directly to the race-preparation phase.

Mesocycle 1: Base Phase

> Week 1: Base 1
>
> Week 2: Base 2
>
> Week 3: Base 3
>
> Week 4: Base 4

Mesocycle 2: Base Phase

> Week 5: Base 1
>
> Week 6: Base 2
>
> Week 7: Base 3
>
> Week 8: Base 4

Mesocycle 3: Race-Preparation Phase

> Week 9: Race prep 1
>
> Week 10: Race prep 2
>
> Week 11: Race prep 3
>
> Week 12: Race prep 4

Mesocycle 4: Race-Preparation Phase

> Week 13: Race prep 1
>
> Week 14: Race prep 2
>
> Week 15: Race prep 3
>
> Week 16: Race prep 4 (taper) with target race

Base Phase

See tables on pages 198 through 205 for base phase training details. The details presume you have increased training tolerance previously.

Race-Preparation Phase

The tables on pages 206 through 221 give a schedule of the main sets for each focused training session. Complete a standard warm-up before and a cool-down afterward. Aerobic sets are not described and can be in a variety of formats. The speed sets are the same as used in the sprint-distance program and are shown the same for weeks 1 to 3. You will increase your speed in these sets, typically once per mesocycle, as adaptation occurs. This should occur if new testing indicates a new set of target speeds or you choose to make a small progression over your previous targets. The other sets are presented in a week-by-week or microcycle-by-microcycle format so that you can see the anticipated progressions. In addition to the warm-up, precede each session with a drill set and progressive alactates in the applicable sport (swim, bike, or run). Ride all bike sessions in race position. Do run and bike race-pace sessions on a measured course. Do run and bike endurance sessions on a race-specific course (hills, turns) on a road or dirt trail (depending on type of race). Make progressions only if adaptation has occurred (see chapters 1 and 5).

Mesocycle 1: Base Phase Week 1

Day	Training session	Specific session details
Monday	No training	
Tuesday	Run intermediate length	7 miles at 12 to 14 RPE Strength endurance: 10 minutes
	Bike intermediate length	20 miles at 12 to 14 RPE Strength endurance: 20 minutes
Wednesday	Swim intermediate length	1,600 yards at 12 to 14 RPE Strength endurance: 400 yards
	Weight training (strength); all swim-, bike-, and run-specific and supplemental movements	1 × 12 reps at 50% 1RM 2 × 6 to 8 reps at 85% 1RM
Thursday	Run intermediate length	7 miles at 12 to 14 RPE Strength endurance: 10 minutes
	Bike intermediate length	20 miles at 12 to 14 RPE Strength endurance: 20 minutes
Friday	Swim intermediate length	1,600 yards at 12 to 14 RPE Strength endurance: 400 yards
Saturday	Bike long	32 miles at <12 RPE Strength endurance: 20 minutes
	Weight training (power and muscular endurance); all swim-, bike-, and run-specific and supplemental movements; plyometrics	1 × 20 reps at 50% 1RM 2 × 6 reps at 50% 1RM explosive
Sunday	Swim long	2,200 yards at <12 RPE Strength endurance: 400 yards
	Run long	9 miles at <12 RPE Strength endurance: 10 minutes

Mesocycle 1: Base Phase Week 2

Day	Training session	Specific session details
Monday	No training	
Tuesday	Run intermediate length	7.5 miles at 12 to 14 RPE Strength endurance: 12 minutes
	Bike intermediate length	22 miles at 12 to 14 RPE Strength endurance: 25 minutes
Wednesday	Swim intermediate length	1,800 yards at 12 to 14 RPE Strength endurance: 500 yards
	Weight training (strength); all swim-, bike-, and run-specific and supplemental movements	1 × 12 reps at 50% 1RM 2 × 6 to 8 reps at 85% 1RM
Thursday	Run intermediate length	7.5 miles at 12 to 14 RPE Strength endurance: 12 minutes
	Bike intermediate length	22 miles at 12 to 14 RPE Strength endurance: 25 minutes
Friday	Swim intermediate length	1,800 yards at 12 to 14 RPE Strength endurance: 500 yards
Saturday	Bike long	36 miles at <12 RPE Strength endurance: 25 minutes
	Weight training (power and muscular endurance); all swim-, bike-, and run-specific and supplemental movements; plyometrics	1 × 20 reps at 50% 1RM 2 × 6 reps at 50% 1RM explosive
Sunday	Swim long	2,400 yards at <12 RPE Strength endurance: 500 yards
	Run long	9.5 miles at <12 RPE Strength endurance: 12 minutes

Mesocycle 1: Base Phase Week 3

Day	Training session	Specific session details
Monday	No training	
Tuesday	Run intermediate length	8 miles at 12 to 14 RPE Strength endurance: 15 minutes
	Bike intermediate length	24 miles at 12 to 14 RPE Strength endurance: 30 minutes
Wednesday	Swim intermediate length	2,000 yards at 12 to 14 RPE Strength endurance: 600 yards
	Weight training (strength); all swim-, bike-, and run-specific and supplemental movements	1 × 12 reps at 50% 1RM 2 × 6 to 8 reps at 85% 1RM
Thursday	Run intermediate length	8 miles at 12 to 14 RPE Strength endurance: 15 minutes
	Bike intermediate length	24 miles at 12 to 14 RPE Strength endurance: 30 minutes
Friday	Swim intermediate length	2,000 yards at 12 to 14 RPE Strength endurance: 600 yards
Saturday	Bike long	40 miles at <12 RPE Strength endurance: 30 minutes
	Weight training (power and muscular endurance); all swim-, bike-, and run-specific and supplemental movements; plyometrics	1 × 20 reps at 50% 1RM 2 × 6 reps at 50% 1RM explosive
Sunday	Swim long	2,600 yards at <12 RPE Strength endurance: 600 yards
	Run long	10 miles at <12 RPE Strength endurance: 15 minutes

Mesocycle 1: Base Phase Week 4 (Restoration)

Day	Training session	Specific session details
Monday	No training	
Tuesday	Run intermediate length	4 miles at 12 to 14 RPE Strength endurance: 8 minutes
	Bike intermediate length	12 miles at 12 to 14 RPE Strength endurance: 15 minutes
Wednesday	Swim intermediate length	1,000 yards at 12 to 14 RPE Strength endurance: 300 yards
	Weight training (strength); all swim-, bike-, and run-specific and supplemental movements	1 × 6 reps at 50% 1RM 2 × 3 or 4 reps at 85% 1RM
Thursday	Run intermediate length	4 miles at 12 to 14 RPE Strength endurance: 8 minutes
	Bike intermediate length	12 miles at 12 to 14 RPE Strength endurance: 15 minutes
Friday	Swim intermediate length	1,000 yards at 12 to 14 RPE Strength endurance: 300 yards
Saturday	Bike long	20 miles at <12 RPE Strength endurance: 15 minutes
	Weight training (power and muscular endurance); all swim-, bike-, and run-specific and supplemental movements; plyometrics	1 × 10 reps at 50% 1RM 1 × 6 reps at 50% 1RM explosive
Sunday	Swim long	1,300 yards at <12 RPE Strength endurance: 300 yards
	Run long	5 miles at <12 RPE Strength endurance: 8 minutes

Mesocycle 2: Base Phase Week 5

Day	Training session	Specific session details
Monday	No training	
Tuesday	Run intermediate length	8 miles at 12 to 14 RPE Strength endurance: 15 minutes
	Bike intermediate length	24 miles at 12 to 14 RPE Strength endurance: 30 minutes
Wednesday	Swim intermediate length	2,000 yards at 12 to 14 RPE Strength endurance: 600 yards
	Weight training (strength); all swim-, bike-, and run-specific and supplemental movements	1 × 12 reps at 50% 1RM 2 × 6 to 8 reps at 85% 1RM
Thursday	Run intermediate length	8 miles at 12 to 14 RPE Strength endurance: 15 minutes
	Bike intermediate length	24 miles at 12 to 14 RPE Strength endurance: 30 minutes
Friday	Swim intermediate length	2,000 yards at 12 to 14 RPE Strength endurance: 600 yards
Saturday	Bike long	40 miles at <12 RPE Strength endurance: 30 minutes
	Weight training (power and muscular endurance); all swim-, bike-, and run-specific and supplemental movements; plyometrics	1 × 20 reps at 50% 1RM 2 × 6 reps at 50% 1RM explosive
Sunday	Swim long	2,600 yards at <12 RPE Strength endurance: 600 yards
	Run long	10 miles at <12 RPE Strength endurance: 15 minutes

Mesocycle 2: Base Phase Week 6

Day	Training session	Specific session details
Monday	No training	
Tuesday	Run intermediate length	8.5 miles at 12 to 14 RPE Strength endurance: 20 minutes
	Bike intermediate length	26 miles at 12 to 14 RPE Strength endurance: 40 minutes
Wednesday	Swim intermediate length	2,200 yards at 12 to 14 RPE Strength endurance: 700 yards
	Weight training (strength); all swim-, bike-, and run-specific and supplemental movements	1 × 12 reps at 50% 1RM 2 × 6 to 8 reps at 85% 1RM
Thursday	Run intermediate length	8.5 miles at 12 to 14 RPE Strength endurance: 20 minutes
	Bike intermediate length	26 miles at 12 to 14 RPE Strength endurance: 40 minutes
Friday	Swim intermediate length	2,200 yards at 12 to 14 RPE Strength endurance: 700 yards
Saturday	Bike long	44 miles at <12 RPE Strength endurance: 40 minutes
	Weight training (power and muscular endurance); all swim-, bike-, and run-specific and supplemental movements; plyometrics	1 × 20 reps at 50% 1RM 2 × 6 reps at 50% 1RM explosive
Sunday	Swim long	2,800 yards at <12 RPE Strength endurance: 700 yards
	Run long	11 miles at <12 RPE Strength endurance: 20 minutes

Mesocycle 2: Base Phase Week 7

Day	Training session	Specific session details
Monday	No training	
Tuesday	Run intermediate length	9 miles at 12 to 14 RPE Strength endurance: 25 minutes
	Bike intermediate length	28 miles at 12 to 14 RPE Strength endurance: 50 minutes
Wednesday	Swim intermediate length	2,400 yards at 12 to 14 RPE Strength endurance: 800 yards
	Weight training (strength); all swim-, bike-, and run-specific and supplemental movements	1 × 12 reps at 50% 1RM 2 × 6 to 8 reps at 85% 1RM
Thursday	Run intermediate length	9 miles at 12 to 14 RPE Strength endurance: 25 minutes
	Bike intermediate length	28 miles at 12 to 14 RPE Strength endurance: 50 minutes
Friday	Swim intermediate length	2,400 yards at 12 to 14 RPE Strength endurance: 800 yards
Saturday	Bike long	48 miles at <12 RPE Strength endurance: 50 minutes
	Weight training (power and muscular endurance); all swim-, bike-, and run-specific and supplemental movements; plyometrics	1 × 20 reps at 50% 1RM 2 × 6 reps at 50% 1RM explosive
Sunday	Swim long	3,000 yards at <12 RPE Strength endurance: 800 yards
	Run long	12 miles at <12 RPE Strength endurance: 25 minutes

Mesocycle 2: Base Phase Week 8 (Restoration)

Day	Training session	Specific session details
Monday	No training	
Tuesday	Run intermediate length	4.5 miles at 12 to 14 RPE Strength endurance: 12 minutes
	Bike intermediate length	14 miles at 12 to 14 RPE Strength endurance: 25 minutes
Wednesday	Swim intermediate length	1,200 yards at 12 to 14 RPE Strength endurance: 400 yards
	Weight training (strength); all swim-, bike-, and run-specific and supplemental movements	1 × 6 reps at 50% 1RM 2 × 3 or 4 reps at 85% 1RM
Thursday	Run intermediate length	4.5 miles at 12 to 14 RPE Strength endurance: 12 minutes
	Bike intermediate length	14 miles at 12 to 14 RPE Strength endurance: 25 minutes
Friday	Swim intermediate length	1,200 yards at 12 to 14 RPE Strength endurance: 400 yards
Saturday	Bike long	24 miles at <12 RPE Strength endurance: 25 minutes
	Weight training (power and muscular endurance); all swim-, bike-, and run-specific and supplemental movements; plyometrics	1 × 10 reps at 50% 1RM 1 × 6 reps at 50% 1RM explosive
Sunday	Swim long	1,500 yards at <12 RPE Strength endurance: 400 yards
	Run long	6 miles at <12 RPE Strength endurance: 12 minutes

Mesocycle 3: Race-Preparation Phase Week 9

Day	Training sessions	Specific session details
Monday	No training	
Tuesday	Run speed focus	**Total-session target volume = 7 miles.** Set 1: 4 × 100 meters (track) or 4 × 20 seconds (treadmill) at target 400-meter velocity with 100-meter walk or jog (track) or 30-second recovery walk off treadmill. Set 2: 400-meter recovery walk or jog (track) or 1- to 2-minute easy jog (treadmill). Set 3: 4 × 200 meters (track) or 4 × 40 seconds (treadmill) at 800-meter target velocity with 100-meter walk or jog (track) or 40-second recovery walk off treadmill. Set 4: 400-meter recovery walk or jog (track) or 1- to 2-minute easy jog (treadmill). Set 5: 4 × 400 meters (track) or 4 × 1:30 (treadmill) at 1,600-meter target velocity with 100-meter walk or jog (track) or 30-second recovery walk off treadmill. Set 6: 400-meter recovery walk or jog (track) or 1- to 2-minute easy jog (treadmill). Set 7: 20-minute strength endurance work using a weighted vest or incline on the treadmill. Combine a speed and grade (and vest weight if used) that allow for a comfortable aerobic heart rate. A 2% grade is a good starting point. Set 8: Additional aerobic running to achieve target volume.
	Bike speed focus	**Total-session target volume = 24 miles.** Set 1: 4 × 0.125 mile at target 0.5-mile velocity or power with equal rest (easy spin recovery). Set 2: 1- to 2-minute easy spin. Set 3: 4 × 0.25 mile at 1-mile target velocity with 30-second spin recovery. Set 4: 1- to 2-minute easy spin. Set 5: 4 × 0.5 mile at 2-mile target velocity with 40-second spin recovery. Set 6: 1- to 2-minute easy spin. Set 7: 30-minute strength endurance set using a gear that produces 40 to 60 rpm at aerobic intensity in race position. Set 8: Additional aerobic cycling to achieve target cycle volume.
Wednesday	Swim speed focus	**Total-session target volume = 2,200 yards.** Set 1: 4 × 25 yards at target 100-yard velocity with equal rest. Set 2: 50-yard easy swim. Set 3: 4 × 50 yards at 200-yard target velocity with 30-second rest. Set 4: 50-yard easy swim. Set 5: 4 × 100 yards at 500-yard target velocity with 40-second rest. Set 6: 100-yard easy swim. Set 7: 800-yard strength endurance swim at aerobic intensity using paddles. Set 8: Aerobic swim or set to achieve target swim volume.

Day	Training sessions	Specific session details
Wednesday *(continued)*	Weight training (strength)	1 × 12 reps at 50% 1RM. 2 × 6 to 8 reps at 85% 1RM. No weight progression—same reps and weight maintained as during the base period. Complete all swim-, bike-, and run-specific and supplemental movements.
Thursday	Bike race-pace focus	**Total-session target volume = 26 miles.** Set 1: 3 × 5 miles at target 24.8-mile (40K) velocity with 1- to 2-minute easy spin. Set 2: 1- to 2-minute easy spin. Use an appropriate cadence target to help select your gears (see chapter 3). Set 3: Additional aerobic cycling to achieve target cycle volume.
	Run race-pace focus	**Total-session target volume = 8 miles.** Set 1: 3 × 2,000 meters at 10,000-meter target velocity with 400-meter recovery walk or jog. Set 2: Additional aerobic running to achieve target volume.
Friday	Swim race-pace focus	**Total-session target volume = 2,200 yards.** Set 1: 3 × 300 yards at target 1,600-yard velocity with 30-second rest. Set 2: 100-yard easy swim. Set 3: Aerobic swim or set to achieve target swim volume.
Saturday	Bike endurance focus	**Total-session target volume = 43 miles.** Set 1: 20 miles or 50 to 75 minutes continuously at target cadence and 56-mile target velocity. Focus on taking in fluids and nutrition as you will in the target race. Set 2: 30-minute strength endurance set using a gear that produces 40 to 60 rpm at aerobic intensity in race position. Set 3: Additional aerobic cycling to achieve target cycle volume.
	Weight training (power and muscular endurance)	1 × 20 reps at 50% 1RM. 2 × 6 reps at 50% 1RM explosive. No weight progression—same reps and weight maintained as during the base period. Complete all swim-, bike-, and run-specific and supplemental movements and plyometrics.
Sunday	Swim endurance focus	**Total-session target volume = 2,700 yards.** Set 1: 20 to 25 minutes or 1,200 yards continuously using at least one head lift per 25 yards or every 12 to 20 strokes at target 3,200-yard velocity. Wear the equipment (goggles, wet suit, race suit) you will wear in the race. Set 2: 800-yard strength endurance swim at aerobic intensity using paddles. Set 3: Aerobic swim or set to achieve target swim volume.
	Run endurance focus	**Total-session target volume = 11 miles.** Set 1: 5 miles or 30 to 40 minutes continuously at half-marathon-mile target velocity. Set 2: 15-minute strength endurance work running up a 2% to 4% grade at aerobic speed. Set 3: Additional aerobic running (likely downhill) to achieve target run volume.

Mesocycle 3: Race-Preparation Phase Week 10

Day	Training sessions	Specific session details
Monday	No training	
Tuesday	Run speed focus	**Total-session target volume = 7 miles.** Set 1: 4 × 100 meters (track) or 4 × 20 seconds (treadmill) at target 400-meter velocity with 100-meter walk or jog (track) or 30-second recovery walk off treadmill. Set 2: 400-meter recovery walk or jog (track) or 1- to 2-minute easy jog (treadmill). Set 3: 4 × 200 meters (track) or 4 × 40 seconds (treadmill) at 800-meter target velocity with 100-meter walk or jog (track) or 40-second recovery walk off treadmill. Set 4: 400-meter recovery walk or jog (track) or 1- to 2-minute easy jog (treadmill). Set 5: 4 × 400 meters (track) or 4 × 1:30 (treadmill) at 1,600-meter target velocity with 100-meter walk or jog (track) or 30-second recovery walk off treadmill. Set 6: 400-meter recovery walk or jog (track) or 1- to 2-minute easy jog (treadmill). Set 7: 20-minute strength endurance work using a weighted vest or incline on the treadmill. Combine a speed and grade (and vest weight if used) that allow for a comfortable aerobic heart rate. A 2% grade is a good starting point. Set 8: Additional aerobic running to achieve target volume.
	Bike speed focus	**Total-session target volume = 24 miles.** Set 1: 4 × 0.125 mile at target 0.5-mile velocity or power with equal rest (easy spin recovery). Set 2: 1- to 2-minute easy spin. Set 3: 4 × 0.25 mile at 1-mile target velocity with 30-second spin recovery. Set 4: 1- to 2-minute easy spin. Set 5: 4 × 0.5 mile at 2-mile target velocity with 40-second spin recovery. Set 6: 1- to 2-minute easy spin. Set 7: 30-minute strength endurance set using a gear that produces 40 to 60 rpm at aerobic intensity in race position. Set 8: Additional aerobic cycling to achieve target cycle volume.
Wednesday	Swim speed focus	**Total-session target volume = 2,200 yards.** Set 1: 4 × 25 yards at target 100-yard velocity with equal rest. Set 2: 50-yard easy swim. Set 3: 4 × 50 yards at 200-yard target velocity with 30-second rest. Set 4: 50-yard easy swim. Set 5: 4 × 100 yards at 500-yard target velocity with 40-second rest. Set 6: 100-yard easy swim. Set 7: 800-yard strength endurance swim at aerobic intensity using paddles. Set 8: Aerobic swim or set to achieve target swim volume.
	Weight training (strength)	1 × 12 reps at 50% 1RM. 2 × 6 to 8 reps at 85% 1RM. Complete all swim-, bike-, and run-specific and supplemental movements.

Day	Training sessions	Specific session details
Thursday	Bike race-pace focus	**Total-session target volume = 26 miles.** Set 1: 4 × 5 miles at target 24.8-mile (40K) velocity with 1- to 2-minute easy spin. Set 2: 1- to 2-minute easy spin. Use an appropriate cadence target to help select your gears. Set 3: Additional aerobic cycling to achieve target cycle volume.
	Run race-pace focus	**Total-session target volume = 8 miles.** Set 1: 4 × 2,000 meters at 10,000-meter target velocity with 400-meter recovery walk or jog. Set 2: Additional aerobic running to achieve target volume.
Friday	Swim race-pace focus	**Total-session target volume = 2,200 yards.** Set 1: 4 × 300 yards at target 1,600-yard velocity with 30-second rest. Set 2: 100-yard easy swim. Set 3: Aerobic swim or set to achieve target swim volume.
Saturday	Bike endurance focus	**Total-session target volume = 43 miles.** Set 1: 24 miles or 60 to 85 minutes continuously at target cadence and 56-mile target velocity. Focus on taking in fluids and nutrition as you will in the target race. Set 2: 40-minute strength endurance set using a gear that produces 40 to 60 rpm at aerobic intensity in race position. Set 3: Additional aerobic cycling to achieve target cycle volume.
	Weight training (power and muscular endurance)	1 × 20 reps at 50% 1RM. 2 × 6 reps at 50% 1RM explosive. Complete all swim-, bike-, and run-specific and supplemental movements and plyometrics.
Sunday	Swim endurance focus	**Total-session target volume = 2,700 yards.** Set 1: 22 to 27 minutes or 1,400 yards continuously using at least one head lift per 25 yards or every 12 to 20 strokes at target 3,200-yard velocity. Wear the equipment (goggles, wet suit, race suit) you will wear in the race. Set 2: 900-yard strength endurance swim at aerobic intensity using paddles. Set 3: Aerobic swim or set to achieve target swim volume.
	Run endurance focus	**Total-session target volume = 11 miles.** Set 1: 6 miles or 35 to 45 minutes continuously at half-marathon-mile target velocity. Set 2: 20-minute strength endurance work running up a 2% to 4% grade at aerobic speed. Set 3: Additional aerobic running (likely downhill) to achieve target run volume.

Mesocycle 3: Race-Preparation Phase Week 11

Day	Training sessions	Specific session details
Monday	No training	
Tuesday	Run speed focus	**Total-session target volume = 7 miles.** Set 1: 4 × 100 meters (track) or 4 × 20 seconds (treadmill) at target 400-meter velocity with 100-meter walk or jog (track) or 30-second recovery walk off treadmill. Set 2: 400-meter recovery walk or jog (track) or 1- to 2-minute easy jog (treadmill). Set 3: 4 × 200 meters (track) or 4 × 40 seconds (treadmill) at 800-meter target velocity with 100-meter walk or jog (track) or 40-second recovery walk off treadmill. Set 4: 400-meter recovery walk or jog (track) or 1- to 2-minute easy jog (treadmill). Set 5: 4 × 400 meters (track) or 4 × 1:30 (treadmill) at 1,600-meter target velocity with 100-meter walk or jog (track) or 30-second recovery walk off treadmill. Set 6: 400-meter recovery walk or jog (track) or 1- to 2-minute easy jog (treadmill). Set 7: 20-minute strength endurance work using a weighted vest or incline on the treadmill. Combine a speed and grade (and vest weight if used) that allow for a comfortable aerobic heart rate. A 2% grade is a good starting point. Set 8: Additional aerobic running to achieve target volume.
	Bike speed focus	**Total-session target volume = 24 miles.** Set 1: 4 × 0.125 mile at target 0.5-mile velocity or power with equal rest (easy spin recovery). Set 2: 1- to 2-minute easy spin. Set 3: 4 × 0.25 mile at 1-mile target velocity with 30-second spin recovery. Set 4: 1- to 2-minute easy spin. Set 5: 4 × 0.5 mile at 2-mile target velocity with 40-second spin recovery. Set 6: 1- to 2-minute easy spin. Set 7: 30-minute strength endurance set using a gear that produces 40 to 60 rpm at aerobic intensity in race position. Set 8: Additional aerobic cycling to achieve target cycle volume.
Wednesday	Swim speed focus	**Total-session target volume = 2,200 yards.** Set 1: 4 × 25 yards at target 100-yard velocity with equal rest. Set 2: 50-yard easy swim. Set 3: 4 × 50 yards at 200-yard target velocity with 30-second rest. Set 4: 50-yard easy swim. Set 5: 4 × 100 yards at 500-yard target velocity with 40-second rest. Set 6: 100-yard easy swim. Set 7: 800-yard strength endurance swim at aerobic intensity using paddles. Set 8: Aerobic swim or set to achieve target swim volume.
	Weight training (strength)	1 × 12 reps at 50% 1RM. 2 × 6 to 8 reps at 85% 1RM. Complete all swim-, bike-, and run-specific and supplemental movements.

Day	Training sessions	Specific session details
Thursday	Bike race-pace focus	**Total-session target volume = 26 miles.** Set 1: 5 × 5 miles at target 24.8-mile (40K) velocity with 1- to 2-minute easy spin. Set 2: 1- to 2-minute easy spin. Use an appropriate cadence target to help select your gears. Set 3: Additional aerobic cycling to achieve target cycle volume.
	Run race-pace focus	**Total-session target volume = 8 miles.** Set 1: 5 × 2,000 meters at 10,000-meter target velocity with 400-meter recovery walk or jog. Set 2: Additional aerobic running to achieve target volume.
Friday	Swim race-pace focus	**Total-session target volume = 2,200 yards.** Set 1: 5 × 300 yards at target 1,600-yard velocity with 30-second rest. Set 2: 100-yard easy swim. Set 3: Aerobic swim or set to achieve target swim volume.
Saturday	Bike endurance focus	**Total-session target volume = 43 miles.** Set 1: 28 miles or 70 to 95 minutes continuously at target cadence and 56-mile target velocity. Focus on taking in fluids and nutrition as you will in the target race. Set 2: 50-minute strength endurance set using a gear that produces 40 to 60 rpm at aerobic intensity in race position. Set 3: Additional aerobic cycling to achieve target cycle volume.
	Weight training (power and muscular endurance)	1 × 20 reps at 50% 1RM. 2 × 6 reps at 50% 1RM explosive. Complete all swim-, bike-, and run-specific and supplemental movements and plyometrics.
Sunday	Swim endurance focus	**Total-session target volume = 2,700 yards.** Set 1: 24 to 30 minutes or 1,600 yards continuously using at least one head lift per 25 yards or every 12 to 20 strokes at target 3,200-yard velocity. Wear the equipment (goggles, wet suit, race suit) you will wear in the race. Set 2: 1,000-yard strength endurance swim at aerobic intensity using paddles. Set 3: Aerobic swim or set to achieve target swim volume.
	Run endurance focus	**Total-session target volume = 11 miles.** Set 1: 7 miles or 40 to 55 minutes continuously at half-marathon-mile target velocity. Set 2: 25-minute strength endurance work running up a 2% to 4% grade at aerobic speed. Set 3: Additional aerobic running (likely downhill) to achieve target run volume.

Mesocycle 3: Race-Preparation Phase Week 12 (Restoration)

Day	Training sessions	Specific session details
Monday	No training	
Tuesday	Run speed focus	**Total-session target volume = 3.5 miles.** Set 1: 2 × 100 meters (track) or 2 × 20 seconds (treadmill) at target 400-meter velocity with 100-meter walk or jog (track) or 30-second recovery walk off treadmill. Set 2: 400-meter recovery walk or jog (track) or 1- to 2-minute easy jog (treadmill). Set 3: 2 × 200 meters (track) or 2 × 40 seconds (treadmill) at 800-meter target velocity with 100-meter walk or jog (track) or 40-second recovery walk off treadmill. Set 4: 400-meter recovery walk or jog (track) or 1- to 2-minute easy jog (treadmill). Set 5: 2 × 400 meters (track) or 2 × 1:30 (treadmill) at 1,600-meter target velocity with 100-meter walk or jog (track) or 30-second recovery walk off treadmill. Set 6: 400-meter recovery walk or jog (track) or 1- to 2-minute easy jog (treadmill). Set 7: 20-minute strength endurance work using a weighted vest or incline on the treadmill. Combine a speed and grade (and vest weight if used) that allow for a comfortable aerobic heart rate. A 2% grade is a good starting point. Set 8: Additional aerobic running to achieve target volume.
	Bike speed focus	**Total-session target volume = 12 miles.** Set 1: 2 × 0.125 mile at target 0.5-mile velocity or power with equal rest (easy spin recovery). Set 2: 1- to 2-minute easy spin. Set 3: 2 × 0.25 mile at 1-mile target velocity with 30-second spin recovery. Set 4: 1- to 2-minute easy spin. Set 5: 2 × 0.5 mile at 2-mile target velocity with 40-second spin recovery. Set 6: 1- to 2-minute easy spin. Set 7: 15-minute strength endurance set using a gear that produces 40 to 60 rpm at aerobic intensity in race position. Set 8: Additional aerobic cycling to achieve target cycle volume.
Wednesday	Swim speed focus	**Total-session target volume = 1,100 yards.** Set 1: 2 × 25 yards at target 100-yard velocity with equal rest. Set 2: 50-yard easy swim. Set 3: 2 × 50 yards at 200-yard target velocity with 30-second rest. Set 4: 50-yard easy swim. Set 5: 2 × 100 yards at 500-yard target velocity with 40-second rest. Set 6: 100-yard easy swim. Set 7: 400-yard strength endurance swim at aerobic intensity using paddles. Set 8: Aerobic swim or set to achieve target swim volume.
	Weight training (strength)	1 × 6 reps at 50% 1RM. 1 × 3 or 4 reps at 85% 1RM. Complete all swim-, bike-, and run-specific and supplemental movements.

Day	Training sessions	Specific session details
Thursday	Bike race-pace focus	**Total-session target volume = 13 miles.** Set 1: 2 × 5 miles at target 24.8-mile (40K) velocity with 1- to 2-minute easy spin. Set 2: 1- to 2-minute easy spin. Use an appropriate cadence target to help select your gears. Set 3: Additional aerobic cycling to achieve target cycle volume.
	Run race-pace focus	**Total-session target volume = 4 miles.** Set 1: 2 × 2,000 meters at 10,000-meter target velocity with 400-meter recovery walk or jog. Set 2: Additional aerobic running to achieve target volume.
Friday	Swim race-pace focus	**Total-session target volume = 1,100 yards.** Set 1: 2 × 300 yards at target 1,600-yard velocity with 30-second rest. Set 2: 100-yard easy swim. Set 3: Aerobic swim or set to achieve target swim volume.
Saturday	Bike endurance focus	**Total-session target volume = 21 miles.** Set 1: 14 miles or 35 to 48 minutes continuously at target cadence and 56-mile target velocity. Focus on taking in fluids and nutrition as you will in the target race. Set 2: 25-minute strength endurance set using a gear that produces 40 to 60 rpm at aerobic intensity in race position. Set 3: Additional aerobic cycling to achieve target cycle volume.
	Weight training (power and muscular endurance)	1 × 10 reps at 50% 1RM. 2× 3 reps at 50% 1RM explosive. Complete all swim-, bike-, and run-specific and supplemental movements and plyometrics.
Sunday	Swim endurance focus	**Total-session target volume = 1,300 yards.** Set 1: 12 to 15 minutes or 800 yards continuously using at least one head lift per 25 yards or every 12 to 20 strokes at target 3,200-yard velocity. Wear the equipment (goggles, wet suit, race suit) you will wear in the race. Set 2: 250-yard strength endurance swim at aerobic intensity using paddles. Set 3: Aerobic swim or set to achieve target swim volume.
	Run endurance focus	**Total-session target volume = 5.5 miles.** Set 1: 3.5 miles or 20 to 27 minutes continuously at half-marathon-mile target velocity. Set 2: 12-minute strength endurance work running up a 2% to 4% grade at aerobic speed. Set 3: Additional aerobic running (likely downhill) to achieve target run volume.

Mesocycle 4: Race-Preparation Phase Week 13

Day	Training sessions	Specific session details
Monday	No training	
Tuesday	Run speed focus	**Total-session target volume = 7 miles.** Set 1: 4 × 100 meters (track) or 4 × 20 seconds (treadmill) at target 400-meter velocity with 100-meter walk or jog (track) or 30-second recovery walk off treadmill. Set 2: 400-meter recovery walk or jog (track) or 1- to 2-minute easy jog (treadmill). Set 3: 4 × 200 meters (track) or 4 × 40 seconds (treadmill) at 800-meter target velocity with 100-meter walk or jog (track) or 40-second recovery walk off treadmill. Set 4: 400-meter recovery walk or jog (track) or 1- to 2-minute easy jog (treadmill). Set 5: 4 × 400 meters (track) or 4 × 1:30 (treadmill) at 1,600-meter target velocity with 100-meter walk or jog (track) or 30-second recovery walk off treadmill. Set 6: 400-meter recovery walk or jog (track) or 1- to 2-minute easy jog (treadmill). Set 7: 20-minute strength endurance work using a weighted vest or incline on the treadmill. Combine a speed and grade (and vest weight if used) that allow for a comfortable aerobic heart rate. A 2% grade is a good starting point. Set 8: Additional aerobic running to achieve target volume.
	Bike speed focus	**Total-session target volume = 26 miles.** Set 1: 4 × 0.125 mile at target 0.5-mile velocity or power with equal rest (easy spin recovery). Set 2: 1- to 2-minute easy spin. Set 3: 4 × 0.25 mile at 1-mile target velocity with 30-second spin recovery. Set 4: 1- to 2-minute easy spin. Set 5: 4 × 0.5 mile at 2-mile target velocity with 40-second spin recovery. Set 6: 1- to 2-minute easy spin. Set 7: 30-minute strength endurance set using a gear that produces 40 to 60 rpm at aerobic intensity in race position. Set 8: Additional aerobic cycling to achieve target cycle volume.
Wednesday	Swim speed focus	**Total-session target volume = 2,200 yards.** Set 1: 4 × 25 yards at target 100-yard velocity with equal rest. Set 2: 50-yard easy swim. Set 3: 4 × 50 yards at 200-yard target velocity with 30-second rest. Set 4: 50-yard easy swim. Set 5: 4 × 100 yards at 500-yard target velocity with 40-second rest. Set 6: 100-yard easy swim. Set 7: 800-yard strength endurance swim at aerobic intensity using paddles. Set 8: Aerobic swim or set to achieve target swim volume.
	Weight training (strength)	1 × 12 reps at 50% 1RM. 2 × 6 to 8 reps at 85% 1RM. Complete all swim-, bike-, and run-specific and supplemental movements.

Day	Training sessions	Specific session details
Thursday	Bike race-pace focus	**Total-session target volume = 26 miles.** Set 1: 3 × 5 miles at new target 24.8-mile (40K) velocity with 1- to 2-minute easy spin. Set 2: 1- to 2-minute easy spin. Use an appropriate cadence target to help select your gears (see chapter 3). Set 3: Additional aerobic cycling to achieve target cycle volume.
	Run race-pace focus	**Total-session target volume = 8 miles.** Set 1: 3 × 2,000 meters at new 10,000-meter target velocity with 400-meter recovery walk or jog. Set 2: Additional aerobic running to achieve target volume.
Friday	Swim race-pace focus	**Total-session target volume = 2,200 yards.** Set 1: 3 × 300 yards at new target 1,600-yard velocity with 30-second rest. Set 2: 100-yard easy swim. Set 3: Aerobic swim or set to achieve target swim volume.
Saturday	Bike endurance focus	**Total-session target volume = 43 miles.** Set 1: 20 miles or 50 to 75 minutes continuously at target cadence and new 56-mile target velocity. Focus on taking in fluids and nutrition as you will in the target race. Set 2: 30-minute strength endurance set using a gear that produces 40 to 60 rpm at aerobic intensity in race position. Set 3: Additional aerobic cycling to achieve target cycle volume.
	Weight training (power and muscular endurance)	1 × 20 reps at 50% 1RM. 2 × 6 reps at 50% 1RM explosive. Complete all swim-, bike-, and run-specific and supplemental movements and plyometrics.
Sunday	Swim endurance focus	**Total-session target volume = 2,700 yards.** Set 1: 20 to 25 minutes or 1,200 yards continuously using at least one head lift per 25 yards or every 12 to 20 strokes at new target 3,200-yard velocity. Wear the equipment (goggles, wet suit, race suit) you will wear in the race. Set 2: 800-yard strength endurance swim at aerobic intensity using paddles. Set 3: Aerobic swim or set to achieve target swim volume.
	Run endurance focus	**Total-session target volume = 11 miles.** Set 1: 5 miles or 30 to 40 minutes continuously at new half-marathon-mile target velocity. Set 2: 15-minute strength endurance work running up a 2% to 4% grade at aerobic speed. Set 3: Additional aerobic running (likely downhill) to achieve target run volume.

Mesocycle 4: Race-Preparation Phase Week 14

Day	Training sessions	Specific session details
Monday	No training	
Tuesday	Run speed focus	**Total-session target volume = 7 miles.** Set 1: 4 × 100 meters (track) or 4 × 20 seconds (treadmill) at target 400-meter velocity with 100-meter walk or jog (track) or 30-second recovery walk off treadmill. Set 2: 400-meter recovery walk or jog (track) or 1- to 2-minute easy jog (treadmill). Set 3: 4 × 200 meters (track) or 4 × 40 seconds (treadmill) at 800-meter target velocity with 100-meter walk or jog (track) or 40-second recovery walk off treadmill. Set 4: 400-meter recovery walk or jog (track) or 1- to 2-minute easy jog (treadmill). Set 5: 4 × 400 meters (track) or 4 × 1:30 (treadmill) at 1,600-meter target velocity with 100-meter walk or jog (track) or 30-second recovery walk off treadmill. Set 6: 400-meter recovery walk or jog (track) or 1- to 2-minute easy jog (treadmill). Set 7: 20-minute strength endurance work using a weighted vest or incline on the treadmill. Combine a speed and grade (and vest weight if used) that allow for a comfortable aerobic heart rate. A 2% grade is a good starting point. Set 8: Additional aerobic running to achieve target volume.
	Bike speed focus	**Total-session target volume = 26 miles.** Set 1: 4 × 0.125 mile at target 0.5-mile velocity or power with equal rest (easy spin recovery). Set 2: 1- to 2-minute easy spin. Set 3: 4 × 0.25 mile at 1-mile target velocity with 30-second spin recovery. Set 4: 1- to 2-minute easy spin. Set 5: 4 × 0.5 mile at 2-mile target velocity with 40-second spin recovery. Set 6: 1- to 2-minute easy spin. Set 7: 30-minute strength endurance set using a gear that produces 40 to 60 rpm at aerobic intensity in race position. Set 8: Additional aerobic cycling to achieve target cycle volume.
Wednesday	Swim speed focus	**Total-session target volume = 2,200 yards.** Set 1: 4 × 25 yards at target 100-yard velocity with equal rest. Set 2: 50-yard easy swim. Set 3: 4 × 50 yards at 200-yard target velocity with 30-second rest. Set 4: 50-yard easy swim. Set 5: 4 × 100 yards at 500-yard target velocity with 40-second rest. Set 6: 100-yard easy swim. Set 7: 800-yard strength endurance swim at aerobic intensity using paddles. Set 8: Aerobic swim or set to achieve target swim volume.
	Weight training (strength)	1 × 12 reps at 50% 1RM. 2 × 6 to 8 reps at 85% 1RM. Complete all swim-, bike-, and run-specific and supplemental movements.

Day	Training sessions	Specific session details
Thursday	Bike race-pace focus	**Total-session target volume = 26 miles.** Set 1: 4 × 5 miles at new target 24.8-mile (40K) velocity with 1- to 2-minute easy spin. Set 2: 1- to 2-minute easy spin. Use an appropriate cadence target to help select your gears. Set 3: Additional aerobic cycling to achieve target cycle volume.
	Run race-pace focus	**Total-session target volume = 8 miles.** Set 1: 4 × 2,000 meters at new 10,000-meter target velocity with 400-meter recovery walk or jog. Set 2: Additional aerobic running to achieve target volume.
Friday	Swim race-pace focus	**Total-session target volume = 2,200 yards.** Set 1: 4 × 300 yards at new target 1,600-yard velocity with 30-second rest. Set 2: 100-yard easy swim. Set 3: Aerobic swim or set to achieve target swim volume.
Saturday	Bike endurance focus	**Total-session target volume = 43 miles.** Set 1: 24 miles or 60 to 85 minutes continuously at target cadence and new 56-mile target velocity. Focus on taking in fluids and nutrition as you will in the target race. Set 2: 40-minute strength endurance set using a gear that produces 40 to 60 rpm at aerobic intensity in race position. Set 3: Additional aerobic cycling to achieve target cycle volume.
	Weight training (power and muscular endurance)	1 × 20 reps at 50% 1RM. 2 × 6 reps at 50% 1RM explosive. Complete all swim-, bike-, and run-specific and supplemental movements and plyometrics.
Sunday	Swim endurance focus	**Total-session target volume = 2,700 yards.** Set 1: 22 to 27 minutes or 1,400 yards continuously using at least one head lift per 25 yards or every 12 to 20 strokes at new target 3,200-yard velocity. Wear the equipment (goggles, wet suit, race suit) you will wear in the race. Set 2: 900-yard strength endurance swim at aerobic intensity using paddles. Set 3: Aerobic swim or set to achieve target swim volume.
	Run endurance focus	**Total-session target volume = 11 miles.** Set 1: 6 miles or 35 to 45 minutes continuously at new half-marathon-mile target velocity. Set 2: 20-minute strength endurance work running up a 2% to 4% grade at aerobic speed. Set 3: Additional aerobic running (likely downhill) to achieve target run volume.

Mesocycle 4: Race-Preparation Phase Week 15

Day	Training sessions	Specific session details
Monday	No training	
Tuesday	Run speed focus	**Total-session target volume = 7 miles.** Set 1: 4 × 100 meters (track) or 4 × 20 seconds (treadmill) at target 400-meter velocity with 100-meter walk or jog (track) or 30-second recovery walk off treadmill. Set 2: 400-meter recovery walk or jog (track) or 1- to 2-minute easy jog (treadmill). Set 3: 4 × 200 meters (track) or 4 × 40 seconds (treadmill) at 800-meter target velocity with 100-meter walk or jog (track) or 40-second recovery walk off treadmill. Set 4: 400-meter recovery walk or jog (track) or 1- to 2-minute easy jog (treadmill). Set 5: 4 × 400 meters (track) or 4 × 1:30 (treadmill) at 1,600-meter target velocity with 100-meter walk or jog (track) or 30-second recovery walk off treadmill. Set 6: 400-meter recovery walk or jog (track) or 1- to 2-minute easy jog (treadmill). Set 7: 20-minute strength endurance work using weighted vest or incline on the treadmill. Combine a speed and grade (and vest weight if used) that allow for a comfortable aerobic heart rate. A 2% grade is a good starting point. Set 8: Additional aerobic running to achieve target volume.
	Bike speed focus	**Total-session target volume = 26 miles.** Set 1: 4 × 0.125 mile at target 0.5-mile velocity or power with equal rest (easy spin recovery). Set 2: 1- to 2-minute easy spin. Set 3: 4 × 0.25 mile at 1-mile target velocity with 30-second spin recovery. Set 4: 1- to 2-minute easy spin. Set 5: 4 × 0.5 mile at 2-mile target velocity with 40-second spin recovery. Set 6: 1- to 2-minute easy spin. Set 7: 30-minute strength endurance set using a gear that produces 40 to 60 rpm at aerobic intensity in race position. Set 8: Additional aerobic cycling to achieve target cycle volume.
Wednesday	Swim speed focus	**Total-session target volume = 2,200 yards.** Set 1: 4 × 25 yards at target 100-yard velocity with equal rest. Set 2: 50-yard easy swim. Set 3: 4 × 50 yards at 200-yard target velocity with 30-second rest. Set 4: 50-yard easy swim. Set 5: 4 × 100 yards at 500-yard target velocity with 40-second rest. Set 6: 100-yard easy swim. Set 7: 800-yard strength endurance swim at aerobic intensity using paddles. Set 8: Aerobic swim or set to achieve target swim volume.
	Weight training (strength)	1 × 12 reps at 50% 1RM. 2 × 6 to 8 reps at 85% 1RM. Complete all swim-, bike-, and run-specific and supplemental movements.

Day	Training sessions	Specific session details
Thursday	Bike race-pace focus	**Total-session target volume = 26 miles.** Set 1: 5 × 5 miles at new target 24.8-mile (40K) velocity with 1- to 2-minute easy spin. Set 2: 1- to 2-minute easy spin. Use an appropriate cadence target to help select your gears. Set 3: Additional aerobic cycling to achieve target cycle volume.
	Run race-pace focus	**Total-session target volume = 8 miles.** Set 1: 5 × 2,000 meters at new 10,000-meter target velocity with 400-meter recovery walk or jog. Set 2: Additional aerobic running to achieve target volume.
Friday	Swim race-pace focus	**Total-session target volume = 2,200 yards.** Set 1: 5 × 300 yards at new target 1,600-yard velocity with 30-second rest. Set 2: 100-yard easy swim. Set 3: Aerobic swim or set to achieve target swim volume.
Saturday	Bike endurance focus	**Total-session target volume = 43 miles.** Set 1: 28 miles or 70 to 95 minutes continuously at target cadence and new 56-mile target velocity. Focus on taking in fluids and nutrition as you will in the target race. Set 2: 50-minute strength endurance set using a gear that produces 40 to 60 rpm at aerobic intensity in race position. Set 3: Additional aerobic cycling to achieve target cycle volume.
	Weight training (power and muscular endurance)	1 × 20 reps at 50% 1RM. 2 × 6 reps at 50% 1RM explosive. Complete all swim-, bike-, and run-specific and supplemental movements and plyometrics.
Sunday	Swim endurance focus	**Total-session target volume = 2,700 yards.** Set 1: 24 to 30 minutes or 1,600 yards continuously using at least one head lift per 25 yards or every 12 to 20 strokes at new target 3,200-yard velocity. Wear the equipment (goggles, wet suit, race suit) you will wear in the race. Set 2: 1,000-yard strength endurance swim at aerobic intensity using paddles. Set 3: Aerobic swim or set to achieve target swim volume.
	Run endurance focus	**Total-session target volume = 11 miles.** Set 1: 7 miles or 40 to 55 minutes continuously at new half-marathon-mile target velocity. Set 2: 25-minute strength endurance work running up a 2% to 4% grade at aerobic speed. Set 3: Additional aerobic running (likely downhill) to achieve target run volume.

Mesocycle 4: Race-Preparation Phase Week 16 (Taper)

Day	Training sessions	Specific session details
Monday	No training	
Tuesday	Run speed focus	**Total-session target volume = 3.5 miles.** Set 1: 2 × 100 meters (track) or 2 × 20 seconds (treadmill) at target 400-meter velocity with 100-meter walk or jog (track) or 30-second recovery walk off treadmill. Set 2: 400-meter recovery walk or jog (track) or 1- to 2-minute easy jog (treadmill). Set 3: 2 × 200 meters (track) or 2 × 40 seconds (treadmill) at 800-meter target velocity with 100-meter walk or jog (track) or 40-second recovery walk off treadmill. Set 4: 400-meter recovery walk or jog (track) or 1- to 2-minute easy jog (treadmill). Set 5: 2 × 400 meters (track) or 2 × 1:30 (treadmill) at 1,600-meter target velocity with 100-meter walk or jog (track) or 30-second recovery walk off treadmill. Set 6: 400-meter recovery walk or jog (track) or 1- to 2-minute easy jog (treadmill). Set 7: 20-minute strength endurance work using a weighted vest or incline on the treadmill. Combine a speed and grade (and vest weight if used) that allow for a comfortable aerobic heart rate. A 2% grade is a good starting point. Set 8: Additional aerobic running to achieve target volume.
	Bike speed focus	**Total-session target volume = 13 miles.** Set 1: 2 × 0.125 mile at target 0.5-mile velocity or power with equal rest (easy spin recovery). Set 2: 1- to 2-minute easy spin. Set 3: 2 × 0.25 mile at 1-mile target velocity with 30-second spin recovery. Set 4: 1- to 2-minute easy spin. Set 5: 2 × 0.5 mile at 2-mile target velocity with 40-second spin recovery. Set 6: 1- to 2-minute easy spin. Set 7: 15-minute strength endurance set using a gear that produces 40 to 60 rpm at aerobic intensity in race position. Set 8: Additional aerobic cycling to achieve target cycle volume.
Wednesday	Swim speed focus	**Total-session target volume = 1,100 yards.** Set 1: 2 × 25 yards at target 100-yard velocity with equal rest. Set 2: 50-yard easy swim. Set 3: 2 × 50 yards at 200-yard target velocity with 30-second rest. Set 4: 50-yard easy swim. Set 5: 2 × 100 yards at 500-yard target velocity with 40-second rest. Set 6: 100-yard easy swim. Set 7: 400-yard strength endurance swim at aerobic intensity using paddles. Set 8: Aerobic swim or set to achieve target swim volume.
	Weight training (strength)	1 × 6 reps at 50% 1RM. 1 × 3 or 4 reps at 85% 1RM. Complete all swim-, bike-, and run-specific and supplemental movements.

Day	Training sessions	Specific session details
Thursday	Bike race-pace focus	**Total-session target volume = 10 miles.** This work is replaced by the race at the end of the week. Do aerobic cycling with one or two 1-minute efforts at race pace to reach your target volume, which is 50% of previous 3 weeks' training sessions.
	Run race-pace focus	**Total-session target volume = 2.0 miles.** This work is replaced by the race at the end of the week. Include aerobic work and one or two 400-meter efforts at race pace only. Volume is 50% or less of the previous week's training sessions.
Friday	Swim race-pace focus	**Total-session target volume = 800 yards.** This work is replaced by the race at the end of the week. Include aerobic work and one or two 50-yard efforts at race pace only. Volume is 50% or less of the previous week's training sessions.
Saturday*	Bike endurance focus	This is replaced by the target race.
	Weight training (power and muscular endurance)	Eliminate weight training and plyometric exercises before race.
Sunday	Swim endurance focus	This is replaced by the target race.
	Run endurance focus	This is replaced by the target race.

*If racing on Sunday, complete a **short** warm-up in each discipline on the course if possible.

Half-Ironman Distance

Term

Minimum 8 weeks to compete at the half-Ironman distance in triathlon in the 1.2-mile swim, 56-mile cycle, and 13.1-mile run range after preparing for an Olympic-distance race.

Training Periodization

For this preparation*, it is assumed that you have completed the Olympic-distance race preparation to build your training tolerance up to the beginning points indicated here. The program makes a fundamental change in preparation resulting from the fact that the target race distance most often exceeds what most triathletes (other than full-time elites) ordinarily do in regular training sessions. To accommodate that fact, the race-preparation mesocycles include a progressively longer race-pace effort at half-Ironman-distance velocities as well as a progressively lengthening endurance effort at Ironman-distance racing velocities. Good nutritional habits become more important during this training. You maintain speed efforts developed during previous training periods by repeating them without progression. This allows adaptive energy to go toward increasing race-specific endurance without sacrificing basic speed.

Mesocycle 1: Race-Preparation Phase

   Week 1: Race prep 1

   Week 2: Race prep 2

   Week 3: Race prep 3

   Week 4: Race prep 4

Mesocycle 2: Race-Preparation Phase

   Week 5: Race prep 1

   Week 6: Race prep 2

   Week 7: Race prep 3 (taper first week running only**)

   Week 8: Race prep 4 (taper) with target race

*This presumes an 8-week block of time and previous buildup in volume from the age-group Olympic-distance program.
**Taper begins earlier for running only due to longer time period needed to reduce accumulated stress in an eccentric loading activity.

Race-Preparation Block Main Sets and Individual Progressions

The tables on pages 224 through 239 give a schedule of the main sets for each focused training session for the half-Ironman preparation program. Complete a standard warm-up before and a cool-down afterward. Aerobic sets are not described and can be of a variety of formats; however, a progression in overall duration is indicated. The speed sets are the same as used in the Olympic-distance program and so are presented only once. You will maintain your current speeds or power outputs for these sets throughout the mesocycle by repeating the sessions without progressions. This allows you to adapt to your race-specific and endurance training sessions as well as to progressively add aerobic training work to your speed-oriented sessions. The sets are presented in a week-by-week or microcycle-by-microcycle format so that you can see the progressions. In addition to the warm-up, precede each session with a drill set and progressive alactates in the applicable sport (swim, bike, or run). Ride all bike sessions in your race position. Do all run and bike race-pace sets on a measured course or using power and time. Do endurance sessions for run and bike on a race-specific course (hills, turns) on a road or dirt trail (depending on type of race). Make progressions only if adaptation has occurred (see chapters 1 and 5).

Mesocycle 1: Race-Preparation Phase Week 1

Day	Training sessions	Specific session details
Monday	No training	
Tuesday	Run speed focus	**Total-session target volume = 9 miles.** Set 1: 4 × 100 meters (track) or 4 × 20 seconds (treadmill) at target 400-meter velocity with 100-meter walk or jog (track) or 30-second recovery walk off treadmill. Set 2: 400-meter recovery walk or jog (track) or 1- to 2-minute easy jog (treadmill). Set 3: 4 × 200 meters (track) or 4 × 40 seconds (treadmill) at 800-meter target velocity with 100-meter walk or jog (track) or 40-second recovery walk off treadmill. Set 4: 400-meter recovery walk or jog (track) or 1- to 2-minute easy jog (treadmill). Set 5: 4 × 400 meters (track) or 4 × 1:30 (treadmill) at 1,600-meter target velocity with 100-meter walk or jog (track) or 30-second recovery walk off treadmill. Set 6: 400-meter recovery walk or jog (track) or 1- to 2-minute easy jog (treadmill). Set 7: 25-minute strength endurance work using a weighted vest or incline on the treadmill. Combine a speed and grade (and vest weight if used) that allow for a comfortable aerobic heart rate. A 2% grade is a good starting point. Set 8: Additional aerobic running to achieve target volume.
	Bike speed focus	**Total-session target volume = 28 miles.** Set 1: 4 × 0.125 mile at target 0.5-mile velocity or power with equal rest (easy spin recovery). Set 2: 1- to 2-minute easy spin. Set 3: 4 × 0.25 mile at 1-mile target velocity with 30-second spin recovery. Set 4: 1- to 2-minute easy spin. Set 5: 4 × 0.5 mile at 2-mile target velocity with 40-second spin recovery. Set 6: 1- to 2-minute easy spin. Set 7: 50-minute strength endurance set using a gear that produces 40 to 60 rpm at aerobic intensity in race position. Set 8: Additional aerobic cycling to achieve target cycle volume.
Wednesday	Swim speed focus	**Total-session target volume = 2,400 yards.** Set 1: 4 × 25 yards at target 100-yard velocity with equal rest. Set 2: 50-yard easy swim. Set 3: 4 × 50 yards at 200-yard target velocity with 30-second rest. Set 4: 50-yard easy swim. Set 5: 4 × 100 yards at 500-yard target velocity with 40-second rest. Set 6: 100-yard easy swim. Set 7: 800-yard strength endurance swim at aerobic intensity using paddles. Set 8: Aerobic swim or set to achieve target swim volume.

Day	Training sessions	Specific session details
Wednesday *(continued)*	Weight training (strength)	1 × 12 reps at 50% 1RM. 2 × 6 to 8 reps at 85% 1RM. No weight progression—same reps and weight maintained as during the base period. Complete all swim-, bike-, and run-specific and supplemental movements.
Thursday	Bike race-pace focus	**Total-session target volume = 28 miles.** Set 1: 3 × 7 miles at target 56-mile velocity with 5-minute easy spin. Set 2: 1- to 2-minute easy spin. Use an appropriate cadence target to help select your gears. Set 3: Additional aerobic cycling to achieve target cycle volume.
	Run race-pace focus	**Total-session target volume = 9 miles.** Set 1: 3 × 2 miles at 13.1-mile target velocity with 400-meter recovery walk or jog. Set 2: Additional aerobic running to achieve target volume.
Friday	Swim race-pace focus	**Total-session target volume = 2,400 yards.** Set 1: 3 × 500 yards at target 2,000-yard velocity with 60-second rest. Set 2: 100-yard easy swim. Set 3: Aerobic swim or set to achieve target swim volume.
Saturday	Bike endurance focus	**Total-session target volume = 48 miles.** Set 1: 28 miles or 85 to 105 minutes continuously at target cadence and 112-mile target velocity. Focus on taking in fluids and nutrition as you will in the target race. Set 2: 50-minute strength endurance set using a gear that produces 40 to 60 rpm at aerobic intensity in race position. Set 3: Additional aerobic cycling to achieve target cycle volume.
	Weight training (power and muscular endurance)	1 × 20 reps at 50% 1RM. 2 × 6 reps at 50% 1RM explosive. Complete all swim-, bike-, and run-specific and supplemental movements and plyometrics.
Sunday	Swim endurance focus	**Total-session target volume = 3,000 yards.** Set 1: 24 to 30 minutes or 1,600 yards continuously using at least one head lift per 25 yards or every 12 to 20 strokes at target 3,200-yard velocity. Wear the equipment (goggles, wet suit, race suit) you will wear in the race. Set 2: 800-yard strength endurance swim at aerobic intensity using paddles. Set 3: Aerobic swim or set to achieve target swim volume.
	Run endurance focus	**Total-session target volume = 12 miles.** Set 1: 7 miles or 60 to 80 minutes continuously at marathon-mile target velocity. Set 2: 25-minute strength endurance work running up a 2% to 4% grade at aerobic speed. Set 3: Additional aerobic running (likely downhill) to achieve target run volume.

Mesocycle 1: Race-Preparation Phase Week 2

Day	Training sessions	Specific session details
Monday	No training	
Tuesday	Run speed focus	**Total-session target volume = 10 miles.** Sets 1-6: Repeat week 1. Set 7: 30-minute strength endurance work using a weighted vest or incline on the treadmill. Combine a speed and grade (and vest weight if used) that allow for a comfortable aerobic heart rate. A 2% grade is a good starting point. Set 8: Additional aerobic running to achieve target volume.
	Bike speed focus	**Total-session target volume = 32 miles.** Sets 1-6: Repeat week 1. Set 7: 60-minute strength endurance set using a gear that produces 40 to 60 rpm at aerobic intensity in race position. Set 8: Additional aerobic cycling to achieve target cycle volume.
Wednesday	Swim speed focus	**Total-session target volume = 2,600 yards.** Sets 1-6: Repeat week 1. Set 7: 900-yard strength endurance swim at aerobic intensity using paddles. Set 8: Aerobic swim or set to achieve target swim volume.
	Weight training (strength)	1 × 12 reps at 50% 1RM. 2 × 6 to 8 reps at 85% 1RM. Complete all swim-, bike-, and run-specific and supplemental movements.
Thursday	Bike race-pace focus	**Total-session target volume = 32 miles.** Set 1: 3 × 8 miles at target 56-mile velocity with 5-minute easy spin. Set 2: 1- to 2-minute easy spin. Use an appropriate cadence target to help select your gears. Set 3: Additional aerobic cycling to achieve target cycle volume.
	Run race-pace focus	**Total-session target volume = 10 miles.** Set 1: 3 × 2.5 miles at 13.1-mile target velocity with 400-meter recovery walk or jog. Set 2: Additional aerobic running to achieve target volume.

Day	Training sessions	Specific session details
Friday	Swim race-pace focus	**Total-session target volume = 2,600 yards.** Set 1: 3 × 600 yards at target 2,000-yard velocity with 60-second rest. Set 2: 100-yard easy swim. Set 3: Aerobic swim or set to achieve target swim volume.
Saturday	Bike endurance focus	**Total-session target volume = 54 miles.** Set 1: 30 miles or 95 to 120 minutes continuously at target cadence and 112-mile target velocity. Focus on taking in fluids and nutrition as you will in the target race. Set 2: 60-minute strength endurance set using a gear that produces 40 to 60 rpm at aerobic intensity in race position. Set 3: Additional aerobic cycling to achieve target cycle volume.
	Weight training (power and muscular endurance)	1 × 20 reps at 50% 1RM. 2 × 6 reps at 50% 1RM explosive. Complete all swim-, bike-, and run-specific and supplemental movements and plyometrics.
Sunday	Swim endurance focus	**Total-session target volume = 3,200 yards.** Set 1: 28 to 34 minutes or 1,800 yards continuously using at least one head lift per 25 yards or every 12 to 20 strokes at target 3,200-yard velocity. Wear the equipment (goggles, wet suit, race suit) you will wear in the race. Set 2: 900-yard strength endurance swim at aerobic intensity using paddles. Set 3: Aerobic swim or set to achieve target swim volume.
	Run endurance focus	**Total-session target volume = 13 miles.** Set 1: 8 miles or 70 to 90 minutes continuously at marathon-mile target velocity. Set 2: 30-minute strength endurance work running up a 2% to 4% grade at aerobic speed. Set 3: Additional aerobic running (likely downhill) to achieve target run volume.

Mesocycle 1: Race-Preparation Phase Week 3

Day	Training sessions	Specific session details
Monday	No training	
Tuesday	Run speed focus	**Total-session target volume = 11 miles.** Sets 1-6: Repeat week 1. Set 7: 35-minute strength endurance work using a weighted vest or incline on the treadmill. Combine a speed and grade (and vest weight if used) that allow for a comfortable aerobic heart rate. A 2% grade is a good starting point. Set 8: Additional aerobic running to achieve target volume.
	Bike speed focus	**Total-session target volume = 36 miles.** Sets 1-6: Repeat week 1. Set 7: 70-minute strength endurance set using a gear that produces 40 to 60 rpm at aerobic intensity in race position. Set 8: Additional aerobic cycling to achieve target cycle volume.
Wednesday	Swim speed focus	**Total-session target volume = 2,800 yards.** Sets 1-6: Repeat week 1. Set 7: 1,000-yard strength endurance swim at aerobic intensity using paddles. Set 8: Aerobic swim or set to achieve target swim volume.
	Weight training (strength)	1 × 12 reps at 50% 1RM. 2 × 6 to 8 reps at 85% 1RM. Complete all swim-, bike-, and run-specific and supplemental movements.
Thursday	Bike race-pace focus	**Total-session target volume = 36 miles.** Set 1: 3 × 9 miles at target 56-mile velocity with 5-minute easy spin. Set 2: 1- to 2-minute easy spin. Use an appropriate cadence target to help select your gears. Set 3: Additional aerobic cycling to achieve target cycle volume.
	Run race-pace focus	**Total-session target volume = 11 miles.** Set 1: 3 × 3 miles at 13.1-mile target velocity with 400-meter recovery walk or jog. Set 2: Additional aerobic running to achieve target volume.

Day	Training sessions	Specific session details
Friday	Swim race-pace focus	**Total-session target volume = 2,800 yards.** Set 1: 3 × 700 yards at target 2,000-yard velocity with 60-second rest. Set 2: 100-yard easy swim. Set 3: Aerobic swim or set to achieve target swim volume.
Saturday	Bike endurance focus	**Total-session target volume = 60 miles.** Set 1: 32 miles or 105 to 135 minutes continuously at target cadence and 112-mile target velocity. Focus on taking in fluids and nutrition as you will in the target race. Set 2: 70-minute strength endurance set using a gear that produces 40 to 60 rpm at aerobic intensity in race position. Set 3: Additional aerobic cycling to achieve target cycle volume.
	Weight training (power and muscular endurance)	1 × 20 reps at 50% 1RM. 2 × 6 reps at 50% 1RM explosive. Complete all swim-, bike-, and run-specific and supplemental movements and plyometrics.
Sunday	Swim endurance focus	**Total-session target volume = 3,400 yards.** Set 1: 32 to 38 minutes or 2,000 yards continuously using at least one head lift per 25 yards or every 12 to 20 strokes at target 3,200-yard velocity. Wear the equipment (goggles, wet suit, race suit) you will wear in the race. Set 2: 1,000-yard strength endurance swim at aerobic intensity using paddles. Set 3: Aerobic swim or set to achieve target swim volume.
	Run endurance focus	**Total-session target volume = 13 miles.** Set 1: 9 miles or 80 to 100 minutes continuously at marathon-mile target velocity. Set 2: 35-minute strength endurance work running up a 2% to 4% grade at aerobic speed. Set 3: Additional aerobic running (likely downhill) to achieve target run volume.

Mesocycle 1: Race-Preparation Phase Week 4 (Restoration)

Day	Training sessions	Specific session details
Monday	No training	
Tuesday	Run speed focus	**Total-session target volume = 5.5 miles.** Set 1: 2 × 100 meters (track) or 2 × 20 seconds (treadmill) at target 400-meter velocity with 100-meter walk or jog (track) or 30-second recovery walk off treadmill. Set 2: 400-meter recovery walk or jog (track) or 1- to 2-minute easy jog (treadmill). Set 3: 2 × 200 meters (track) or 2 × 40 seconds (treadmill) at 800-meter target velocity with 100-meter walk or jog (track) or 40-second recovery walk off treadmill. Set 4: 400-meter recovery walk or jog (track) or 1- to 2-minute easy jog (treadmill). Set 5: 2 × 400 meters (track) or 2 × 1:30 (treadmill) at 1,600-meter target velocity with 100-meter walk or jog (track) or 30-second recovery walk off treadmill. Set 6: 400-meter recovery walk or jog (track) or 1- to 2-minute easy jog (treadmill). Set 7: 17-minute strength endurance work using a weighted vest or incline on the treadmill. Combine a speed and grade (and vest weight if used) that allow for a comfortable aerobic heart rate. A 2% grade is a good starting point. Set 8: Additional aerobic running to achieve target volume.
	Bike speed focus	**Total-session target volume = 18 miles.** Set 1: 2 × 0.125 mile at target 0.5-mile velocity or power with equal rest (easy spin recovery). Set 2: 1- to 2-minute easy spin. Set 3: 2 × 0.25 mile at 1-mile target velocity with 30-second spin recovery. Set 4: 1- to 2-minute easy spin. Set 5: 2 × 0.5 mile at 2-mile target velocity with 40-second spin recovery. Set 6: 1- to 2-minute easy spin. Set 7: 35-minute strength endurance set using a gear that produces 40 to 60 rpm at aerobic intensity in race position. Set 8: Additional aerobic cycling to achieve target cycle volume.
Wednesday	Swim speed focus	**Total-session target volume = 1,400 yards.** Set 1: 2 × 25 yards at target 100-yard velocity with equal rest. Set 2: 50-yard easy swim. Set 3: 2 × 50 yards at 200-yard target velocity with 30-second rest. Set 4: 50-yard easy swim. Set 5: 2 × 100 yards at 500-yard target velocity with 40-second rest. Set 6: 100-yard easy swim. Set 7: 500-yard strength endurance swim at aerobic intensity using paddles. Set 8: Aerobic swim or set to achieve target swim volume.
	Weight training (strength)	1 × 6 reps at 50% 1RM. 1 × 3 or 4 reps at 85% 1RM. Complete all swim-, bike-, and run-specific and supplemental movements.

Day	Training sessions	Specific session details
Thursday	Bike race-pace focus	**Total-session target volume = 18 miles.** Set 1: 3 × 4.5 miles at target 56-mile velocity with 3-minute easy spin. Set 2: 1- to 2-minute easy spin. Use an appropriate cadence target to help select your gears. Set 3: Additional aerobic cycling to achieve target cycle volume.
	Run race-pace focus	**Total-session target volume = 5.5 miles.** Set 1: 3 × 1.5 miles at 13.1-mile target velocity with 400-meter recovery walk or jog. Set 2: Additional aerobic running to achieve target volume.
Friday	Swim race-pace focus	**Total-session target volume = 1,400 yards.** Set 1: 3 × 350 yards at target 2,000-yard velocity with 60-second rest. Set 2: 100-yard easy swim. Set 3: Aerobic swim or set to achieve target swim volume.
Saturday	Bike endurance focus	**Total-session target volume = 30 miles.** Set 1: 16 miles or 105 to 135 minutes continuously at target cadence and 112-mile target velocity. Focus on taking in fluids and nutrition as you will in the target race. Set 2: 35-minute strength endurance set using a gear that produces 40 to 60 rpm at aerobic intensity in race position. Set 3: Additional aerobic cycling to achieve target cycle volume.
	Weight training (power and muscular endurance)	1 × 10 reps at 50% 1RM. 1 × 6 reps at 50% 1RM explosive. Complete all swim-, bike-, and run-specific and supplemental movements and plyometrics.
Sunday	Swim endurance focus	**Total-session target volume = 1,700 yards.** Set 1: 16 to 19 minutes or 1,000 yards continuously using at least one head lift per 25 yards or every 12 to 20 strokes at target 3,200-yard velocity. Wear the equipment (goggles, wet suit, race suit) you will wear in the race. Set 2: 500-yard strength endurance swim at aerobic intensity using paddles. Set 3: Aerobic swim or set to achieve target swim volume.
	Run endurance focus	**Total-session target volume = 7 miles.** Set 1: 4.5 miles or 40 to 50 minutes continuously at marathon-mile target velocity. Set 2: 17.5-minute strength endurance work running up a 2% to 4% grade at aerobic speed. Set 3: Additional aerobic running (likely downhill) to achieve target run volume.

Mesocycle 2: Race-Preparation Phase Week 5

Day	Training sessions	Specific session details
Monday	No training	
Tuesday	Run speed focus	**Total-session target volume = 11 miles.** Sets 1-6: Repeat week 1. Set 7: 35-minute strength endurance work using a weighted vest or incline on the treadmill. Combine a speed and grade (and vest weight if used) that allow for a comfortable aerobic heart rate. A 2% grade is a good starting point. Set 8: Additional aerobic running to achieve target volume.
	Bike speed focus	**Total-session target volume = 36 miles.** Sets 1-6: Repeat week 1. Set 7: 70-minute strength endurance set using a gear that produces 40 to 60 rpm at aerobic intensity in race position. Set 8: Additional aerobic cycling to achieve target cycle volume.
Wednesday	Swim speed focus	**Total-session target volume = 2,800 yards.** Sets 1-6: Repeat week 1. Set 7: 1,000-yard strength endurance swim at aerobic intensity using paddles. Set 8: Aerobic swim or set to achieve target swim volume.
	Weight training (strength)	1×12 reps at 50% 1RM. 2×6 to 8 reps at 85% 1RM. Complete all swim-, bike-, and run-specific and supplemental movements.
Thursday	Bike race-pace focus	**Total-session target volume = 36 miles.** Set 1: 3×9 miles at target 56-mile velocity with 5-minute easy spin. Set 2: 1- to 2-minute easy spin. Use an appropriate cadence target to help select your gears. Set 3: Additional aerobic cycling to achieve target cycle volume.
	Run race-pace focus	**Total-session target volume = 11 miles.** Set 1: 3×3 miles at 13.1-mile target velocity with 400-meter recovery walk or jog. Set 2: Additional aerobic running to achieve target volume.

Day	Training sessions	Specific session details
Friday	Swim race-pace focus	**Total-session target volume = 2,800 yards.** Set 1: 2 × 800 and 1 × 400 yards at target 2,000-yard velocity with 60-second rest. Set 2: 100-yard easy swim. Set 3: Aerobic swim or set to achieve target swim volume.
Saturday	Bike endurance focus	**Total-session target volume = 60 miles.** Set 1: 32 miles or 110 to 145 minutes continuously at target cadence and 112-mile target velocity. Focus on taking in fluids and nutrition as you will in the target race. Set 2: 70-minute strength endurance set using a gear that produces 40 to 60 rpm at aerobic intensity in race position. Set 3: Additional aerobic cycling to achieve target cycle volume.
	Weight training (power and muscular endurance)	1 × 20 reps at 50% 1RM. 2 × 6 reps at 50% 1RM explosive. Complete all swim-, bike-, and run-specific and supplemental movements and plyometrics.
Sunday	Swim endurance focus	**Total-session target volume = 3,400 yards.** Set 1: 32 to 38 minutes or 2,000 yards continuously using at least one head lift per 25 yards or every 12 to 20 strokes at target 3,200-yard velocity. Wear the equipment (goggles, wet suit, race suit) you will wear in the race. Set 2: 1,000-yard strength endurance swim at aerobic intensity using paddles. Set 3: Aerobic swim or set to achieve target swim volume.
	Run endurance focus	**Total-session target volume = 14 miles.** Set 1: 9 miles or 80 to 100 minutes continuously at marathon-mile target velocity. Set 2: 35-minute strength endurance work running up a 2% to 4% grade at aerobic speed. Set 3: Additional aerobic running (likely downhill) to achieve target run volume.

Mesocycle 2: Race-Preparation Phase Week 6

Day	Training sessions	Specific session details
Monday	No training	
Tuesday	Run speed focus	**Total-session target volume = 12 miles.** Sets 1-6: Repeat week 1. Set 7: 40-minute strength endurance work using a weighted vest or incline on the treadmill. Combine a speed and grade (and vest weight if used) that allow for a comfortable aerobic heart rate. A 2% grade is a good starting point. Set 8: Additional aerobic running to achieve target volume.
	Bike speed focus	**Total-session target volume = 40 miles.** Sets 1-6: Repeat week 1. Set 7: 80-minute strength endurance set using a gear that produces 40 to 60 rpm at aerobic intensity in race position. Set 8: Additional aerobic cycling to achieve target cycle volume.
Wednesday	Swim speed focus	**Total-session target volume = 3,000 yards.** Sets 1-6: Repeat week 1. Set 7: 1,100-yard strength endurance swim at aerobic intensity using paddles. Set 8: Aerobic swim or set to achieve target swim volume.
	Weight training (strength)	1 × 12 reps at 50% 1RM. 2 × 6 to 8 reps at 85% 1RM. Complete all swim-, bike-, and run-specific and supplemental movements.
Thursday	Bike race-pace focus	**Total-session target volume = 40 miles.** Set 1: 3 × 10 miles at target 56-mile velocity with 5-minute easy spin. Set 2: 1- to 2-minute easy spin. Use an appropriate cadence target to help select your gears. Set 3: Additional aerobic cycling to achieve target cycle volume.
	Run race-pace focus	**Total-session target volume = 12 miles.** Set 1: 3 × 3.5 miles at 13.1-mile target velocity with 400-meter recovery walk or jog. Set 2: Additional aerobic running to achieve target volume.

Day	Training sessions	Specific session details
Friday	Swim race-pace focus	**Total-session target volume = 3,000 yards.** Set 1: 2 × 900 and 1 × 200 yards at target 2,000-yard velocity with 60-second rest. Set 2: 100-yard easy swim. Set 3: Aerobic swim or set to achieve target swim volume.
Saturday	Bike endurance focus	**Total-session target volume = 66 miles.** Set 1: 34 miles or 115 to 150 minutes continuously at target cadence and 112-mile target velocity. Focus on taking in fluids and nutrition as you will in the target race. Set 2: 80-minute strength endurance set using a gear that produces 40 to 60 rpm at aerobic intensity in race position. Set 3: Additional aerobic cycling to achieve target cycle volume.
	Weight training (power and muscular endurance)	1 × 20 reps at 50% 1RM. 2 × 6 reps at 50% 1RM explosive. Complete all swim-, bike-, and run-specific and supplemental movements and plyometrics.
Sunday	Swim endurance focus	**Total-session target volume = 3,800 yards.** Set 1: 36 to 42 minutes or 2,200 yards continuously using at least one head lift per 25 yards or every 12 to 20 strokes at target 3,200-yard velocity. Wear the equipment (goggles, wet suit, race suit) you will wear in the race. Set 2: 1,100-yard strength endurance swim at aerobic intensity using paddles. Set 3: Aerobic swim or set to achieve target swim volume.
	Run endurance focus	**Total-session target volume = 15 miles.** Set 1: 10 miles or 90 to 110 minutes continuously at marathon-mile target velocity. Set 2: 40-minute strength endurance work running up a 2% to 4% grade at aerobic speed. Set 3: Additional aerobic running (likely downhill) to achieve target run volume.

Mesocycle 2: Race-Preparation Phase Week 7

This is the first week of taper for the run only.

Day	Training sessions	Specific session details
Monday	No training	
Tuesday	Run speed focus	**Total-session target volume = 8 miles.** Set 1: 2 × 100 meters (track) or 2 × 20 seconds (treadmill) at target 400-meter velocity with 100-meter walk or jog (track) or 30-second recovery walk off treadmill. Set 2: 400-meter recovery walk or jog (track) or 1- to 2-minute easy jog (treadmill). Set 3: 2 × 200 meters (track) or 2 × 40 seconds (treadmill) at 800-meter target velocity with 100-meter walk or jog (track) or 40-second recovery walk off treadmill. Set 4: 400-meter recovery walk or jog (track) or 1- to 2-minute easy jog (treadmill). Set 5: 2 × 400 meters (track) or 2 × 1:30 (treadmill) at 1,600-meter target velocity with 100-meter walk or jog (track) or 30-second recovery walk off treadmill. Set 6: 400-meter recovery walk or jog (track) or 1- to 2-minute easy jog (treadmill). Set 7: 25-minute strength endurance work using a weighted vest or incline on the treadmill. Combine a speed and grade (and vest weight if used) that allow for a comfortable aerobic heart rate. A 2% grade is a good starting point. Set 8: Additional aerobic running to achieve target volume.
	Bike speed focus	**Total-session target volume = 44 miles.** Sets 1-6: Repeat week 1. Set 7: 90-minute strength endurance set using a gear that produces 40 to 60 rpm at aerobic intensity in race position. Set 8: Additional aerobic cycling to achieve target cycle volume.
Wednesday	Swim speed focus	**Total-session target volume = 3,200 yards.** Sets 1-6: Repeat week 1. Set 7: 1,200-yard strength endurance swim at aerobic intensity using paddles. Set 8: Aerobic swim or set to achieve target swim volume.
	Weight training (strength)	1 × 12 reps at 50% 1RM. 2 × 6 to 8 reps at 85% 1RM. Complete all swim-, bike-, and run-specific and supplemental movements.

Day	Training sessions	Specific session details
Thursday	Bike race-pace focus	**Total-session target volume = 44 miles.** Set 1: 3 × 11 miles at target 56-mile velocity with 5-minute easy spin. Set 2: 1- to 2-minute easy spin. Use an appropriate cadence target to help select your gears. Set 3: Additional aerobic cycling to achieve target cycle volume.
	Run race-pace focus	**Total-session target volume = 8 miles.** Set 1: 3 × 1.5 miles at 13.1-mile target velocity with 400-meter recovery walk or jog. Set 2: Additional aerobic running to achieve target volume.
Friday	Swim race-pace focus	**Total-session target volume = 3,200 yards.** Set 1: 2 × 1,000 yards at target 2,000-yard velocity with 60-second rest. Set 2: 100-yard easy swim. Set 3: Aerobic swim or set to achieve target swim volume.
Saturday	Bike endurance focus	**Total-session target volume = 72 miles.** Set 1: 36 miles or 120 to 155 minutes continuously at target cadence and 112-mile target velocity. Focus on taking in fluids and nutrition as you will in the target race. Set 2: 90-minute strength endurance set using a gear that produces 40 to 60 rpm at aerobic intensity in race position. Set 3: Additional aerobic cycling to achieve target cycle volume.
	Weight training (power and muscular endurance)	1 × 20 reps at 50% 1RM. 2 × 6 reps at 50% 1RM explosive. Complete all swim-, bike-, and run-specific and supplemental movements and plyometrics.
Sunday	Swim endurance focus	**Total-session target volume = 4,000 yards.** Set 1: 40 to 46 minutes or 2,400 yards continuously using at least one head lift per 25 yards or every 12 to 20 strokes at target 3,200-yard velocity. Wear the equipment (goggles, wet suit, race suit) you will wear in the race. Set 2: 1,200-yard strength endurance swim at aerobic intensity using paddles. Set 3: Aerobic swim or set to achieve target swim volume.
	Run endurance focus	**Total-session target volume = 8 miles.** Set 1: 5 miles or 45 to 55 minutes continuously at marathon-mile target velocity. Set 2: 25-minute strength endurance work running up a 2% to 4% grade at aerobic speed. Set 3: Additional aerobic running (likely downhill) to achieve target run volume.

Mesocycle 2: Race-Preparation Phase Week 8 (Taper)

This is the second week of taper for the run.

Day	Training sessions	Specific session details
Monday	No training	
Tuesday	Run speed focus	**Total-session target volume = 4 miles.** Include aerobic work, several alactates, and one or two 400-meter efforts at race pace only. Volume is 30% or less of the previous week's training sessions.
	Bike speed focus	**Total-session target volume = 14 miles.** Include aerobic work, several alactates, and one or two 1-minute efforts at race pace only. Volume is 30% or less of the previous week's training sessions.
Wednesday	Swim speed focus	**Total-session target volume = 1,600 yards.** Set 1: 2 × 25 yards at target 100-yard velocity with equal rest. Set 2: 50-yard easy swim. Set 3: 2 × 50 yards at 200-yard target velocity with 30-second rest. Set 4: 50-yard easy swim. Set 5: 2 × 100 yards at 500-yard target velocity with 40-second rest. Set 6: 100-yard easy swim. Set 7: Aerobic swim or set to achieve target swim volume.
	Weight training (strength)	1 × 6 reps at 50% 1RM. 1 × 3 or 4 reps at 85% 1RM. Complete all swim-, bike-, and run-specific and supplemental movements.
Thursday	Bike race-pace focus	**Total-session target volume = 10 miles.** This work is replaced by the race at the end of the week. Do aerobic cycling with one or two 1-minute efforts at race pace to reach your target volume, which is 50% of previous 3 weeks' training sessions.
	Run race-pace focus	**Total-session target volume = 3 miles.** This work is replaced by the race at the end of the week. Include aerobic work and one or two 400-meter efforts at race pace only. Volume is 30% or less of the previous week's training sessions.

Day	Training sessions	Specific session details
Friday	Swim race-pace focus	**Total-session target volume = 1,200 yards.** Include aerobic work, several alactates, and one or two 50-yard efforts at race pace only. Volume is 30% or less of the previous week's training sessions.
Saturday*	Bike endurance focus	This is replaced by the target race.
	Weight training (power and muscular endurance)	Eliminate weight training and plyometric exercises before race.
Sunday	Swim endurance focus	This is replaced by the target race.
	Run endurance focus	This is replaced by the target race.

If racing on Sunday, complete a **short** warm-up in all three sports on the course Saturday.

Ironman Distance

Term

Minimum 12 weeks to complete the Ironman distance in triathlon in the 2.4-mile swim, 112-mile bicycle, and 26.2-mile run range after preparing for a half-Ironman-distance race.

Training Periodization

This program* assumes an earlier period of preparation for half-Ironman-distance racing or that you have developed your training tolerance to the starting points indicated. As with the half-Ironman program, the race-preparation period extends your general aerobic endurance as well as your one-day endurance to the point where you can race an Ironman-length competition. Basic speed is maintained as in the half-Ironman program. You maintain a range of race-specific speeds by introducing the concept of rotating race-pace training sets at different distances across microcycles in a mesocycle. You progress in endurance efforts in a series of cycles to allow for increased restoration time as you exceed your typical training distances by proportionately greater amounts with your longest endurance sessions.

Mesocycle 1: Race-Preparation Phase

Week 1: Race prep 1

Week 2: Race prep 2

Week 3: Race prep 3

Week 4: Race prep 4

Mesocycle 2: Race-Preparation Phase

Week 5: Race prep 1

Week 6: Race prep 2

Week 7: Race prep 3

Week 8: Race prep 4

Mesocycle 3: Race-Preparation Phase

Week 9: Race prep 1

Week 10: Race prep 2

Week 11: Race prep 3 (taper first week running only**)

Week 12: Race prep 4 (taper) with target race

*Presumes a 12-week block of time and previous buildup in volume from the age-group half-Ironman-distance program.
**Taper begins earlier for running only due to longer time period required for reducing accumulated stress in an eccentric loading activity.

Race-Preparation Block Main Sets and Individual Progressions

The tables on pages 242 through 265 give a schedule of the main sets for each focused training session. Complete a standard warm-up before the workout and a cool-down afterward. Aerobic sets are not described and can be of a variety of formats; however, a progression in overall duration is indicated. The speed sets are the same as used in previous programs. The assumption is that you will maintain your current speeds or power outputs for these sets throughout the mesocycle by repeating the sessions without progressions. This allows you to adapt to your race-specific training sessions, which in this case are the endurance-focused sessions as well.

The race-pace sets rotate sprint distance, Olympic distance, and half-Ironman distance across the spectrum of each mesocycle. They are also maintenance sets based on the level of work established in the previous programs. Progressions here would be in speed of the set if adaptation indicates the need to do so. The endurance-focused sets are presented in a week-by-week or microcycle-by-microcycle format so that you can see the progressions. Ride all bike sessions in your race position. Do run and bike race-pace sessions on a measured course. Do run and bike endurance sessions on a race-specific course (hills, turns) on a road or dirt trail (depending on type of race). Make progressions only if adaptation has occurred (see chapters 1 and 5).

Mesocycle 1: Race-Preparation Phase Week 1

Day	Training sessions	Specific session details
Monday	No training	
Tuesday	Run speed focus	**Total-session target volume = 12 miles.** Set 1: 4 × 100 meters (track) or 4 × 20 seconds (treadmill) at target 400-meter velocity with 100-meter walk or jog (track) or 30-second recovery walk off treadmill. Set 2: 400-meter recovery walk or jog (track) or 1- to 2-minute easy jog (treadmill). Set 3: 4 × 200 meters (track) or 4 × 40 seconds (treadmill) at 800-meter target velocity with 100-meter walk or jog (track) or 40-second recovery walk off treadmill. Set 4: 400-meter recovery walk or jog (track) or 1- to 2-minute easy jog (treadmill). Set 5: 4 × 400 meters (track) or 4 × 1:30 (treadmill) at 1,600-meter target velocity with 100-meter walk or jog (track) or 30-second recovery walk off treadmill. Set 6: 400-meter recovery walk or jog (track) or 1- to 2-minute easy jog (treadmill). Set 7: 40-minute strength endurance work using a weighted vest or incline on the treadmill. Combine a speed and grade (and vest weight if used) that allow for a comfortable aerobic heart rate. A 2% grade is a good starting point. Set 8: Additional aerobic running to achieve target volume.
	Bike speed focus	**Total-session target volume = 45 miles.** Set 1: 4 × 0.125 mile at target 0.5-mile velocity or power with equal rest (easy spin recovery). Set 2: 1- to 2-minute easy spin. Set 3: 4 × 0.25 mile at 1-mile target velocity with 30-second spin recovery. Set 4: 1- to 2-minute easy spin. Set 5: 4 × 0.5 mile at 2-mile target velocity with 40-second spin recovery. Set 6: 1- to 2-minute easy spin. Set 7: 60-minute strength endurance set using a gear that produces 40 to 60 rpm at aerobic intensity in race position. Set 8: Additional aerobic cycling to achieve target cycle volume.
Wednesday	Swim speed focus	**Total-session target volume = 3,200 yards.** Set 1: 4 × 25 yards at target 100-yard velocity with equal rest. Set 2: 50-yard easy swim. Set 3: 4 × 50 yards at 200-yard target velocity with 30-second rest. Set 4: 50-yard easy swim. Set 5: 4 × 100 yards at 500-yard target velocity with 40-second rest. Set 6: 100-yard easy swim. Set 7: 1,200-yard strength endurance swim at aerobic intensity using paddles. Set 8: Aerobic swim or set to achieve target swim volume.

Day	Training sessions	Specific session details
Wednesday (continued)	Weight training (strength)	1 × 12 reps at 50% 1RM. 2 × 6 to 8 reps at 85% 1RM. No weight progression—same reps and weight maintained as during the base period. Complete all swim-, bike-, and run-specific and supplemental movements.
Thursday	Bike race-pace focus	**Total-session target volume = 45 miles.** Set 1: 4 × 3 miles at target 12.4-mile (20K) velocity with 1-minute easy spin. Set 2: 1- to 2-minute easy spin. Use an appropriate cadence target to help select your gears. Set 3: Additional aerobic cycling to achieve target cycle volume.
	Run race-pace focus	**Total-session target volume = 12 miles.** Set 1: 6 × 800 meters at 3.1-mile (5K) target velocity with 400-meter recovery walk or jog. Set 2: Additional aerobic running to achieve target volume.
Friday	Swim race-pace focus	**Total-session target volume = 3,200 yards.** Set 1: 5 × 100 yards at target 500-yard velocity with 30-second rest. Set 2: 100-yard easy swim. Set 3: 1,200-yard strength endurance set. Set 4: Aerobic swim or set to achieve target swim volume.
Saturday	Bike endurance focus	**Total-session target volume = 75 miles.** Set 1: 36 miles or 108 to 144 minutes continuously at target cadence and 112-mile target velocity. Focus on taking in fluids and nutrition as you will in the target race. Set 2: 60-minute strength endurance set using a gear that produces 40 to 60 rpm at aerobic intensity in race position. Set 3: Additional aerobic cycling to achieve target cycle volume.
	Weight training (power and muscular endurance)	1 × 20 reps at 50% 1RM. 2 × 6 reps at 50% 1RM explosive. No weight progression—same reps and weight maintained as during the base period. Complete all swim-, bike-, and run-specific and supplemental movements and plyometrics.
Sunday	Swim endurance focus	**Total-session target volume = 4,500 yards.** Set 1: 35 to 50 minutes or 2,500 yards continuously using at least one head lift per 25 yards or every 12 to 20 strokes at target 4,000-yard velocity. Wear the equipment (goggles, wet suit, race suit) you will wear in the race. Divide this into shorter efforts to allow for food breaks. Set 2: 1,200-yard strength endurance swim at aerobic intensity using paddles. Set 3: Aerobic swim or set to achieve target swim volume.
	Run endurance focus	**Total-session target volume = 15 miles.** Set 1: 10 miles or 80 to 100 minutes continuously at marathon-mile target velocity. Include a short walk break (1 to 2 minutes) every mile to allow for partial recovery and a faster overall pace. Set 2: 45-minute strength endurance work running up a 2% to 4% grade at aerobic speed. Set 3: Additional aerobic running (likely downhill) to achieve target run volume.

Mesocycle 1: Race-Preparation Phase Week 2

Day	Training sessions	Specific session details
Monday	No training	
Tuesday	Run speed focus	**Total-session target volume = 11 miles.** Sets 1-6: Repeat week 1. Set 7: 35-minute strength endurance work using a weighted vest or incline on the treadmill. Combine a speed and grade (and vest weight if used) that allow for a comfortable aerobic heart rate. A 2% grade is a good starting point. Set 8: Additional aerobic running to achieve target volume.
	Bike speed focus	**Total-session target volume = 40 miles.** Sets 1-6: Repeat week 1. Set 7: 55-minute strength endurance set using a gear that produces 40 to 60 rpm at aerobic intensity in race position. Set 8: Additional aerobic cycling to achieve target cycle volume.
Wednesday	Swim speed focus	**Total-session target volume = 3,000 yards.** Sets 1-6: Repeat week 1. Set 7: 1,100-yard strength endurance swim at aerobic intensity using paddles. Set 8: Aerobic swim or set to achieve target swim volume.
	Weight training (strength)	1×12 reps at 50% 1RM. 2×6 to 8 reps at 85% 1RM. Complete all swim-, bike-, and run-specific and supplemental movements.
Thursday	Bike race-pace focus	**Total-session target volume = 40 miles.** Set 1: 3×8 miles at target 24.8-mile (40K) velocity with 5-minute easy spin. Set 2: 1- to 2-minute easy spin. Use an appropriate cadence target to help select your gears. Set 3: Additional aerobic cycling to achieve target cycle volume.
	Run race-pace focus	**Total-session target volume = 11 miles.** Set 1: $6 \times 1,600$ meters at 6.2-mile (10K) target velocity with 400-meter recovery walk or jog. Set 2: Additional aerobic running to achieve target volume.

Day	Training sessions	Specific session details
Friday	Swim race-pace focus	**Total-session target volume = 3,000 yards.** Set 1: 4 × 300 yards at target 1,600-yard velocity with 30-second rest. Set 2: 100-yard easy swim. Set 3: 1,200-yard strength endurance set. Set 4: Aerobic swim or set to achieve target swim volume.
Saturday	Bike endurance focus	**Total-session target volume = 66 miles.** Set 1: 32 miles or 96 to 128 minutes continuously at target cadence and 112-mile target velocity. Focus on taking in fluids and nutrition as you will in the target race. Set 2: 55-minute strength endurance set using a gear that produces 40 to 60 rpm at aerobic intensity in race position. Set 3: Additional aerobic cycling to achieve target cycle volume.
	Weight training (power and muscular endurance)	1 × 20 reps at 50% 1RM. 2 × 6 reps at 50% 1RM explosive. Complete all swim-, bike-, and run-specific and supplemental movements and plyometrics.
Sunday	Swim endurance focus	**Total-session target volume = 4,000 yards.** Set 1: 28 to 40 minutes or 2,000 yards continuously using at least one head lift per 25 yards or every 12 to 20 strokes at target 4,000-yard velocity. Wear the equipment (goggles, wet suit, race suit) you will wear in the race. Divide this into shorter efforts to allow for food breaks. Set 2: 1,200-yard strength endurance swim at aerobic intensity using paddles. Set 3: Aerobic swim or set to achieve target swim volume.
	Run endurance focus	**Total-session target volume = 13 miles.** Set 1: 8 miles or 64 to 80 minutes continuously at marathon-mile target velocity. Include a short walk break (1 to 2 minutes) every mile to allow for partial recovery and a faster overall pace. Set 2: 40-minute strength endurance work running up a 2% to 4% grade at aerobic speed. Set 3: Additional aerobic running (likely downhill) to achieve target run volume.

Mesocycle 1: Race-Preparation Phase Week 3

Day	Training sessions	Specific session details
Monday	No training	
Tuesday	Run speed focus	**Total-session target volume = 12 miles.** Sets 1-6: Repeat week 1. Set 7: 40-minute strength endurance work using a weighted vest or incline on the treadmill. Combine a speed and grade (and vest weight if used) that allow for a comfortable aerobic heart rate. A 2% grade is a good starting point. Set 8: Additional aerobic running to achieve target volume.
	Bike speed focus	**Total-session target volume = 50 miles.** Sets 1-6: Repeat week 1. Set 7: 60-minute strength endurance set using a gear that produces 40 to 60 rpm at aerobic intensity in race position. Set 8: Additional aerobic cycling to achieve target cycle volume.
Wednesday	Swim speed focus	**Total-session target volume = 3,200 yards.** Sets 1-6: Repeat week 1. Set 7: 1,000-yard strength endurance swim at aerobic intensity using paddles. Set 8: Aerobic swim or set to achieve target swim volume.
	Weight training (strength)	1×12 reps at 50% 1RM. 2×6 to 8 reps at 85% 1RM. Complete all swim-, bike-, and run-specific and supplemental movements.
Thursday	Bike race-pace focus	**Total-session target volume = 50 miles.** Set 1: 2×18 miles at target 56-mile velocity with 5-minute easy spin. Set 2: 1- to 2-minute easy spin. Use an appropriate cadence target to help select your gears. Set 3: Additional aerobic cycling to achieve target cycle volume.
	Run race-pace focus	**Total-session target volume = 12 miles.** Set 1: 3×3 miles at 13.1-mile target velocity with 800-meter recovery walk or jog. Set 2: Additional aerobic running to achieve target volume.

Day	Training sessions	Specific session details
Friday	Swim race-pace focus	**Total-session target volume = 3,200 yards.** Set 1: 2 × 800 yards or other equivalent set at target 2,000-yard velocity with 60-second rest. Set 2: 100-yard easy swim. Set 3: 1,200-yard strength endurance set. Set 4: Aerobic swim or set to achieve target swim volume.
Saturday	Bike endurance focus	**Total-session target volume = 85 miles.** Set 1: 44 miles or 105 to 135 minutes continuously at target cadence and 112-mile target velocity. Focus on taking in fluids and nutrition as you will in the target race. Set 2: 60-minute strength endurance set using a gear that produces 40 to 60 rpm at aerobic intensity in race position. Set 3: Additional aerobic cycling to achieve target cycle volume.
	Weight training (power and muscular endurance)	1 × 20 reps at 50% 1RM. 2 × 6 reps at 50% 1RM explosive. Complete all swim-, bike-, and run-specific and supplemental movements and plyometrics.
Sunday	Swim endurance focus	**Total-session target volume = 5,000 yards.** Set 1: 42 to 60 minutes or 3,000 yards continuously using at least one head lift per 25 yards or every 12 to 20 strokes at target 4,000-yard velocity. Wear the equipment (goggles, wet suit, race suit) you will wear in the race. Divide this into shorter efforts to allow for food breaks. Set 2: 1,200-yard strength endurance swim at aerobic intensity using paddles. Set 3: Aerobic swim or set to achieve target swim volume.
	Run endurance focus	**Total-session target volume = 17 miles.** Set 1: 11 miles or 88 to 110 minutes continuously at marathon-mile target velocity. Include a short walk break (1 to 2 minutes) every mile to allow for partial recovery and a faster overall pace. Set 2: 40-minute strength endurance work running up a 2% to 4% grade at aerobic speed. Set 3: Additional aerobic running (likely downhill) to achieve target run volume.

Mesocycle 1: Race-Preparation Phase Week 4 (Restoration)

Day	Training sessions	Specific session details
Monday	No training	
Tuesday	Run speed focus	**Total-session target volume = 6 miles.** Set 1: 2 × 100 meters (track) or 2 × 20 seconds (treadmill) at target 400-meter velocity with 100-meter walk or jog (track) or 30-second recovery walk off treadmill. Set 2: 400-meter recovery walk or jog (track) or 1- to 2-minute easy jog (treadmill). Set 3: 2 × 200 meters (track) or 2 × 40 seconds (treadmill) at 800-meter target velocity with 100-meter walk or jog (track) or 40-second recovery walk off treadmill. Set 4: 400-meter recovery walk or jog (track) or 1- to 2-minute easy jog (treadmill). Set 5: 2 × 400 meters (track) or 2 × 1:30 (treadmill) at 1,600-meter target velocity with 100-meter walk or jog (track) or 30-second recovery walk off treadmill. Set 6: 400-meter recovery walk or jog (track) or 1- to 2-minute easy jog (treadmill). Set 7: 20-minute strength endurance work using a weighted vest or incline on the treadmill. Combine a speed and grade (and vest weight if used) that allow for a comfortable aerobic heart rate. A 2% grade is a good starting point. Set 8: Additional aerobic running to achieve target volume.
	Bike speed focus	**Total-session target volume = 25 miles.** Set 1: 2 × 0.125 mile at target 0.5-mile velocity or power with equal rest (easy spin recovery). Set 2: 1- to 2-minute easy spin. Set 3: 2 × 0.25 mile at 1-mile target velocity with 30-second spin recovery. Set 4: 1- to 2-minute easy spin. Set 5: 2 × 0.5 mile at 2-mile target velocity with 40-second spin recovery. Set 6: 1- to 2-minute easy spin. Set 7: 30-minute strength endurance set using gear that produces 40 to 60 rpm at aerobic intensity in race position. Set 8: Additional aerobic cycling to achieve target cycle volume.
Wednesday	Swim speed focus	**Total-session target volume = 1,600 yards.** Set 1: 2 × 25 yards at target 100-yard velocity with equal rest. Set 2: 50-yard easy swim. Set 3: 2 × 50 yards at 200-yard target velocity with 30-second rest. Set 4: 50-yard easy swim. Set 5: 2 × 100 yards at 500-yard target velocity with 40-second rest. Set 6: 100-yard easy swim. Set 7: 600-yard strength endurance swim at aerobic intensity using paddles. Set 8: Aerobic swim or set to achieve target swim volume.
	Weight training (strength)	1 × 6 reps at 50% 1RM. 1 × 3 or 4 reps at 85% 1RM. Complete all swim-, bike-, and run-specific and supplemental movements.

Day	Training sessions	Specific session details
Thursday	Bike race-pace focus	**Total-session target volume = 25 miles.** Set 1: 2 × 9 miles at target 56-mile velocity with 3-minute easy spin. Set 2: 1- to 2-minute easy spin. Use an appropriate cadence target to help select your gears. Set 3: Additional aerobic cycling to achieve target cycle volume.
	Run race-pace focus	**Total-session target volume = 6 miles.** Set 1: 2 × 1.5 miles at 13.1-mile target velocity with 800-meter recovery walk or jog. Set 2: Additional aerobic running to achieve target volume.
Friday	Swim race-pace focus	**Total-session target volume = 1,600 yards.** Set 1: 3 × 350 yards at target 2,000-yard velocity with 60-second rest. Set 2: 100-yard easy swim. Set 3: Aerobic swim or set to achieve target swim volume.
Saturday	Bike endurance focus	**Total-session target volume = 42 miles.** Set 1: 22 miles or 66 to 88 minutes continuously at target cadence and 112-mile target velocity. Focus on taking in fluids and nutrition as you will in the target race. Set 2: 30-minute strength endurance set using a gear that produces 40 to 60 rpm at aerobic intensity in race position. Set 3: Additional aerobic cycling to achieve target cycle volume.
	Weight training (power and muscular endurance)	1 × 10 reps at 50% 1RM. 1 × 6 reps at 50% 1RM explosive. Complete all swim-, bike-, and run-specific and supplemental movements and plyometrics.
Sunday	Swim endurance focus	**Total-session target volume = 2,500 yards.** Set 1: 21 to 30 minutes or 1,500 yards continuously using at least one head lift per 25 yards or every 12 to 20 strokes at target 4,000-yard velocity. Wear the equipment (goggles, wet suit, race suit) you will wear in the race. Divide this into shorter efforts to allow for food breaks. Set 2: 600-yard strength endurance swim at aerobic intensity using paddles. Set 3: Aerobic swim or set to achieve target swim volume.
	Run endurance focus	**Total-session target volume = 8.5 miles.** Set 1: 4 miles or 32 to 40 minutes continuously at marathon-mile target velocity. Include a short walk break (1 to 2 minutes) every mile to allow for partial recovery and a faster overall pace. Set 2: 20-minute strength endurance work running up a 2% to 4% grade at aerobic speed. Set 3: Additional aerobic running (likely downhill) to achieve target run volume.

Mesocycle 2: Race-Preparation Phase Week 5

Day	Training sessions	Specific session details
Monday	No training	
Tuesday	Run speed focus	**Total-session target volume = 13 miles.** Sets 1-6: Repeat week 1. Set 7: 45-minute strength endurance work using a weighted vest or incline on the treadmill. Combine a speed and grade (and vest weight if used) that allow for a comfortable aerobic heart rate. A 2% grade is a good starting point. Set 8: Additional aerobic running to achieve target volume.
	Bike speed focus	**Total-session target volume = 55 miles.** Sets 1-6: Repeat week 1. Set 7: 70-minute strength endurance set using a gear that produces 40 to 60 rpm at aerobic intensity in race position. Set 8: Additional aerobic cycling to achieve target cycle volume.
Wednesday	Swim speed focus	**Total-session target volume = 3,400 yards.** Sets 1-6: Repeat week 1. Set 7: 1,000-yard strength endurance swim at aerobic intensity using paddles. Set 8: Aerobic swim or set to achieve target swim volume.
	Weight training (strength)	1 × 12 reps at 50% 1RM. 2 × 6 to 8 reps at 85% 1RM. Complete all swim-, bike-, and run-specific and supplemental movements.
Thursday	Bike race-pace focus	**Total-session target volume = 55 miles.** Set 1: 4 × 3 miles at target 12.4-mile (20K) velocity with 1-minute easy spin. Set 2: 1- to 2-minute easy spin. Use an appropriate cadence target to help select your gears. Set 3: Additional aerobic cycling to achieve target cycle volume.
	Run race-pace focus	**Total-session target volume = 13 miles.** Set 1: 6 × 800 meters at 3.1-mile (5K) target velocity with 400-meter recovery walk or jog. Set 2: Additional aerobic running to achieve target volume.

Day	Training sessions	Specific session details
Friday	Swim race-pace focus	**Total-session target volume = 3,400 yards.** Set 1: 5 × 100 yards at target 500-yard velocity with 30-second rest. Set 2: 100-yard easy swim. Set 3: 1,300-yard strength endurance set. Set 4: Aerobic swim or set to achieve target swim volume.
Saturday	Bike endurance focus	**Total-session target volume = 95 miles.** Set 1: 52 miles or 156 to 208 minutes continuously at target cadence and 112-mile target velocity. Focus on taking in fluids and nutrition as you will in the target race. Set 2: 70-minute strength endurance set using a gear that produces 40 to 60 rpm at aerobic intensity in race position. Set 3: Additional aerobic cycling to achieve target cycle volume.
	Weight training (power and muscular endurance)	1 × 20 reps at 50% 1RM. 2 × 6 reps at 50% 1RM explosive. Complete all swim-, bike-, and run-specific and supplemental movements and plyometrics.
Sunday	Swim endurance focus	**Total-session target volume = 5,000 yards.** Set 1: 42 to 60 minutes or 3,000 yards continuously using at least one head lift per 25 yards or every 12 to 20 strokes at target 4,000-yard velocity. Wear the equipment (goggles, wet suit, race suit) you will wear in the race. Divide this into shorter efforts to allow for food breaks. Set 2: 1,300-yard strength endurance swim at aerobic intensity using paddles. Set 3: Aerobic swim or set to achieve target swim volume.
	Run endurance focus	**Total-session target volume = 19 miles.** Set 1: 12 miles or 96 to 120 minutes continuously at marathon-mile target velocity. Include a short walk break (1 to 2 minutes) every mile to allow for partial recovery and a faster overall pace. Set 2: 45-minute strength endurance work running up a 2% to 4% grade at aerobic speed. Set 3: Additional aerobic running (likely downhill) to achieve target run volume.

Mesocycle 2: Race-Preparation Phase Week 6

Day	Training sessions	Specific session details
Monday	No training	
Tuesday	Run speed focus	**Total-session target volume = 11 miles.** Set 1: 3 × 100 meters (track) or 3 × 20 seconds (treadmill) at target 400-meter velocity with 100-meter walk or jog (track) or 30-second recovery walk off treadmill. Set 2: 400-meter recovery walk or jog (track) or 1- to 2-minute easy jog (treadmill). Set 3: 3 × 200 meters (track) or 3 × 40 seconds (treadmill) at 800-meter target velocity with 100-meter walk or jog (track) or 40-second recovery walk off treadmill. Set 4: 400-meter recovery walk or jog (track) or 1- to 2-minute easy jog (treadmill). Set 5: 3 × 400 meters (track) or 3 × 1:30 (treadmill) at 1,600-meter target velocity with 100-meter walk or jog (track) or 30-second recovery walk off treadmill. Set 6: 400-meter recovery walk or jog (track) or 1- to 2-minute easy jog (treadmill). Set 7: 35-minute strength endurance work using a weighted vest or incline on the treadmill. Combine a speed and grade (and vest weight if used) that allow for a comfortable aerobic heart rate. A 2% grade is a good starting point. Set 8: Additional aerobic running to achieve target volume.
	Bike speed focus	**Total-session target volume = 45 miles.** Set 1: 3 × 0.125 mile at target 0.5-mile velocity or power with equal rest (easy spin recovery). Set 2: 1- to 2-minute easy spin. Set 3: 3 × 0.25 mile at 1-mile target velocity with 30-second spin recovery. Set 4: 1- to 2-minute easy spin. Set 5: 3 × 0.5 mile at 2-mile target velocity with 40-second spin recovery. Set 6: 1- to 2-minute easy spin. Set 7: 60-minute strength endurance set using a gear that produces 40 to 60 rpm at aerobic intensity in race position. Set 8: Additional aerobic cycling to achieve target cycle volume.
Wednesday	Swim speed focus	**Total-session target volume = 3,200 yards.** Set 1: 3 × 25 yards at target 100-yard velocity with equal rest. Set 2: 50-yard easy swim. Set 3: 3 × 50 yards at 200-yard target velocity with 30-second rest. Set 4: 50-yard easy swim. Set 5: 3 × 100 yards at 500-yard target velocity with 40-second rest. Set 6: 100-yard easy swim. Set 7: 1,200-yard strength endurance swim at aerobic intensity using paddles. Set 8: Aerobic swim or set to achieve target swim volume.
	Weight training (strength)	1 × 12 reps at 50% 1RM. 2 × 6 to 8 reps at 85% 1RM. Complete all swim-, bike-, and run-specific and supplemental movements.

Day	Training sessions	Specific session details
Thursday	Bike race-pace focus	**Total-session target volume = 45 miles.** Set 1: 3 × 8 miles at target 24.8-mile (40K) velocity with 5-minute easy spin. Set 2: 1- to 2-minute easy spin. Use an appropriate cadence target to help select your gears. Set 3: Additional aerobic cycling to achieve target cycle volume.
	Run race-pace focus	**Total-session target volume = 11 miles.** Set 1: 6 × 1,600 meters at 6.2-mile (10K) target velocity with 400-meter recovery walk or jog. Set 2: Additional aerobic running to achieve target volume.
Friday	Swim race-pace focus	**Total-session target volume = 3,200 yards.** Set 1: 5 × 300 yards at target 1,600-yard velocity with 30-second rest. Set 2: 100-yard easy swim. Set 3: 1,200-yard strength endurance set. Set 4: Aerobic swim or set to achieve target swim volume.
Saturday	Bike endurance focus	**Total-session target volume = 70 miles.** Set 1: 36 miles or 108 to 144 minutes continuously at target cadence and 112-mile target velocity. Focus on taking in fluids and nutrition as you will in the target race. Set 2: 60-minute strength endurance set using a gear that produces 40 to 60 rpm at aerobic intensity in race position. Set 3: Additional aerobic cycling to achieve target cycle volume.
	Weight training (power and muscular endurance)	1 × 20 reps at 50% 1RM. 2 × 6 reps at 50% 1RM explosive. Complete all swim-, bike-, and run-specific and supplemental movements and plyometrics.
Sunday	Swim endurance focus	**Total-session target volume = 4,500 yards.** Set 1: 35 to 50 minutes or 2,500 yards continuously using at least one head lift per 25 yards or every 12 to 20 strokes at target 4,000-yard velocity. Wear the equipment (goggles, wet suit, race suit) you will wear in the race. Divide this into shorter efforts to allow for food breaks. Set 2: 1,200-yard strength endurance swim at aerobic intensity using paddles. Set 3: Aerobic swim or set to achieve target swim volume.
	Run endurance focus	**Total-session target volume = 14 miles.** Set 1: 9 miles or 72 to 90 minutes continuously at marathon-mile target velocity. Include a short walk break (1 to 2 minutes) every mile to allow for partial recovery and a faster overall pace. Set 2: 40-minute strength endurance work running up a 2% to 4% grade at aerobic speed. Set 3: Additional aerobic running (likely downhill) to achieve target run volume.

Mesocycle 2: Race-Preparation Phase Week 7

This is the first week of taper for the run only.

Day	Training sessions	Specific session details
Monday	No training	
Tuesday	Run speed focus	**Total-session target volume = 13 miles.** Sets 1-6: Repeat week 1. Set 7: 40-minute strength endurance work using a weighted vest or incline on the treadmill. Combine a speed and grade (and vest weight if used) that allow for a comfortable aerobic heart rate. A 2% grade is a good starting point. Set 8: Additional aerobic running to achieve target volume.
	Bike speed focus	**Total-session target volume = 60 miles.** Sets 1-6: Repeat week 1. Set 7: 70-minute strength endurance set using a gear that produces 40 to 60 rpm at aerobic intensity in race position. Set 8: Additional aerobic cycling to achieve target cycle volume.
Wednesday	Swim speed focus	**Total-session target volume = 3,600 yards.** Sets 1-6: Repeat week 1. Set 7: 1,400-yard strength endurance swim at aerobic intensity using paddles. Set 8: Aerobic swim or set to achieve target swim volume.
	Weight training (strength)	1 × 12 reps at 50% 1RM. 2 × 6 to 8 reps at 85% 1RM. Complete all swim-, bike-, and run-specific and supplemental movements.
Thursday	Bike race-pace focus	**Total-session target volume = 60 miles.** Set 1: 3 × 18 miles at target 56-mile velocity with 5-minute easy spin. Set 2: 1- to 2-minute easy spin. Use an appropriate cadence target to help select your gears. Set 3: Additional aerobic cycling to achieve target cycle volume.
	Run race-pace focus	**Total-session target volume = 13 miles.** Set 1: 3 × 3 miles at 13.1-mile target velocity with 800-meter recovery walk or jog. Set 2: Additional aerobic running to achieve target volume.

Day	Training sessions	Specific session details
Friday	Swim race-pace focus	**Total-session target volume = 3,600 yards.** Set 1: 2 × 900 yards or equivalent set at target 2,000-yard velocity with 60-second rest. Set 2: 100-yard easy swim. Set 3: 1,400-yard strength endurance set. Set 4: Aerobic swim or set to achieve target swim volume.
Saturday	Bike endurance focus	**Total-session target volume = 105 miles.** Set 1: 60 miles or 180 to 240 minutes continuously at target cadence and 112-mile target velocity. Focus on taking in fluids and nutrition as you will in the target race. Set 2: 70-minute strength endurance set using a gear that produces 40 to 60 rpm at aerobic intensity in race position. Set 3: Additional aerobic cycling to achieve target cycle volume.
	Weight training (power and muscular endurance)	1 × 20 reps at 50% 1RM. 2 × 6 reps at 50% 1RM explosive. Complete all swim-, bike-, and run-specific and supplemental movements and plyometrics.
Sunday	Swim endurance focus	**Total-session target volume = 6,000 yards.** Set 1: 49 to 70 minutes or 3,500 yards continuously using at least one head lift per 25 yards or every 12 to 20 strokes at target 4,000-yard velocity. Wear the equipment (goggles, wet suit, race suit) you will wear in the race. Divide this into shorter efforts to allow for food breaks. Set 2: 1,400-yard strength endurance swim at aerobic intensity using paddles. Set 3: Aerobic swim or set to achieve target swim volume.
	Run endurance focus	**Total-session target volume = 21 miles.** Set 1: 13 miles or 104 to 130 minutes continuously at marathon-mile target velocity. Include a short walk break (1 to 2 minutes) every mile to allow for partial recovery and a faster overall pace. Set 2: 45-minute strength endurance work running up a 2% to 4% grade at aerobic speed. Set 3: Additional aerobic running (likely downhill) to achieve target run volume.

Mesocycle 2: Race-Preparation Phase Week 8 (Restoration)

Day	Training sessions	Specific session details
Monday	No training	
Tuesday	Run speed focus	**Total-session target volume = 6.5 miles.** Set 1: 2 × 100 meters (track) or 2 × 20 seconds (treadmill) at target 400-meter velocity with 100-meter walk or jog (track) or 30-second recovery walk off treadmill. Set 2: 400-meter recovery walk or jog (track) or 1- to 2-minute easy jog (treadmill). Set 3: 2 × 200 meters (track) or 2 × 40 seconds (treadmill) at 800-meter target velocity with 100-meter walk or jog (track) or 40-second recovery walk off treadmill. Set 4: 400-meter recovery walk or jog (track) or 1- to 2-minute easy jog (treadmill). Set 5: 2 × 400 meters (track) or 2 × 1:30 (treadmill) at 1,600-meter target velocity with 100-meter walk or jog (track) or 30-second recovery walk off treadmill. Set 6: 400-meter recovery walk or jog (track) or 1- to 2-minute easy jog (treadmill). Set 7: 20-minute strength endurance work using a weighted vest or incline on the treadmill. Combine a speed and grade (and vest weight if used) that allow for a comfortable aerobic heart rate. A 2% grade is a good starting point. Set 8: Additional aerobic running to achieve target volume.
	Bike speed focus	**Total-session target volume = 30 miles.** Set 1: 2 × 0.125 mile at target 0.5-mile velocity or power with equal rest (easy spin recovery). Set 2: 1- to 2-minute easy spin. Set 3: 2 × 0.25 mile at 1-mile target velocity with 30-second spin recovery. Set 4: 1- to 2-minute easy spin. Set 5: 2 × 0.5 mile at 2-mile target velocity with 40-second spin recovery. Set 6: 1- to 2-minute easy spin. Set 7: 30-minute strength endurance set using a gear that produces 40 to 60 rpm at aerobic intensity in race position. Set 8: Additional aerobic cycling to achieve target cycle volume.
Wednesday	Swim speed focus	**Total-session target volume = 1,600 yards.** Set 1: 2 × 25 yards at target 100-yard velocity with equal rest. Set 2: 50-yard easy swim. Set 3: 2 × 50 yards at 200-yard target velocity with 30-second rest. Set 4: 50-yard easy swim. Set 5: 2 × 100 yards at 500-yard target velocity with 40-second rest. Set 6: 100-yard easy swim. Set 7: 700-yard strength endurance swim at aerobic intensity using paddles. Set 8: Aerobic swim or set to achieve target swim volume.
	Weight training (strength)	1 × 6 reps at 50% 1RM. 1 × 3-4 reps at 85% 1RM. Complete all swim-, bike-, and run-specific and supplemental movements.

Day	Training sessions	Specific session details
Thursday	Bike race-pace focus	**Total-session target volume = 30 miles.** Set 1: 2 × 9 miles at target 56-mile velocity with 3-minute easy spin. Set 2: 1- to 2-minute easy spin. Use an appropriate cadence target to help select your gears. Set 3: Additional aerobic cycling to achieve target cycle volume.
	Run race-pace focus	**Total-session target volume = 6.5 miles.** Set 1: 3 × 1.5 miles at 13.1-mile target velocity with 800-meter recovery walk or jog. Set 2: Additional aerobic running to achieve target volume.
Friday	Swim race-pace focus	**Total-session target volume = 1,600 yards.** Set 1: 3 × 300 yards at target 2,000-yard velocity with 60-second rest. Set 2: 100-yard easy swim. Set 3: Aerobic swim or set to achieve target swim volume.
Saturday	Bike endurance focus	**Total-session target volume = 52 miles.** Set 1: 30 miles or 90 to 120 minutes continuously at target cadence and 112-mile target velocity. Focus on taking in fluids and nutrition as you will in the target race. Set 2: 35-minute strength endurance set using a gear that produces 40 to 60 rpm at aerobic intensity in race position. Set 3: Additional aerobic cycling to achieve target cycle volume.
	Weight training (power and muscular endurance)	1 × 10 reps at 50% 1RM. 1 × 6 reps at 50% 1RM explosive. Complete all swim-, bike-, and run-specific and supplemental movements and plyometrics.
Sunday	Swim endurance focus	**Total-session target volume = 3,000 yards.** Set 1: 28 to 40 minutes or 2,000 yards continuously using at least one head lift per 25 yards or every 12 to 20 strokes at target 4,000-yard velocity. Wear the equipment (goggles, wet suit, race suit) you will wear in the race. Divide this into shorter efforts to allow for food breaks. Set 2: 700-yard strength endurance swim at aerobic intensity using paddles. Set 3: Aerobic swim or set to achieve target swim volume.
	Run endurance focus	**Total-session target volume = 10.5 miles.** Set 1: 5 miles or 40 to 50 minutes continuously at marathon-mile target velocity. Include a short walk break (1 to 2 minutes) every mile to allow for partial recovery and a faster overall pace. Set 2: 20-minute strength endurance work running up a 2% to 4% grade at aerobic speed. Set 3: Additional aerobic running (likely downhill) to achieve target run volume.

Mesocycle 3: Race-Preparation Phase Week 9

Day	Training sessions	Specific session details
Monday	No training	
Tuesday	Run speed focus	**Total-session target volume = 13 miles.** Sets 1-6: Repeat week 1. Set 7: 40-minute strength endurance work using a weighted vest or incline on the treadmill. Combine a speed and grade (and vest weight if used) that allow for a comfortable aerobic heart rate. A 2% grade is a good starting point. Set 8: Additional aerobic running to achieve target volume.
	Bike speed focus	**Total-session target volume = 60 miles.** Sets 1-6: Repeat week 1. Set 7: 70-minute strength endurance set using a gear that produces 40 to 60 rpm at aerobic intensity in race position. Set 8: Additional aerobic cycling to achieve target cycle volume.
Wednesday	Swim speed focus	**Total-session target volume = 3,600 yards.** Sets 1-6: Repeat week 1. Set 7: 1,400-yard strength endurance swim at aerobic intensity using paddles. Set 8: Aerobic swim or set to achieve target swim volume.
	Weight training (strength)	1 × 12 reps at 50% 1RM. 2 × 6 to 8 reps at 85% 1RM. Complete all swim-, bike-, and run-specific and supplemental movements.
Thursday	Bike race-pace focus	**Total-session target volume = 60 miles.** Set 1: 4 × 3 miles at target 12.4-mile (20K) velocity with 1-minute easy spin Set 2: 1- to 2-minute easy spin. Use an appropriate cadence target to help select your gears. Set 3: Additional aerobic cycling to achieve target cycle volume.
	Run race-pace focus	**Total-session target volume = 13 miles.** Set 1: 6 × 800 meters at 3.1-mile (5K) target velocity with 400-meter recovery walk or jog. Set 2: Additional aerobic running to achieve target volume.

Day	Training sessions	Specific session details
Friday	Swim race-pace focus	**Total-session target volume = 3,600 yards.** Set 1: 5 × 100 yards at target 500-yard velocity with 30-second rest. Set 2: 100-yard easy swim. Set 3: 1,400-yard strength endurance set. Set 4: Aerobic swim or set to achieve target swim volume.
Saturday	Bike endurance focus	**Total-session target volume = 110 miles.** Set 1: 68 miles or 204 to 272 minutes continuously at target cadence and 112-mile target velocity. Focus on taking in fluids and nutrition as you will in the target race. Set 2: 70-minute strength endurance set using a gear that produces 40 to 60 rpm at aerobic intensity in race position. Set 3: Additional aerobic cycling to achieve target cycle volume.
	Weight training (power and muscular endurance)	1 × 20 reps at 50% 1RM. 2 × 6 reps at 50% 1RM explosive. Complete all swim-, bike-, and run-specific and supplemental movements and plyometrics.
Sunday	Swim endurance focus	**Total-session target volume = 6,000 yards.** Set 1: 42 to 60 minutes or 3,000 yards continuously using at least one head lift per 25 yards or every 12 to 20 strokes at target 4,000-yard velocity. Wear the equipment (goggles, wet suit, race suit) you will wear in the race. Divide this into shorter efforts to allow for food breaks. Set 2: 1,400-yard strength endurance swim at aerobic intensity using paddles. Set 3: Aerobic swim or set to achieve target swim volume.
	Run endurance focus	**Total-session target volume = 23 miles.** Set 1: 14 miles or 112 to 140 minutes continuously at marathon-mile target velocity. Include a short walk break (1 to 2 minutes) every mile to allow for partial recovery and a faster overall pace. Set 2: 45-minute strength endurance work running up a 2% to 4% grade at aerobic speed. Set 3: Additional aerobic running (likely downhill) to achieve target run volume.

Mesocycle 3: Race-Preparation Phase Week 10

This is the first week of a gradual taper.

Day	Training sessions	Specific session details
Monday	No training	
Tuesday	Run speed focus	**Total-session target volume = 11 miles.** Set 1: 3 × 100 meters (track) or 3 × 20 seconds (treadmill) at target 400-meter velocity with 100-meter walk or jog (track) or 30-second recovery walk off treadmill. Set 2: 400-meter recovery walk or jog (track) or 1- to 2-minute easy jog (treadmill). Set 3: 3 × 200 meters (track) or 3 × 40 seconds (treadmill) at 800-meter target velocity with 100-meter walk or jog (track) or 40-second recovery walk off treadmill. Set 4: 400-meter recovery walk or jog (track) or 1- to 2-minute easy jog (treadmill). Set 5: 3 × 400 meters (track) or 3 × 1:30 (treadmill) at 1,600-meter target velocity with 100-meter walk or jog (track) or 30-second recovery walk off treadmill. Set 6: 400-meter recovery walk or jog (track) or 1- to 2-minute easy jog (treadmill). Set 7: 30-minute strength endurance work using a weighted vest or incline on the treadmill. Combine a speed and grade (and vest weight if used) that allow for a comfortable aerobic heart rate. A 2% grade is a good starting point. Set 8: Additional aerobic running to achieve target volume.
	Bike speed focus	**Total-session target volume = 50 miles.** Set 1: 3 × 0.125 mile at target 0.5-mile velocity or power with equal rest (easy spin recovery). Set 2: 1- to 2-minute easy spin. Set 3: 3 × 0.25 mile at 1-mile target velocity with 30-second spin recovery. Set 4: 1- to 2-minute easy spin. Set 5: 3 × 0.5 mile at 2-mile target velocity with 40-second spin recovery. Set 6: 1- to 2-minute easy spin. Set 7: 60-minute strength endurance set using a gear that produces 40 to 60 rpm at aerobic intensity in race position. Set 8: Additional aerobic cycling to achieve target cycle volume.
Wednesday	Swim speed focus	**Total-session target volume = 3,200 yards.** Set 1: 3 × 25 yards at target 100-yard velocity with equal rest. Set 2: 50-yard easy swim. Set 3: 3 × 50 yards at 200-yard target velocity with 30-second rest. Set 4: 50-yard easy swim. Set 5: 3 × 100 yards at 500-yard target velocity with 40-second rest. Set 6: 100-yard easy swim. Set 7: 1,200-yard strength endurance swim at aerobic intensity using paddles. Set 8: Aerobic swim or set to achieve target swim volume.
	Weight training (strength)	1 × 12 reps at 50% 1RM. 2 × 6 to 8 reps at 85% 1RM. Complete all swim-, bike-, and run-specific and supplemental movements.

Day	Training sessions	Specific session details
Thursday	Bike race-pace focus	**Total-session target volume = 50 miles.** Set 1: 2 × 8 miles at target 24.8-mile (40K) velocity with 5-minute easy spin. Set 2: 1- to 2-minute easy spin. Use an appropriate cadence target to help select your gears. Set 3: Additional aerobic cycling to achieve target cycle volume.
	Run race-pace focus	**Total-session target volume = 11 miles.** Set 1: 4 × 1,600 meters at 6.2-mile (10K) target velocity with 400-meter recovery walk or jog. Set 2: Additional aerobic running to achieve target volume.
Friday	Swim race-pace focus	**Total-session target volume = 3,200 yards.** Set 1: 4 × 300 yards at target 1,600-yard velocity with 30-second rest. Set 2: 100-yard easy swim. Set 3: 1,200-yard strength endurance set. Set 4: Aerobic swim or set to achieve target swim volume.
Saturday	Bike endurance focus	**Total-session target volume = 100 miles.** Set 1: 60 miles or 180 to 240 minutes continuously at target cadence and 112-mile target velocity. Focus on taking in fluids and nutrition as you will in the target race. Set 2: 60-minute strength endurance set using a gear that produces 40 to 60 rpm at aerobic intensity in race position. Set 3: Additional aerobic cycling to achieve target cycle volume.
	Weight training (power and muscular endurance)	1 × 20 reps at 50% 1RM. 2 × 6 reps at 50% 1RM explosive. Complete all swim-, bike-, and run-specific and supplemental movements and plyometrics.
Sunday	Swim endurance focus	**Total-session target volume = 5,000 yards.** Set 1: 35 to 50 minutes or 2,500 yards continuously using at least one head lift per 25 yards or every 12 to 20 strokes at target 4,000-yard velocity. Wear the equipment (goggles, wet suit, race suit) you will wear in the race. Divide this into shorter efforts to allow for food breaks. Set 2: 1,200-yard strength endurance swim at aerobic intensity using paddles. Set 3: Aerobic swim or set to achieve target swim volume.
	Run endurance focus	**Total-session target volume = 18 miles.** Set 1: 12 miles or 96 to 120 minutes continuously at marathon-mile target velocity. Include a short walk break (1 to 2 minutes) every mile to allow for partial recovery and a faster overall pace. Set 2: 40-minute strength endurance work running up a 2% to 4% grade at aerobic speed. Set 3: Additional aerobic running (likely downhill) to achieve target run volume.

Mesocycle 3: Race-Preparation Phase Week 11

This is the second week of taper.

Day	Training sessions	Specific session details
Monday	No training	
Tuesday	Run speed focus	**Total-session target volume = 8 miles.** Set 1: 2 × 100 meters (track) or 2 × 20 seconds (treadmill) at target 400-meter velocity with 100-meter walk or jog (track) or 30-second recovery walk off treadmill. Set 2: 400-meter recovery walk or jog (track) or 1- to 2-minute easy jog (treadmill). Set 3: 2 × 200 meters (track) or 2 × 40 seconds (treadmill) at 800-meter target velocity with 100-meter walk or jog (track) or 40-second recovery walk off treadmill. Set 4: 400-meter recovery walk or jog (track) or 1- to 2-minute easy jog (treadmill). Set 5: 2 × 400 meters (track) or 2 × 1:30 (treadmill) at 1,600-meter target velocity with 100-meter walk or jog (track) or 30-second recovery walk off treadmill. Set 6: 400-meter recovery walk or jog (track) or 1- to 2-minute easy jog (treadmill). Set 7: 20-minute strength endurance work using a weighted vest or incline on the treadmill. Combine a speed and grade (and vest weight if used) that allow for a comfortable aerobic heart rate. A 2% grade is a good starting point. Set 8: Additional aerobic running to achieve target volume.
	Bike speed focus	**Total-session target volume = 25 miles.** Set 1: 2 × 0.125 mile at target 0.5-mile velocity or power with equal rest (easy spin recovery). Set 2: 1- to 2-minute easy spin. Set 3: 2 × 0.25 mile at 1-mile target velocity with 30-second spin recovery. Set 4: 1- to 2-minute easy spin. Set 5: 2 × 0.5 mile at 2-mile target velocity with 40-second spin recovery. Set 6: 1- to 2-minute easy spin. Set 7: 30-minute strength endurance set using a gear that produces 40 to 60 rpm at aerobic intensity in race position. Set 8: Additional aerobic cycling to achieve target cycle volume.
Wednesday	Swim speed focus	**Total-session target volume = 1,600 yards.** Set 1: 2 × 25 yards at target 100-yard velocity with equal rest. Set 2: 50-yard easy swim. Set 3: 2 × 50 yards at 200-yard target velocity with 30-second rest. Set 4: 50-yard easy swim. Set 5: 2 × 100 yards at 500-yard target velocity with 40-second rest. Set 6: 100-yard easy swim. Set 7: 600-yard strength endurance swim at aerobic intensity using paddles. Set 8: Aerobic swim or set to achieve target swim volume.

Day	Training sessions	Specific session details
Wednesday *(continued)*	Weight training (strength)	1 × 12 reps at 50% 1RM. 2 × 6 to 8 reps at 85% 1RM. Complete all swim-, bike-, and run-specific and supplemental movements.
Thursday	Bike race-pace focus	**Total-session target volume = 25 miles.** Set 1: 1 × 18 miles at target 56-mile velocity with 5-minute easy spin. Set 2: 1- to 2-minute easy spin. Use an appropriate cadence target to help select your gears. Set 3: Additional aerobic cycling to achieve target cycle volume.
	Run race-pace focus	**Total-session target volume = 8 miles.** Set 1: 2 × 1.5 miles at 13.1-mile target velocity with 400-meter recovery walk or jog. Set 2: Additional aerobic running to achieve target volume.
Friday	Swim race-pace focus	**Total-session target volume = 1,600 yards.** Set 1: 1 × 600 yards or other equivalent set at target 2,000-yard velocity with 60-second rest. Set 2: 100-yard easy swim. Set 3: 600-yard strength endurance set. Set 4: Aerobic swim or set to achieve target swim volume.
Saturday	Bike endurance focus	**Total-session target volume = 50 miles.** Set 1: 30 miles or 90 to 120 minutes continuously at target cadence and 112-mile target velocity. Focus on taking in fluids and nutrition as you will in the target race. Set 2: 30-minute strength endurance set using a gear that produces 40 to 60 rpm at aerobic intensity in race position. Set 3: Additional aerobic cycling to achieve target cycle volume.
	Weight training (power and muscular endurance)	1 × 20 reps at 50% 1RM. 2 × 6 reps at 50% 1RM explosive. Complete all swim-, bike-, and run-specific and supplemental movements and plyometrics.
Sunday	Swim endurance focus	**Total-session target volume = 3,000 yards.** Set 1: 28 to 40 minutes or 2,000 yards continuously using at least one head lift per 25 yards or every 12 to 20 strokes at target 4,000-yard velocity. Wear the equipment (goggles, wet suit, race suit) you will wear in the race. Divide this into shorter efforts to allow for food breaks. Set 2: 600-yard strength endurance swim at aerobic intensity using paddles. Set 3: Aerobic swim or set to achieve target swim volume.
	Run endurance focus	**Total-session target volume = 11.5 miles.** Set 1: 5.5 miles or 44 to 55 minutes continuously at marathon-mile target velocity. Include a short walk break (1 to 2 minutes) every mile to allow for partial recovery and a faster overall pace. Set 2: 20-minute strength endurance work running up a 2% to 4% grade at aerobic speed. Set 3: Additional aerobic running (likely downhill) to achieve target run volume.

Mesocycle 3: Race-Preparation Phase Week 12 (Taper)

This is the final week of a full taper.

Day	Training sessions	Specific session details
Monday	No training	
Tuesday	Run speed focus	**Total-session target volume = 3.0 miles.** Include aerobic work, several alactates, and one or two 400-meter efforts at race pace only. Volume is 30% or less of the previous week's training sessions.
	Bike speed focus	**Total-session target volume = 15 miles.** Include aerobic work, several alactates, and one or two 1-minute efforts at race pace only. Volume is 30% or less of the previous week's training sessions.
Wednesday	Swim speed focus	**Total-session target volume = 1,000 yards.** Set 1: 1 × 25 yards at target 100-yard velocity with equal rest. Set 2: 50-yard easy swim. Set 3: 1 × 50 yards at 200-yard target velocity with 30-second rest. Set 4: 50-yard easy swim. Set 5: 1 × 100 yards at 500-yard target velocity with 40-second rest. Set 6: 100-yard easy swim. Set 7: Aerobic swim or set to achieve target swim volume.
	Weight training (strength)	1 × 6 reps at 50% 1RM. 1 × 3 or 4 reps at 85% 1RM. Complete all swim-, bike-, and run-specific and supplemental movements.
Thursday	Bike race-pace focus	**Total-session target volume = 15 miles.** This work is replaced by the race at the end of the week. Do aerobic cycling with one or two 1-minute efforts at race pace to reach your target volume, which is 50% of previous 3 weeks' training sessions.
	Run race-pace focus	**Total-session target volume = 3 miles.** Include aerobic work and one or two 400-meter efforts at race pace only. Volume is 30% or less of the week 6 training sessions.

Day	Training sessions	Specific session details
Friday	Swim race-pace focus	**Total-session target volume = 1,000 yards.** Include aerobic work, several alactates, and one or two 50-yard efforts at 2,000-yard race pace only. Volume is 30% or less of the previous week's training sessions.
Saturday*	Bike endurance focus	This is replaced by the target race.
	Weight training (power and muscular endurance)	Eliminate weight training and plyometric exercises before race.
Sunday	Swim endurance focus	This is replaced by the target race.
	Run endurance focus	This is replaced by the target race.

If your race is on Sunday, then you should do a **short** warm-up in all three sports on the course Saturday.

Summary

Prepackaged training programs such as those presented here can provide the basis for becoming a triathlete. You should address a full range of training intensities in a tolerable approach based on your own abilities and allow yourself the time to engage in an adaptive process before making progressions. Then, be sure to make those progressions in a realistic manner. Always remember that triathlon training must be individualized to your lifestyle, age, adaptive capability, and racing interests to be completely effective and to allow you to reach your potential.

The training plans presume a complete understanding of the training concepts described in previous chapters. Also note that there is a glossary of terms in the back of the book. Finally, be sure to use the training programs—don't let them use you.

Health and Fueling for Optimal Performance

9

Research in epidemiology, medicine, and exercise physiology over the last 30 years has demonstrated relationships between lack of physical activity and many of the major causes of disease and death common in Western society. Multisport activity and racing provide an antidote. By creating an environment where physical activity is diversified, enjoyable, and self-actualizing, multisports offer tremendous potential to create optimal health—or as it is commonly called now, a state of wellness. But multisport athletes commonly experience a variety of ailments that are a direct result of overextending themselves. This chapter addresses these issues so that your triathlon or duathlon experience can be one that brings about wellness rather than one that brings about disability or sickness. You can think of this as a means of improving your performance potential. As discussed earlier in the book, the most important variable in training success is consistency, so avoiding injury and sickness allows you to fully realize training progressions.

Because you ask yourself to deal with considerable physical and mental stress through the process of training for triathlon, it's important that you maximize those preventive behaviors. For optimal health, human beings need to be physically active in such a way that protects the immune system and creates muscular balance, get adequate sleep, eat nutritious food, avoid environmental toxins (such as cigarette smoke and pollution), and create happy, self-actualizing experiences. Before engaging in a demanding program of training, you should also consider completing a health screening. Because the training for triathlon is very specific in nature, you must develop a strategy to minimize the possibility of musculoskeletal injury by creating balance in your approach. Depending on how you do it, participation in endurance sport can both help and hinder you in engaging in all of these elements of healthy living.

Protecting the Immune System

Physical training can stimulate your immune response, create muscular balance, increase bone and soft-tissue density, improve organ function (heart and lungs), and create psychological health and feelings of satisfaction. The key to creating a training program that stimulates the immune system, rather than suppresses it, is to avoid overtraining, as discussed in chapter 5. Your immune system does become temporarily suppressed when your efforts in training and racing greatly exceed previous efforts or efforts that you are not prepared to do. For example, running a marathon when you have previously run only a 10K in training is likely to leave you immunosuppressed for a time afterward and vulnerable to both tissue-level injury and infectious diseases. If you run such a race fully prepared, you are less likely to experience the negatives. Taking on epic training efforts without gradually working up to them can bring about the same outcome. Even though that monumental five-hour mountain bike ride (when you normally ride only an hour or less) often seems like a good idea at the time, the long-term result is often illness and an overall loss of training progress.

When you overextend yourself frequently, temporary suppression of the immune response becomes chronic. This can precipitate ongoing minor illnesses and potentially chronic illness, such as Epstein-Barr syndrome, various upper-respiratory problems, and other more serious diseases. To avoid both acute and chronic immune suppression, you must avoid attempting training and racing efforts when underprepared and make progressions in training in small increments. A model for training based on adaptation will go a long way in eliminating this type of immunosuppression and any resulting illness.

Getting Enough Good Sleep

Once you begin to see multisport training as a process of adapting to physical training rather than simply training harder, you can recognize the value of sleep in the process. You need only miss a few hours of sleep or have poor sleep for a night or two to see how it affects adaptation. Sleep is your most important and basic recuperative process. Adequate sleep allows your hormone levels to recharge, your digestive system to absorb nutrients, your cellular proteins to be rebuilt, and your mind to decompress. Achieving adequate sleep in today's society is much more difficult than you might think. In particular, the type of person so often attracted to triathlon—the high-achieving, heavily committed adult—is often the most likely person to have sleep problems as well. This can seriously interfere with, if not derail, the training process.

Exercise itself is one of the most fundamental techniques for improving sleep quality. However, this is a double-edged sword in regard to the training programs of triathletes. Overtraining, created by training excessively without short-term adaptation, also creates chronically high levels of stress hormones circulating in the blood. The hormones can then interfere with sleeping. A loss in sleep quality is a distinct signal of overtraining or the presence of other stressors beyond a level that you can handle. Furthermore, the short-term effect of higher-level training is an increase in stress hormones and your general metabolic level. So if you are not a morning exerciser, you should finish training several hours or more before bedtime. Of course, each person has unique sensitivities to individual training schedules in regard to sleep. For some, nearly all training should occur in the morning. Others may find that early-evening training sessions still allow for high-quality sleep. And you need to take other considerations into account when setting up your training schedule, from simply preferring either the morning or late afternoon or early evening time to having to pick one or the other because of work, school, or family responsibilities.

The following are additional commonly suggested strategies to improve sleep quality:

- Play background noise, particularly if your room is not quiet. It should be relaxing and monotonous white noise, such as wave sounds.

- Sleep in complete darkness or as close to it as possible. Darkness is the basic stimulus for melatonin, the hormone that creates sleepiness. Even short exposure to a bathroom light can inhibit your ability to fall or stay asleep.

- Avoid a high level of visual or mental stimulation, such as TV, computer games, or work, right before bed. Both the light from the TV and thought processes resulting from working, watching television, or doing other stimulating activities inhibit a restful mind and easy sleep process. Engage in some relaxing activity before bedtime, such as reading, listening to relaxing music, or taking a warm bath.

- Keep the temperature in the bedroom relatively cool. A temperature around 70 degrees Fahrenheit (21 degrees Celsius) results in the highest quality of sleep for most people.

- Avoid using caffeine, nicotine, and alcohol because these substances interfere with sleep. Caffeine and nicotine are stimulants that make sleep more difficult. Alcohol may make you drowsy, but it also inhibits sleep later during the night.

- Don't drink any fluids within two hours of going to bed, then go to the bathroom just before retiring. This makes it less likely you'll need to wake up to urinate. Particularly as people get older, nighttime bathroom needs can become a significant source of lost sleep time.

- Use your bed for sleeping and sex only. This behavioral concept allows you to associate your bed with these activities only, making both more likely to occur.

- Establish a prebedtime routine and stick to it. Go to sleep and wake up at the same times, including on weekends. By maintaining this rhythm, you enhance the quality of your sleep. Deviation from this rhythm is the main reason long travel to different time zones for a race is difficult to accommodate. Attempt to duplicate the ritual in those situations as well.

- Find the amount of sleep time it takes you to awaken feeling refreshed. This may differ with age and from person to person, but most of the scientific literature on this topic suggests that a minimum of eight hours is necessary for optimal physical performance. Athletes training at high loads commonly report the need for even more sleep. Unfortunately, many busy age-group triathletes find that early-morning training times and conflicting life demands reduce sleep time to six or seven hours. In such situations, regular napping during the day can be beneficial. Naps should occur on a regular cycle as well. When you have adequate time to sleep at night, avoiding napping may increase the quality and length of your nighttime sleep.

Ensuring Proper Nutrition

There are many good books on nutrition, but there are also plenty of bad ones. Most of the good books are written by qualified nutritionists and specialists in preventive medicine. For sport nutrition in particular, there are a number of fine books by recognized and qualified sport nutritionists, such as Louise Burke's *Practical Sports Nutrition*, Susanne Girard Eberle's *Endurance Sports Nutrition*, and Nancy Clark's *Sports Nutrition Guidebook*. Both of the latter authors also write regularly for several endurance sport magazines. This chapter presents a broad-based approach to sport nutrition as well as specifics on energy bars, drinks, and gels (which change every year as new ones come out and old ones go by the wayside). For more resources on sport nutrition, check out the bibliography at the end of this book.

It has taken a while to arrive at just what constitutes healthful eating. Many people growing up in the 1960s were raised to believe that the egg was a perfect food. By the '70s and on into the '80s, the egg had come to be considered a precursor to heart attacks. Currently, it appears to be an acceptable food if eaten in moderation, although it is not considered ideal as a staple of the diet. Some swimming coaches used to encourage their athletes to eat steak before swim meets. Of course, steak would now be the last thing most swimmers would eat just before a race. Currently the food pyramid promoted by the U.S. Departments of Agriculture and Health and Human Services recommends that people consume the bulk of their calories from grains, fruits, and vegetables, with a relatively modest amount of protein and fat.

Some nutritional concepts have withstood the test of time and make sense. No one specific diet is recommended here—that task is for the sport nutritionists and registered dietitians who are appropriately qualified. This chapter does provide some nutritional concepts and principles that may assist you in becoming a healthier multisport athlete and a higher-performing one as well.

Nutrition Principles

Within the last several decades a theory regarding the optimization of human nutrition has been developed that not only seems logical but also is supported by the results of many of the studies conducted in recent years. The theory is that for optimal health, your diet should be similar to the diet humans were consuming when they began to live in organized communities (Cordain et al. 2002; O'Keefe and Cordain 2004). This pattern of eating is sometimes referred to as the Paleolithic diet, meaning the diet of the Stone Age humans living during that time. The basis for this theory is that for the majority of the time that human beings have existed on earth (millions of years), food was obtained through hunting and gathering. Agriculture is a fairly late development, going back only about 10,000 years. In Western societies, the highly industrialized food creation and distribution systems people rely on now have been in place for only a blink of the eye.

People are still encoded genetically to do best by consuming the kind of diet consumed during the Paleolithic period. By examining anthropological and archeological data as well as current-day populations that have remained in relative isolation from "civilization," you can come to some generalizations about this dietary pattern. This means that you should consume plant foods in an unrefined state (not to include typically mass-produced grain products) and meat as obtained from nondomesticated animals. Humans should eat neither dairy products produced from domesticated animals nor other food products created through domestication, industrialization, or significant refinement.

Of course the immediate reaction to this theory is that modern agriculture, domestication of animals, and industrialization have for modern societies largely eliminated starvation. Adequate and diversified nutrition also strengthens the immune system to fight against the major infectious diseases of the bygone days. However, the theory suggests that in the current state of abundant availability of food, the nature of the food is more important to health and performance than its availability, which is currently virtually unlimited for the typical triathlete.

One major controversy about this theory concerns what types of food the Paleolithic human was most likely to eat. Those conclusions are largely based on scientific methods that "look backward," an imperfect process at best. Consider how you might obtain food and survive if there were no towns, no supermarkets, and no McDonald's. You might immediately suggest that you would hunt. If you watch *Survivor*-type shows on television, you might also suggest you would set traps and gather whatever food you could. You might quickly come to the conclusion that you would eat mainly plants with some smaller animals. If you have more bravado, you might suggest that you would create weapons and then capture and eat a larger animal as well. This would allow you to gorge yourself periodically. However, in most cases you would simply eat as you found things, grazing continually. The result would be a diet composed mainly of native plants (those that are nontoxic) with an occasional meat feast.

Of course, the theory regarding optimal eating based on evolutionary need has to be balanced against the practical realities of food availability and the clearly nonevolutionary needs of athletes choosing to train for triathlons. Cultivated grain products are the most commonly available source of energy. Systematic exercise training requires an excessive intake of energy, best in the form of carbohydrate. Thus it is almost impossible to imagine a triathlete exclusively using a diet that parallels the diet of Paleolithic ancestors, which is likely to have been somewhat low in carbohydrate simply due to the sheer difficulty of obtaining a large mass of plant foods by foraging. However, the swing toward very low-fat, low-protein, and excessively high-carbohydrate diets that resounded through endurance sports in the 1970s and '80s also seems misplaced at this point, especially since the bulk of carbohydrate that is readily available is of the processed variety. People now seem to have reached a state of balance, supported by current nutrition science, on which the following recommendations are based.

■   **Eat a large amount of plant foods in as close to their natural state as is reasonable.** Fresh and frozen vegetables, fruits, and whole-grain products are vital sources of carbohydrate. They replace the constant turnover of stored carbohydrate (liver and muscle glycogen) that your body relies on so heavily for fuel during exercise.

■   **Eat meat that comes from animals that swim, run, or fly.** This means game birds, fish, venison, buffalo, and wild fowl rather than domesticated pork, lamb, veal, and beef. Animals such as these are generally leaner, meaning you consume less fat when you eat them, and in most cases are more likely to have been consuming their natural diet as well. In a less-than-ideal world, where the consumption of domesticated animals is necessary, those animals that have been fed by grasses naturally rather than by grains in a more industrialized setting might be a healthier choice because they are likely to have more optimal ratios of beneficial omega-3 fat.

■   **Balance your plate with two-thirds or more of plant foods and one-third or less of protein sources.** The largest portion of your diet (in terms of weight) should come from plant foods that retain their natural fiber and vitamin content and provide carbohydrate for training.

■   **Maximize the variety of colors on your plate.** As reaffirmed in the scientific research, fruits and vegetables with deep, full color exhibit nature's signs of high nutritional value. This does not apply to your meat intake, however.

■   **Eat a variety of foods.** Variety provides both moderation in the intake of any one food or nutrient as well as a full range of available nutrients. Experimenting with new and different foods is one of the elements of eating that makes it most interesting as well as beneficial.

■   **Combine macronutrients—carbohydrate, protein, and fat—in meals.** This approach helps to reduce hunger caused by high insulin levels and keeps your energy level high. Protein and fat reduce the glycemic, or blood-sugar-raising, capacity of carbohydrate foods by slowing their absorption. This reduces the stimulating effect of meals on insulin production. The only time this effect may not be relevant for triathletes is when eating in the midst of training or competition. At those times, the elevation of the blood epinephrine (adrenaline) level blocks the receptors that allow high blood sugar levels to cause the release of insulin. Because carbohydrate consumption is directly related to immediate performance capacity during exercise, consume foods that maximize delivery of carbohydrate to the bloodstream. This basically means that sugar is optimal in the triathlon training setting.

■ **Reduce or avoid highly processed foods.** This approach helps to control the intake of many foods that people typically consume in an inappropriate balance and that are not present in high quantities in natural, unrefined foods. These include sugar in its various forms (including corn starch, high-fructose corn syrup, maltose), salt, additives, dyes, other preservatives (besides salt), and fillers.

■ **Eat healthy types of fat rather than unhealthy types.** First, choose liquid rather than solid fat where possible, such as using oil to cook with rather than butter or margarine. This reduces your intake of solid saturated and trans fat in favor of liquid unsaturated fat. Second, choose unsaturated (liquid) fat sources that include a high percentage of monounsaturated fat, such as olive oil, rather than other more typical oils, such as canola or corn oil. The current science suggests that monounsaturated fat is more beneficial than polyunsaturated fat. Finally, increase your intake of omega-3 fat rather than the more commonly available omega-6 fat. Omega-3 fat is found in greater concentrations in animals that do not consume grain products. It is especially concentrated in cold-water fish such as salmon and tuna. However, if you choose to eat a significant amount of fish, you must also consider the level of mercury present.

■ **Graze throughout the day rather than eat just a few large meals.** This means starting out the day eating (even before training), eating while you train, and eating all the rest of the time. If you are following the first several concepts, this will promote a high energy level, support training, and create leanness rather than fat. By contrast, large meals eaten infrequently when you are very hungry maximize energy storage as fat and create fluctuations in energy levels as insulin is overproduced, resulting in blood sugar levels falling below normal sometime later (LeBlanc, Mercier, and Nadeau 1993; Speechly and Buffenstein 1999). Amounts will vary with the amount of training you are doing.

Changing Your Eating Habits

The approach to eating described here sounds optimal, but it might be difficult for athletes with the "I do triathlon so I can eat anything I want" mentality to adopt such changes. Following are several suggestions derived from concepts presented in chapter 2 regarding behavior change.

- **Separate emotional hunger from physiological hunger.** Many poor food choices are made to satisfy psychological hunger created because the food looks and smells good or is associated with a pleasurable experience, rather than because you actually need fuel. By eating small amounts frequently and by combining macronutrients, you can reduce the occurrence of both physiological hunger and psychological hunger. But do not completely avoid sugar and fat. Rather, include them judiciously with other foods so you avoid the feeling of deprivation as well as cravings.

- **Reperceive newly desired foods: focus on their positive rather than negative aspects.** This is how coffee drinkers, for example, learn to appreciate the aroma and taste of coffee along with how they feel drinking it. They focus on those attributes rather than on its inherent bitterness and potential for creating nervousness. If you can learn to love coffee, surely you can learn to love vegetables, whether cooked or in salads. If you focus on the positive aspects of vegetables, such as their distinctive tastes and textures, vitamin content, and potential for making you healthier, rather than on less rational belief systems such as "all vegetables are bland," you will find that you enjoy eating them more. You can also rev up the taste of vegetables by using spices, nuts, small grains, raisins, and dried cranberries in moderation.

- **Make small changes in your diet one at a time rather than big changes all at once.** This is the behavioral concept of gradual change. Take something you feel confident you can change and are committed to change and then do so gradually. For example, you could reduce your consumption of whole milk by gradually mixing it with lower-fat varieties in progressively increasing concentrations. Keep in mind that any improvement in diet is worthwhile. When you make large-scale behavioral changes and then fail to continue them, at some point the rule-violation effect, which is the common irrational belief that once the rule is broken it no longer exists, comes into play to sabotage your efforts.

- **Don't forget the primary reward driving eating behavior—taste.** The immediate satisfaction to be gained by eating food that tastes good can more than offset all potential negatives of healthy eating. That's part of the reason why sugar is so addictive—it tastes so good. Use this to your advantage by finding ways to make changes in the right direction that don't sacrifice taste. This takes the development of some culinary skills and the willingness to try new things. Always keep in mind that by making progressive changes, you can change your tastes gradually in ways that may not even be noticeable. Of course, many tastes for food are acquired over time. Were this not so, how could people enjoy smoking cigarettes, drinking coffee, drinking beer, or eating olives and liver? Taste is greatly enhanced by appetite as well, which makes this an easier process for triathletes, who are always a little hungry.

Food as Fuel

Participation in triathlons, particularly long-distance ones, shows just how close you are at any one time to running on an empty tank. As possibly the most overfed society on earth, along with being among the least active, many Westerners have never experienced an empty energy tank. However, two hours or more of extended effort in a triathlon without proper fueling can bring on that experience in a hurry. While your body, even at its leanest, carries enough stored fuel in the form of fat to last for days and days of low-level activity, during high-level exercise you rapidly expend the relatively limited stores of carbohydrate from the muscles and liver.

Because your brain operates on carbohydrate, if you experience a sudden drop in this energy supply, mental energy level declines quickly. Further, as your carbohydrate levels drop, it becomes increasingly difficult to burn fat for energy. Then your pace slows considerably and your sense of effort increases. With training you can expand on this glycogen (carbohydrate) storage capacity. But to optimize performance over an hour or more, you also need to consume carbohydrate as you go. The benefits of this approach have been demonstrated experimentally so many times now as to be regarded as scientific fact.

Further, during the training process, you continually expend and then attempt to replace this important fuel source (glycogen) from training session to training session. To the degree that you do so successfully, training can proceed and adaptation can occur. However, when you fail to adequately replace your stored glycogen over time, progressive fatigue develops and you fail to adapt to the training process. This is the rationale behind incorporating a relatively large amount of carbohydrate in the training diet of triathletes.

This nutritional approach can compromise health when carried out inappropriately or to excess. The negative effects include dental cavities, an overactive pancreas and elevated insulin response, a large number of empty calories in the diet, and a variety of other less obvious health issues thought to be associated with a high carbohydrate intake (especially of the unhealthful variety). However, failure to provide the needed energy directly affects both the training process and racing performance. A study illustrates that the supplementation of carbohydrate while cycling contributes to a reduction in the loss of glycogen (stored carbohydrate) in the muscles after exercise (Halson et al. 2004).

It should be obvious that to succeed in training as well as racing, it is necessary to keep the energy tank as full as possible as much of the time as possible. You should seek to maximize the replacement of muscle and liver glycogen during training as well as after it by consuming carbohydrate-containing foods before exercise, during exercise, and relatively quickly after exercise. This approach allows you to reduce fatigue and improve your adaptability.

Practical Strategies for Eating to Train and Race

Optimal eating involves consuming food and water before exercise, during exercise, and immediately after exercise, and then throughout the day. This process replaces glycogen and allows for new muscle cell synthesis to occur, resulting in training adaptations. The types of fuel consumed throughout the day should reflect those principles for an optimal diet discussed previously. But the fuel consumed just before, during, and immediately after exercise is a different matter.

Eating Before Training and Racing

Although it has long been believed that eating highly glycemic foods (those carbohydrate-containing foods that elevate blood sugar rapidly) in the hour or so before training will cause an increase in insulin production, resulting in reduced performance, recent research has not completely supported this belief (Febbraio et al. 2000). The increased glucose (sugar) delivery created by eating a larger meal several hours before exercise or a smaller meal just before exercise offsets any substantial negative effect of increased insulin on performance in most athletes. However, a more moderately glycemic pretraining meal may also reduce reliance on the current storage of muscle glycogen during training and improve endurance performance and recovery (Kirwan et al. 2001).

Another concern is potential gastrointestinal stress and any negative effect on the training or racing session. So the prerace meal should consist of an easily digestible high-carbohydrate food with lower fat and protein content. A more immediate prerace option might be an easily digestible beverage designed to deliver both water and carbohydrate. These foods should also be familiar to you so that you know how much to eat or drink and how they will make you feel. You should evaluate all prerace meals by eating the same foods and beverages before training sessions.

The most interesting question, not yet examined in sport science literature, is whether or not a person can "train" the digestive tract to tolerate an increased intake of food both before and during exercise. With practice, you can learn to tolerate both solid foods and beverages before and during exercise, although this may be as much a psychological phenomenon as a physiological one. Key to this is that meals during exercise should be smaller and more frequent so that the gastrointestinal tract is never subjected to a very large bolus of food and drink all at once. In addition, avoid foods that produce gas, constipation, or bloating.

It is possible to significantly increase the body's water content before training or racing. This process, referred to as hyperhydrating, allows for a greater volume of water to be held temporarily in the blood plasma to improve sweating capacity and cardiovascular efficiency. It results in a lower heart rate and improved heat tolerance during the race. Hyperhydrating may be most useful when racing or training in hotter or more humid conditions than what you are currently accustomed to. You hyperhydrate by consuming fluids with a high enough concentration of solids (osmolality) over several hours before the race or training to avoid excessive urinating. This might be accomplished with a typical race drink containing glucose and salt or with a more specialized drink containing glycerol, a carbohydrate form that occurs naturally in the blood.

You must practice increasing your water content during training to determine effective concentrations for the drink and how much you can consume and how quickly without creating gastrointestinal upset, excessive bloating, or nausea. For sure, if you drink plain water in this way, the result will be multiple trips to the Porta-Potties.

Eating During Training and Racing

The principle here is that consuming carbohydrate during training and racing will improve performance by sparing glycogen supplied by the liver to keep the blood sugar level elevated. This not only extends work capacity, but it also makes you feel better while exercising. By sparing glycogen during training, you will be better able to recover full glycogen levels before the next training session. And by finishing training sessions without producing extreme hunger, you tend to make better food choices for posttraining meals.

By consuming carbohydrate, you also need to replace lost water. Doing so improves immediate exercise performance, especially when sweat rates are high, and helps you avoid excessive dehydration after exercise. Both strategies require the regular intake of fluid and carbohydrate, something you can accomplish efficiently with either typical drinks, such as orange juice, or engineered energy-replacement drinks, such as Gatorade. While there is a large volume of scientific and pseudoscientific research examining the utility of various drink combinations, the honest interpretation of this array of information is still relatively simple. During exercise you should drink fluids with relatively low concentrations (about 8 to 12 percent) of carbohydrate.

The drinks should be palatable to you, and you should consume them frequently enough to offset as much of the water weight lost during exercise as possible. Weigh yourself before and after training sessions to determine the amount of fluid you've lost. Fluid lost can then be replaced at a rate of two cups for every pound of weight lost, assuming you drink gradually and use a fluid that will not promote diuresis. You should also develop a strategy to drink more fluids to offset your weight loss during training. An easy approach is to set a timer on your watch for some fixed interval so that it will beep and remind you to drink. The drinks can be either homemade or manufactured. The amount of energy that you can consume and digest will never fully match your energy requirements during racing and training, so you should seek to find the highest rate of energy absorption you can tolerate comfortably.

In very long training sessions or races lasting several hours, especially in hot conditions where sweat rates are high, you should not consume only plain water. Doing so in excess will gradually lower blood sodium levels and put you at risk for developing hyponatremia. Severe hyponatremia can be a fatal condition. In cases where sweat losses will be large due to heat or length of training, you can add a small amount of salt (to taste) to your drink, or you can use commercial drinks with electrolytes. This is not essential for more typical training session lasting less than a few hours. It is also not prudent, relative to the eating guidelines presented previously, to regularly consume electrolyte-containing beverages for nontraining or nonracing purposes, because this increases your overall sodium consumption needlessly.

For longer training sessions and races (typically three hours or more), many athletes choose to eat some solid foods as well. This alleviates the boredom of consuming only a drink, no matter how tasty it may have been early in the day. The foods should also be easily digestible and contain large amounts of carbohydrate. A vast industry produces innumerable types of energy bars and gels for this purpose. Keep in mind that you need to drink water with the food so that you do not overconcentrate your gut—reducing absorption and creating discomfort. Eating such bars as a dietary staple is not recommended in the context of an optimal diet because of their high carbohydrate content. Rather, you should use energy bars primarily for training or long-distance racing purposes.

Also consider that science has failed to illustrate any nutritional advantage of such commercially engineered foods over foods you might prepare yourself, beyond their simple convenience. In addition, most such bars are relatively sticky (so that the ingredients stick together yet are malleable), which means they also tend to adhere to your teeth—a likely culprit in rapidly advancing tooth decay. When using such bars, rinse your mouth with water each time you chew and swallow a piece. It is certainly possible to train and race effectively using more typical high-carbohydrate foods such as fruit or items you prepare yourself.

Training and Racing Foods You Can Prepare Yourself

If you are planning to eat your own foods while training and competing in triathlon, the primary issues are to deliver carbohydrate and avoid gastrointestinal distress. Test any food you plan to eat while racing (including the manufactured types) for palatability and ease of digestion during training in similar conditions. Important considerations for avoiding gastrointestinal distress include avoiding foods that have high fiber content, foods that contain artificial sweeteners, dairy products for those with lactose intolerance, and foods that are high in caffeine, especially in hot conditions. Bananas, oranges, grapes, and melons are relatively low-fiber fruit possibilities that are high in sugar. Certain refined-carbohydrate foods, such as cookies, bagels, and some breads, are also low in fiber and easily digestible. Various milk alternatives, such as soy products or those containing yogurt cultures, reduce the tendency to create discomfort in those who respond poorly to lactose-containing products. Peppermints are easy to suck on while moving and offer a side benefit of aiding digestion. While manufactured foods offer both convenience of use and an optimal formulation for providing energy, humans need variety in their diets.

Eating After Training and Racing

A body of scientific literature now supports the concept that eating immediately after training or racing will enhance the resynthesis of muscle and liver glycogen, allowing for a quicker recovery (Jeukendrup, Jentjens, and Moseley 2005). Originally it was suggested that the meals should consist primarily of fluids and carbohydrate. More recent work suggests that the addition of a small amount of protein may increase glycogen resynthesis and, theoretically at least, allow for enhanced restructuring of muscle protein (Berardi et al. 2006). On a practical level, these foods need to be highly palatable because many athletes are in a state of appetite suppression after exercise. This is particularly so after racing or training at higher levels of effort or with a subsequent increase in body temperature and relative dehydration. Milk or milk-based products, such as low-fat chocolate milk, and flavored calorie-replacement drinks offer high palatability and an optimal blend of carbohydrate, fluid, and protein with low fat levels. Numerous postexercise energy-replacement drinks have also been commercially produced for this purpose. It also appears to be very helpful for glycogen resynthesis if a more normal meal can be consumed within a few hours after racing or training. Of course, you should also gradually drink fluids with a goal of regaining prerace or pretraining weight and normal hydration levels.

Eating to Improve Body Composition

Body composition is an important factor in your success as a triathlete simply because a leaner body can more efficiently move itself forward, particularly in running. However, a lighter body is not necessarily the same thing as a leaner body. Thus a focus on simply reducing body weight for this purpose by eating less can be counterproductive to the overall training and racing process in triathlon. The concept of limiting eating with the intent to reduce body weight also very likely precipitates the development of other nonproductive behaviors, such as bulimia and anorexia, in susceptible people. These conditions occur at alarming rates in weight-related endurance-sport athletes, particularly in young women.

With that in mind, focus on increasing leanness, using a three-pronged approach: resistance training to increase movement-specific muscle mass and strength and the metabolic use of energy, endurance training to increase caloric consumption beyond the basal metabolic rate, and an optimal fueling approach to allow training sessions to be completed with maximum effectiveness. The training and eating approach advocated throughout this book supports that focus on increasing and maintaining leanness.

You should not attempt to reduce total food consumption (that is, diet) except in the case of those who overeat for emotional or psychological reasons. In those cases, the eating issue is best addressed with a psychologist rather than a weight-loss professional.

For people who begin the process of triathlon training significantly overfat, the three-pronged approach will result in a reduction of body weight. As lean

Doughnut Eater to Leader

Late in 2004, Hunter Kemper had won a World Cup race and been pro national champion in the United States on multiple occasions. He had competed in both the Sydney and Athens Olympic Games and was the top American in every Olympic Trials race to date. But he wanted more. He wanted to reach the top rank in the World Cup. His highest rank to date had been fifth. The difference between a fifth-place rank and the first-place rank is considerable. Previously he had been renowned as a regular consumer of the undeniably delicious Krispy Kreme doughnut. He had not been particularly concerned with dietary improvement.

Hunter Kemper

AP Photo/Andy King

Because he wanted to go from fifth to first, and because he came to recognize the importance of healthful eating in improving his race performance, Hunter decided that improving his diet was essential. He was motivated by the potential for performance improvement he saw through becoming leaner and being better fueled for training. Not surprisingly, he was also fascinated by the effects of Lance Armstrong's dietary adjustments on his string of Tour de France victories. Hunter set about achieving this goal by first consulting with a USOC sport nutritionist. He then set about making the suggested basic improvements in his diet by focusing on eating more vegetables and fruits and fewer doughnuts. At the end of 2005 he was leaner, stronger, fitter, and the Triathlon World Cup champion. Little else had changed in his training approach. In his own mind, the most important factor in that year's improvement was dietary change.

body mass is developed, it will be eventually offset by a relatively larger loss in body fat storage, determining the resulting body weight. In people who are not particularly overfat to begin with, this process may actually increase or stabilize body weight as increases in lean mass offset relatively smaller losses in stored body fat. In regard to running in particular, you should run "lighter" by being stronger in the running movements relative to your body weight rather than simply by being lighter overall.

In cycling, the same concept may be thought of in terms of the ratio between your power output and drag for flat and downhill cycling. Regarding uphill cycling, the ratio between your power output and weight indicates relative climbing lightness similar to that in running. Of course, the loss of buoyancy created by having greater leanness in swimming can be offset by efficient technique or the use of wet suits.

Special Dietary Needs of Multisport Athletes

As a multisport athlete, you have considerably higher energy requirements than most other people. As a result, you subject your cells to higher levels of oxidative stress than less active people. Oxidative stress refers to the idea that your body is aged by the same process you use to metabolize (break down) food—that is, the removal of various atoms from the cells in the presence of oxygen. This is basically the same process by which steel rusts in the presence of oxygen. This destabilizing cellular effect is offset to some degree by antioxidants, substances that absorb the highly reactive oxygen atoms that tend to destabilize the structures of your cells by absorbing them into their own structure.

A healthy diet contains high levels of antioxidants. However, there is some reason to believe that endurance athletes may also benefit by taking supplemental amounts of key antioxidants, such as vitamin E, vitamin C, and beta-carotene. Many other substances may also exert this effect as well. The research addressing this question is somewhat equivocal, because your cells clearly also develop enhanced biochemical protection systems if regularly exposed to the higher oxygen flow rate that occurs when you exercise. Many endurance athletes take a daily supplement of 400 IUs (inernational units) of vitamin E along with 500 to 1,000 milligrams of vitamin C in hopes of reducing the potential effects of high-level training.

You have to consider also that the high energy intake of triathletes, coupled with a relatively greater percentage of less nutritious carbohydrate calories in the diet for training purposes, may result in a lower nutrient density of the diet overall, particularly in terms of vitamins and minerals. In other words, your diet may be providing fewer key nutrients per calorie than those of less active people who are consuming smaller amounts of total calories and carbohydrate to meet their lower metabolic needs. Many engineered sport foods contain high levels of vitamin and mineral supplements, in which case this will likely be a nonissue. For those who think that their diets are less than nutritious, taking a daily multivitamin supplement may be prudent.

Endurance athletes also have a higher need for iron in their diets than less active people. This is particularly true of women who use running as part of their training process and who live at higher altitudes than sea level. All three factors—menstruation, altitude residence, and foot-strike hemolysis (red blood cell destruction) from running—increase the turnover of red blood cells. Because iron is in the hemoglobin protein in the red blood cells that carry oxygen, triathletes turn iron over faster than less active people do. They also require a higher intake of it to keep their storage levels, referred to as ferritin iron, at the optimum for peak performance.

Because iron can be stored in your bodily tissues and can reach toxic levels, it is important not to consume supplemental iron if it is not necessary. If you are a heavily training triathlete, you should have your iron status checked periodically by a physician, particularly when you exhibit one or more of the risk factors mentioned previously. Also, you should never take supplemental iron without a physician's guidance.

Reducing Exposure to Infectious Disease

All people are exposed to multiple infectious and noninfectious pathogens on a daily basis, but endurance athletes increase this exposure by breathing large quantities of air during training. These include bacteria, viruses, molds, and fungi. In addition, if you train in a way that creates acute or chronic immunosuppression, you will become increasingly vulnerable to infectious disease. The body's most basic defense to this exposure is through the filtering process that occurs when you breathe through your nasal passage (as advocated in chapter 3). The nasal passage secretes mucus that captures and holds particles contained in the air you breathe. Further, it warms and humidifies the air to the body's normal ranges before it passes to the lungs. This process prevents the bronchi and lung tissues from becoming the filter, as occurs when you inhale cigarette smoke through the mouth or breathe through the mouth.

When the nasal cavity is used overtime, as would occur by breathing through your nose during training, excess mucus and pathogenic materials tend to cluster in the sinus cavities. This process creates a platform for infections that occur both within your sinuses and in the upper-respiratory tract in general. As explained in chapter 3, nasal breathing offers many benefits for those engaged in endurance training; a remedy for this problem is the age-old process of sinus flushing. Sinus flushing is simply the draining of fluid through the nasal passage and sinuses on a regular basis using what is called a Neti Pot.

The modern Neti Pot is a small plastic pot, like a little teapot, that you fill with warm water. You mix the water with a small amount of salt, which has antimicrobial properties, and baking soda, which nullifies the stinging of the salt water in your nose. You drain the liquid through one nostril and out the other by tilting the head. While this process takes a little practice to master, it holds tremendous benefits for your daily health. This is especially true if you have allergies, breathe through your nose in training, or have frequent sinus and upper-respiratory infections. The process is analogous to preventing dental infections by brushing and flossing on a regular basis rather than simply waiting for them to occur and then treating them with medications and surgical procedures.

Inland open-water swimming offers exposure to increased levels of bacteria and other pathogens. As discussed in chapter 3, swimming offers less opportunity to breathe nasally, and water is often inhaled in the process. Some evidence suggests that the development of low-level bacterial infections, which are not widely recognized or diagnosed, may be one of the pitfalls of swimming in inland lakes and rivers. When possible, check the bacterial counts of such bodies of water with the local health department before making decisions about whether to swim in them. It is also possible to take an inoculation for such infections as hepatitis A when risk is high yet you still make a decision to participate in such an event. This will always involve a physician's consultation, of course. This problem is not relevant to saltwater ocean swims (although it is relevant to tidal-river swims).

Dealing With Exposure to Environmental Toxins

Because they breathe at high rates on a daily basis, multisport athletes are exposed to environmental toxins on a disproportionate level in comparison with less active people. Of most immediate concern are the remnants of oxidation (burning), such as car exhaust, industrial pollution, and cigarette smoke, although there are many other toxins in the air. The various chemicals formed by these processes have various negative long-term effects on health. Carbon monoxide, a gas formed in virtually all commercial burning processes, creates an acute (immediate) reduction in your ability to transport oxygen by binding to hemoglobin so that the ability of your red blood cells to carry oxygen is reduced. This immediately, although transiently, reduces performance capability.

Nasal breathing offers a form of protection against harmful particulate matter in the air, although it will have little to no effect on toxic gases such as carbon monoxide. Multisport athletes must make measured decisions about where and when to train. In particular, cycling and running routes that parallel those taken by commuters driving to and from work dramatically increase exposure to car exhaust. In addition, local pollution levels vary with time of day, temperature, and other weather patterns. This problem is so significant in larger cities that ratings of air quality are regularly posted. Consult these postings often. One remedy is to train inside on days when your own limitations prevent training within acceptable exposure levels. Another approach is to schedule training for early morning before the beginning of major commute time (as long as it is light enough to train safely). For some it is also possible to establish training routes that are less traveled by cars. For example, you could adapt much of your outdoor cycle and run training to local trail networks not open to automobile traffic.

Maintaining Joint Integrity

A lack of appropriate muscular balance is a significant factor (some would argue the most significant factor) in many musculoskeletal injuries. When muscles working in opposition to each other across a joint develop an inappropriate balance of strength and endurance, not only is the resting posture of the joint affected but its dynamic movement pattern is as well. This produces small but meaningful negative changes in movement over time. These postural changes not only impair performance ability but also often lead to chronic pain or injury as the joint is used at the limits of its normal tolerances. For example, runners inevitably develop the muscles that externally rotate and abduct their hips more so than those that internally rotate and adduct them. This is because the primary hip extensor, the gluteus maximus, is also an external rotator and abductor because of its angular alignment. This leads to an external rotation in the hip that you can observe in your feet pointing out from the midline when standing and running. Repositioning of the hip reduces running efficiency by directing forces laterally with each stride. Some would argue that it is also a compensating motion created when you lack adequate range of motion in the hip. An externally rotated hip creates a rotary movement in the knee, for which it is not designed, when you extend it under load, as when cycling or running. This may extend to the ankle and foot. Your joints can initially tolerate undue rotations, but over time problems begin to appear, which you might recognize initially as ankle or foot pain, knee pain, or hip pain.

While your training program is designed to create muscular balance in the basic propulsive movements of swimming, cycling, and running and offset the postural imbalances that may occur (as described in chapter 4), general postural imbalances in the hips and shoulders, ankles, and vertebral column can still develop. This occurs as a consequence of the sheer volume of repetition of the movements involved in swimming, cycling, and running, particularly if you maintain poor posture.

The most common concerns involve the development of hip flexor tightness and external hip rotation from running, the resulting hyperflexed (excessive) lumbar (lower back) curve while running, long periods of time spent with reduced lumbar curve (rounded back) and hyperflexed cervical (neck) curve while cycling, and the development of a winged (forwardly rotated) shoulder blade associated with swimming freestyle and using aerobars while cycling. These are exacerbated by extended sitting at a computer or driving with poor posture. Many triathletes can benefit from a combination of stretching, soft-tissue release work, and compensating exercises that maintain or redevelop the posture that optimizes the ability to move without pain. A detailed discussion of evaluating and responding to these joint alignment issues, beyond what is addressed in the basic training program in chapter 4, exceeds the scope here. *Pain Free*, a book describing the self-help approach to musculoskeletal pain developed by Peter Egoscue (1998), is a good recommendation on the issue.

Treating Musculoskeletal Injuries

Although injuries should not be an inevitable outcome of the multisport training process, the scientific data on the topic would tend to indicate otherwise. Studies examining injury in triathlon report it as an epidemic problem; some show that up to 50 percent of triathletes will sustain some kind of musculoskeletal injury yearly and up to 75 percent will sustain an injury sometime during their participation in the sport (Burns, Keenan, and Redmond 2003; Egermann et al. 2003). Other than those caused by external trauma, many of the injuries are attributed to technique deficiencies, muscular and postural imbalances, overextending during the training process, and the misguided use of heavily cushioned and overly controlling running shoes. Human beings are subject to frailties and fully capable of acting without complete rationality, so here is a discussion of what to do if you become injured.

First and foremost, do not ignore pain. Posttraining musculoskeletal pain, whether muscular or joint related, is a red flag indicating that tissue is failing to adapt. This a different pain than the muscular discomfort associated with training itself. Many people consider that postexercise muscular pain is a necessary consequence of the training process, but it is a result of an inconsistent training process rather than an effective one. Extreme delayed-onset muscular soreness (DOMS, or pain that increases over the 48 hours after training) is usually an indication that you attempted to train too hard and that your body is struggling to adapt. While this might be an acceptable outcome of a race, it is not something you should strive for regularly in training. Again, you can avoid this problem by using small progressions only when adaptation occurs.

You should also recognize that the greatest vulnerability to this kind of pain occurs after activities that create eccentric muscular contractions, such as running and weight training. Eccentric (lengthening) muscular contractions occur as you lower your body or a weight toward the ground. This type of contraction creates greater muscular damage than a similar-intensity concentric (shortening) contraction. The highest-risk activities for overextending yourself are running and lifting. Downhill running exaggerates this risk. When postexercise musculoskeletal pain does occur, it is a signal to revise your training process to allow for greater recovery time, such as would occur normally after racing.

Joint-related pain is also a signal of a developing problem, albeit for most people a clearer one than muscular pain. Although it is common to ignore joint pain initially, it is not a good idea. By responding quickly, you can often completely avoid a significant injury and minimally upset the training process. First and foremost, do not respond by simply taking anti-inflammatories and continuing on as before, even though such drugs are widely advocated for this purpose. This approach simply masks the pain and allows you to further the process that created it, likely leading to a significant injury that will require a substantially longer downtime from training.

Following is a summary of what you should do:

- Consult with someone who has the appropriate medical expertise, such as your physician, physical therapist, or alternative health care practitioner, before continuing to train in the activities associated with the pain.

- Attempt to discern the likely mechanism driving the process and then modify it. In many cases this will be muscular imbalance and the resulting postural problems. It may also be related to technique, training conditions, or equipments, so an experienced triathlon coach may be useful.

- Attempt to remedy the situation by employing various healing techniques under the guidance of your health care practitioner. These could include complementary exercises, deliberate technique modifications (when not simply compensating for pain), equipment changes, and the use of healing modalities such as icing or various methods to increase blood flow. Do not ignore the simple therapeutic value of using your own hands (or those of others) to manipulate the area of injury. Direct manual pressure encourages blood flow to an area of the body. Increased blood flow is the primary mechanism by which you heal yourself.

- If taking anti-inflammatory medications, cease or greatly reduce the activities associated with pain for which you are seeking relief until the course of medication is completed.

- Do not give up. This process can take time and be multifaceted in nature. If one method is not successful, given adequate time, then look for another.

An example of the process might be found in responding to plantar fasciitis, a fairly common overuse injury in those who run a good deal. Plantar fasciitis often begins as a relatively minor pain just forward of and under the heel. When ignored, this pain often progresses and becomes debilitating, sometimes even making walking difficult and persisting for many years. It is caused by tearing of the plantar fascia, the sheath that helps to support the foot's normal arched position, near the heel. It can be the result of inappropriate forces created by poor running mechanics (a heel-striking pattern that results in pronation, or the heel angling inward and the arch collapsing, to distribute impact forces) and exacerbated by excessive increases in running training load, the use of worn-out shoes, and the use of shoes that promote excessive pronation through their design.

Conventional forms of treatment, including anti-inflammatory medications combined with calf stretching and conventional orthotics, may resolve the condition once it develops. However, many athletes do have persistent problems with it over many years. In these cases, further consultation with an appropriate health practitioner, such as a knowledgeable orthopedist or podiatrist (and the key word is *knowledgeable*), can lead to a relatively rapid reduction of initial symptoms using alternative approaches. These include an initial resting period created by using an orthotic that completely reestablishes the optimal position of the foot; a change in the biomechanics of running toward the model described in chapter 3; regular soft-tissue work on the site of the injury, particularly before rising in the morning; an increase in the strength of the feet created by barefoot walking and running, and the redevelopment of balance in muscular strength and range of motion in the calf and anterior ankle through stretching and strengthening exercises for dorsiflexion. This kind of approach, given adequate healing time, can resolve the current injury and reduce the possibility of reinjury. A side benefit is that you become a faster and more injury-free runner in general. However, none of this should be regarded as medical advice. Rather, if conventional approaches don't work for you, seek a health care practitioner who is experienced with using these interventions.

Considering Health Screening

If you are reading this book, you are most likely to be a physically fit adult. Unfortunately, you are also at an increased risk for a fatal coronary event while you are training or racing, in spite of the fact that the training process itself will reduce your overall mortality risk. This double-edged sword occurs because although exercise training helps to reduce the general deterioration of your cardiovascular system created by atherosclerosis, it also increases the likelihood that any underlying health issue that you are not currently aware of will surface during the training. These issues most often involve the electrical regulation of your heart, referred to as its cardiac conduction system. The second concept is analogous to identifying problems with the operation of your car by running the engine through the full range of its capability. The good news is that the decrease in risk of heart disease over the course of your life as a result of regular training is much greater than the increase of risk for having an acute cardiac event during any given training session. The majority of those who experience fatal sudden cardiac events during exercise are in the "weekend warrior" category, meaning that they do not exercise regularly. If you fully engage in the training methods suggested here, you will also add one or more elements of high-intensity training to your approach. This further increases your immediate training risk. Take heart: These risks are still very low for most people, say in comparison to the probability of being in a car wreck. But such deaths, while very rare, do occur in triathlon every year. Do not assume that simply because you are fit you do not need to be concerned. High-level fitness does not completely modify the presence of other risk factors based on your genetics, diet, age, stress level, blood pressure, or consumption of tobacco. You should perform the risk factor assessment endorsed by the American College of Sports Medicine. A version of this appears in the sidebar.

Health Risk Assessment

Before beginning a full spectrum of intensity in training for or racing in a triathlon, establish your level of health risk and seek medical clearance before doing so if indicated. You can establish your health risk by assessing the following ACSM risk factors.

1. A family history of cardiovascular disease as defined by these factors:
   - Heart attack, bypass surgery, or sudden death in a first-degree male relative (brother, father, son) before age 55
   - Heart attack, bypass surgery, or sudden death in a first-degree female relative (sister, mother, daughter) before age 65
2. A current cigarette smoker or have quit within the last 6 months
3. A blood pressure at rest at or above 140/90 (confirmed on two separate occasions) or use of blood pressure medication
4. A total blood cholesterol reading at or above 200 mg/dl or HDL cholesterol at or below 35 mg/dl
5. A fasting blood glucose at or above 110 mg/dl confirmed by measurements on two separate occasions
6. A body mass index (BMI) above 30 kg/m2 or a waist girth greater than 100 cm

>> continued

7. A sedentary lifestyle as defined by the failure to accumulate 30 minutes or more of moderate physical activity most days of the week

8. Any other known chronic illness*

You should also consider whether or not you have experienced any of the following signs or symptoms of cardiovascular or pulmonary disease:

- Pain or discomfort in the chest, neck, jaw, arms, or other areas that may be due to poor blood flow

- Shortness of breath at rest or with mild exertion

- Periodic dizziness

- Swelling in the ankles

- Unusual heartbeat, heart murmur, or episodes of rapid heart rate

- Previous episodes of blood clot formation

- Unusual fatigue with normal activities

Based on your answers to these items, you can classify yourself into one of the following health risk categories. These categories help you to determine your need for further medical clearance or evaluation before beginning a rigorous triathlon training program:

- **Low risk** is a person who exhibits one or no risk factors and no signs or symptoms of cardiovascular disease and is either a male under 45 years of age or a female under 55 years of age. While a physical examination within the past year would be considered appropriate, you are considered safe to participate in exercise at all of the intensities described in these ACSM standards without it.

- **Moderate risk** is a person who exhibits two or more of the risk factors described or is either a male over 45 years of age or a female over 55 years of age but has no signs or symptoms of cardiovascular or pulmonary disease. A prior physical examination is appropriate. However, only those who plan to participate in vigorous exercise training or competition need medical clearance. Keep in mind that participation in the triathlon training approach advocated in this book requires vigorous exercise. Should this be the case for you, then you should precede your triathlon training with a medical examination.

- **High risk** is a person who exhibits any of the signs or symptoms of cardiovascular or pulmonary disease listed previously. A physical examination and medical clearance are considered essential before anyone in this group participates in exercise programs of any intensity.**

Despite the advice given here about the relative risks of exercise, if you have the slightest reservation about your ability to exercise with minimal risk to health, you should consult a physician. Should your status relative to the ACSM risk factors or signs and symptoms of cardiovascular or pulmonary disease change after starting or modifying your triathlon training program, consult your physician.

*Adapted, by permission, from American College of Sports Medicine, 2006, *ACSM's guidelines for exercise testing and prescription,* 7th ed. (Philadelphia, PA: Lippincott, Williams & Wilkins), 22.
**Adapted from American College of Sports Medicine, 2006, *ACSM's guidelines for exercise testing and prescription*, 7th ed. (Philadelphia, PA: Lippincott, Williams & Wilkins), 23-26.

Basic risk factor screenings are also available in fitness and health facilities through personal trainers and some triathlon coaches. If you have an unacceptable level of risk as defined by the ACSM, the recommendation is that you consult with a physician before engaging in exercise training. It is also appropriate to consult with your physician about the safety of your triathlon training without having taken the health risk assessment, particularly if you plan to race or do higher-intensity forms of training.

Summary

Participation in triathlon training provides a platform for wellness. But it can also create increased health risk and ongoing injury or infectious disease if not carried out properly. Optimal training involves avoiding overtraining and muscular imbalance, eating a healthful and performance-boosting diet, controlling exposure to pathogens and environmental contaminants, and avoiding musculoskeletal injuries. If injuries do occur, do not ignore them or mask them with medications. Rather, engage in a proactive process of change. Also carry out a health screening process before engaging in training or competition. A well-thought-out plan that encompasses all of the components discussed in this book can help you achieve your triathlon goals and compete in a way that's healthy for you. The result is a sustainable and satisfying physical lifestyle.

Glossary

aerobic speed—The current velocity or power output range at which a person can move aerobically; current velocity at the aerobic threshold. See *aerobic training*.

aerobic training—Training velocities or power outputs that can be completed at comfortable levels of exertion whereby the athlete provides energy using predominantly aerobic metabolic pathways. This is often defined by an upper limit for heart rate at the aerobic or first lactate threshold.

alactate—Referring to short (less than 20 seconds), relatively intense training efforts that are not carried out long enough to produce significant increases in blood lactate, acidity, or exertional pain.

alveoli—The small saclike cells of the lungs through which gases such as oxygen and carbon dioxide diffuse to and from the bloodstream.

kinetic chain—The series of joints and associated muscles that link the movements of the body's trunk to the movements of the limbs.

macrocycle—The largest cyclical block in a periodized training plan. These are defined by the combination of multiple mesocycles to culminate in a target race or racing period. Most periodized training programs in triathlon include one to three major macrocycles per training year.

mesocycle—The second-largest block in a periodization plan combining multiple microcycles, most typically three or four. The mesocycle usually has a single theme (such as base or race preparation). The microcycles represent workload progressions related to that theme.

microcycle—The short-term cycle that is the smallest block of cyclical training in a periodization plan. This cycle is typically 7 to 10 days.

restoration cycle—A cycle of training (at the microcycle, mesocycle, or macrocycle level) that represents a planned attempt to reduce cumulative training fatigue by reducing training workloads, typically by 50 percent.

speed endurance training—Training slightly below race velocity or power output for any given distance that increases endurance for those same velocities or power outputs.

speed-focused training—Training at the higher end of a current velocity or power fatigue curve. This training is designed primarily to increase speed.

strength endurance training—Aerobic training using greater-than-normal movement resistance, which reduces stride rate, stroke rate, and pedal rate at a given power output or speed.

target velocity or power—The rate of work (expressed in watts) or the speed of movement (most often expressed in miles or kilometers per hour or as minutes per mile or kilometer) associated with any given targeted training distance or time frame as determined by the athlete's current velocity or power curve or through physiological testing. For instance, an athlete might project the ability to run 1 mile in 6 minutes based on his fatigue curve. His target velocity for that distance in training would then be 6 minutes per mile or 10 mph. Another athlete might project the ability to cycle at 250 watts at his anaerobic threshold based on a lactate curve. His target power for training at anaerobic threshold would then be 250 watts.

tissue acidity—A higher-than-normal concentration of hydrogen ions (low pH) in the muscle tissue. The presence of a high level of hydrogen ions is thought to create acute reductions in work capacity (fatigue) as well as discomfort.

training periodization—The training plan an athlete uses to create cycles of training that emphasize distinct elements of the training process. This approach makes use of three primary organizational blocks: macrocycle, mesocycle, microcycle.

training tolerance—The total training load (volume and intensity) that an athlete can absorb (adapt to).

velocity or power fatigue curve—The projected series of times, velocities, or power outputs an athlete is theoretically capable of producing over successive distances based on current performance in at least two distances.

velocity or power fatigue rate—The rate, expressed as a percentage, at which an athlete's velocity or power drops off as the time or distance of effort is doubled.

Bibliography

Adams, M. April-June 2001. *Swimming technique: A superior model for swimming success.* Online at www.limmatsharks.com/superior_technique.html.

Aguilo, A., P. Tauler, A. Sureda, N. Cases, J. Tur, and A. Pons. 2007. Antioxidant diet supplementation enhances aerobic performance in amateur sportsmen. *Journal of Sports Sciences* 25(11): 1203-1210.

Arendse, R.E., T.D. Noakes, L.B. Azevedo, N. Romanov, M.P. Schwellnus, and G. Fletcher. 2004. Reduced eccentric loading of the knee with the pose running method. *Medicine and Science in Sports and Exercise* 36(2): 272-277.

Argentin, S., C. Hausswirth, T. Bernard, F. Bieuzen, J.M. Leveque, A. Couturier, and R. Lepers. 2006. Relation between preferred and optimal cadences during two hours of cycling in triathletes. *British Journal of Sports Medicine* 40(4): 293-298.

Armstrong, L.E. 2003. *Exertional heat illnesses.* Champaign, IL: Human Kinetics.

Atkinson, G., R. Davison, A. Jeukendrup, and L. Passfield. 2003. Science and cycling: Current knowledge and future directions for research. *Journal of Sports Sciences* 21(9): 767-787.

Baker, J., J. Côté, and J. Deakin. 2005a. Cognitive characteristics of expert, middle of the pack, and back of the pack ultra-endurance triathletes. *Psychology of Sport & Exercise* 6(5): 551-558.

Baker, J., J. Côté, and J. Deakin. 2005b. Expertise in ultra-endurance triathletes early sport involvement, training structure, and the theory of deliberate practice. *Journal of Applied Sport Psychology* 17(1): 64-78.

Baker, J., J. Côté, and J. Deakin. 2005c. On the utility of deliberate practice: Predicting performance in ultra-endurance triathletes from training indices. *International Journal of Sport Psychology* 36(3): 225-240.

Banister, E.W., J.B. Carter, and P.C. Zarkadas. 1999. Training theory and taper: Validation in triathlon athletes. *European Journal of Applied Physiology and Occupational Physiology* 79(2): 182-191.

Batt, M.E., R. Jaques, and M. Stone. 2004. Preparticipation examination (screening): Practical issues as determined by sport: A United Kingdom perspective. *Clinical Journal of Sport Medicine: Official Journal of the Canadian Academy of Sport Medicine* 14(3): 178-182.

Bell, G.J., S.R. Petersen, J. Wessel, K. Bagnall, and H.A. Quinney. 1991. Physiological adaptations to concurrent endurance training and low velocity resistance training. *International Journal of Sports Medicine* 12(4): 384-390.

Bentley, D.J., G.R. Cox, D. Green, and P.B. Laursen. 2007. Maximising performance in triathlon: Applied physiological and nutritional aspects of elite and non-elite competitions. *Journal of Science and Medicine in Sport / Sports Medicine Australia.* www.sciencedirect.com.

Bentley, D.J., G.P. Millet, V.E. Vleck, and L.R. McNaughton. 2002. Specific aspects of contemporary triathlon: Implications for physiological analysis and performance. *Sports Medicine* (Auckland, NZ) 32(6): 345-359.

Bentley, D.J., G.J. Wilson, A.J. Davie, and S. Zhou. 1998. Correlations between peak power output, muscular strength and cycle time trial performance in triathletes. *Journal of Sports Medicine and Physical Fitness* 38(3): 201-207.

Berardi, J.M., T.B. Price, E.E. Noreen, and P.W. Lemon. 2006. Postexercise muscle glycogen recovery enhanced with a carbohydrate-protein supplement. *Medicine and Science in Sports and Exercise* 38(6): 1106-1113.

Bernhardt, G. 2007. *Training plans for multisport athletes.* 2nd ed. Boulder, CO: VeloPress.

Billat, L.V. 2001. Interval training for performance: A scientific and empirical practice. Special recommendations for middle- and long-distance running. Part I: Aerobic interval training. *Sports Medicine* (Auckland, NZ) 31(1): 13-31.

Brown, R.C. 2002. Nutrition for optimal performance during exercise: Carbohydrate and fat. *Current Sports Medicine Reports* 1(4): 222-229.

Bunc, V., M. Ejem, V. Kucera, and P. Moravec. 1992. Assessment of predispositions for endurance running from field tests. *Journal of Sports Sciences* 10(3): 237-242.

Burke, L. 2007. *Practical sports nutrition.* Champaign, IL: Human Kinetics.

Burns, J., A.M. Keenan, and A.C. Redmond. 2003. Factors associated with triathlon-related overuse injuries. *Journal of Orthopaedic and Sports Physical Therapy* 33(4): 177-184.

Chapman, A.R., B. Vicenzino, P. Blanch, and P.W. Hodges. 2007. Leg muscle recruitment during cycling is less developed in triathletes than cyclists despite matched cycling training loads. *Experimental Brain Research. Experimentelle Hirnforschung. Experimentation Cerebrale* 181(3): 503-518.

Chtara, M., K. Chamari, M. Chaouachi, A. Chaouachi, D. Koubaa, Y. Feki, G.P. Millet, and M. Amri. 2005. Effects of intra-session concurrent endurance and strength training sequence on aerobic performance and capacity. *British Journal of Sports Medicine* 39(8): 555-560.

Clingman, J.M., and D.V. Hilliard. 1987. Some personality characteristics of the super-adherer: Following those who go beyond fitness. *Journal of Sport Behavior* 10(3): 123-136.

Clingman, J.M., and D.V. Hilliard. 1988. Triathletes' self-perceptions: To finish is to win. *Journal of Sport Behavior* 11(2): 89-98.

Cogan, K. 2005. Sport psychology library: Triathlon. *Sport Psychologist* 19(4): 459-460.

Collins, M., and G. Rodrigues, directors. 2003. *Open water swimming.* Louisville, KY: Endurance Films.

Colwin, C. 2002. *Breakthrough swimming.* Champaign, IL: Human Kinetics.

Cook, C.M., and M.D. Haub. 2007. Low-carbohydrate diets and performance. *Current Sports Medicine Reports* 6(4): 225-229.

Cordain, L., S.B. Eaton, J.B. Miller, N. Mann, and K. Hill. 2002. The paradoxical nature of hunter-gatherer diets: Meat-based, yet non-atherogenic. *European Journal of Clinical Nutrition* 56(suppl 1): S42-52.

Cronin, J., and G. Sleivert. 2005. Challenges in understanding the influence of maximal power training on improving athletic performance. *Sports Medicine* (Auckland, NZ) 35(3): 213-234.

Dallam, G.M., S. Jonas, and T.K. Miller. 2005. Medical considerations in triathlon competition: Recommendations for triathlon organisers, competitors and coaches. *Sports Medicine* (Auckland, NZ) 35(2): 143-161.

Dallam, G.M., R.L. Wilber, K. Jadelis, G. Fletcher, and N. Romanov. 2005. Effect of a global alteration of running technique on kinematics and economy. *Journal of Sports Sciences* 23(7): 757-764.

Daniels, J., R. Fitts, and G. Sheehan. 1978. *Conditioning for distance running.* American College of Sports Medicine Series. New York: Wiley.

Davison, G., M. Gleeson, and S. Phillips. 2007. Antioxidant supplementation and immuno-endocrine responses to prolonged exercise. *Medicine and Science in Sports and Exercise* 39(4): 645-652.

De Wit, B., D. De Clercq, and P. Aerts. 2000. Biomechanical analysis of the stance phase during barefoot and shod running. *Journal of Biomechanics* 33(3): 269-278.

DeBate, R. DiGioacchino, H. Wethington, and R. Sargent. 2002. Sub-clinical eating disorder characteristics among male and female triathletes. *Eating and Weight Disorders* 7(3): 210-220.

Delextrat, A., T. Bernard, C. Hausswirth, F. Vercruyssen, and J. Brisswalter. 2003. Effects of swimming with a wet suit on energy expenditure during subsequent cycling. *Canadian Journal of Applied Physiology* 28(3): 356-369.

Divert, C., G. Mornieux, H. Baur, F. Mayer, and A. Belli. 2005. Mechanical comparison of barefoot and shod running. *International Journal of Sports Medicine* 26(7): 593-598.

Douglas, R., H. Hemila, E. Chalker, and B. Treacy. 2007. Vitamin C for preventing and treating the common cold. *Cochrane Database of Systematic Reviews* 3(3): CD000980.

Durell, D.L., T.J. Pujol, and J.T. Barnes. 2003. A survey of the scientific data and training methods utilized by collegiate strength and conditioning coaches. *Journal of Strength and Conditioning Research* 17(2): 368-373.

Ebben, W.P., A.G. Kindler, K.A. Chirdon, N.C. Jenkins, A.J. Polichnowski, and A.V. Ng. 2004. The effect of high-load vs. high-repetition training on endurance performance. *Journal of Strength and Conditioning Research* 18(3): 513-517.

Egermann, M., D. Brocai, C.A. Lill, and H. Schmitt. 2003. Analysis of injuries in long-distance triathletes. *International Journal of Sports Medicine* 24(4): 271-276.

Egoscue, P. 1998. *Pain free*. New York: Random House.

Esfarjani, F., and P.B. Laursen. 2007. Manipulating high-intensity interval training: Effects on $\dot{V}O_2$max, the lactate threshold and 3000 m running performance in moderately trained males. *Journal of Science and Medicine in Sport* 10(1): 27-35.

Esteve-Lanao, J., C. Foster, S. Seiler, and A. Lucia. 2007. Impact of training intensity distribution on performance in endurance athletes. *Journal of Strength and Conditioning Research* 21(3): 943-949.

Esteve-Lanao, J., A.F. San Juan, C.P. Earnest, C. Foster, and A. Lucia. 2005. How do endurance runners actually train? Relationship with competition performance. *Medicine and Science in Sports and Exercise* 37(3): 496-504.

Faria, E.W., D.L. Parker, and I.E. Faria. 2005a. The science of cycling: Physiology and training—Part 1. *Sports Medicine* (Auckland, NZ) 35(4): 285-312.

Faria, E.W., D.L. Parker, and I.E. Faria. 2005b. The science of cycling: Factors affecting performance—Part 2. *Sports Medicine* (Auckland, NZ) 35(4): 313-337.

Farkas, G.M. 1989. Exposure and response prevention in the treatment of an okeanophobic triathlete. *Sport Psychologist* 3(3): 189-195.

Febbraio, M.A., J. Keenan, D.J. Angus, S.E. Campbell, and A.P. Garnham. 2000. Preexercise carbohydrate ingestion, glucose kinetics, and muscle glycogen use: Effect of the glycemic index. *Journal of Applied Physiology* 89(5): 1845-1851.

Friel, J. 1996. *The cyclist's training bible: A complete training guide for the competitive road cyclist*. Boulder, CO: VeloPress.

Friel, J. 2004. *The triathlete's training bible*. 2nd ed. Boulder, CO: VeloPress.

Girold, S., D. Maurin, B. Dugue, J.C. Chatard, and G. Millet. 2007. Effects of dry-land vs. resisted- and assisted-sprint exercises on swimming sprint performances. *Journal of Strength and Conditioning Research* 21(2): 599-605.

Grandjean, A.C., and J.S. Ruud. 1994. Nutrition for cyclists. *Clinics in Sports Medicine* 13(1): 235-247.

Granskog, J. 1992. Tri-ing together: An exploratory analysis of the social networks of female and male triathletes. *Play & Culture* 5(1): 76-91.

Gulbin, J.P., and P.T. Gaffney. 1999. Ultraendurance triathlon participation: Typical race preparation of lower level triathletes. *The Journal of Sports Medicine and Physical Fitness* 39(1): 12-15.

Halson, S.L., G.I. Lancaster, J. Achten, M. Gleeson, and A.E. Jeukendrup. 2004. Effects of carbohydrate supplementation on performance and carbohydrate oxidation after intensified cycling training. *Journal of Applied Physiology* 97(4): 1245-1253.

Heil, D.P., A.R. Wilcox, and C.M. Quinn. 1995. Cardiorespiratory responses to seat-tube angle variation during steady-state cycling. *Medicine and Science in Sports and Exercise* 27(5): 730-735.

Hendy, H.M., and B.J. Boyer. 1993. Gender differences in attributions for triathlon performance. *Sex Roles* 29(7): 527-543.

Hew-Butler, T.D., K. Sharwood, M. Collins, D. Speedy, and T. Noakes. 2006. Sodium supplementation is not required to maintain serum sodium concentrations during an Ironman triathlon. *British Journal of Sports Medicine* 40(3): 255-259.

Hilliard, D.C. 1988. Finishers, competitors, and pros: A description and speculative interpretation of the triathlon scene. *Play & Culture* 1(4): 300-313.

Hoch, A.Z., J.E. Stavrakos, and J.E. Schimke. 2007. Prevalence of female athlete triad characteristics in a club triathlon team. *Archives of Physical Medicine and Rehabilitation* 88(5): 681-682.

Hue, O., A. Valluet, S. Blonc, and C. Hertogh. 2002. Effects of multicycle-run training on triathlete performance. *Research Quarterly for Exercise and Sport* 73(3): 289-295.

Hughson, R.L., C.J. Orok, and L.E. Staudt. 1984. A high velocity treadmill running test to assess endurance running potential. *International Journal of Sports Medicine* 5(1): 23-25.

Izquierdo, M., J. Ibanez, J.J. Gonzalez-Badillo, K. Hakkinen, N.A. Ratamess, W.J. Kraemer, D.N. French, et al. 2006. Differential effects of strength training leading to failure versus not to failure on hormonal responses, strength, and muscle power gains. *Journal of Applied Physiology* 100(5): 1647-1656.

Jeukendrup, A.E., R.L. Jentjens, and L. Moseley. 2005. Nutritional considerations in triathlon. *Sports Medicine* (Auckland, NZ) 35(2): 163-181.

Jonas, S. 1996. *The essential triathlete.* New York: Lyons and Burford.

Jonas, S. 2006. *Triathloning for ordinary mortals.* 2nd ed. New York: Norton.

Jones, A.M., and H. Carter. 2000. The effect of endurance training on parameters of aerobic fitness. *Sports Medicine* (Auckland, NZ) 29(6): 373-386.

Joseph, A.M., H. Pilegaard, A. Litvintsev, L. Leick, and D.A. Hood. 2006. Control of gene expression and mitochondrial biogenesis in the muscular adaptation to endurance exercise. *Essays in Biochemistry* 42: 13-29.

Jung, A.P. 2003. The impact of resistance training on distance running performance. *Sports Medicine* (Auckland, NZ) 33(7): 539-552.

Kerr, C.G., T.A. Trappe, R.D. Starling, and S.W. Trappe. 1998. Hyperthermia during Olympic triathlon: Influence of body heat storage during the swimming stage. *Medicine and Science in Sports and Exercise* 30(1): 99-104.

Kirwan, J.P., D. Cyr-Campbell, W.W. Campbell, J. Scheiber, and W.J. Evans. 2001. Effects of moderate and high glycemic index meals on metabolism and exercise performance. *Metabolism: Clinical and Experimental* 50(7): 849-855.

Knez, W.L., D.G. Jenkins, and J.S. Coombes. 2007. Oxidative stress in half and full Ironman triathletes. *Medicine and Science in Sports and Exercise* 39(2): 283-288.

Knopfli, B.H., M. Luke-Zeitoun, S.P. von Duvillard, A. Burki, C. Bachlechner, and H. Keller. 2007. High incidence of exercise-induced bronchoconstriction in triathletes of the Swiss national team. *British Journal of Sports Medicine* 41(8): 486-91.

Kraemer, W.J., and R.U. Newton. 1994. Training for improved vertical jump. *Sports Science Exchange* 7(6), 1-12.

Kraemer, W.J., N. Ratamess, A.C. Fry, T. Triplett-McBride, L.P. Koziris, J.A. Bauer, J.M. Lynch, and S.J. Fleck. 2000. Influence of resistance training volume and periodization on physiological and performance adaptations in collegiate women tennis players. *American Journal of Sports Medicine* 28(5): 626-633.

LaChausse, R.G. 2006. Motives of competitive and non-competitive cyclists. *Journal of Sport Behavior* 29(4): 304-314.

Lambert, E.V., and J.H. Goedecke. 2003. The role of dietary macronutrients in optimizing endurance performance. *Current Sports Medicine Reports* 2(4): 194-201.

Laughlin, T. 2002. *Triathlon swimming made easy: The total immersion way for anyone to succeed in triathlon (or open-water swimming)*. New Paltz, NY: Total Immersion.

Laursen, P.B., C.M. Shing, J.M. Peake, J.S. Coombes, and D.G. Jenkins. 2005. Influence of high-intensity interval training on adaptations in well-trained cyclists. *Journal of Strength and Conditioning Research* 19(3): 527-533.

Laursen, P.B., C.M. Shing, J.M. Peake, J.S. Coombes, and D.G. Jenkins. 2002. Interval training program optimization in highly trained endurance cyclists. *Medicine and Science in Sports and Exercise* 34(11): 1801-1807.

LeBlanc, J., I. Mercier, and A. Nadeau. 1993. Components of postprandial thermogenesis in relation to meal frequency in humans. *Canadian Journal of Physiology and Pharmacology* 71(12): 879-883.

Leibovitch, I., and Y. Mor. 2005. The vicious cycling: Bicycling related urogenital disorders. *European Urology* 47(3): 277-286; discussion 286-287.

Lemon, P.W. 1991. Effect of exercise on protein requirements. *Journal of Sports Sciences* 9 Spec No: 53-70.

Li, L. 2004. Neuromuscular control and coordination during cycling. *Research Quarterly for Exercise and Sport* 75(1): 16-22.

Maglischo, E.W. 1993. *Swimming even faster*. Mountain View, CA: Mayfield.

Mangla, P.K., and M.P. Menon. 1981. Effect of nasal and oral breathing on exercise-induced asthma. *Clinical Allergy* 11(5): 433-439.

Martin, D.E., and P.N. Coe. 1997. *Better training for distance runners*. 2nd ed. Champaign, IL: Human Kinetics.

Martin, D.E., and P.N. Coe. 1991. *Training distance runners*. Champaign, IL: Leisure Press.

Marx, J.O., N.A. Ratamess, B.C. Nindl, L.A. Gotshalk, J.S. Volek, K. Dohi, J.A. Bush, et al. 2001. Low-volume circuit versus high-volume periodized resistance training in women. *Medicine and Science in Sports and Exercise* 33(4): 635-643.

Maughan, R.J. 2005. The limits of human athletic performance. *Annals of Transplantation* 10(4): 52-54.

McArdle, W.D., F.I. Katch, and V.L. Katch. 2001. *Exercise physiology: Energy, nutrition, and human performance*. 5th ed. Philadelphia: Lippincott Williams & Wilkins.

McMurray, R.G., D.K. Williams, and C.L. Battaglini. 2006. The timing of fluid intake during an Olympic distance triathlon. *International Journal of Sport Nutrition and Exercise Metabolism* 16(6): 611-619.

Mellion, M.B. 1991. Common cycling injuries. Management and prevention. *Sports Medicine* (Auckland, NZ) 11(1): 52-70.

Mikkola, J.S., H.K. Rusko, A.T. Nummela, L.M. Paavolainen, and K. Hakkinen. 2007. Concurrent endurance and explosive type strength training increases activation and fast force production of leg extensor muscles in endurance athletes. *Journal of Strength and Conditioning Research* 21(2): 613-620.

Mikkola, J.S., H.K. Rusko, A.T. Nummela, T. Pollari, and K. Hakkinen. 2007. Concurrent endurance and explosive type strength training improves neuromuscular and anaerobic characteristics in young distance runners. *International Journal of Sports Medicine* 28(7): 602-611.

Millet, G.P., R.B. Candau, B. Barbier, T. Busso, J.D. Rouillon, and J.C. Chatard. 2002. Modelling the transfers of training effects on performance in elite triathletes. *International Journal of Sports Medicine* 23(1): 55-63.

Millet, G.P., B. Jaouen, F. Borrani, and R. Candau. 2002. Effects of concurrent endurance and strength training on running economy and $\dot{V}O_2$ kinetics. *Medicine and Science in Sports and Exercise* 34(8): 1351-1359.

Millman, D. 2006. *Way of the peaceful warrior: A book that changes lives.* Tiburon, CA: H J Kramer.

Mora, J. 1999. *Triathlon 101: Essentials for multisport success.* Champaign, IL: Human Kinetics.

Mora-Rodriguez, R., and R. Aguado-Jimenez. 2006. Performance at high pedaling cadences in well-trained cyclists. *Medicine and Science in Sports and Exercise* 38(5): 953-957.

Morgan, J., S.L. Bornstein, A.M. Karpati, M. Bruce, C.A. Bolin, C.C. Austin, C.W. Woods, et al. 2002. Outbreak of leptospirosis among triathlon participants and community residents in Springfield, Illinois, 1998. *Clinical Infectious Diseases* 34(12): 1593-1599.

Mujika, I., and S. Padilla. 2003. Scientific bases for precompetition tapering strategies. *Medicine and Science in Sports and Exercise* 35(7): 1182-1187.

Nader, G.A. 2006. Concurrent strength and endurance training: From molecules to man. *Medicine and Science in Sports and Exercise* 38(11): 1965-1970.

Nieman, D.C. 1998. Influence of carbohydrate on the immune response to intensive, prolonged exercise. *Exercise Immunology Review* 4: 64-76.

Niess, A.M., A. Hipp, S. Thoma, and H. Striegel. 2007. Performance food in sports. *Therapeutische Umschau. Revue Therapeutique* 64(3): 181-185.

Noakes, T. 2003. *Lore of running.* 4th ed. Champaign, IL: Human Kinetics.

O'Keefe, J.H., and L. Cordain. 2004. Cardiovascular disease resulting from a diet and lifestyle at odds with our paleolithic genome: How to become a 21st-century hunter-gatherer. *Mayo Clinic Proceedings. Mayo Clinic* 79(1): 101-108.

O'Toole, M.L., and P.S. Douglas. 1995. Applied physiology of triathlon. *Sports Medicine* (Auckland, NZ) 19(4): 251-267.

Paavolainen, L.M., K. Hakkinen, I. Hamalainen, A.T. Nummela, and H.K. Rusko. 1999. Explosive-strength training improves 5-km running time by improving running economy and muscle power. *Journal of Applied Physiology* 86(5): 1527-1533.

Paavolainen, L.M., A.T. Nummela, and H.K. Rusko. 1999. Neuromuscular characteristics and muscle power as determinants of 5-km running performance. *Medicine and Science in Sports and Exercise* 31(1): 124-130.

Papsin, B., and A. McTavish. 2003. Saline nasal irrigation: Its role as an adjunct treatment. *Canadian Family Physician (Medecin De Famille Canadien)* 49: 168-173.

Paton, C.D., and W.G. Hopkins. 2005. Combining explosive and high-resistance training improves performance in competitive cyclists. *Journal of Strength and Conditioning Research* 19(4): 826-830.

Paton, C.D., and W.G. Hopkins. 2004. Effects of high-intensity training on performance and physiology of endurance athletes. *Sportscience* 8: 25-40.

Peeling, P.D., D.J. Bishop, and G.J. Landers. 2005. Effect of swimming intensity on subsequent cycling and overall triathlon performance. *British Journal of Sports Medicine* 39(12): 960-964.

Peeling, P.D., and G.J. Landers. 2007. The effect of a one-piece competition speedsuit on swimming performance and thermoregulation during a swim-cycle trial in triathletes. *Journal of Science and Medicine in Sport* 10(5): 327-33.

Rhea, M.R., S.D. Ball, W.T. Phillips, and L.N. Burkett. 2002. A comparison of linear and daily undulating periodized programs with equated volume and intensity for strength. *Journal of Strength and Conditioning Research* 16(2): 250-255.

Rhea, M.R., W.T. Phillips, L.N. Burkett, W.J. Stone, S.D. Ball, B.A. Alvar, and A.B. Thomas. 2003. A comparison of linear and daily undulating periodized programs with equated volume and intensity for local muscular endurance. *Journal of Strength and Conditioning Research* 17(1): 82-87.

Rietjens, G.J., H. Kuipers, J.J. Adam, W.H. Saris, E. van Breda, D. van Hamont, and H.A. Keizer. 2005. Physiological, biochemical and psychological markers of strenuous training-induced fatigue. *International Journal of Sports Medicine* 26(1): 16-26.

Robbins, S.E., G.J. Gouw, J. McClaran, and E. Waked. 1993. Protective sensation of the plantar aspect of the foot. *Foot & Ankle* 14(6): 347-352.

Robbins, S.E., and A.M. Hanna. 1987. Running-related injury prevention through barefoot adaptations. *Medicine and Science in Sports and Exercise* 19(2): 148-156.

Robbins, S.E., and E. Waked. 1997. Hazard of deceptive advertising of athletic footwear. *British Journal of Sports Medicine* 31(4): 299-303.

Robins, A. 2007. Nutritional recommendations for competing in the Ironman triathlon. *Current Sports Medicine Reports* 6(4): 241-248.

Romanov, N.S. 2006. Pose method. www.posetech.com/pose_method.

Romanov, N.S. 2002. *Pose method: Strength conditioning hamstring and hips exercises booklet.* 2nd ed. Miami, FL: PoseTech Press.

Romanov, N.S., and G. Fletcher. 2007. Runners do not push off the ground but fall forwards via a gravitational torque. *Sports Biomechanics* 6(3): 434-452.

Schofield, G., G. Dickson, K. Mummery, and H. Street. 2002. Dysphoria, linking, and pre-competitive anxiety in triathletes. *Athletic Insight: Online Journal of Sport Psychology* 4(2).

Shaw, T., P. Howat, M. Trainor, and B. Maycock. 2004. Training patterns and sports injuries in triathletes. *Journal of Science and Medicine in Sport* 7(4): 446-450.

Shturman-Ellstein, R., R.J. Zeballos, J.M. Buckley, and J.F. Souhrada. 1978. The beneficial effect of nasal breathing on exercise-induced bronchoconstriction. *American Review of Respiratory Disease* 118(1): 65-73.

Smith, T.P., J.S. Coombes, and D.P. Geraghty. 2003. Optimising high-intensity treadmill training using the running speed at maximal O_2 uptake and the time for which this can be maintained. *European Journal of Applied Physiology* 89(3-4): 337-343.

Snyder, A.C. 1998. Overtraining and glycogen depletion hypothesis. *Medicine and Science in Sports and Exercise* 30(7): 1146-50.

Speechly, D.P., and R. Buffenstein. 1999. Greater appetite control associated with an increased frequency of eating in lean males. *Appetite* 33(3): 285-297.

Sports injury bulletin. N.d. Pose running technique: A beginner's guide. www.sportsinjurybulletin.com/archive/pose-running-technique.html.

Spriet, L.L., and M.J. Gibala. 2004. Nutritional strategies to influence adaptations to training. *Journal of Sports Sciences* 22(1): 127-141.

Spurrs, R.W., A.J. Murphy, and M.L. Watsford. 2003. The effect of plyometric training on distance running performance. *European Journal of Applied Physiology* 89(1): 1-7.

Stewart, A.M., and W.G. Hopkins. 2000. Seasonal training and performance of competitive swimmers. *Journal of Sports Sciences* 18(11): 873-884.

Stray-Gunderson, J., R.F. Chapman, and B.D. Levine. 2001. "Living high–training low" altitude training improves sea level performance in male and female elite runners. *Journal of Applied Physiology* 91(3): 1113-1120.

Takaishi, T., T. Yamamoto, T. Ono, T. Ito, and T. Moritani. 1998. Neuromuscular, metabolic, and kinetic adaptations for skilled pedaling performance in cyclists. *Medicine and Science in Sports and Exercise* 30(3): 442-449.

Tanaka, H., and T. Swensen. 1998. Impact of resistance training on endurance performance. A new form of cross-training? *Sports Medicine* (Auckland, NZ) 25(3): 191-200.

Tanaka, Y., T. Morikawa, and Y. Honda. 1988. An assessment of nasal functions in control of breathing. *Journal of Applied Physiology* 65(4): 1520-1524.

Taylor-Mason, A.M. 2005. High-resistance interval training improves 40-km time-trial performance in competitive cyclists. *Sportscience* 9: 27-31. http://sportsci.org/2005/index.html.

Telford, R.D., G.J. Sly, A.G. Hahn, R.B. Cunningham, C. Bryant, and J.A. Smith. 2003. Footstrike is the major cause of hemolysis during running. *Journal of Applied Physiology* 94(1): 38-42.

Thelwell, R.C., and I.A. Greenlees. 2003. Developing competitive endurance performance using mental skills training. *Sport Psychologist* 17(3): 318.

Thomas, C., S. Perrey, H. Ben Saad, M. Delage, A.M. Dupuy, J.P. Cristol, and J. Mercier. 2007. Effects of a supplementation during exercise and recovery. *International Journal of Sports Medicine* 28(8): 703-712.

Tomikawa, M., Y. Shimoyama, and T. Nomura. 2007. Factors related to the advantageous effects of wearing a wetsuit during swimming at different submaximal velocity in triathletes. *Journal of Science and Medicine in Sport*. www.sciencedirect.com.

Topp, R., M. Fahlman, and D. Boardley. 2004. Healthy aging: Health promotion and disease prevention. *Nursing Clinics of North America* 39(2): 411-422.

Toussaint, H.M. 1990. Differences in propelling efficiency between competitive and triathlon swimmers. *Medicine and Science in Sports and Exercise* 22(3): 409-415.

Toussaint, H.M., and P.J. Beek. 1992. Biomechanics of competitive front crawl swimming. *Sports Medicine* (Auckland, NZ) 13(1): 8-24.

VanHelder, T., and M.W. Radomski. 1989. Sleep deprivation and the effect on exercise performance. *Sports Medicine* (Auckland, NZ) 7(4): 235-247.

Villavicencio, A.T., S. Burneikiene, T.D. Hernandez, and J. Thramann. 2006. Back and neck pain in triathletes. *Neurosurgical Focus* 21(4): E7.

Villavicencio, A.T., T.D. Hernandez, S. Burneikiene, and J. Thramann. 2007. Neck pain in multisport athletes. *Journal of Neurosurgery. Spine* 7(4): 408-413.

Vleck, V.E., D.J. Bentley, G.P. Millet, and A. Burgi. 2007. Pacing during an elite Olympic distance triathlon: Comparison between male and female competitors. *Journal of Science and Medicine in Sport*. www.sciencedirect.com.

Walker, B.J. 1999. *An exploratory examination of the utilization of psychological skills employed by triathletes*. Vol. 59. ProQuest Information & Learning. http://proquest.umi.com/pqdweb?did=732842631&sid=1&Fmt=2&clientId=19460&RQT=309&VName=PQD&cfc=1.

Warburton, M. 2001. Barefoot running. *Sportscience* 5(3). http://sportsci.org/jour/0103/mw.htm.

Weil, A. Nasal flushing to reduce sinus problems. www.dfwcfids.org/healing/nasal-flush.htm.

Weinberg, R.S., and D. Gould. 2007. *Foundations of sport and exercise psychology*. 4th ed. Champaign, IL: Human Kinetics.

Whiting, W.C. 2002. The differences between successful and less-successful triathletes on imagery usage. Dissertation, Springfield College, Springfield, MA.

Whitmarsh, B.G., and R.B. Alderman. 1993. Role of psychological skills training in increasing athletic pain tolerance. *Sport Psychologist* 7(4): 388-399.

Wilber, R.L. 2001. Current trends in altitude training. *Sports Medicine* (Auckland, NZ) 31(4): 249-265.

Wilber, R.L., P.L. Holm, D.M. Morris, G.M. Dallam, A.W. Subudhi, D.M. Murray, and S.D. Callan. 2004. Effect of FIO_2 on oxidative stress during interval training at moderate altitude. *Medicine and Science in Sports and Exercise* 36(11): 1888-1894.

Wood, R.E., S. Hayter, D. Rowbottom, and I. Stewart. 2005. Applying a mathematical model to training adaptation in a distance runner. *European Journal of Applied Physiology* 94(3): 310-316.

Zaryski, C., and D.J. Smith. 2005. Training principles and issues for ultra-endurance athletes. *Current Sports Medicine Reports* 4(3): 165-170.

Zinn, L. 2007. *Zinn & the art of triathlon bikes*. Boulder, CO: VeloPress.

Zoladz, J.A., A.C. Rademaker, and A.J. Sargeant. 2000. Human muscle power generating capability during cycling at different pedalling rates. *Experimental Physiology* 85(1): 117-124.

Index

Note: The italicized *f* and *t* following pages numbers refer to figures and tables, respectively.

About the Authors

George Dallam, PhD, is the longtime coach of Hunter Kemper, the number-one-ranked triathlete in the ITU World Cup during 2005 and most of 2006. He is the founding member of the National Coaching Commission of USA Triathlon, the sport's national governing body, and was USA Triathlon's first national team coach. In 2004, he was a finalist for the Doc Counsilman Award for Science in Coaching category of the United States Olympic Committee's Coach of the Year Award. In 2005, he was USA Triathlon's Elite Coach of the Year.

Dallam is an associate professor of exercise science and health promotion at Colorado State University at Pueblo. As a sport scientist, he has authored and coauthored numerous scientific papers relating to triathlon. During his career at CSU-Pueblo, he has received each of the university-wide awards for teaching, scholarship, and service, becoming the only faculty member in the history of the institution to receive all three awards.

During his 16-year triathlon coaching career, Dallam has served as a personal coach to several elite triathletes, including Amanda Stevens, Marcel Vifian, Callahan Hatfield, Michael Smedley, and Ryan Bickerstaff. As the USA Triathlon national team coach, he also served as the Olympic Training Center resident and collegiate programs coach for Olympians Nick Radkewich and Susan Williams as well as perennial international stars Laura Reback, Becky Lavelle, and Doug Friman. Before focusing on triathlon, he coached at various levels in swimming, water polo, and cross country. He resides in Colorado Springs.

Steven Jonas, MD, MPH, MS, FNYAS, has been a regular columnist and contributor to *The East Coast Triathlete, Triathlon Today, Triathlon Times,* and *American TRI.* Since 2006, he has written a column titled "Ordinary Mortals: Talking Triathlon with Steve Jonas" for *USA Triathlon Life.* He is the author of *Triathloning for Ordinary Mortals* and *The Essential Triathlete.* He also currently serves as editor in chief for *American Medical Athletic Association Journal* and has been a member of the editorial board of *ACSM's Health & Fitness Journal* since 1999.

Jonas is a professor of preventive medicine in the School of Medicine at Stony Brook University in New York. As author, coauthor, editor, and coeditor, he has published more than 25 books and 135 academic papers on health policy, health promotion, disease prevention, and fitness and exercise.

The year 2007 marked Jonas' 25th season as a recreational triathlete. He has competed in over 185 multisport races, including 115 triathlons, at distances up to the Ironman. He is also a certified professional ski instructor. Jonas resides in Port Jefferson, New York.

You'll find other outstanding triathlon resources at

http://triathlon.humankinetics.com

In the U.S. call 1-800-747-4457

Australia 08 8372 0999 • Canada 1-800-465-7301
Europe +44 (0) 113 255 5665 • New Zealand 0064 9 448 1207

HUMAN KINETICS
The Premier Publisher for Sports & Fitness
P.O. Box 5076 • Champaign, IL 61825-5076 USA